Contemporary Metaethics

For my mother and father, John and Isabella

Contemporary Metaethics

An Introduction

Second Edition

Alexander Miller

polity

The right of Alexander Miller to be identified as Author of this Work has been asserted in accordance with the UK Copyright, Designs and Patents Act 1988.

First published in 2013 by Polity Press

First edition published in 2003 by Polity Press

Polity Press
65 Bridge Street
Cambridge CB2 1UR, UK

Polity Press
350 Main Street
Malden, MA 02148, USA

ISBN-13: 978-0-7456-4658-9
ISBN-13: 978-0-7456-4659-6(pb)

A catalogue record for this book is available from the British Library.

Typeset in 10 on 11.5pt Palatino
by Servis Filmsetting Ltd, Stockport, Cheshire
Printed and bound by the MPG Printgroup, UK

The publisher has used its best endeavours to ensure that the URLs for external websites referred to in this book are correct and active at the time of going to press. However, the publisher has no responsibility for the websites and can make no guarantee that a site will remain live or that the content is or will remain appropriate.

Every effort has been made to trace all copyright holders, but if any have been inadvertently overlooked the publisher will be pleased to include any necessary credits in any subsequent reprint or edition.

For further information on Polity, visit our website: www.politybooks.com

Contents

Detailed Chapter Contents

Preface to the First Edition (2003)

This book is intended to provide a critical overview of some main themes and issues in contemporary metaethics. I set the scene with discussions of Moore and Ayer, and follow up with discussions of more recent figures: Blackburn, Gibbard, Mackie, Wright, Harman, Sturgeon, Railton, Wiggins, Jackson, Pettit, Smith and McDowell. It will be apparent to anyone with a knowledge of the rich scene presented by contemporary metaethics that many important figures and issues do not get discussed in the book. In a work of this length and scope that could not be helped. In addition, it seemed to me that a substantial discussion of some main facets of the territory would be more interesting, and ultimately more helpful, than a superficial tour of a much larger area. And where possible I have tried to make small contributions to the ongoing debates, which I hope will be of interest to the professional as well as the student.

I had the idea for this book shortly after completing my PhD dissertation at the University of Michigan, Ann Arbor, in 1995. In that dissertation I attempted to defend what I took to be McDowell's take on Wittgenstein's 'rule-following considerations'. Initially, my plan was to start with Moore, then get clear on the inadequacies of his non-naturalist position before showing that both naturalistic cognitivism and non-cognitivism are likewise implausible. Courtesy of the rule-following arguments, McDowell would emerge at the end of the book as a defender of a form of non-naturalism not prone to the difficulties of Moore's position or of its naturalistic competitors. In fact, the book has turned out to be the opposite of this. I still begin by arguing that Moore's non-naturalism is inadequate, but then I try to show that many of the objections against naturalistic cognitivism (especially reductionist versions) and non-cognitivism (especially Blackburn's quasi-realism) are at least less compelling than they initially seem. In particular, I argue that the 'rule-following' arguments and their like do nothing to undermine Railton's naturalistic cognitivism or Blackburn's quasi-realism, nor do they save McDowell from the charge that his non-naturalism is ultimately no more plausible than Moore's.

Versions of parts of the book have been read at seminars at: Cambridge, Cardiff, Durham, Stirling, and Macquarie University in Sydney; and also at the 2001 graduate metaethics conference at Leeds and Martin Kusch's 2002 workshop on meaning and normativity at the Wissenschaftskolleg zu Berlin. The audiences at these events provided many helpful responses. I used early versions of the manuscript as the basis for lecture courses at Birmingham in 1996 and 1997, and at Cardiff in 2001. I would like to thank the students in those classes for their useful feedback. For comments on parts of the manuscript I am grateful to John Divers, Mark Nelson, Penelope Mackie, Chris Norris, Robin Attfield, Duncan McFarland and Bob Hale. For detailed comments on the entire manuscript I am very grateful to Phillip Stratton-Lake and two other (anonymous) readers for Polity Press, and also to Andrew Fisher and Simon Kirchin. Needless to say, I have not been able to deal with all of these comments in the final version, and I am alone responsible for any errors that remain. I have found Michael Smith's *The Moral Problem* wonderfully helpful; I am grateful to Michael for his patience with my attempts to criticize some of his arguments. The bulk of the book was written during my tenure as senior research fellow at Cardiff University. I am grateful to the university for its support, and in particular to David Skilton of the School of English, Communication and Philosophy for being an ideal head of school. I also thank my colleagues in the Philosophy section at Cardiff for providing me with such a stimulating and friendly environment in which to work: Andrew Belsey, Robin Attfield, Chris Norris, Alessandra Tanesini, Alison Venables, Christine Southwell, Barry Wilkins, Peter Sedgwick and Andrew Edgar. That such an excellent department could be so undervalued is a sign of more than mere degeneracy on the part of the British philosophical establishment. For help and encouragement that extend beyond the covers of this volume, I am indebted to Crispin Wright, Philip Pettit, Bob Kirk, John Divers, Alan Weir and Brian Leiter. Finally, and most of all, I am grateful to Jean and Rosa for providing me with the perfect escape route from the thorny paths of contemporary metaethics.

Preface to the Second Edition (2013)

For this second edition I have added new sections on Richard Joyce's 'revolutionary moral fictionalism' and Mark Kalderon's 'hermeneutic moral fictionalism'. I have also revised each chapter, in the process hopefully improving on the first (2003) edition. The guides to further reading at the end of each chapter have been updated, and can be read in conjunction with my entry in *Oxford Bibliographies Online*. Such is the vibrancy of the current metaethical scene, there have been many interesting recent developments that I've simply had no space to discuss – for example, 'hybrid' or 'ecumenical' theories of moral judgement, Mark Schroeder's work on the Frege-Geach problem, the 'cognitivist expressivism' of Horgan and Timmons, the moral realism of Russ Shafer-Landau. I'm hoping to take these up in a sequel to the current book, *An Introduction to Advanced Metaethics*.

Since the first edition, I've given talks on metaethical themes at a number of departments and conferences, including: ANU, Wellington, Auckland, Christchurch, the Oxford Moral Philosophy Seminar, the 2006 Ethical Naturalism conference at Durham, Turku, Szczecin, Nottingham, Seoul National University, the 2011 Nottingham Ethics and Explanation conference, and the University of Otago. I'm grateful to audiences at these events for helpful feedback, and also to the students in my classes at Macquarie and Birmingham. I'm also very grateful to the reviewers who commented on the whole manuscript for Polity Press, and especially to Simon Kirchin for extremely helpful comments and advice. Thanks, too, to postgraduate supervisees working on metaethical themes: Andrew Field, Callum Hood, and the inimitable Kirk Surgener. I'm very grateful to Helen Gray for her invaluable copy-editing.

I would like to thank John Haldane for some helpful guidance when

I was planning the original version, and special thanks are due to Allan Anderson, Janet Elwell, Martin Kusch, Brian Leiter, Philip Pettit, Mark Walker and Crispin Wright. As with the first edition, thanks most of all to Jean Cockram and Rosa Heloise Miller.

Later on I asked Marlow why he wished to cultivate this chance acquaintance. He confessed apologetically that it was the commonest curiosity. I flatter myself that I understand all sorts of curiosity – curiosity about daily facts, daily things, about daily men. It is the most respectable faculty of the human mind – in fact, I cannot conceive the uses of an incurious mind. It would be like a chamber perpetually locked up.

Joseph Conrad, Chance

1

Introduction

In this chapter, I provide a brief account of the territory covered in metaethics, and of the main philosophical positions in metaethics to be covered in detail in the course of the book.

1.1 What is Metaethics?

Suppose I am debating with a friend the question whether or not we ought to give to famine relief, whether or not we are morally obliged to give to famine relief. The sorts of questions philosophers raise about this kind of debate fall roughly into two groups. First, there are *first-order* questions about which party in the debate, if any, is right, and why. Then, there are *second-order* questions about what the parties in the debate are doing when they engage in it. Roughly, the first-order questions are the province of *normative ethics*, and the second-order questions are the province of *metaethics*. As one recent writer puts it:

> In metaethics, we are concerned not with questions which are the province of normative ethics like 'Should I give to famine relief?' or 'Should I return the wallet I found in the street?' but with questions about questions like these. (Smith 1994a: 2)

It is important to be clear that in normative ethics we do not just look for an answer to the question 'Should we give to famine relief?'; we also look for some insight into *why* the right answer is right. It is in their answers to this latter sort of 'why?' question that the classic theories in normative ethics disagree. Examples of such theories include: *act-utilitarianism* (one ought to give to famine relief because that particular action, of those possible, contributes most to the greater happiness of the greatest number), *rule-utilitarianism* (one ought to give to famine relief because giving to famine relief is prescribed by a rule the general observance of which contributes most to the greater happiness of the greatest number), and *Kantianism* (one ought to give to famine relief because universal refusal to give to famine relief would generate some kind of inconsistency). Normative ethics thus seeks to discover the general principles underlying moral practice, and in this way potentially impacts upon practical moral problems: different general principles may yield different verdicts in particular cases. In this book we are not concerned with questions or theories in normative ethics. Rather, we are concerned with questions about the following:[1]

(a) *Meaning*: what is the *semantic function* of moral discourse? Is the function of moral discourse to state *facts*, or does it have some other non-fact-stating role?

(b) *Metaphysics*: do moral facts (or properties) exist? If so, what are they like? Are they identical or reducible to natural facts (or properties) or are they irreducible and *sui generis*?

(c) *Epistemology* and *justification*: is there such a thing as moral knowledge? How can we know whether our moral judgements are true or false? How can we ever justify our claims to moral knowledge?

(d) *Phenomenology*: how are moral qualities represented in the experience of an agent making a moral judgement? Do they appear to be 'out there' in the world?

(e) *Moral psychology*: what can we say about the motivational state of someone making a moral judgement? What sort of connection is there between making a moral judgement and being motivated to act as that judgement prescribes?

(f) *Objectivity*: can moral judgements really be correct or incorrect? Can we work towards finding out the moral truth?

Obviously, this list is not intended to be exhaustive, and the various questions are not all independent (for example, a positive answer to (f) looks, on the face of it, to presuppose that the function of moral discourse is to state facts). But it is worth noting that the list is much wider than many philosophers forty or fifty years ago would have thought. For example, one such philosopher writes:

> [Metaethics] is not about what people ought to do. It is about what they are doing when they talk about what they ought to do. (Hudson 1970: 1)

The idea that metaethics is exclusively about language was no doubt due to the once prevalent idea that philosophy as a whole has no function other than the study of ordinary language and that 'philosophical problems' only arise from the application of words out of the contexts in which they are ordinarily used. Fortunately, this 'ordinary language' conception of philosophy has long since ceased to hold sway, and the list of metaethical concerns – in metaphysics, epistemology, phenomenology, moral psychology, as well as in semantics and the theory of meaning – bears this out.

Positions in metaethics can be defined in terms of the answers they give to these sorts of question. Some examples of metaethical theories are: *moral realism, non-cognitivism, error-theory,* and *moral anti-realism.* The task of this book is to explain and evaluate these theories. In this chapter I give thumbnail sketches of the various theories and try to convey an idea of the sorts of questions they address. These preliminary sketches are then developed at more length in the remainder of the book.

1.2 Cognitivism and Non-Cognitivism

Consider a particular moral judgement, such as the judgement that murder is wrong. What sort of psychological state does this express? Some philosophers, called *cognitivists,* think that a moral judgement like this expresses a *belief.* Beliefs can be true or false: they are *truth-apt,* or apt to be assessed in terms of truth and falsity. So cognitivists think that moral judgements are capable of being true or false. On the other hand, *non-cognitivists* think that moral judgements express non-cognitive states like emotions or desires.[2] Desires and emotions are not truth-apt. So moral judgements are not capable of being true or false. (Note that although it may be true *that I have* a desire for a pint of beer and false *that I have* a desire to see England win the World Cup, this does not imply that desires *themselves* can be true or false.) In many ways, it is the battle between cognitivism and non-cognitivism that takes centre-stage in this book: chapters 3–5 concern non-cognitivism and its problems, while cognitivism and its problems are the topic of chapter 2 and chapters 6–10.

1.3 Strong Cognitivism: Naturalism

A *strong cognitivist* theory is one which holds that moral judgements (a) are apt for evaluation in terms of truth and falsity, and (b) can be the upshot of cognitively accessing the facts which render them true. Strong cognitivist theories can be either *naturalist* or *non-naturalist.* According to a naturalist, a moral judgement is rendered true or false by a natural state of affairs, and it is this natural state of affairs to which a true moral judgement affords us access. But what is a natural state of affairs? In this book I will follow G. E. Moore's characterization:

> By nature then I do mean and have meant that which is the subject matter
> of the natural sciences, and also of psychology. (Moore 1903: 92)

A natural property is a property which figures in one of the natural
sciences or in psychology: examples might include the property of
being conducive to the greatest happiness of the greatest number and
the property of being conducive to the preservation of the human
species. A natural state of affairs is simply a state of affairs that consists
in the instantiation of a natural property.

Naturalist cognitivists hold that moral properties are identical to
(or reducible to) natural properties. The *Cornell Realists* (e.g., Nicholas
Sturgeon, Richard Boyd and David Brink: see Sturgeon 1988; Boyd
1988; and Brink 1989) think that moral properties are *irreducible* natural
properties in their own right. *Naturalist reductionists* (e.g., Richard
Brandt, Peter Railton: see Brandt 1979; Railton 1986a, b) think that
moral properties are reducible to the sorts of natural properties that
are the subject matter of the natural sciences and psychology. Both the
Cornell Realists and the naturalist reductionists are *moral realists*: they
think that there really are moral facts and moral properties, and that the
existence of these moral facts and instantiation of these moral properties is constitutively independent of human opinion. The non-reductive
naturalism of the Cornell Realists is discussed in chapter 8 and naturalist reductionism is the subject of chapter 9.

1.4 Strong Cognitivism: Non-Naturalism

Non-naturalists think that moral properties are not identical to or
reducible to natural properties. They are irreducible and *sui generis*. We
will look at two types of strong cognitivist non-naturalism: Moore's
ethical non-naturalism, as developed in his *Principia Ethica* (first published in 1903), according to which the property of moral goodness is
non-natural, simple, and unanalysable; and the contemporary version
of non-naturalism that has been developed by John McDowell and
David Wiggins (roughly from the 1970s to the present day: see
McDowell 1998; Wiggins 1987). Again, both types of non-naturalist are
moral realists: they think that there really are moral facts and moral
properties, and that the existence of these moral facts and instantiation of these moral properties is constitutively independent of human
opinion.[3] Moore's non-naturalism, and his attack on naturalism, are
discussed in chapters 2 and 3; the non-naturalism of McDowell is
discussed in chapter 10.

1.5 Strong Cognitivism without Moral Realism: Mackie's Error-Theory

John Mackie has argued that although moral judgements are apt to be true or false, and that moral judgements, if true, would afford us cognitive access to moral facts, moral judgements are in fact always *false* (Mackie 1973). This is because there simply are no moral facts or properties in the world of the sort required to render our moral judgements true: we have no plausible epistemological account of how we could access such facts and properties, and, moreover, such properties and facts would be *metaphysically queer*, unlike anything else in the universe as we know it. A moral property would have to be such that the mere apprehension of it by a moral agent would be sufficient to motivate that agent to act. Mackie finds this idea utterly problematic. He concludes that there are no moral properties or moral facts, so that (positive, atomic) moral judgements are uniformly false: our moral thinking involves us in a radical *error*. Because Mackie denies that there are moral facts or properties, he is not a moral realist, but a *moral anti-realist*. Mackie's error-theory is the subject of chapter 6. In that chapter, we also look at some related fictionalist accounts of moral judgement (Joyce 2001; Kalderon 2005a).

1.6 Weak Cognitivism about Morals without Moral Realism: Response-Dependence Theories

A *weak cognitivist* theory is one which holds that moral judgements (a) are apt for evaluation in terms of truth and falsity, but (b) cannot be the upshot of cognitive access to moral properties and states of affairs. Weak cognitivism thus agrees with strong cognitivism in virtue of (a), but disagrees in virtue of (b). An example of a weak cognitivist theory would be a 'response-dependence' view which held that our best judgements about morals *determine* the extensions of moral predicates, rather than based upon some faculty which *tracks*, *detects* or *cognitively accesses* facts about the instantiation of moral properties. (The extension of a predicate is the class of things, events, or objects, to which that predicate may correctly be applied.) Moral judgements are thus capable of being true or false, even though they are not based on a faculty with a tracking, accessing or detecting role, in other words, even though true moral judgements are not the upshot of cognitive access to moral states of affairs. This view thus rejects moral realism, not by denying the existence of moral facts (like the error-theory), but by denying that those facts are constitutively independent of human opinion. In chapter 7, I will discuss weak cognitivist theories of this type in the context of Crispin Wright's work on *anti-realism* (e.g., Wright 1988a).

1.7 Non-Cognitivism

Non-cognitivists deny that moral judgements are even apt to be true
or false. Non-cognitivists thus disagree with both weak and strong
cognitivism. We shall look at a number of arguments which the non-
cognitivist uses against cognitivism. An example of such an argument
is the *argument from moral psychology*:

Suppose that moral judgements can express beliefs, as the cognitivist claims. Being motivated to do something or to pursue a course of
action is always a matter of having a belief and a desire. For example,
I am motivated to reach for the fridge because I believe that it contains
beer and I have a desire for a beer. But it is an internal and necessary
fact about an agent that if she sincerely judges that X is morally right,
she is motivated to pursue the course of action X. So if a moral judgement expressed a belief, it would have to be a belief which sustained
an internal and necessary connection to a desire: it would have to be
a necessary truth that an agent who possessed the belief would inter
alia possess the desire. But no belief is necessarily connected to a desire
because, as Hume claimed, 'beliefs and desires are distinct existences',
and it is impossible to have a necessary connection between distinct
existences (Hume 1739). So it cannot be the case that moral judgements
express beliefs. So moral judgements are not truth-apt.[4]

If moral judgements cannot express beliefs, what do they express?
We shall look at three versions of non-cognitivism which give different
answers to this question: A. J. Ayer's *emotivism* (1936), according to
which moral judgements express emotions, or sentiments of approval
or disapproval; Simon Blackburn's *quasi-realism* (1984), according to
which moral judgements express our dispositions to form sentiments
of approval or disapproval; and Allan Gibbard's *norm-expressivism*
(1990, 2003), according to which our moral judgements express our
acceptance of norms.

Perhaps the main challenge to non-cognitivism is what is called the
Frege–Geach problem. According to emotivism, for example, judging
that murder is wrong is really just like shouting 'Boo for murder!'
(When I shout 'Boo!' I am evincing my disapproval; I am not attempting to *describe* something.) But what about 'If murder is wrong, then
it is wrong to murder your mother-in-law'? This makes sense. But on
the emotivist interpretation it doesn't (what would it sound like on
an emotivist interpretation?). We shall look at how quasi-realism and
norm-expressivism try to solve this problem for non-cognitivism, as
well as a range of other problems that threaten the non-cognitivist.
Non-cognitivism is the subject of chapters 3, 4 and 5.

1.8 Internalism and Externalism, Humeanism and Anti-Humeanism

One of the premises in the argument from moral psychology above is the claim that there is an internal and necessary connection between sincerely making a moral judgement and being motivated to act in the manner prescribed by that judgement. This claim is known as *internalism*: because it says that there is an *internal* or *conceptual* connection between moral judgement and motivation. Some cognitivist philosophers (e.g., Railton, Brink) respond to the argument from moral psychology by denying internalism. They claim that the connection between judgement and motivation is only external and contingent. Such philosophers are known as *externalists*. Other cognitivist philosophers (e.g., McDowell, Wiggins) respond to the argument from moral psychology by denying another premise of the argument, the claim that motivation always involves the presence of *both* beliefs and desires (this premise is known as the *Humean Theory of Motivation*, since it received a classic exposition by Hume). McDowell and Wiggins advance an *Anti-Humean Theory of Motivation*, according to which beliefs themselves can be intrinsically motivating. The debates between internalism and externalism, and Humeanism and Anti-Humeanism, are the subject of 9.9–9.10 and 10.4.

1.9 Further Reading

The following surveys of recent and contemporary metaethics may be found useful: Sayre-McCord (1986); Darwall, Gibbard and Railton (1992); Little (1994a, 1994b); Railton (1996a). A nice book that may ease readers unfamiliar with metaethics into the present text is Fisher (2011). For those entirely new to philosophical ethics, Blackburn (2001) and Shafer-Landau (2003a) are excellent and concise introductions. Benn (1998) and Kirchin (2012) are also useful. Useful collections of essays on the metaethical topics covered in this book are Fisher and Kirchin (2006), and Shafer-Landau and Cuneo (2007).

1.10 Flowchart of Main Metaethical Theories[5]

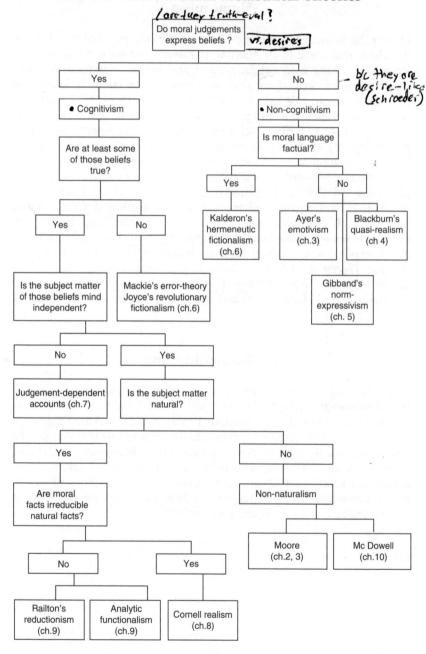

2

Moore's Attack on Ethical Naturalism

2.1 Moore's Strong Cognitivism and Account of 'Natural'

In chapter 1, I distinguished between two forms of strong cognitivism: naturalistic strong cognitivism and non-naturalistic strong cognitivism. We can view these theories as theories about the *truth-conditions* of moral statements. Naturalistic strong cognitivism holds that the truth-conditions of moral sentences are determined by facts about the instantiation of natural properties, while non-naturalistic strong cognitivism holds that the truth-conditions of moral sentences are determined by facts about the instantiation of non-natural properties. In *Principia Ethica*, Moore argues for a version of non-naturalistic strong cognitivism. His argument is mainly negative: he argues for non-naturalism by arguing *against* naturalism. He claims that all naturalistic theories of morals are flawed, because they commit a fallacy, which he labels 'The naturalistic fallacy'.

Before outlining Moore's argument against naturalism, two comments are in order.

Comment 1: Moore on 'natural'

Moore's understanding of 'natural' is as follows:

> By 'nature', then, I do mean and have meant that which is the subject matter of the natural sciences and also of psychology. It may be said to include all that has existed, does exist, or will exist in time. (Moore 1993: 92)

This characterization has some obvious drawbacks. First, we require some account of what makes a particular science 'natural', an account which begs no questions against ethical naturalism. In addition, the implication in the passage is that psychology is not, in whatever sense Moore had in mind, a 'natural' science. So why characterize the subject matter of psychology as 'natural'? This suggests that there is some deeper characterization of 'nature' such that the subject matters of both the 'natural' sciences and psychology count as part of it. So what is this more fundamental characterization? One commentator suggests the following:

> [F]or a property to be natural is for it to be causal, that is, to be such that its presence, in suitable conditions, brings about certain effects. (Baldwin 1993: xxii)

While another suggests:

> [Moore] was willing to accept a criterion for 'non-natural' which suggested that a non-natural property was one which could not be discerned by the senses. (Warnock 1960: 15)

Rather than digress into a discussion of how these suggestions relate to each other, I will simply take natural properties to be those which are either causal or detectable by the senses. Natural properties, thus characterized, will either be dealt with by typical 'natural' sciences or by psychology. So, if a property is natural on our characterization, it will also be natural on Moore's. Conversely, properties dealt with by the 'natural' sciences or by psychology, on any plausible characterization of 'natural' science, will be either causal or detectable by the senses. So, if a property is natural on Moore's characterization, it will also be natural on ours. Non-natural properties, on our characterization, are simply properties which are neither causal nor detectable by the senses.

Comment 2: Was Moore a strong cognitivist?

Recall that there are two components to strong cognitivism: (a) moral judgements are truth-apt, and (b) moral judgements can be the upshot of cognitively accessing the facts which render them true. Moore says certain things that make it sound as if he rejects (b), so that he should really be classed as a weak cognitivist:

> I wish it to be observed that, when I call [moral] propositions 'intuitions', I mean merely to assert that they are incapable of proof; I imply nothing whatever as to the manner or origin of our cognition of them. (Moore 1903: 37)

However, in practice, Moore seems to adhere to some form of strong cognitivism. For example, the uneasiness one might feel on realizing that one's moral judgements are incapable of proof is replied to as follows:

> The mere fact that in certain cases proof is impossible does not usually give us the least uneasiness. For instance, nobody can prove that this is a chair beside me; yet I do not suppose that anyone is much dissatisfied for that reason. (Moore 1903: 127)

Recall that what distinguishes strong from weak cognitivism is the idea that true moral judgements can be the upshot of cognitive access to the facts which render them true. Now, a judgement can be the upshot of cognitive access to a state of affairs if and only if that judgement is the deliverance of a cognitive faculty. And, of course, the judgement that there is a chair beside me is an example par excellence of a judgement based on the deliverances of a cognitive faculty, namely, sense-perception. If we are to take the analogy seriously, then, we would have to view moral judgements as based on the deliverances of some cognitive faculty and as the possible upshot of cognitive access to moral states of affairs. In other words, we would have to be strong cognitivists.[1]

2.2 The Naturalistic Fallacy and the Classical Open-Question Argument

Moore sets out to argue that moral terms such as 'good' are not definable in terms of natural properties, such as pleasure, desire, or desiring to desire. Moore's target is thus what we might call *definitional naturalism*: the view that moral properties are identical or reducible to natural properties as a matter of definitional or conceptual fact. An example of definitional naturalism would be the view about the meaning of 'good' proposed by Hobbes:

> Whatsoever is the object of any man's appetite or desire; that is it which he for his part calleth good; and the object of his hate and aversion, evil. (1651, part 1, chapter 6)

Moore is not concerned with how we actually use the word 'good': his concern is with attempts to analyse the concept good. In other words, his concern is with attempts to apply the method of *conceptual analysis* to 'good':

> I shall therefore use 'good' in the sense in which I think it is ordinarily used; but at the same time I am not anxious to discuss whether I am right in thinking that it is so used. My business is solely with that object or idea, which I hold rightly or wrongly, that the word is generally used

to stand for. What I want to discover is the nature of that object or idea, and about this I am extremely anxious to arrive at an agreement. (Moore 1993: 58)[2]

Moore claims that any attempt to define 'good' in terms of natural properties commits what he calls the 'naturalistic fallacy'. It is clear that the reason Moore thinks that 'good' is not definable in terms of natural properties is that he thinks that it is not definable *at all*, not even in terms of non-natural properties, such as metaphysical properties (e.g., such as the property of being approved by God):

> It should be observed that the fallacy, by reference to which I define 'Metaphysical Ethics', is the same in kind; and I give it but one name, the naturalistic fallacy. (Moore 1903: 91)

And even if good were a natural property, one would still commit the naturalistic fallacy in attempting to define it:

> Even if [good] were a natural object, that would not alter the nature of the fallacy nor diminish its importance one whit. All that I have said about it would remain quite equally true: only the name which I have called it would not be so appropriate as I think it is. (Moore 1903: 65)

The naturalistic fallacy is thus committed by anyone who tries to give any sort of definition of 'good' or analysis of the concept which it expresses. So where is the fallacy? Why is it a mistake to think that a definition of 'good' can be given? Let's look at the claim that 'good' can be defined or analysed in terms of some natural property N, and attempt to reconstruct the argument of 12–13 of *Principia Ethica*. I'll refer to this as the 'Classical Open-Question Argument' (COQA). Let's say that a question is *closed* if sincerely asking the question implies that you don't understand some of the meanings or concepts involved in its formulation: in other words, that you are prey to some linguistic or conceptual confusion (an example might be 'Are bachelors unmarried?'). A question is open if it is not closed.

(1) Suppose that the predicate 'good' is synonymous with, or analytically equivalent to, the naturalistic predicate 'N'.

Then:

(2) It is part of the meaning of the claim that 'x is N' that x is good.

But then:

(3) Someone who seriously asked 'Is an x which is N also good?'

would betray some conceptual confusion. The question would be closed.

But:

(4) For, given any natural property N, it is always an *open question* whether an x which is N is good. That is to say, asking the question 'Is an x which is N also good?' betrays no conceptual confusion.

(For example, it makes sense to ask 'Is a pleasurable action good?' or 'Is something which we desire to desire good?' Someone asking these questions betrays no conceptual confusion.)[3]

So:

(5) It cannot be the case that 'good' is synonymous with, or analytically equivalent to, 'N'.

So:

(6) The property of *being good* cannot as a matter of conceptual necessity be identical to the property of *being N*.

This argument is often referred to as 'the Open-Question Argument', because of step (4). Note that the same argument could be run against the attempt to define 'good' in terms of some metaphysical property. To see this, we can just choose a metaphysical property M, and substitute M for N in the argument above. Thus:

(7) Suppose that the predicate 'good' is synonymous with, or analytically equivalent to, the metaphysical predicate 'is approved by God'.

Then:

(8) It is part of the meaning of the claim that 'x is approved by God' that x is good.

But then:

(9) Someone who seriously asked 'Is an x which is approved by God also good?' would betray some conceptual confusion.

But:

(10) Asking the question 'Is an x which is approved by God also good?' betrays no conceptual confusion. It is an open question.

So:

(11) It cannot be the case that 'good' is synonymous with, or analytically equivalent to, 'approved by God'.

So:

(12) The property of *being good* cannot as a matter of conceptual necessity be identical to the property of *being approved by God*.

How plausible is the COQA?[4]

2.3 Three Objections to the Classical Open-Question Argument

In this section, I'll outline three objections to Moore's open-question argument.

Objection 1: Frankena's objection

Frankena writes:

> [T]he charge of committing the naturalistic fallacy can be made, if at all, only as a conclusion from the discussion and not as an instrument of deciding it. (1938: 465)

There are at least two ways of taking Frankena's objection that Moore's argument begs the question against the analytical naturalist.

First, we can only appeal to our conviction that there is an open question at step (4) if that conviction is well-founded. But if analytical naturalism is correct, that conviction is not well-founded: seriously asking of an x which is N whether it is also good *will* betray a conceptual confusion, even though we erroneously think that it does not. So we can only appeal to the open question at step (4) if we have *already* established that analytical naturalism is incorrect. Since that is the intended conclusion of Moore's reasoning, he cannot use the COQA against analytical naturalism without simply begging the question.

Second, we can view Frankena as complaining along the following lines. Certainly, it is an open question whether pleasant actions are good, and it is an open question whether things that we desire to desire are good. But generalizing from these few examples to the conclusion that for *any* natural property N, it is an open question whether N-things are good is unwarranted unless we already assume the falsity of analytical naturalism. So, again, the argument presented by Moore is question-begging.

Objection 2: The 'no interesting analyses' objection

The open-question argument assumes that it is impossible for a conceptual analysis to be true but informative and interesting. Take any concept P and suppose that it can be analysed in terms of some other concept P*. If the analysis is to be informative and interesting, it must be possible to question meaningfully whether something which is P* is P. According to Moore, the analysis of P in terms of P* can be correct only if the question whether something which is P* is P is closed: in other words, if sincerely asking the question implies that you don't understand it. So Moore's argument implies that the analysis of P in terms of P* can be correct only if it is completely uninformative and uninteresting. However, this implication is false: analyses patently can be informative and interesting. For example, mathematics and logic are arguably full of unobvious a priori and analytic truths, and there are also many candidates for interesting and informative philosophical analyses (e.g., the dispositional analysis of colours in terms of our dispositions to see things in certain ways, the analysis of knowledge as justified true belief and so on).[5] So there is something amiss with Moore's argument.

Moore might reply to this objection as follows. The open-question argument is not flawed, because in fact it *is* impossible for there to be an analysis which is simultaneously correct, informative and interesting. This is shown by the 'paradox of analysis'. Suppose we are trying to analyse some concept C in terms of some other concept C*. *Ex hypothesi*, we understand concept C. So we know what concept C means. So we know what is included in the meaning of C. If C can be analysed in terms of C*, then C* is part of the meaning of C. So we already know that C* is part of the meaning of C. So if C can be correctly analysed in terms of C*, this analysis cannot be interesting or informative. So the objection in question is not a good objection, after all, because the paradox of analysis shows that there *are* no interesting and informative analyses.

But the 'paradox of analysis' is in fact no paradox at all. To see this, ask: how can one grasp a concept without being consciously aware of what is involved in the correct analysis of that concept? If we can answer this question satisfactorily, we can show that there is no 'paradox of analysis'. One way to answer it is to distinguish between *knowledge how* (the possession of an ability) and *knowledge that* (propositional knowledge), and then to argue that grasp of a concept consists in the possession of knowledge how, whereas knowledge of a correct analysis is a species of knowledge that. The explanation of how grasp of a concept can coexist with lack of knowledge of its correct analysis would then be simply that in most cases of knowledge how, it is possible to possess the relevant ability without possessing any propositional knowledge describing that ability. For example, someone might know how to drive a car round a bend without knowing the (highly complex) propositions which correctly describe what driving a car round a bend involves. Another example: someone can know how to speak grammatically without being able to state in propositional form the extremely complicated grammatical rules which underlie that ability. These reflections suggest that there is no 'paradox of analysis', and that Moore thus has no defence against the 'no interesting analyses' objection.[6]

Objection 3: The 'sense-reference' objection

Frege famously distinguished two different elements in the intuitive conception of meaning: *sense* and *reference*. He used the example of the evening star and the morning star. We know what the name 'Hesperus' means, we also know what the name 'Phosphorus' means, and 'Hesperus' and 'Phosphorus' mean the same thing. So how can we *discover* that Hesperus actually *is* Phosphorus? How can it be an 'open question' whether Hesperus is Phosphorous? Frege says that the names 'Hesperus' and 'Phosphorus' have the *same reference* but *different senses*. So what we should actually say is: we know the sense of 'Hesperus', we know the sense of 'Phosphorus', but 'Hesperus' and 'Phosphorus' do not have the same sense. They have different senses which nevertheless pick out the same reference, and the fact that they possess the same reference is something that we can discover, *because we can understand the sense of an expression without knowing its reference*. For example, I understand the sense of 'the cleverest student in year 3'. But I do not know which person is picked out by that phrase: that is something I have to discover.[7]

Perhaps the ethical naturalist can apply Frege's sense-reference distinction to the case of 'good' and 'N'. According to the naturalist, we know what 'N' means, we know what 'good' means, and 'good' and 'N' mean the same thing. So how can we discover that goodness actually is property N? How can it be an 'open question' whether something which possesses N actually is good? Well, can't we say that 'good' and 'N', like 'Hesperus' and 'Phosphorus', have the same reference but different senses? Then we could say: we know the sense of 'good' and we know the sense of 'N', but 'good' and 'N' do not have the same sense. They have different senses but nevertheless refer to the same property, and the fact that they refer to the same property is something that we can discover, because we can understand the sense of a predicate without knowing which property it stands for.

How plausible are the three objections to the COQA? The 'sense-reference' objection is problematic. Moore's argument is directed against versions of ethical naturalism that argue that the property of being good is identical or reducible to the property of being N in virtue of a conceptual or analytic equivalence between 'good' and 'N'. Two expressions are analytically equivalent if they have the same sense. So, in conceding that 'good' and 'N' do not have the same sense, the 'sense-reference' objection effectively concedes to Moore the implausibility of definitional or analytic naturalism. In short, the version of naturalism which the 'sense-reference' objection preserves in the face of the open-question argument is not the intended target of that argument. But although the 'sense-reference' objection can be said to fail in this way, Moore's victory is somewhat hollow, for what that objection shows is that there is a version of ethical naturalism apparently left untouched by the open-question argument. Is this version of naturalism – what we might call 'metaphysical' or 'synthetic' as opposed to definitional or analytic naturalism – independently plausible, or is there a version of the COQA which applies even to it? For the moment we must leave these questions up in the air: we will return to them in chapters 8 and 9.

However, it seems to me that Moore has no good reply to Frankena's objection, and that Moore's reply to the 'no interesting analyses' objection ultimately fails. So, can we salvage anything from the COQA, or do these objections show that Moore's argument is completely useless as a philosophical tool?

2.4 Can the Open-Question Argument Be Salvaged?

We shall look at two attempts to retrieve something from the open-question argument. The aim of these attempts is to use something like Moore's argument, not to decisively refute definitional ethical naturalism, but to establish a presumption against it. And they try to do this in a way which avoids both Frankena's charge of question-begging and the idea that no analysis can be both correct and informative.

(a) Baldwin's 'open-question' argument

Thomas Baldwin writes:

> If a conceptual analysis is correct, then, once we have encountered it, it should come to seem to us entirely appropriate to guide our thoughts and judgements in accordance with it, even if at first the analysis strikes

us as unobvious; and Moore's objection to proposed analyses of intrinsic value is precisely that we do not find ourselves able to move to this reflective assimilation of them. (1993: xix)

And:

> [I]t is reasonable to demand of an analysis of meaning that it should illuminate the concepts in such a way that, because it enhances our understanding, we come to find it natural for us to guide our judgements according to it. It is in the light of this requirement that the persisting sense of the significance of Moore's questions is problematic for the ethical reductionist. It is evidence that his reductive analysis is simply not persuasive, and therefore not correct. . . . This establishes a presumption against the reductionist, but no more. (1990: 89)

The argument is:

(13) If 'good' and 'N' are analytically equivalent, then *ceteris paribus* competent speakers should – after conceptual reflection – come to find it natural to guide their evaluative judgements by the analysis.

(14) After conceptual reflection, the conviction that 'Is an x which is N also good?' is an open question persists among competent speakers. So, after conceptual reflection, they do not come to find it natural to guide their evaluative judgements by the analysis of 'good' in terms of 'N'.

So:

(15) We can conclude that 'good' and 'N' are not analytically equivalent, unless *ceteris* isn't *paribus* (i.e., there is some other explanation of why competent speakers do not come to find it natural to guide their evaluative judgements by the analysis).

The argument establishes only a presumption against the analytic naturalist, because it is of course open to the naturalist to attempt to 'explain away' our persisting conviction that the question is indeed open – perhaps in terms of 'our attachment to an illusory conception of distinctive ethical meaning' (Baldwin 1990: 89). But if there is no plausible deflationary explanation, the presumption has to be against the naturalist's claim of analytic equivalence. Note that the argument does not turn on the claim that the conviction that the question is open is correct or well-founded, merely that it persists even after conceptual reflection, and that it does so for the range of instances of 'N' that we have so far considered. So Frankena's charge of question-begging is avoided. Nor is there any assumption to the effect that analyses cannot be both correct and informative. Indeed, the idea behind (13) is that we come to find it natural to guide our practice according to an analysis precisely because it is informative and illuminating.

We could object to Baldwin's argument as follows: 'if analytical naturalism is correct then anyone who fails, after conceptual reflection, to find it natural to guide his practice by the purported analysis is not fully competent with the relevant concepts'. But this is weak. The objection can be pressed only on pain of holding that otherwise competent speakers are nevertheless not fully competent only because they do not find it natural to guide their practice by means of the purported analysis. Unless the objector can find some *independent* reason to convict of some conceptual shortcoming those who don't find it natural to guide their practice by the purported analysis, the objection on behalf of the analytical naturalist looks very ad hoc.

So it appears that Baldwin's argument does at least establish a presumption against the analytical naturalist.

(b) Darwall, Gibbard and Railton's 'open-question' argument

Stephen Darwall, Allan Gibbard and Peter Railton try to save something from the open-question argument by responding to Frankena's objection:

> *First*, one should not claim utter conviction [that there really is an open question], but merely observe that the open question argument is compelling for otherwise competent, reflective speakers of English, who appear to have no difficulty imagining what it would be like to dispute whether P [some natural property] is good. *Second*, one should articulate a philosophical explanation of why this might be so. Here is one such explanation. Attributions of goodness appear to have a conceptual link with the guidance of action, a link exploited whenever we gloss the open question 'Is P really good?' as 'Is it clear that, other things being equal, we really ought to, or must, devote ourselves to bringing about P?' Our confidence that the openness of the open question does not depend upon any error or oversight may stem from our seeming ability to imagine, for any naturalistic property R, clear-headed beings who would fail to find appropriate reason or motive to action in the mere fact that R obtains (or is seen to be in the offing). Given this imaginative possibility, it has not been logically secured that P is action-guiding (even if, as a matter of fact, we all do find R psychologically compelling). And this absence of a logical or conceptual link to action shows us exactly where there is room to ask, intelligibly, whether R really is good. (1992: 117)

On my understanding, the argument is as follows:

(16) There is a *conceptual* or *internal* link between making a moral judgement and being motivated, *ceteris paribus*, to act as that

judgement prescribes. (This is *internalism*.[8])Absent some weakness of will or other psychological affliction, judging that a type of action is morally good entails being motivated to perform actions of that type. Someone with no psychological afflictions, etc., who (apparently) judges that a type of action is morally good but consistently claims that he sees no reason to perform actions of that type doesn't grasp the concept of moral goodness.

(17) Competent and reflective speakers of English are convinced that they are able to imagine clear-headed (and otherwise psychologically healthy) beings who judge that R (some naturalistic property) obtains, but who fail to find appropriate reason or motive to act in accordance with that judgement.

(18) If there were no conceptual link between judging that R obtains and being motivated to act accordingly, we would expect competent and reflective speakers of English to have the conviction described in (17).

So:

(19) Unless there is some other explanation of the conviction described in (17), we are entitled to conclude that there is no conceptual link between judging that R obtains and being motivated to act accordingly.

So:

(20) Unless there is some other explanation of the conviction described in (17), we are entitled to conclude that the judgement that R obtains isn't a *moral* judgement (from (16)).

So:

(21) Unless there is some other explanation of the conviction mentioned in (17), we are entitled to conclude that the property of being morally good is not identical or reducible to the property of being R as a matter of conceptual necessity.

Note that this version of the argument escapes Frankena's objection, since it turns on the claim (17) that competent and reflective speakers *have* the relevant conviction, not on the question-begging assumption that that conviction is correct. Note also that Darwall, Gibbard and Railton are clear that this is not a knock-down argument against analytical naturalism, nor a claim that the analytical naturalist commits a fallacy:

Moore had discovered not a proof of a fallacy, but rather an argumentative device that implicitly brings to the fore certain characteristic features of 'good' – and of other normative vocabulary – that seem to stand in the way of our accepting any known naturalistic or metaphysical definition as unquestionably right, as definitions, at least when fully understood, seemingly should be. (1992: 116)

The characteristic feature is the intrinsically action-guiding nature of moral judgement alleged in (16). The argument establishes only a presumption against naturalism: the naturalist can overturn that presumption by finding some alternative explanation of the conviction described in (17).

Let's pause for a moment. Baldwin's argument may seem to be the stronger of the two, since unlike the Darwall–Gibbard–Railton version, it doesn't depend on an internalist premise about moral judgement and motivation. But, in fact, Baldwin's version is implicitly internalistic. Recall that the argument went as follows:

(13) If 'good' and 'N' are analytically equivalent, then *ceteris paribus* competent speakers should – after conceptual reflection – come to find it natural to guide their evaluative judgements by the analysis.

(14) After conceptual reflection, the conviction that 'Is an x which is N also good?' is an open question persists among competent speakers. So after conceptual reflection they do not come to find it natural to guide their evaluative judgements by the analysis of 'good' in terms of 'N'.

So:

(15) We can presume that 'Good' and 'N' are not genuinely analytically equivalent, unless *ceteris* isn't *paribus* (i.e., there is some other explanation of why competent speakers do not come to find it natural to guide their evaluative judgements by the analysis).

If the argument is just left like this, the naturalist can retort: 'Sure, I have left an explanatory obligation undischarged: I have provided no explanation of why otherwise competent speakers do not find it natural to guide their practice by means of my proposed analysis. But if, as you claim, competent speakers do not come to find it natural to guide their practice by means of the naturalistic analysis, you need to provide some explanation of why that is so. And you cannot just say "because 'good' and 'N' are analytically inequivalent". That is no explanation at all.' Thus, if Baldwin's argument is left as it stands, we get at best a stand-off between the naturalist and his opponent: neither view is superior, since both leave substantial explanatory obligations unfulfilled. To get more than a stand-off, Baldwin will have to do something to provide an explanation of why competent speakers do not find it natural to guide their practice with 'good' by the naturalistic analysis. And this is where the Darwall–Gibbard–Railton line comes into play. Judgements about good are intrinsically motivating, judgements about N are not, so no wonder speakers do not find it natural to guide their practice with 'good' by the proposed analysis. The presumption against the analytic equivalence of 'good' and 'N' thus falls out in a way which avoids a simple stand-off. Unless there is a better explanation of why speakers do not find it natural to guide their practice with 'good' via the proposed analysis, we are entitled to presume that 'good' and 'N' are not analytically equivalent. At bottom, then, there is no substantial difference between Baldwin's argument and the Darwall–Gibbard–Railton argument. So from now on I'll focus on the latter.

How strong is the presumption established against the naturalist in this argument? I will not address here the question of whether the naturalist can find some suitable explanation of the fact that speakers have the conviction described in (17). Suffice it to say that the naturalist can take two other steps to deflect the argument. First, many modern naturalists respond by denying premise (16), internalism. They put forward the externalist claim that although there is a relation between moral judgement and being motivated to act accordingly, it is only a *contingent* and *external* relation. It is only a *contingent* and *external* fact that someone who judges that x is good is, *ceteris paribus*, motivated to act accordingly. The debate between internalists and externalists is one of the most hotly contested debates in modern metaethics, as we'll see in 9.9. Given this, the presumption that the new open-question argument establishes against the analytic naturalist is at best highly provisional, depending as it does on the outcome of this debate. Second, the naturalist has the option of discarding the idea that moral goodness is identical or reducible to some naturalistic property as a matter of conceptual necessity. That is, giving up *analytic* naturalism in favour of metaphysical or synthetic naturalism will block the move from step (20) to the denial of naturalism. Metaphysical naturalism is the view, introduced in the 'sense-reference' objection to Moore in 2.3, that 'good' and 'N', although analytically *in*equivalent, stand for the same property, a fact which is discoverable a posteriori. Again, this style of naturalism is hotly debated in modern metaethics, as we shall see in detail in later chapters. Once more, the presumption that the new open-question argument establishes against naturalism is at most provisional, depending as it does on the outcome of that debate.

2.5 Further Reading

The classic text here is Moore ([1903] 1993), especially chapter 1. Note that Moore would have liked to have revised much of what he attempted to say in the first edition (1903). He never did this because it seemed to him that the only way to do it properly would have involved rewriting the entire book, and when the book was reprinted in 1922 the only revisions were grammatical and typographical. However, an idea of the sorts of major alterations which Moore envisioned can be gleaned from the extended preface to the revised edition, which Moore never published (it was published in 1993 in the second edition). Also useful in this regard are the exchanges between Moore and his critics, in Schillp (1942). This volume also contains Moore's short autobiography. Frankena (1938) is a classic.

More recent discussions of Moore's arguments against naturalism can be found in Warnock (1960: chapters 1 and 2); Baldwin (1990: especially chapter 3, 1993); Darwall, Gibbard and Railton (1992: especially section 1); Soames (2003: chapters 3 and 4); Altman (2004); and Strandberg (2004). Two useful collections, both published to mark the 100th anniversary of the publication of *Principia Ethica*, are the 2003 special issue of the journal *Ethics* and Horgan and Timmons (eds) (2006).

Non-analytic naturalism and the debate between internalism and externalism are discussed in chapters 8 and 9 of this volume.

3

Emotivism and the Rejection of Non-Naturalism

3.1 Introduction to Ayer's Emotivism

The central claim of cognitivism is that moral judgements express beliefs, and that those judgements are therefore truth-apt. The first version of non-cognitivism we will look at is emotivism, as propounded by A. J. Ayer in *Language, Truth and Logic*. Ayer's version of emotivism is the simplest and most provocative version of non-cognitivism: more sophisticated versions were later developed by Charles Stevenson, Richard Hare, Simon Blackburn and Allan Gibbard. Some of these will be discussed in due course. We'll begin with a brief exposition of Ayer's view.

Ayer denies that moral judgements express beliefs: rather, moral judgements express emotions, or sentiments, of approval and disapproval. Since these emotions and sentiments are unlike beliefs in that they do not even purport to represent how the world is, the judgements which express them are not truth-apt. Compare your belief that there are children in the street, which purports to represent how the world is, with your horror at the fact that the children are torturing a cat. The belief has a representative function: it purports to represent how the world is, and it is true if and only if the world actually is as it represents it. The emotion of horror, on the other hand, has no such representative function: it is not the sort of thing that can even be assessed for truth or falsity. In short, moral judgements are neither true nor false: they do not state anything, but rather express our emotions and feelings. As Ayer puts it in a famous passage:

> If I say to someone, 'You acted wrongly in stealing that money', I am not stating anything more than if I had simply said, 'You stole that money'. In adding that this action is wrong, *I am not making any further statement*

about it. I am simply evincing my moral disapproval of it. It is as if I had said, 'You stole that money', in a peculiar tone of horror, or written it with the addition of some special exclamation marks. The tone, or the exclamation marks, adds nothing to the literal meaning of the sentence. *It merely serves to show that the expression of it is attended by certain feelings in the speaker.* (Ayer [1936] 1946: 107, emphases added)

It follows that:

If I now generalise my previous statement and say, 'Stealing money is wrong,' I produce a sentence which has no factual meaning – that is, expresses no proposition that can be either true or false. ([1936] 1946: 107)

But what about moral disagreement? If I say 'Stealing money is wrong' and someone else says 'Stealing money is not wrong', isn't this a case of us contradicting each other? And how can we make sense of this except by seeing the judgements we make as true or false: we *contradict* each other because if what I say is true, what the other person says is false, and vice versa. Ayer realizes that this model of moral disagreement is only available to the cognitivist, and rejects it:

When someone disagrees with us about the moral value of a certain action or type of action, we do admittedly resort to argument in order to win him over to our way of thinking. But we do not attempt to show by our arguments that he has the 'wrong' ethical feeling towards a situation whose nature he has correctly apprehended. What we attempt to show is that he is mistaken about the facts of the case. . . . [I]f our opponent happens to have undergone a different process of moral 'conditioning' from ourselves, so that, even when he acknowledges all the facts, he still disagrees with us about the moral value of the actions under discussion, then we abandon the attempt to convince him by argument. . . . It is because argument fails us when we come to deal with pure questions of value, as distinct from questions of fact, that we finally resort to mere abuse. ([1936] 1946: 111)

Moral disagreement is not a case of having contradictory beliefs, but rather a matter of having a clash of feelings.

Ayer's argument for emotivism basically takes the following form: he considers various forms of cognitivism, both naturalistic and non-naturalistic, and finds that they are implausible. Given that all the known forms of cognitivism fail, he concludes that the best way to make sense of moral judgement is to opt for a version of non-cognitivism, namely, emotivism. Ayer's rejection of naturalistic cognitivism turns on an application of Moore's COQA. For example, Ayer deals with utilitarian analyses of 'x is good' as follows:

[S]ince it is not self-contradictory to say that some pleasant things are not good, or that some bad things are desired, it cannot be the case that the sentence 'x is good' is equivalent to 'x is pleasant', or to 'x is desired'. And to every other variant of utilitarianism with which I am acquainted the same objection can be made. ([1936] 1946: 105)

Even though we found that the 'open-question' argument does not have the sort of force which Moore attributed to it, for the sake of argument, we'll grant Ayer the conclusion that naturalistic cognitivism is implausible. But what about Moore's own non-naturalistic brand of cognitivism? We found that his arguments against naturalism were far from conclusive, but we haven't yet discussed the plausibility of his own non-naturalistic position. Ayer does discuss Moorean non-naturalism, and rejects it, and we discuss this in the next section.

3.2 Ayer's Argument Against Non-Naturalism

Ayer was a logical positivist. According to logical positivism, there were only two ways in which a statement could be *literally significant*: by being *empirically verifiable*, or by being *analytic* (roughly, true by definition). Thus, 'There are over 300 pubs in Birmingham' is literally significant because it is in principle verifiable by observation: we can go round the streets of the city, use our eyes, and count the pubs. Also, 'All bachelors are unmarried' is literally significant, because it is true in virtue of the definitions of the terms it contains: roughly 'bachelor' means 'an unmarried male of marriageable age'. When the logical positivists speak of literal significance, they mean roughly what we mean when we speak of a judgement being truth-apt. Thus, if a putative statement is neither analytic nor empirically verifiable, it is not literally significant, not apt for assessment in terms of truth and falsity. According to the logical positivists, moral judgements come into this category: they are neither analytic nor empirically verifiable, so they are not literally significant.

Ayer uses this account of literal significance to dispose of Moore's non-naturalism. Moore claims that moral judgements are truth-apt, and that they are rendered true or false by facts about the instantiation of the non-natural, simple and unanalysable property of moral goodness. Ayer rejects this on the grounds that it conflicts with the logical positivist account of literal significance: Moore agrees that moral judgements are not analytic, so if he claims that they are literally significant, he needs to be able to defend the claim that they are empirically verifiable. According to Ayer, it is indefensible to claim that moral judgements, thus construed, are empirically verifiable:

In admitting that normative ethical concepts are irreducible to empirical concepts, we seem to be leaving the way clear for the 'absolutist' view of ethics – that is, the view that statements of value are not controlled by observation, as ordinary empirical propositions are, but only by a mysterious 'intellectual intuition'. A feature of this theory, which is seldom recognized by its advocates, is that it makes statements of value unverifiable. For it is notorious that what seems intuitively certain to one person may seem doubtful, or even false, to another. So that unless it is possible to provide some criterion by which one may decide between conflicting intuitions, a mere appeal to intuition is worthless as a test of a proposition's validity. But in the case of moral judgements, no such criterion can be given. Some moralists claim to settle the matter by saying that they 'know' that their own moral judgements are correct. But such an assertion is of purely psychological interest, and has not the slightest tendency to prove the validity of any moral judgement. For dissentient moralists may equally well 'know' that their ethical views are correct. And, as far as subjective certainty goes, there will be nothing to choose between them. ([1936] 1946: 106)

Given that naturalism has been rejected, and given that non-naturalism would require a literally significant judgement which was synthetic (i.e., not analytic) and empirically unverifiable, the only option is to give up the claim that moral judgements are literally significant.

A number of comments can be made about this argument. First, the argument against non-naturalism is based on the logical positivist theory of literal significance, according to which the only statements which are literally significant are those which are analytic, or in principle empirically verifiable. But there seem to be many statements which are intuitively literally significant, but neither analytic nor in principle empirically verifiable. Michael Smith gives the following example: 'Before the big bang all the objects in the Universe converged on a single point' (Smith 1994a: 20). Simple examples like this cast doubt on the logical positivist theory of literal significance.

Second, when Ayer actually tried to spell out what it means to say that a statement is in principle empirically verifiable, he ran into all sorts of trouble. It proved impossible to state a criterion for empirical verifiability which did not count any arbitrary 'nonsensical' statement as empirically significant (see Miller 2007: chapter 3).

Given that Ayer's argument against non-naturalism is based on a theory of literal significance which faces these problems, the argument is not persuasive. And in addition to these problems, which stem from problems with the logical positivism upon which it is based, Ayer's argument is also subject to pressures from within the logical positivist theory of meaning. To see this, we need to be clear about the status of Ayer's conclusion that moral statements are not literally significant. He sometimes describes this conclusion as the claim that 'ethical concepts are mere pseudo-concepts' ([1936] 1946: 107). This might suggest that he was claiming that ethics is *nonsense*. This is further suggested by his remarks on metaphysical statements (such as 'We have an enduring self' or 'Reality is one substance and not many'): he concludes from the fact that these are neither analytic nor empirically verifiable that they are 'nonsensical', and that metaphysics ought therefore to be eliminated. The title of chapter 1 of *Language, Truth and Logic* is 'The Elimination of Metaphysics'. So why isn't chapter 6 of that work entitled 'The Elimination of Ethics'? Why doesn't Ayer simply conclude from the fact that moral judgements are neither analytic nor empirically verifiable that they are *verbiage*? Ayer realizes that this moral nihilism might be taken to be an implication of the emotive theory and, in the Introduction to the second edition of *Language, Truth and Logic*, writes:

> In putting forward the principle of verification as a criterion of meaning, I do not overlook the fact that the word 'meaning' is commonly used in a variety of senses, and I do not wish to deny that in some of these senses a statement may properly be said to be meaningful even though it is neither analytic nor empirically verifiable. ([1936] 1946: 15)

Ayer's idea seems to be this: although moral judgements are not literally significant, they are not nonsensical, because they possess some other sort of significance, *emotive significance*. Two questions now loom. First, by what criterion does Ayer distinguish between judgements which possess emotive significance and those which are nonsensical (and which therefore ought to be eliminated)?; and, second, can that criterion be stated in such a way that it grants emotive significance to ethical judgements, but refuses it to the putative judgements of the metaphysicians? Ayer nowhere attempts to answer these questions, and as a consequence his position – combining an eliminativist view of traditional metaphysics with a rejection of moral nihilism – seems only dubiously consistent.[1]

3.3 Some Better Objections to Non-Naturalism

So it looks as if Ayer's case against non-naturalism is pretty shaky. Can we do better? Recall that Moore was a strong cognitivist: he held, not only that moral judgements are truth-apt, but that making a moral judgement can be the upshot of the exercise of a cognitive faculty: my making a correct moral judgement can be based on detecting or accessing the non-natural moral facts, in much the same way that my judgement that there is a table in front of me can be based on my perceiving that there is a table in front of me. This idea faces a number of problems.

Problem 1: The a priori supervenience of the moral on the natural

Philosophers often want to say that properties of one sort *supervene* on properties of a different sort. What does it mean to say that the moral properties of an object supervene on its natural properties? It means if two things have exactly the same natural properties, then they also have exactly the same moral properties. If you find that two things have different moral properties, you must also find that they differ in some way in respect of their natural properties.

Now let's introduce the notion of *necessity*. We say that the proposition that $2 + 2 = 4$ is a *necessary* truth. It did not just turn out to be the case that $2 + 2 = 4$: in some sense it *had* to turn out that way, it *could not* have turned out otherwise. Contrast this with a *contingent* truth, such as the proposition that there is a postbox at the end of Grosvenor Street. This is true, but it might have been otherwise: we can quite easily conceive of situations in which it is false. Here we are talking about *logical* or *conceptual* necessity. There are different kinds of necessity: e.g., *physical* necessity. It is physically impossible for me to jump over the moon (I'd have to violate the laws of physics) but it is still logically possible (my doing so would not violate the laws of logic). Thus, a proposition is physically necessary if its denial is physically impossible: a proposition is logically or conceptually necessary if someone who denies it violates a logical law or displays some conceptual shortcoming.

What sort of necessity is involved in the claim that moral properties supervene on natural properties in this sense? Plausibly, it is *logical or conceptual* necessity: someone who self-consciously gave differing moral evaluations of two acts or events without thinking that he had to point to some natural difference between those acts or events would be displaying his lack of competence with moral concepts. Think about it: how could you say that Jones's action was not as good as Smith's, even though the two actions were exactly alike in terms of their natural properties and the natural circumstances in which they were conducted? Someone who thought in this way would soon be accused of lacking an understanding of the concept of moral goodness.

What has all this to do with non-naturalism? The non-naturalist claims that making a correct moral judgement can be the upshot of something like sense-perception: we can sometimes perceive that a particular action is bad and move from that perception to a judgement to that effect. Likewise, we can sometimes perceive that a particular action has certain natural features and thereby perceive that that action has a certain non-natural moral property. For example, (a) I perceive that Jones is deliberately inflicting pain just for the fun of it on the cat, and thereby perceive that what Jones is doing to the cat is wrong; likewise, (b) I perceive that Smith is deliberately inflicting pain just for the fun of it on the child, and thereby perceive that what Smith is doing to the child is wrong. Now, given that the supervenience of the moral on the natural is a priori, the following is a priori also:

(1)   Any two actions which are deliberate acts of inflicting pain just for the fun of it (and otherwise identical in their naturalistic properties) must receive the same moral evaluation.

But there seems to be no way that we could get to the a priori (1) from (a), (b), and the like: no matter how many more instances of pointless deliberate cruelty we perceive, the inductive generalization to (1) will yield at best an a posteriori truth. So non-naturalism in effect renders mysterious the a priori supervenience of the moral on the natural. Given that 'recognition of the way in which the moral supervenes on the natural is a constraint on the proper use of moral concepts' (Smith 1994a: 22), non-naturalism is thereby thrown into doubt.

It seems to me that there is a genuine problem for non-naturalism here, but that Smith somewhat overstates the strength of the worry (1994a: 21–4). Smith writes as though non-naturalism were somehow *incompatible* with the a priori supervenience of the moral on the natural.[2] But the argument above shows at most that the non-naturalist cannot *use* the idea that we detect moral properties to underwrite the a priori supervenience of the moral on the natural: it remains open to the non-naturalist to find some other way of grounding the claim about a priori supervenience and to find some other explanatory work for the analogy with perception to carry out. The argument does not establish that non-naturalism is false: it just shows that it cannot use its distinctive claims about moral perception *by themselves* to ground one important fact about moral concepts.

Although Smith overstates the force of the objection, it does nevertheless illustrate that there is a question so far unanswered by the non-naturalist: how can you account for the a priori supervenience of the moral on the natural in a way that is consistent with the claim that we can sometimes cognitively access or 'perceive' facts involving non-natural moral properties?[3]

Problem 2: The role of 'perception' in moral deliberation

A distinct problem – which Smith appears to run together with problem 1 from above (1994a: 23–4) – is that the 'perceptual' model seems ill equipped to account for what actually goes on in moral deliberation. Blackburn puts the point as follows:

> Literal talk of perception runs into many problems. One is that the ethical very commonly, and given its function in guiding choice, even typically, concerns imagined or described situations, not perceived ones. We reach

ethical verdicts about the behaviour of the described agents or actions in the light of general standards. And it is stretching things to see these standards as perceptually maintained. Do I see that ingratitude is base only on occasions when I see an example of ingratitude? How can I be sure of the generalization to examples I did not see? (1993a: 170)

Reflection on what is involved in, for example, the deliberate infliction of pain just for the fun of it by itself is sufficient to ground the general claim that all actions which deliberately inflict pain just for the fun of it are morally bad: 'perception' seems to play no role at all. The idea that we move from the likes of (a) and (b) to general moral standards simply misdescribes what goes on in moral deliberation. Reflection takes us to the general claim or standard, not 'perception' of particular actions or agents.[4]

Like problem 1, this is not a knock-down argument against the non-naturalist. The point is not that non-naturalism is incompatible with the fact that general standards play the role that they do in moral deliberation. Rather, the non-naturalist is challenged to account for the role that general standards play in moral deliberation in a way that is consistent with his 'perceptual' model of moral knowledge.[5]

Problem 3: Non-naturalism and moral motivation

To the extent that Moore's OQA poses a threat to naturalism, it also poses a threat to his own non-naturalism:

The [open-question] argument came to bite the hand that first fed it, and, eventually, to count Intuitionism among its victims. For, it appears no easier to see how an appropriate link to motivation or action could be logically secured if we were to substitute '*sui generis*, simple, nonnatural property Q' for 'naturalistic property R'. (Darwall, Gibbard and Railton 1992: 118)

That is to say, we can rerun the 'new' version of the open-question argument in the following way:

(2) There is a *conceptual* or *internal* link between making a moral judgement and being motivated, *ceteris paribus*, to act as that judgement prescribes.
(3) Competent and reflective speakers of English are convinced that they are able to imagine clear-headed (and otherwise psychologically healthy) beings who judge that Q (some indefinable *sui generis* non-natural property) obtains, but who fail to find appropriate reason or motive to act in accordance with that judgement.
(4) If there were no conceptual link between judging that Q obtains and being motivated to act accordingly, we would expect

competent and reflective speakers of English to have the conviction described in (3).

So:

(5) Unless there is some other explanation of the conviction described in (3), we are entitled to conclude that there is no conceptual link between judging that Q obtains and being motivated to act accordingly.

So:

(6) Unless there is some other explanation of the conviction described in (3), we are entitled to conclude that the judgement that Q obtains isn't a *moral* judgement (from (2)).

So:

(7) Unless there is some other explanation of the conviction mentioned in (3), we are entitled to conclude that the property of being morally good is not identical to the property of being Q as a matter of conceptual necessity.

So the non-naturalist faces the same pressing question as the naturalist: how to account for the internal link between moral judgement and motivation?

Problem 4: Epistemological bankruptcy

For Moore, 'good' denotes a simple, unanalysable, non-natural property, which is not part of the causal order. A fact which consists in the instantiation of that property is not part of the causal order and is not detectable by the senses. In the case of the judgement that there is a table in front of me, we have a story about which cognitive faculty allows us to access the fact that there is a table in front of us: namely, sense-perception. We also have a detailed story about how that faculty manages to do what it does: perceiving a chair is a causal process, and cognitive psychology goes into some detail about what that causal process involves. But what cognitive faculty allows us to access the fact that justice is good? And can we tell a detailed story about how that faculty works? *Ex hypothesi*, the fact that justice is good is not part of the causal order, so the cognitive faculty involved is not sense-perception. So what is it? Moore's followers describe it as 'intuition' (see Dancy 1991). But what does that mean? There appear to be two options. It could mean either (a) the capacity for making correct moral judgements, or (b) a cognitive faculty similar to sense-perception in some respects, but unlike sense-perception insofar as the states of affairs perceived are not part of the causal order. But neither of these options seems plausible: (a) is useless as an attempt at explaining how correct moral judgement allows us to access the moral facts – 'correct moral judgements access the moral facts because they are the upshot of exercises of the capacity to form correct moral judgements' is trivial and completely unexplanatory. And (b) as it stands just seems obscurantist: it amounts to the claim that 'intuition' is like sense-perception in some respects, but unlike it insofar as the states of affairs it detects are not detectable by the senses. This tells us nothing. Neither (a) nor (b) amounts to a plausible non-naturalist account of moral epistemology. Non-naturalism appears to be epistemologically bankrupt.[6]

3.4 Clarificatory Comments on Emotivism

Those are just some of the problems facing non-naturalism. Before looking at some of the problems which emotivism itself faces, three clarificatory comments are in order.

Comment 1: Metaphysical and epistemological solvency

The problems reviewed in 3.3 suggest that Moore's non-naturalist cognitivism is unable to discharge its epistemological debts: it can't give a plausible account of how we come to have moral knowledge, because it can't give a plausible account of how we are related to the non-natural facts which allegedly confer truth upon our moral judgements. Emotivism is designed to avoid incurring any such epistemological debt: since there *are* no moral facts, and moral judgements are viewed as playing some non-fact-stating role, there is no need to give an account of how people could be related to those facts in some way that results in moral knowledge. Likewise, emotivism does not incur any expensive metaphysical debts: since it denies that there *are* moral facts, it is under no obligation to give an account of the *nature* of those facts, or of the relationship they stand in to the non-moral facts.

Comment 2: Emotivism and subjectivism

It is very important not to confuse emotivism with *subjectivism*. According to a simple form of subjectivism, when make a moral judgement I am really saying something about my emotions or sentiments: e.g., 'Murder is wrong' comes out as saying 'I disapprove of murder'. On more complex forms of subjectivism, when I make a moral judgement I am saying something about the emotions or sentiments of the community at large: e.g., 'Murder is wrong' comes out as saying 'Most people in my community disapprove of murder'. According to subjectivism, then, moral judgements say something about our emotions or sentiments: they report something about those emotions and sentiments. Despite some superficial similarity, emotivism differs quite radically from subjectivism, for emotivism denies that moral judgements are reports or propositions at all. *They are not reports or propositions at all, and so a fortiori they are not reports or propositions about our sentiments or emotions.*

Ayer explicitly rejects subjectivism on the grounds that it falls to the same sort of objection as he wielded against utilitarian naturalism:

> We reject the subjectivist view that to call . . . a thing good, is to say that it is generally approved of, because it is not self-contradictory to assert that some . . . things which are generally approved of are not good, and we reject the alternative subjectivist view that a man who asserts that . . . a certain thing is good is saying that he himself approves of it, on the ground that a man who confessed that he sometimes approved of what was bad or wrong would not be contradicting himself. ([1936] 1946: 104; see also Stevenson 1937: 274–5)

According to emotivism, when I judge that murder is wrong I am not *saying* anything: I am rather *expressing* or *evincing* my disapproval. This is why versions of non-cognitivism are sometimes called *expressivism*. According to emotivism, when I judge that murder is wrong, I am no more saying or reporting that I disapprove of murder than I say or report that I am in pain when I cry '@*%$!' after standing on a nail. My utterance of '@*%$!' is not a report, and so a fortiori not a report that I am in pain: it is an expression of pain, not a saying about it.[7]

Comment 3: Emotivism and the 'speech-act fallacy'

Expressivist theories such as emotivism have often been accused of the 'speech-act fallacy': the fallacy of inferring, from the fact that the making of a certain judgement expresses an attitude, that it does not also say something. Since there are plenty of cases of sayings which are inter alia the expressions of attitudes, this inference is invalid. Thus, if one attempts to argue for emotivism on the basis of the fact that moral judgements express feelings, one would be relying on an invalid argument. But, as Simon Blackburn points out, the arguments for emotivism, and for expressivism generally, do not need to take this shape:

> It is frequently pointed out that a term may occur in an utterance which *both* is a description of how things are, *and* expresses an attitude. If I say that there is a bull in the next field I may be threatening you, or warning

you, or expressing timidity, or challenging you to cross, or doing any of a range of other things, and expressing any of a range of subtle attitudes and emotions. But none of these things has any bearing on the meaning or content of my remark, which is true or false in a determinate range of circumstances, and is a paradigm of a saying with a truth-condition. But it would be wrong to infer that *no* description is given from the fact that an attitude is *also* expressed. . . . However, this fallacy need not be committed. First of all, an expressive theory should not infer that the attitude gives the role of the saying from the fact that it is expressed when the saying is made. So long as the attitude *may* give the role, the argument for saying that it does is the superior explanation of the commitments which we then arrive at. There is no inference of the form 'this attitude is expressed, *so* these remarks have no truth-conditions', but only 'this attitude is expressed; if we see the remark as having no truth-conditions the philosophy improves [because, e.g., we are relieved of the metaphysical and epistemological debts of cognitivism]; so let us see the remark as expressive rather than descriptive'. There is no fallacy here. And there is a second point. We can see that it does not matter at all if an utterance is descriptive as well as expressive, provided that its *distinctive* meaning is expressive. It is the *extra import* making the term evaluative as well as descriptive, which must be given an expressive role. It is only if that involves an extra truth-condition that expressivism about values is impugned. (1984: 169–70)

We can now proceed to the problems faced by emotivism.

3.5 Problems for Emotivism

Problem 1: The implied error problem

Emotivism is a form of *projectivism*: when we use 'is wrong' in an evaluative judgement, e.g., when we judge that murder is wrong, we are treating 'wrong' as if it is a predicate akin to the non-evaluative predicates of our language. In other words, we view *wrongness* as a property of the act of murder. Thus we take 'murder is wrong' to be on a par with 'gold is a metal' in the sense that both 'wrong' and 'metal' are, as it were, genuine predicates, picking out genuine features of things. However, according to emotivism, in the case of 'murder is wrong' this is inaccurate: and what we are doing when we treat wrongness as a genuine feature of things is *project our sentiments or emotions on to the world*. Wrongness is not really a property of things in the world: rather it is something we *project* on to the world when we form an attitude or sentiment towards it. As Blackburn puts it:

> We project an attitude or habit or other commitment which is not descriptive onto the world, when we speak and think as though there were a property of things which our sayings describe, which we can reason

about, know about, be wrong about, and so on. Projecting is what Hume referred to when he talks of 'gilding and staining all natural objects with the colours borrowed from internal sentiment', or of the mind 'spreading itself on the world'. (1984: 170–1)

The problem for the emotivist is to explain how this projection can be anything other than a *mistake* or an *error*. If we speak and think as if there is a property of goodness, although there actually is not, why isn't our speaking and thinking in that way simply *flawed*? And isn't the rational reaction to this to demand that our practice of moralizing be *eliminated* or, at the very least *revised* so that the error is avoided?

This sort of worry is familiar from everyday life and literature. In Joseph Conrad's *Victory*, for example, the narrator and Captain Davidson wonder about Axel Heyst's motive in rescuing Lena from Zangiocomo's travelling orchestra: did Heyst represent the action to himself as taking advantage of a beautiful young woman in a tight situation or as the rescue of a distressed human being? Heyst has a tendency to 'project' sentiments of his on the world, and the narrator and Davidson therefore worry whether Heyst thereby makes the mistake of representing his action as the rescue of a distressed human being when it is really just an act of taking advantage of a beautiful young woman in a tight situation:

> Davidson shared my suspicion that this was in its essence the rescue of a distressed human being. Not that we were two romantics, tingeing the world to the hue of our temperament, but both of us had been acute enough to discover a long time ago that Heyst was. (1915: 66–7)

Thus Davidson and the narrator absolve Heyst of any error: but the presumption is that his tendency to 'tinge' the world with his temperament makes him susceptible to mistakes of the relevant sort.

As a more prosaic illustration, consider something which literally projects: an overhead projector. Suppose an anatomy lecturer is using an overhead projector to show slides of the human brain to his students. He sets the projector up so that it shines on a plain white wall. During the class the lecturer and students talk 'as if' there were a picture of a human brain on the wall. For example, the lecturer asks one student which part of the picture represents the cerebellum, and another student asks the lecturer to point out to him the picture of the brain stem. But, of course, there is no picture *really* on the wall, just an image cast by the projector. In a sense, this doesn't worry us in the case at hand: speaking 'as if' there really were a picture on the wall is just a convenient and harmless fiction. But the idea that we are 'projecting' when we judge that Smith's torturing the cat is wrong is much more unsettling: can we really accept that Smith's act is not *really* wrong and that its wrongness is just a projection of our discomfiture or horror?

So: how can one be a projectivist about moral qualities and avoid the implication that ascribing moral qualities to things always involves us in error?[8]

Problem 2: The Frege–Geach problem

This problem is named after Peter Geach, who provided the classic modern exposition of the problem in his 1960 and 1965 (see the latter for Geach's attribution of the objection to Frege). According to emotivism, when I sincerely utter the sentence 'Murder is wrong' I am not expressing a belief or making an assertion, but rather expressing some non-cognitive sentiment or feeling, incapable of being true or false.

Thus, the emotivist claims that in contexts where 'Murder is wrong' is apparently being used to assert that murder is wrong, it is in fact being used to express a sentiment or feeling of disapproval towards murder. But what about contexts in which it is not even apparently the case that 'Murder is wrong' is being used to make an assertion? An example of such a sentence would be 'If murder is wrong, then getting little brother to murder people is wrong.' In the antecedent of this, 'Murder is wrong' is clearly not even apparently being used to make an assertion. So what account can the emotivist give of the use of 'Murder is wrong' within 'unasserted contexts', such as the antecedent of the conditional above? Since it is not there used to express disapproval of murder, the account of its semantic function must be different from that given for the apparently straightforward assertion expressed by 'Murder is wrong'. But now there is a problem in accounting for the following valid inference:

(8) Murder is wrong.
(9) If murder is wrong, then getting your little brother to murder people is wrong.

Therefore:

(10) Getting your little brother to murder people is wrong.

If the semantic function of 'Murder is wrong' as it occurs within an asserted context in (8) is different from its semantic function as it occurs within an unasserted context in (9), isn't someone arguing in this way simply guilty of *equivocation*? In order for the argument to be valid, the occurrence of 'murder is wrong' in (8) has to *mean the same thing as* the occurrence of 'murder is wrong' in (9). But if 'murder is wrong' has a different semantic function in (8) and (9), then it certainly doesn't mean the same thing in (8) and (9). So the above argument is apparently no more valid than:

(11) My beer has a head on it.
(12) If something has a head on it, then it must have eyes and ears.

Therefore:

(13) My beer must have eyes and ears.

This argument is obviously invalid because it relies on an equivocation on two senses of 'head', in (11) and (12) respectively.

Another way of putting the problem: in elementary logic, how would we try to figure out how a given argument is valid? One way would be to construct a truth-table, and check whether there are any cases in which all of the premises are true and yet the conclusion is false. If there are, the argument is invalid; if there are not, the argument is valid. But how can this procedure even make sense when some of the premises (e.g. (8)) in the argument are not even assessable in terms of truth and falsity?

It is perhaps worth stressing why the Frege-Geach problem doesn't afflict cognitivist ethical theories, theories which see 'Murder is wrong' as having truth-conditions, and sincere utterances of 'Murder is wrong' as capable of expressing beliefs. According to cognitivism, moral *modus ponens* arguments such as the argument above from (8) and (9) to (10) are just like non-moral cases of *modus ponens* such as:

(14) It is raining.
(15) If it is raining then the streets are wet.

Therefore,

(16) The streets are wet.

Why is this non-moral case of *modus ponens* not similarly invalid in virtue of the fact that 'It is raining' is asserted in (14), but not in (15)? The answer is of course that the state of affairs asserted to obtain by 'It is raining' in (14) is the same as that merely introduced hypothetically by the antecedent of (15). In (14) 'It is raining' is used to assert that a state of affairs obtains (it's raining), and in (15) it is asserted that if that state of affairs obtains, so does another (the streets being wet). Throughout, the semantic function of the sentences concerned is given in terms of the states of affairs asserted to obtain in simple assertoric contexts. And it is difficult to see how an emotivist can say anything analogous to this with respect to the argument from (8) and (9) to (10): it is difficult to see how the semantic function of 'Murder is wrong' in the antecedent of (9) could be given in terms of the sentiment it allegedly expresses in (8).

The Frege-Geach challenge to the emotivist is thus: how can you give an emotivist account of the occurrence of moral sentences in 'unasserted contexts' – such as the antecedents of conditionals – without jeopardizing the intuitively valid patterns of inference in which those sentences figure?

Problem 3: The problem of the schizoid attitude

How can we take rightness and wrongness seriously, if they are just projections of our own sentiments and attitudes? Blackburn puts the problem thus:

> Can the projectivist take such things as obligations, duties, the 'stern daughter of the voice of God', seriously? How can he if he denies that these represent external, independent, authoritative requirements? Mustn't he in some sense have a schizoid attitude to his own moral commitments – holding them, but also holding that they are ungrounded? (1984: 197)

> Can the consistent projectivist really avoid ending up with the morals of a French gangster? (1984: ibid.)

Problem 4: The problem of mind-dependence

If rightness and wrongness are, as Hume might have put it, 'the children of our sentiments' (Blackburn 1981: 164–5), doesn't it follow that rightness and wrongness become *dependent* on our sentiments in a problematic way? Doesn't emotivism entail that if our sentiments were to change, rightness and wrongness would change as well (in much the same way that changing what is on the overhead projector changes what is 'on' the white wall)? Likewise, doesn't emotivism entail that if our sentiments were to vanish, so would rightness and wrongness (in the same way as destroying the overhead projector destroys what is 'on' the white wall)? Can emotivism avoid making morals mind-dependent in an unsatisfactory way?

3.6 The Moral Attitude Problem and the Open-Question Argument Revisited

In addition to the four problems outlined above, emotivism faces the following problem. The central claim of emotivism is that moral judgements do not express beliefs, bur rather non-cognitive sentiments, emotions or feelings. But what *sort* of sentiment, emotion or feeling does a moral judgement express? Unless the emotivist has a plausible answer to this question, his account of moral judgement will begin to sound hollow.

Ayer quite clearly takes moral judgement to express a special sort of feeling, ethical feeling. Note the references to 'moral' disapproval, 'peculiar' horror and 'special' exclamation marks in the quote from *Language, Truth and Logic* given above in 3.1:

> In adding that this action is wrong, I am not making any further statement about it. I am simply evincing my *moral* disapproval about it. It is as if I had said, 'You stole that money', in a *peculiar* tone of horror, or written with the addition of some *special* exclamation marks. (Ayer [1936] 1946: 107, emphases added)

Also:

> a *special* sort of *moral* disapproval is the feeling which is being expressed. ([1936] 1946: 107, emphases added)

> Ethical symbols ... occur in sentences which simply express *ethical* feeling about a certain type of action or situation. ([1936] 1946: 108, emphasis added)

And Ayer was still writing of distinctively moral sentiments in the 1980s:

> [W]hen [people] make moral judgements of the kind envisaged by the emotive theory, they are merely expressing their moral sentiments and encouraging others to share them. (Ayer 1984: 30)

But what exactly is the distinctively ethical feeling or sentiment of moral disapproval to which Ayer here refers? There seem to be two options open to Ayer. On the one hand, he could claim that the feeling or sentiment expressed by a moral judgement is *irreducibly* moral: it is simply an *unanalysable* and *sui generis* ethical feeling. Or, on the other hand, he could claim that the feeling or sentiment expressed by a moral judgement is analysable in terms of non-moral feelings and sentiments. I'll argue that neither of these options will work.[9]

Why can't Ayer simply claim that moral judgements express *sui generis* or irreducibly ethical feelings? If we say that moral judgements express irreducible, *sui generis*, unanalysable *ethical* feelings we can't explain moral judgement in terms of feeling. What are moral judgements? Those which express ethical feelings. What are ethical feelings? Those expressed by moral judgements. This is hopeless. Moreover, the idea that moral judgements express irreducibly ethical or moral modes of feeling does not sit well with Ayer's verificationism. We can see this by looking at Ayer's views about the ascription of mental states to other people. He writes:

> [T]he distinction between a conscious man and an unconscious machine resolves itself into a distinction between different types of perceptible behaviour. The only ground I can have for asserting that an object which

appears to be a conscious being is not really a conscious being, but only a dummy or a machine, is that it fails to satisfy one of the empirical tests by which the presence or absence of consciousness is determined. If I know that an object behaves in every way as a conscious being must, by definition, behave, then I know that it is really conscious. . . . [W]hen I assert that an object is conscious I am asserting no more than that it would, in response to any conceivable test, exhibit the empirical manifestations of consciousness. ([1936] 1946: 130)

So the statement that Jones is in pain, for example, is literally significant because there are observable patterns of behaviour, the occurrence of which would verify the proposition. Now the problems associated with this type of behaviourist analysis are well documented (see, e.g., Carruthers 1986), but even putting problems of this nature to one side, the idea that moral judgements express irreducible and *sui generis* feelings looks especially problematic from the perspective of Ayer's verificationism and behaviourism. Are there observable behavioural occurrences which would constitute the expression of this special sort of moral or ethical emotion? It is difficult see how Ayer could answer this in the affirmative: we can perhaps imagine patterns of observable behaviour which would express disapproval, but what observable behaviour could possibly manifest the presence of a distinctively *moral* or *ethical* sort of disapproval? In the absence of a plausible answer to this question, the idea that moral judgements express *sui generis* ethical feelings looks at best dubiously consistent with Ayer's verificationism and behaviourism.

There is an even more powerful worry looming for the suggestion that moral judgements express irreducible and *sui generis* feelings or sentiments: careful attention to our experiences of moral deliberation suggest that there are no such feelings. This point has been well made by Crispin Wright:

[I]t seems to me very moot whether there is . . . any distinctive mode of *moral* emotional concern, identified purely phenomenologically and distinguished from what we feel for other kinds of values. Virtue is satisfied when one is concerned for the right reasons about the right kinds of thing: it is not necessary also to feel a particular *timbre* of concern. . . . What I doubt is whether we can find anything of sufficient rawness in the phenomenology of moral judgement to give the notion of 'moral experience' any serious work to do. (1988a: 11–12)

Of course, we could attempt to explain ethical feelings as those which an agent possesses when he is deliberating about some moral judgement: but this is of no use to the emotivist, since he wants to explain moral judgement in terms of moral feeling and not vice versa. Can we make sense of the idea of an irreducibly ethical feeling, explicable independently of the notion of moral judgement? Another way of asking this question would be to enquire whether we can make sense of the idea of someone *not* capable of making a moral judgement – a very young child, perhaps – nevertheless experiencing a distinctively ethical type of feeling. Again, the problem is well expressed by Wright:

> Very small children, to whom we should hesitate to ascribe any concept of humour, will laugh at grimaces and other forms of clowning and may harmlessly be described as finding them funny. What would be a comparable, pre-conceptual finding of moral value? Suppose such a child is distressed by the sight of a jockey whipping his horse. Should that count as a primitive sentiment of moral disapprobation? It should be obvious that the question is underdetermined. Perhaps the child is frightened by the thundering of the horse's hooves, or the jockey's mask, or feels himself threatened. (1988a: 11–12)

A sentiment is moral because it is the upshot of a process of *moral* deliberation, of coming to form a *moral* judgement. But the emotivist requires some sense to be made of a sentiment's being moral *independently* of its being the upshot of coming to form a moral judgement, because he wants to *explain* moral judgement in terms of the sort of sentiment or feeling it expresses. If we have to explain moral feeling in terms of moral judgement, this will not be possible.

So there are a number of reasons why Ayer cannot simply say that moral judgements express *sui generis* and irreducibly ethical feelings or sentiments. But mightn't Ayer simply drop the idea that the feeling or attitude expressed by a moral judgement is a distinctively ethical feeling or sentiment? This would blunt the force of the three objections outlined above. If we construed the judgement that murder is wrong as simply expressing 'common-or-garden' disapproval of murder, with no suggestion that the feeling of disapproval is somehow distinctively ethical, then there would appear to be no special worries about whether one could verify by empirical means that an agent had this feeling.[10] Moreover, such feelings do uncontroversially exist, so Wright's worry would be assuaged.

However, this suggestion faces a number of objections of its own. I will outline two such objections here.

The implicit elimination of moral judgement

The suggestion appears to entail that there is no class of judgements with distinctively moral content. My judgement that murder is wrong becomes of a piece with my judgement that the Spice Girls' latest single is awful and my judgement that jellied eels aren't nice. Just as these latter two judgements express my distaste for a certain sort of crass music and a certain sort of foodstuff, my judgement that murder is wrong will simply express my distaste for murderous actions. The strength of the distaste may be stronger in the latter case, but that will be the only difference: there will be no qualitative difference in the sentiment expressed. But now it seems that we are close to denying that there is such a thing as moral judgement, at least as ordinarily conceived: as ordinarily conceived, the judgement that murder is wrong does have a different sort of content from the judgements concerning the Spice Girls and jellied eels. So isn't this just the elimination of moral judgement by the back door?[11]

Ayer could attempt to hold on to the claim that the sentiment expressed when I judge that murder is wrong is qualitatively of a piece with those expressed when I make the judgements concerning the Spice Girls and jellied eels, and yet preserve the idea that there is a distinctive class of moral judgements, by arguing that what makes a judgement a moral judgement as opposed to some other sort of judgement isn't the type of sentiment expressed, but rather the distinctive *reasons* for the expression of the sentiment. The three judgements mentioned in the previous paragraph all express the same feeling of disapproval, but the reasons for their expression will be markedly different. Won't this give us a way of accommodating distinctive classes of moral, aesthetic and gustatory judgement?

Whatever merits this suggestion may have in its own right, it is clearly not available to Ayer's emotivist. This is clear from the account of moral disagreement that we saw Ayer outlining above (3.1):

> It is because argument fails us when we come to deal with pure questions of value, as distinct from questions of fact, that we finally resort to mere abuse. ([1936] 1946: 111)

In the sense of 'argument' used here, to argue with someone is to reason with him. Ayer's account of moral disputes entails, then, that although it is possible to reason with people about their views on matters of fact – about their beliefs, in other words – it is not possible to reason with people about their non-cognitive feelings and attitudes. If it were possible, Ayer's official account of moral disagreement would be undermined. This shows that the move suggested above is not available to Ayer. We cannot distinguish between moral, aesthetic and gustatory judgements by claiming that, although they express the same type of sentiment, these sentiments are expressed for different reasons: according to Ayer our sentiments – as opposed to our beliefs about matters of fact – simply have no rational basis.[12]

Emotivism and the open-question argument

As pointed out in 3.1, Ayer's main argument against naturalistic versions of cognitivism was Moore's open-question argument.

Interestingly, the very same argument can be reapplied against the view that moral judgements express common-or-garden sentiments of approval and disapproval. Consider:

(17) Suppose, for *reductio*, that 'Jones judged that murder is wrong' is revealed by conceptual analysis to be equivalent to 'Jones expressed a non-cognitive sentiment of disapproval of murder'.[13]

Then:

(18) It is part of the meaning of 'Jones expressed a non-cognitive senti-ment of disapproval of murder' that Jones judged that murder is wrong.

But then:

(19) Someone who seriously asked 'Jones expressed a non-cognitive sentiment of disapproval of murder but did he judge that murder is wrong?' would betray some conceptual confusion.

And

(20) For any 'common-or-garden' non-cognitive sentiment of disap-proval it is always an *open question* whether an act of expressing that sentiment amounts to the making of a moral judgement. That is to say, it is always an open question whether the person express-ing the sentiment is making a moral judgement, or an aesthetic judgement, or a prudential judgement, or whatever. One can ask this sort of question without betraying conceptual confusion.

So:

(21) It cannot be the case that 'Jones judged that murder is wrong' is analytically equivalent to 'Jones expressed a non-cognitive senti-ment of disapproval of murder'.

As noted above, this argument faces some very serious difficulties (2.3), but the point I wish to make here is simply the following *ad hominem* one: the very argument which Ayer himself uses against naturalistic cognitivism can actually be reapplied against the view that moral judgements express common-or-garden feelings or attitudes of approval and disapproval.[14]

Despite the failure of Moore's open-question argument there is, as we saw in 2.4, a modern variant of the argument, by Darwall, Gibbard and Railton, which at least makes a provisional case against analytic naturalism. Can this version be used to put pressure on Ayer's emotivist? We can move towards an analogous argument against Ayer's emotivism by focusing upon the fact that a clear function of moral discourse is to convince others, specifically to motivate others to act in certain ways. As Peter Kivy has observed, this feature of moral discourse is well captured in the version of emotivism developed by Charles Stevenson:

> The direct purpose of ethical argumentation is implied in the exhortative moment of moral value terms: what the late Charles L. Stevenson called their 'quasi-imperative' part. These terms evince our approval; but they also urge our attitudes upon others. 'I approve; do so as well', was Stevenson's rough analysis of 'good'. (Kivy 1992: 311; see also Stevenson 1937 and 1944)

It appears to be a conceptual fact that when I judge that Jones has judged that x is good (bad), I will expect Jones to be disposed, *ceteris paribus*, to demand that I *share* his non-cognitive sentiments of approval (disapproval) towards x.[15] This is part of what distinguishes my judging that Jones has made a moral judgement from my judging that he has made an aesthetic judgement, or some other non-moral judgement of taste. In the case of Jones's making an aesthetic judgement, for example, the demand that I share his non-cognitive attitudes towards the object of the judgement appears to be idle and unmotivated. It is difficult to imagine a clear-headed and psychologically healthy agent judging that murder is wrong but not caring about whether I approve of murder; but it is much easier to imagine a clear-headed and psychologically healthy agent judging that jellied eels aren't nice, but not caring whether I am partial to them, or judging that the *Missa Solemnis* is sublime, but not caring about whether it engages positively with the non-cognitive side of my nature. As Kivy puts the point:

> We can quite understand why the expression of moral approval should, at the same time, be an exhortation to agreement. My end, in expressing my moral attitude, is to get others to act in certain ways; for it lies close to the heart of the whole institution of morality that it protect various interests, prevent injury, promote human welfare, ensure fair treatment, and so on. Where is the analogue in aesthetics, to explain the existence of 'aesthetic imperatives'? Why should I be the least bit interested in exhorting others to share my aesthetic tastes and attitudes, when no interest of mine or anyone else's depends upon it; where no course of action, of any concern to anyone involved, would be seen to be motivated by it? (1992: 313; see also Kivy 1980, esp. 358–64; and Railton 1993a: 286)

Given this, we can now run the following open-question-style argument against the view that moral judgements express common-or-garden non-cognitive sentiments:

(22) There is a *conceptual* link between judging that Jones has judged that x is morally good and expecting Jones to be disposed, *ceteris paribus*, to demand that you *share* his non-cognitive sentiment of approval of x (*modified internalism*).

(23) Competent and reflective speakers of English are convinced that they are able to imagine clear-headed (and otherwise psychologically healthy beings) who judge that Jones expresses a sentiment of approval towards x, but who fail to expect Jones to be disposed, *ceteris paribus*, to demand that they share his non-cognitive sentiment of approval towards x.

The beings imagined may genuinely wonder whether Jones is expressing aesthetic, gustatory or some other form of approval or disapproval.[16]

(24) If there were no conceptual link between judging that Jones has expressed a non-cognitive sentiment of approval towards x and expecting Jones to be disposed, *ceteris paribus*, to demand that you share his non-cognitive sentiment of approval of x, we would expect competent and reflective speakers of English to have the conviction described in (23).

So:

(25) Unless there is some better explanation of the conviction described in (23), we are entitled to conclude that there is no conceptual link between judging that Jones has expressed a non-cognitive sentiment of approval towards x and expecting Jones to demand that you share his non-cognitive sentiments.

So:

(26) Unless there is some better explanation of the conviction described in (23), we are entitled to conclude that the judgement that Jones has judged that x is good is not identical to the judgement that Jones has expressed a non-cognitive sentiment of approval towards x.

So:

(27) Unless there is some better explanation of the conviction described in (23), we are entitled to conclude that judging that x is good cannot be analysed in terms of the expression of a non-cognitive sentiment of approval towards x.

As before, this does not give us a knock-down argument, but rather poses the emotivist a challenge. Given that the option of looking for some non-analytic identity between moral judgement and the expression of feeling is foreclosed to Ayer, his only option would appear to be to deny that the relationship in (22) is a conceptual or internal relationship, and argue instead that there is at most a contingent and external relation between judging that Jones has made a moral judgement about x and expecting Jones to demand that you share his non-cognitive attitude towards x. It is an interesting question, which I cannot pursue here, whether this latter line of argument can provide Ayer's emotivist[17] with a plausible response to the argument.[18]

Thus, in conclusion, Ayer doesn't provide a satisfactory answer to the question: what is the non-cognitive attitude expressed by a moral judgement? So, is there any viable form of non-cognitivism which avoids the problems rehearsed in 3.5, as well as the moral attitude problem? In the next two chapters, we'll look at Simon Blackburn's quasi-realism and Allan Gibbard's norm-expressivism.

3.7 Further Reading

The *locus classicus* for emotivism is Ayer ([1936] 1946: chapter 6). Later work of Ayer's on ethics includes Ayer (1954, 1984). For an introduction to logical positivism, see Miller (2007: chapter 3), and Soames (2003: chapters 12 and 13). For a nice paper on logical positivism and ethics, see Sayre-McCord (1985). For Stevenson's emotivism, see Stevenson (1937, 1944). For the classic exposition of the Frege-Geach problem, see Geach (1960, 1965). For a very useful overview of the genesis of the Frege-Geach problem, see Schroeder (2008).

There is a useful discussion of Ayer's emotivism in Smith (1994a: chapter 2). A philosopher who develops a view often described as a successor to emotivism is R. M. Hare. For an overview of Hare's views, see Hare (1991).There is a useful discussion of emotivism, placing it in the context of other forms of non-cognitivism, in Schroeder (2010: especially chapter 2). See also Soames (2003: chapter 14).

4

Blackburn's Quasi-Realism

4.1 Introduction

In the previous chapter I looked at problems for emotivism, and I discussed emotivism in terms of the metaphor of projection. Emotivism is a version of projectivism. Blackburn's quasi-realism is also a version of projectivism, explicitly designed to meet the problems raised for emotivism. But what is the difference between a *mere* projectivist and a quasi-realist? What does quasi-realism *add* to projectivism? Blackburn explains the distinction as follows:

> Projectivism is the philosophy of evaluation which says that evaluative properties are projections of our own sentiments (emotions, reactions, attitudes, commendations). Quasi-realism is the enterprise of explaining why our discourse has the shape it does, in particular by way of treating evaluative predicates like others, if projectivism is true. It thus seeks to explain, and justify, the realistic-seeming nature of our talk of evaluations – the way we think we can be wrong about them, that there is a truth to be found, and so on. (1984: 180)

In other words, quasi-realism is the project of explaining how we can legitimately say things like 'It's true that murder is wrong', 'It's false that breaking promises is the right thing to do', 'Jones believes that murder is wrong' and so on, even though we do not *begin* with the assumption that moral predicates refer to properties, or the assumption that moral judgements express beliefs, or the assumption that moral evaluations are truth-apt. It is the project of explaining how we can legitimately talk *as if* we were entitled to the assumption that there is a distinctively moral reality, even though we are not: it is the project of explaining how we can legitimately talk *as if* we were entitled to assume that moral predicates express properties and so on, even though we are not.[1]

4.2 Blackburn's Arguments For Projectivism

Before looking in detail at how Blackburn develops his own quasi-realist brand of projectivism, I'll run through three of the arguments Blackburn uses in order to motivate the adoption of projectivism in the first place.

Argument 1: Metaphysical and epistemological solvency

This is simply the familiar argument (also utilized by the emotivist in 3.4) that projectivism betters cognitivism on the score of metaphysical and epistemological economy:

> The projective theory intends to ask no more from the world than what we know is there – the ordinary features of things on the basis of which we make decisions about them, like or dislike them, fear them and avoid them, desire them and seek them out. It asks no more than this: a natural world, and patterns of reaction to it. (1984: 182)

Projectivism thus differs from cognitivism, which has to posit a realm of distinctively moral facts, as well as a mechanism which accounts for our awareness of those facts. Non-cognitivism can get by with much less.[2] Blackburn is a naturalist, in the sense that he 'tries to see man as a part of nature and tries to explain morality as arising out of man's nature and situation'.[3] But he tries to do this without *reducing* moral facts to natural facts:

> [T]he problem is one of finding room for ethics, or placing ethics within the disenchanted, non-ethical order which we inhabit, and of which we are a part. 'Finding room' means understanding how we think ethically, and why it offends against nothing in the rest of our world-view for us to do so. It does not necessarily mean 'reducing' ethics to something else. (1998a: 49)

Blackburn is thus a Humean, or explanatory, or methodological naturalist, but not a substantive naturalist about ethics.

Argument 2: Supervenience and the ban on mixed worlds

In 3.3 I introduced the idea that, as a matter of conceptual or logical necessity, the moral features of a situation supervene on its natural features: someone who gave differing moral evaluations of two situations without thinking that he had to point to some natural difference between them would thereby display his lack of competence with moral concepts. Blackburn uses this idea to develop an ingenious argument in favour of projectivism.

Before introducing that argument, a few remarks on the notion of logical necessity are required. One way to explicate the notion of logical necessity is as follows: a statement that P is *necessarily true* if it is true in *all possible worlds*. Likewise, a statement that P is *contingent* if it is true at *some* possible worlds but false at others; necessarily false if there are *no* possible worlds in which it is true. Thus, the statement that $2+2=4$ is necessarily true because there are no possible worlds at which it is false (can you imagine one?); the statement that there is a red postbox at the end of Grosvenor Street is contingently true, because although it is true at *this* world, the *actual* world, there are other possible worlds in which it is false (it is easy to imagine one).

We can summarize as follows the claim that the moral supervenes on the natural as a matter of conceptual necessity. Let N be a complete description of all of the natural properties of an act, event or situation. Then, if two acts, events or situations are N, if they both have the same complete naturalistic description, then they must also receive the same moral evaluation.

Now contrast this notion of supervenience with a stronger notion, *necessitation*. To say that natural properties necessitate moral properties is to say that in any possible world, all of the moral properties of an act or event are determined by its complete naturalistic description N. To explain further, necessitation means that for a given moral property M, it is necessarily the case that: if an act, event or situation has N, then it has M.

It may appear at first sight that there is no difference between necessitation and supervenience. But they are different. First, although we have seen that the moral status of a situation plausibly supervenes on its complete naturalistic description, it is less plausible that the complete naturalistic description necessitates the moral evaluation. Blackburn puts this latter point as follows:

> It does not seem a matter of conceptual or logical necessity that any given total natural state of a thing gives it some particular moral property. For to tell which moral quality results from a given natural state means using standards whose correctness cannot be shown by conceptual means alone. It means moralizing, and bad people moralize badly, but need not be confused. (1984: 184)

Someone could be quite competent with all of the concepts implicated in the naturalistic description N, and yet move from the judgement that a situation is N to the wrong moral evaluation of that situation. Lyndon

B. Johnson understood the naturalistic concepts involved in the complete naturalistic description of the use of napalm in the Vietnam War, but he still managed to come to the erroneous judgement that its use was morally permissible. Johnson was not confused about any of the relevant naturalistic concepts: rather, he was a morally base individual.[4]

Second, supervenience allows some sorts of possible worlds which necessitation rules out. For example, consider a world containing only one individual object b:

World W1: b is N and b is not M.

Supervenience allows W1: it only says that if two things are alike in point of N, they must also be alike in point of M. Since there is only one thing which is N in W1, namely b, W1 respects supervenience.[5]

What supervenience does rule out is the possibility of 'mixed worlds', such as:

World W2: a is N and a is M, c is N but c is not M.

Supervenience 'bans' mixed worlds. Now suppose you believed that moral properties supervene on natural properties, but that natural properties do not necessitate moral properties. Then you would have to explain the ban on mixed worlds: given that God could have created a world W1 in which b is N but not M, why could he not have chosen to create a world in which c is N but not M even though in that world a is N and also M? What is the explanation of the fact that there are no mixed worlds?[6]

Why does this constitute an argument in favour of projectivism? According to Blackburn the ban on mixed worlds looks especially hard to explain from a cognitivist base:

> These questions are especially hard for a realist. For he has the conception of an actual moral state of affairs, which might or might not distribute in a particular way across the naturalistic states. Supervenience [and the ban on mixed worlds] then becomes a mysterious fact, and one of which he will have no explanation (or no right to rely on). It would be as though some people are N and doing the right thing, and others are N but doing the wrong thing, but there is a ban on them travelling to the same place: completely inexplicable. (1984: 185–6)

On the other hand, claims Blackburn, the projectivist has a straightforward explanation of supervenience and the associated ban on mixed worlds:

> When we announce our moral commitments we are projecting, we are neither reacting to a given distribution of moral properties, nor

speculating about one. So the supervenience can be explained in terms of the constraints upon proper projection. Our purpose in projecting value predicates may demand that we respect supervenience. If we allowed ourselves a system (schmoralizing) which was like ordinary evaluative practice, but subject to no such constraint, then it would allow us to treat naturally identical cases in morally different ways. . . . That would unfit schmoralizing from being any kind of guide to practical decision making (a thing could be properly deemed schbetter than another although it shared with it all the features relevant to choice or desirability). (1984: 186)[7]

Argument 3: Moral judgement and motivation

Suppose you accept the *Humean Theory of Motivation*: the view that explanation of rational action always requires the citation of both beliefs and desires. How do we explain someone's morally motivated actions? Suppose Jones decides not to steal the exam papers from his tutor's desk. In explanation of this, we might say something like 'Jones judges that stealing is wrong'. Now does his moral judgement express a belief or some non-cognitive sentiment, such as a desire? If it is the former, then the story we just gave as to why he was motivated not to steal the exam papers would, according to the Humean Theory of Motivation, require supplementation with reference to some desire which Jones possesses (presumably the desire not to do wrong). But it seems to need no such supplementation: so long as Jones is sincere in making his moral judgements, no reference to a desire is necessary. If the latter, we would expect his judgement to need supplementation by mention of a belief. And this is exactly what we find: our explanation of Jones's motivation needs to cite his judgement that stealing is wrong and his belief that taking the exam papers would be stealing. The conclusion is thus that non-cognitivism sits better with the best account of moral motivation, the Humean Theory of Motivation.[8]

How convincing are Blackburn's arguments in favour of projectivism? I will not attempt a serious assessment here, but offer instead a few comments in passing. Argument 2, from supervenience and the ban on mixed worlds, deserves more discussion than I can attempt here, but the curious reader will wonder why the explanation of the ban on mixed worlds which Blackburn offers on behalf of the projectivist cannot be co-opted by the cognitivist:

[T]he supervenience can be explained in terms of the constraints upon the proper formation of moral belief. Our purpose in forming moral beliefs may demand that we respect supervenience. If we allowed ourselves a system (schmoralizing) which was like ordinary evaluative practice, but subject to no such constraint, then it would allow us to treat

naturally identical cases in morally different ways. . . . That would unfit
schmoralizing from being any kind of guide to practical decision making.

What is wrong with this argument? Perhaps Blackburn will reply that it
only works if we can view moral beliefs as essentially practical in their
upshot, an assumption that the Humean Theory of Motivation will
disallow. What is important for supervenience is that we take different
evaluative stances only towards situations that differ in some natural
respect: for the Humean, an evaluative stance is always the product
of a belief and a distinct desire, so constraining moral belief to respect
supervenience will not by itself ensure that supervenience is respected.
Evaluative stances which differ only in respect of the attendant desires
can, so far as the constraints on the formation of moral belief go, fail to
differ with respect to naturalistically identical situations. So unless we
reject the Humean Theory of Motivation, the suggested explanation
fails to ensure that supervenience is respected. I have no idea whether
Blackburn would actually proffer this style of response to the suggestion: but, if he does, even if the response is sound it will depend on a
result in favour of the Humean in the province of moral psychology.
So until we discuss these matters in chapter 10, the argument from
supervenience and the ban on mixed worlds can at best be accorded
provisional credence. A fortiori, the same comment applies to argument 3, from moral judgement and motivation.

Argument 1, from metaphysical and epistemological solvency,
depends on the success of the positive aspect of the quasi-realist
project: these considerations only have the force intended by Blackburn
if the quasi-realist reconstruction of the 'realistic-seeming' aspects of
our moral practice is successful. So an evaluation of argument 1 must
wait until we have a proper assessment of Blackburn's reconstructive
project, and its capacity to see off the objections which beset emotivism.
It is to this that I now turn.

4.3 Blackburn's Response to the Frege-Geach Problem

Can the quasi-realist give a projectivist account of, for example, the
semantic function of 'Murder is wrong' as it appears in an unasserted
context such as:

(2) If murder is wrong, then getting little brother to murder is wrong.

Blackburn writes:

> Can [projectivism] explain what we are up to when we make these
> remarks? Unasserted contexts show us treating moral predicates like

others, as though by their means we can introduce objects of doubt, belief, knowledge, things which can be supposed, queried, pondered. Can the projectivist say why we do this? (1984: 191)

And, of course, a constraint on the projectivist's account of why we do this must be that it doesn't convict logically valid arguments like

(1) Murder is wrong.
(2) If murder is wrong, then getting little brother to murder is wrong.

So:

(3) Getting little brother to murder is wrong.

of a fallacy of equivocation.

So what is the projectivist account of what we are doing when we say things like (2)? Recall that one source of the problem was that we normally give an account of (material) conditionals as follows: a conditional is false if it has a true antecedent and a false consequent, true otherwise. But how can we invoke this account in cases like (2), which at this stage in the story cannot be assumed, by the projectivist, to be assessable in terms of truth and falsity? In order to work towards getting round this problem, Blackburn asks us to consider a simpler connective than 'if ... then ...', namely 'and'. The normal account of the semantics of conjunctions goes as follows: a conjunction is true when both of its conjuncts are true, false otherwise. But we nevertheless clearly do use 'and' to conjoin commitments. As Blackburn points out:

> [We should] expand the way we think of 'and'. We have to do this anyway, for it can link utterances when they certainly do not express beliefs which are genuinely susceptible of truth-value e.g. commands: 'hump that barge and tote that bale'. We would instead say something like this: 'and' links commitments to give an overall commitment which is accepted only if each component is accepted. (1984: 191–2)

The projectivist account of, for example, 'Murder is wrong and the sanctions against Iran are morally despicable' is thus as follows: this conjunctive sentence serves to express my disapproval of both murder and the sanctions against Iran.

Can the projectivist do something similar for *conditionals*? What attitude am I expressing when I say that if murder is wrong, then getting little brother to murder people is wrong? According to Blackburn, I am expressing an attitude about a *moral sensibility*.[9] What is a moral sensibility? David McNaughton explains this notion as follows:

Each of us, on the non-cognitivist picture, is disposed to respond to various situations with different attitudes – we may, for example, be outraged by cruelty, amused by adultery, exalted by physical bravery, and so on. The complete set of such dispositions we may call that person's moral sensibility. It is important that we can not only take up an attitude towards people's actions but also towards their moral sensibilities. These can be coarse or sensitive, inflexible or fickle, admirable or despicable. (1988: 183)

According to Blackburn, when I say that if murder is wrong, then getting little brother to murder people is wrong, I am expressing my attitude of approval towards moral sensibilities which combine disapproval of murder with disapproval of getting little brother to murder people. *My utterance of the conditional thus serves to express an attitude, but an attitude to a moral sensibility itself.*

The question now is whether Blackburn can use this story to account for the validity of the inference from (1) and (2) to (3). In order to see how Blackburn tries to deal with this question, let's draw a distinction between the *surface form* of a discourse and the *deep form* of a discourse. The surface form of a discourse is the way that discourse initially appears, in other words whatever is suggested by its surface syntax. Thus, the surface form of moral discourse is *propositional or cognitive*: 'Murder is wrong', 'Euthanasia is permissible' and so on, are *declarative sentences*; 'wrong', 'permissible' and so on, are *predicates*; and 'Jim believes that murder is wrong', 'John believes that abortion is permissible' are *syntactically well-formed*. All of this suggests that moral sentences represent states of affairs, moral predicates denote properties and moral judgements express beliefs. But, of course, the projectivist wants to deny that the surface form of moral discourse is an accurate guide to its *deep* form: although moral statements appear propositional or cognitive on the surface, their fundamental role is actually expressive. So one way of framing the problem faced by projectivism is as follows: *how can you earn the right to the propositional or cognitive surface of moral discourse on the basis of the claim that its deep form is expressive?* In answering this question we will see, inter alia, how Blackburn hopes to solve the Frege-Geach problem.

In order to focus on the question of how moral discourse can have a propositional or cognitive surface even though its deep structure or form is expressive, Blackburn asks us to imagine a language E_{ex} which is unlike English in that its surface form is explicitly expressive:

It might contain a 'hooray!' operator and a 'boo!' operator (H!, B!) which attach to descriptions of things to result in expressions of attitude. H!(the playing of Tottenham Hotspur) would express the attitude towards the playing, B!(lying) would express the contrary attitude towards lying, and so on. (1984: 193)

Blackburn now introduces the following conventions. In order to talk about an attitude of approval or disapproval we put its expression inside square-brackets, so that [H!(the playing of Tottenham Hotspur)] refers to the sentiment of approval at the playing of Tottenham Hotspur. Also, in order to denote the coupling of two attitudes with each other, we place a semi-colon between expressions referring to them: thus [[H!(the playing of Glasgow Celtic)]; [B!(the playing of Glasgow Rangers)]] refers to the coupling of the attitude of approval towards the playing of Glasgow Celtic with the attitude of disapproval towards the playing of Glasgow Rangers.

Now what would a conditional like (2) in our original argument look like in E_{ex}? Recall that the projectivist interpretation of (2) was as the expression of approval of moral sensibilities which combine disapproval of murder with disapproval of getting little brother to murder. Thus (2) would be represented in E_{ex} as: H![[B!(murder)]; [B!(getting little brother to murder)]]. So the argument from (1) and (2) to (3) would come out as:

(1_{ex}) B!(murder)
(2_{ex}) H! [[B!(murder)]; [B!(getting little brother to murder)]]

Therefore:

(3_{ex}) B! (getting little brother to murder).

Now what can we say about the validity of the argument thus interpreted? Well, what would be the position of someone who combined commitment to the premises with no commitment to the conclusion? *He would fail to have a combination of attitudes of which he himself approves*: he would lack the combination of disapproval towards murder and disapproval towards getting little brother to murder, whilst approving of having that combination. As Blackburn puts it, such a person has attitudes which 'clash', and:

> [H]as a fractured sensibility which cannot itself be an object of approval. The 'cannot' here follows not . . . because such a sensibility must be out of line with the moral facts it is trying to describe, but because such a sensibility cannot fulfil the practical purposes for which we evaluate things. E_{ex} will want to signal this. It will want a way of expressing the thought that it is a logical mistake that is made, if someone holds the first two commitments, and not the commitment to disapproval of getting little brother [to murder]. (1984: 195)

Someone who combined commitment to the premises with lack of commitment to the conclusion would thus be indulging himself in a 'fractured' set of attitudes, and Blackburn's thought is that this would account, on an expressive basis, for the intuitive validity of

(1_{ex}), (2_{ex}); therefore, (3_{ex}).

So, if we view ordinary English as having the deep form of E_{ex}, we can account for the validity of inferences like this on an expressive basis. Thus, the validity of

(1), (2): therefore, (3)

is accounted for by the validity of

(1_{ex}), (2_{ex}); therefore (3_{ex}).

Why don't we use E_{ex} instead of ordinary English? Mainly because English is easier and more elegant. But Blackburn thinks that this question in the end doesn't really matter:

> E_{ex} needs to become an instrument of serious, reflective, evaluative practice, able to express concern for improvements, clashes, implications, and coherence of attitudes. Now one way of doing this is to become like ordinary English. That is, it would invent a predicate answering to the attitude, and treat commitments as if they were judgements, and then use all the natural devices for debating truth. If this is right, then our use of indirect contexts does not prove that an expressive theory of morality is wrong; it merely proves us to have adopted a form of expression adequate to our needs. *This is what is meant by 'projecting' attitudes onto the world*. (1984: 195)

This shows how the quasi-realist responds to the Frege-Geach problem, and, if correct, it thereby shows how the quasi-realist can respond to the charge that projectivism implies some *error-theory* about moral discourse. The implication to the error-theory is blocked because we can show how the right to the propositional surface can be earned on a purely expressive basis.

4.4 The Central Objection to Blackburn's Solution to the Frege-Geach Problem

Does Blackburn succeed in showing that the argument:

(1) Murder is wrong.
(2) If murder is wrong, then getting little brother to murder is wrong.

So:

(3) Getting little brother to murder is wrong

is logically valid? Crispin Wright thinks not:

> Anything worth calling the validity of an inference has to reside in
> the inconsistency of accepting its premises but denying its conclusion.
> Blackburn does indeed speak of the 'clash of attitudes' involved in
> endorsing the premises of the modus ponens example, construed as he
> construes it, but in failing to endorse the conclusion. But nothing worth
> regarding as inconsistency seems to be involved. Those who do that
> merely fail to have every combination of attitudes of which they them-
> selves approve. That is a *moral* failing, not a logical one. (1988b: 33; see
> also Schueler 1988)

On behalf of the quasi-realist, Hale (1986) suggests a way of attempting
to deflect this worry. Instead of taking

(2) If murder is wrong, then getting little brother to murder people is
     wrong

to express approval of sensibilities that combine disapproval of murder
with disapproval of getting little brother to murder people, we could
take it to express *disapproval* of sensibilities which combine disapproval
of murder with *lack* of disapproval of getting little brother to murder
people. Just as we can refer to the sentiment of disapproval towards
murder by [B!(murder)] we can refer to the lack of such disapproval
by –[B!(murder)]. The argument from (1) and (2) to (3) will come out
in E_{ex} as:

(1_{ex}) B!(murder)
(2_{ex}) B! [[B!(murder)]; –B![(getting little brother to murder)]]

Therefore:

(3_{ex}) B! (getting little brother to murder).

Someone endorsing the premises, and yet failing to endorse the conclusion of the argument *would have a combination of attitudes of which he
himself disapproves*. Someone who combined commitment to the premises with lack of commitment to the conclusion would thus be indulging
himself in an inconsistent set of attitudes, and this would account, on an
expressive basis, for the intuitive validity of the argument. As before,
if we view ordinary English as having the deep form of E_{ex}, we can
account for the validity of its inferences on an expressive basis.

However, as Hale himself points out (1986: 74), this manoeuvre only postpones the problem. Even on this interpretation, someone who endorses the premises but fails to endorse the conclusion of the argument is guilty of a *moral* failing, that is, guilty of violating a *moral* principle like 'Don't do what you Boo!' The account thus fails to capture the fact that one who endorses the premises and yet refuses to endorse the conclusion of the argument is guilty of some *logical* failing.

4.5 Commitment-Theoretic Semantics and the Frege-Geach Problem[10]

Blackburn, in his 1988 'Attitudes and Contents', and chapter 3 of his recent (1998a) book, *Ruling Passions,* has developed a different answer to the Frege-Geach problem, designed specifically to neutralize the objection rehearsed in the previous section. The approach is complex, but here I will simplify in order to convey the general idea. This is that we give an account of what we are doing when we use ethical statements in unasserted contexts, not in terms of expressing higher-order attitudes, but in terms of 'tying ourselves to trees' of commitments.

Take a straightforward example of non-moral *modus ponens*, such as:

(A) Jones is in Southwark.
(B) If Jones is in Southwark then Jones is in London.

So:

(C) Jones is in London.

Here the sentences involved can all be assumed to be straightforwardly factual or descriptive, and their meanings given in terms of their *truth-conditions*. In particular, the truth-condition of (B) can be given in terms of the truth-conditions of its constituents: (B) is true if and only if there are no situations in which the truth-condition of the antecedent obtains whilst the truth-condition of the consequent fails to obtain. Someone who makes an assertoric utterance of 'Jones is in Southwark' thereby commits himself to the belief that the truth-condition of 'Jones is in Southwark' obtains. What of someone who makes an assertoric utterance of 'If Jones is in Southwark then Jones is in London'? Blackburn writes:

> To avow anything of the form 'If p then q' is to commit oneself to the combination 'Either not-p or q'. (1998a: 72)

Thus, according to Blackburn, someone who makes an assertoric utterance of 'If Jones is in Southwark then Jones is in London' commits himself either to believing that the truth-condition of the antecedent does not obtain or to believing that the truth-condition of the consequent does obtain.

Now, what of someone who endorses the premises (A) and (B) yet fails to endorse the conclusion (C)? We can write these commitments in a list:

Commitment to the belief that Jones is in Southwark.
Commitment either to believing that Jones is not in Southwark or to believing that Jones is in London.
Lack of commitment to believing that Jones is in London.

Is this combination of commitments inconsistent (as we would expect if the argument from (A) and (B) to (C) were logically valid)? Since the middle 'conditional commitment' generates a 'branch' (see the 'tree diagram' below), the set of commitments will be inconsistent only if each branch of the conditional commitment itself issues in an inconsistent set of commitments. It's easy to see that this is the case:

Commitment either to believing that Jones is not in Southwark or to believing that Jones is in London.
   Branch 1
   Commitment to believing that Jones is not in Southwark.
   Commitment to believing that Jones is in Southwark.
   Lack of commitment to believing that Jones is in London.
   X
   Branch 2
   Commitment to believing that Jones is in Southwark.
   Commitment to believing that Jones is in London.
   Lack of commitment to believing that Jones is in London.
   X

On either branch, we end up with an inconsistent set of commitments, signalled by 'X'. On the first branch, we are committed both to believing that Jones is not in Southwark and to believing that Jones is in Southwark, while on the second branch we are both committed to believing that Jones is in London and not committed to believing that Jones is in London. This accounts for the logical validity of the argument from (A) and (B) to (C).

Blackburn aims to extend this strategy to cover cases where the sentences involved are not genuinely factual or descriptive. There are two parts to this strategy. First, in the purely factual case, the commitments are commitments to believing that the truth-conditions of factual sentences obtain. So, since evaluative sentences are assumed to lack truth-conditions, we need some analogue of 'belief'. Following Hale's suggestion (2002: 146), we do this by employing the neutral term 'accept'. Thus, whereas I can believe the proposition expressed by a factual sentence, I can analogously accept the (non-cognitive) attitude expressed by an evaluative sentence. Second, in the purely factual case, we have a ready-made notion of consistency to hand: two beliefs are inconsistent if the truth of one rules out the truth of the other, if, that is, they cannot both be true. So we would need some analogous notion of consistency to apply to cases where the commitments involved are assumed not to be truth-apt. One way to do this would be to model the inconsistency of a set of non-cognitive attitudes on the inconsistency of a set of desires: two desires are inconsistent if the satisfaction or realization of one precludes the satisfaction or realization of the other, if, that is, they cannot be simultaneously satisfied or realized. Suppose that both parts of this strategy can be carried out. Then we could apply it to account for the logical validity of:

(D) Murder is wrong
(E) If murder is wrong, then getting little brother to murder is wrong

So:

(F) Getting little brother to murder is wrong.

Someone who endorsed the premises but failed to endorse the conclusion would have the following commitments:

Commitment to accepting the attitude expressed by 'Murder is wrong'.
Commitment to either rejecting the attitude expressed by 'Murder is wrong' or accepting the attitude expressed by 'Getting little brother to murder people is wrong'.[11]
Lack of commitment to accepting the attitude expressed by 'Getting little brother to murder people is wrong'.

Again, the relevant tree-structure shows that this set is inconsistent.

Branch 1a
Commitment to accepting the attitude expressed by 'Murder is wrong'.
Commitment to rejecting the attitude expressed by 'Murder is wrong'.
Lack of commitment to accepting the attitude expressed by 'Getting little brother to murder people is wrong'.
X

Branch 2a

Commitment to accepting the attitude expressed by 'Murder is wrong'.

Commitment to accepting the attitude expressed by 'Getting little brother to murder people is wrong'.

Lack of commitment to accepting the attitude expressed by 'Getting little brother to murder people is wrong'.

X

Just as in the purely factual case, someone who endorses the premises (D) and (E) whilst refusing to endorse the conclusion (F) embraces an inconsistent set of commitments. As before, the logical validity of the argument is accounted for. Blackburn writes:

> There has been some scepticism about whether this approach can deliver the mighty 'musts' of logic. But we now see that it can do so perfectly well. Consider the example made famous by Geach, of inference according to the pattern of modus ponens. Someone saying each of 'p' and 'If p then q' has the premises of a modus ponens whose conclusion is 'q'. He is logically committed to q, if he is committed to the premises. To put it another way, if anyone represented themselves as holding the combination of 'p' and 'If p then q' and 'not-q' we would not know what to make of them. Logical breakdown means failure of understanding. Is this result secured, on my account, for an evaluative antecedent, p? Yes, because the person represents themselves as tied to a tree of possible combinations of belief and attitude, but at the same time represents themselves as holding a combination that the tree excludes. So what is given at one moment is taken away at the next, and we can make no intelligible interpretation of them. (1998a: 72)

Thus, this account avoids the central objection to the approach adopted in Blackburn (1984). How successful is Blackburn's attempt to use commitment-theoretic semantics in order to tame 'the mighty "musts" of logic'? Bob Hale has argued that even if the quasi-realist could successfully execute the parts of the strategy dealing with the notion of acceptance and attitudinal inconsistency, the commitment-theoretic account would still be problematic. Recall again that for Blackburn

> To avow anything of the form 'If p then q' is to commit oneself to the combination 'Either not-p or q'. (1998a: 72)

Hale points out that this means that Blackburn's account causes problems for the uncontroversial idea that we should accept all instances of the law of identity *If p then p*. On Blackburn's account, commitment to this amounts to having the commitment, for any choice of p, either to accepting not-p or accepting p. But, as Hale points out, 'in states of information neutral with respect to a given proposition p, we should neither accept that not-p nor accept that p' (2002: 148). Thus, unless we rule, implausibly, that it is impossible to be in a state of information which warrants neither not-p nor p, we will be unable, on Blackburn's account, to account for the status of *If p then p* as a theorem of logic. Given that the account cannot secure *that*, even when the components are assumed to be straightforwardly factual, it is unlikely that the account will be able to secure the validity of intuitively valid patterns of argument which involve evaluative constituents.[12]

It is time to leave the commitment-theoretic approach to the Frege-Geach problem. In the next section, I return to Blackburn's (1984) attempt at solving the problem.

4.6 How Compelling is the Central Objection?

Consider again the 'moral *modus ponens*' argument

(1) Murder is wrong.
(2) If murder is wrong, then getting little brother to murder is wrong.

So:

(3) Getting little brother to murder is wrong.

Wright's objection to Blackburn's account of the validity of this argument hinges on the claim that, on Blackburn's account, someone endorsing its premises and yet failing to endorse its conclusion is guilty of at most a moral shortcoming, whereas what we require the account to yield is that such a person is irrational, or prey to some logical failing.

Of what sort of failing is someone who endorses the premises of the moral *modus ponens* but fails to endorse its conclusion actually guilty? This is a question about how best to *interpret* an agent's actions; and this, like any such question, is simply *indeterminate* in the absence of a lot of background information concerning the agent's mental states and actions.[13] If someone tells me that Jones endorses the premises (1) and (2) and yet refuses to endorse the conclusion (3), and then asks me to specify the sort of fault Jones is prey to, the only reasonable thing for me to say is: 'I need to know quite a bit more background information about Jones before I can even begin to answer that question.'.So what happens when we fill in the background information? Jones, suppose, endorses the premises of the moral *modus ponens* argument, yet refuses to endorse its conclusion. Is Jones's failing moral or logical? Well, contrast the following situations (whilst supposing that the standard account of the validity of non-moral *modus ponens* holds good: the arguments are valid because the truth of their premises rules out the falsity of their conclusions).

Situation 1

Jones, when presented with a large number of *non-moral modus ponens* arguments, has invariably endorsed both the premises of the arguments and their conclusions. However, when presented with the 'moral *modus ponens'* argument above, Jones endorses the premises yet refuses to endorse the conclusion. Suppose that Jones grasps all of the concepts implicated in the components of the arguments. In attempting to make sense of Jones, what sort of failing shall we attribute to him? I think that in this sort of case, it *is* plausible to convict Jones of a moral, as opposed to a logical, shortcoming. What is the best explanation for the fact that in the non-moral cases he draws the inference, yet in the moral case fails to do so? The best explanation, I suggest, is that he is guilty of *moral* inconsistency (disapproving of a combination of attitudes which he himself possesses). Why else would he draw the relevant inferences in all of the non-moral cases and yet fail to draw the inference only in cases where some of the premises contain evaluative components? So in this sort of case, Blackburn's account, which would convict Jones of a moral failing, appears to be on target: that is the sort of failing which a plausible attempt at interpretation of Jones would attribute to him. Indeed, convicting Jones of a *logical* mistake appears not to be an option: if Jones were guilty of a logical mistake, how could we make sense of his drawing the correct inferences in the non-moral cases?

Situation 2

Jones, when presented with a large number of *non-moral modus ponens* arguments, invariably endorses the premises of the arguments and *refuses* to endorse their conclusions. Moreover, when presented with the 'moral *modus ponens'* argument, Jones in similar fashion endorses the premises yet refuses to endorse the conclusion. Again, suppose that Jones grasps all of the concepts implicated in the components of the arguments. In attempting to make sense of Jones, what sort of failing shall we attribute to him as regards his failure to endorse the conclusion of the moral *modus ponens* argument? Is he there guilty of a logical failing or of a moral shortcoming? I think the only way to answer this question is to consider what would have happened in counterfactual situations in which he endorses the conclusion in all of the non-moral cases. There are two such cases to consider:

2 (i) If Jones had drawn the inference in the non-moral cases, he would still have failed to draw the conclusion in the moral examples.

If this were true, the most plausible interpretation of Jones would put his failure to draw the inference in the moral examples, as above, down to a moral shortcoming: that of 'doing what you Boo!'.

2 (ii) If Jones had drawn the inference in the non-moral cases, he would also have drawn the inference in the moral cases.

If this were true, the most plausible interpretation of Jones's failure to endorse the conclusion of the moral *modus ponens* argument would be, I think, to convict him of a logical failing: lack of grasp of *modus ponens*. In other words, to attribute to him a systematic tendency to endorse the premises of arguments with the logical form of *modus ponens*, while failing to endorse their conclusions. But in this case the quasi-realist too can see this failing as operative in Jones's failure to endorse the conclusion of the moral *modus ponens*: we already think that he can't get his head round the rule of *modus ponens*, the 'moral *modus ponens*' has the *same syntactic form* as the non-moral cases, so it is no wonder that Jones fails to draw the inference in the moral case. Thus, in this case, Jones is guilty of a logical failing: but the quasi-realist has an obvious explanation ready to hand of why this is so.

Suppose that situations 1 and 2 exhausted all of the possible cases. Then matters would stand as follows. In the cases where our best interpretation of Jones is that he is, in refusing to endorse (3) whilst endorsing (1) and (2), guilty of a moral shortcoming, the quasi-realist account can accommodate this fact; and in the cases where our best interpretation of Jones is that he is, in refusing to endorse (3) whilst endorsing (1) and (2), guilty of a logical shortcoming, the quasi-realist account can accommodate this also. So Wright's objection would be rendered toothless.

But of course situations 1 and 2 do not exhaust all of the possible cases. There are two more to consider.

Situation 3

Jones refuses to endorse the conclusion of cases of non-moral *modus ponens* yet never refuses to endorse the conclusion in cases of 'moral *modus ponens*'. It is difficult to see what sense could be made of an agent who displayed this sort of combination: how would you respond to a student in an elementary logic class who exemplified this case? But to the extent that we *can* make any sense of what is going on here, I think that it is the quasi-realist who is in the better position. We convict the agent of failing to grasp *modus ponens* on the strength of his refusal to endorse the conclusion in the non-moral cases. But now what can we say about what keeps the agent 'on track' in the 'moral *modus ponens*' cases? The quasi-realist can cite his account of the validity of such cases and claim that the agent is driven by moral consistency: the agent has no combinations of attitudes of which he himself disapproves. That is why he 'gets it right' in the moral cases, despite getting it wrong in the non-moral cases.

Finally:

Situation 4

Jones draws the relevant inferences, whether moral or not. In this sort of case, we will most likely attribute to Jones a grasp of the rule of *modus ponens*, as well as the virtue of ethical consistency. Which of these – logical acumen or moral consistency – is the dominant factor in explaining why Jones draws the relevant inferences in the moral cases? We can only tell this by looking at counterfactual scenarios in which Jones fails to draw the 'moral *modus ponens*' inference. If the following counterfactual holds

4(i) If Jones had failed to draw the inferences in the moral cases, then he would also have failed to draw the inferences in the non-moral cases

then plausibly logical acumen is the dominant factor. If, on the other hand, the following holds

4(ii) If Jones had failed to draw the inferences in the moral cases, then he would not have failed to draw the inferences in the non-moral cases

then moral consistency has the upper hand. As above, in neither case will we find ourselves saying anything which the quasi-realist account of indirect contexts cannot accommodate: and, in fact, in the case of 4(ii), the quasi-realist seems better placed to capture the sense, if any, in which Jones's behaviour is intelligible.

In conclusion, in all the cases where best interpretation convicts Jones, in endorsing (1) and (2) and yet refusing to endorse (3), of a logical failing, the quasi-realist too can convict him of a logical failing; and in all the cases where best interpretation convicts Jones, in endorsing (1) and (2) and yet refusing to endorse (3), of a moral shortcoming, the quasi-realist too can convict him of a moral shortcoming. Since, in the remaining cases, the quasi-realist can mesh his account of 'moral *modus ponens*' with the deliverances of interpretation, Wright's objection fails. Or at least, if Wright's objection is correct, it is no longer clear why exactly that is so.

It is worth pausing to take stock. In response to the central criticism of his 1984 solution to the Frege-Geach problem, Blackburn (in his

1993a: chapter 10) in effect attempts to widen the notion of a logical fault by broadening the notion of inconsistency, so that, for example, a set of desires can be deemed inconsistent if there is no possible world in which all of its members can be realized. He then attempts to construct a logic to go with this wider notion of inconsistency, and, by utilizing a commitment-theoretic semantics, to preserve the idea that someone who asserts the premises, but not the conclusion, of a moral *modus ponens* argument is guilty of a logical failing. As we saw in the previous section, this approach has problems of its own. In effect, what I am proposing here involves leaving the notion of inconsistency as it is: only sets of truth-apt states such as beliefs can be inconsistent, when there is no possible world in which all of their members can be true. Instead, we widen the notion of a logical fault in a different way: a fault is now a logical fault if it either (a) consists in holding a set of inconsistent beliefs, or (b) is best *explained* by the attribution of a disposition to hold logically inconsistent beliefs. With (b), the quasi-realist can now, as I suggest above, convict agents of logical faults in the appropriate cases where they endorse the premises, but not the conclusions, of arguments such as moral *modus ponens*.[14]

4.7 Blackburn's Response to the Problem of Mind-Dependence

Can projectivism avoid making morals mind-dependent in an unsatisfactory way? An essential part of Blackburn's quasi-realism is his response to this problem. The quasi-realist has to protect our ordinary commitment to the thought that values are mind-independent. But what does this mean? Well, someone who thought that values were mind-dependent would claim things such as the following:

(4) If we think that kicking dogs is right, then kicking dogs is right.
(5) If murder is right, then we think that murder is right.
(6) If we think that murder is wrong, then murder is wrong.
(7) If stealing is wrong, then we think that stealing is wrong.

Intuitively, we want to deny conditionals such as these: the connection they express between our attitudes and rightness and wrongness is much closer than anything we feel comfortable with. Note that the problem with (4) and (5) is not that the moral judgements involved in their respective consequents and antecedents are judgements from which we would dissent: we would want to reject (6) and (7) just as much, even though the judgements that figure in their consequents and antecedents are judgements we would be quite happy to accept. The problem is that even if murder is wrong, it is not merely our thinking it wrong which makes it so; and, even if stealing is wrong, there is no guarantee that we will think that it is. Thus, in order to preserve our right to the thought that values are mind-independent, Blackburn has to preserve our right to the following:

(8) It's not the case that if we think that kicking dogs is right, then kicking dogs is right.

(9) It's not the case that if murder is right, then we think that murder is right.

(10) It's not the case that if we think that murder is wrong, then murder is wrong.

(11) It's not the case that if stealing is wrong, we think that stealing is wrong.

So how can the quasi-realist ground our right to (8)–(11), and our right to reject (4)–(7)? Blackburn's move here is very similar to the move we saw him making in 4.3 in response to the Frege-Geach problem. In order to respond to that problem he had to give an attitudinal account of our conditional commitments, and the way he did this was to view the conditionals (e.g., 'If lying is wrong, then getting little brother to lie is wrong') as expressions of attitudes to moral sensibilities themselves. *Now Blackburn attempts to rule out (4)–(7) because (a) they are components of a repugnant moral sensibility, and (b) we can express our repugnance at these sensibilities within the projectivist framework.* Just as I can express a higher-order moral attitude (an attitude of approval or disapproval towards a moral sensibility itself) in the case of 'If lying is wrong, then getting little brother to lie is wrong', I can also express a higher-order attitude concerning 'It's not the case that if we think kicking dogs is right, then kicking dogs is right'. According to Blackburn, the higher-order attitude expressed by 'It's not the case that if we think kicking dogs is right, then kicking dogs is right' is an attitude of approval for sensibilities which, when given the belief that kicking dogs causes them pain as input, yields disapproval for kicking them as output; or disapproval of sensibilities which needs some belief about our attitudes *as well as* the belief that kicking dogs causes them pain in order to yield disapproval of kicking dogs as output.

Thus, although moral values, and our practice of moral theorizing, are to be explained on an attitudinal basis, the explanation does not entail that we are committed to conditionals such as (4)–(7):

> Values are the children of our sentiments in the sense that the full expla-
> nation of what we do when we moralize cites only the natural properties
> of things and natural reactions to them. But they are not the children of
> our sentiments in the sense that were our sentiments to vanish, the moral
> truths would alter as well. The way in which we gild or stain the world
> with the colours borrowed from internal sentiment gives our creations its

own life, and its own dependence on facts. So we should not say or think that were our sentiments to alter or disappear, moral facts would do so as well. (1984: 219, n. 21)

How plausible is Blackburn's account of how the quasi-realist can earn the right to the idea that morals are mind-independent? I shall now consider an objection to that account.

Zangwill's objection to Blackburn

Nick Zangwill (in his 1994) has objected to Blackburn's account of mind-independence in the following way. There intuitively is some sort of status difference between, for example, (8) and ordinary moral commitments. Intuitively, (8) does not *just* express a moral commitment. Zangwill suggests:

(i)   that (8), or at least the generalized version of (8), expresses a conceptual truth;
(ii)   that this is the only plausible way in which the status difference between (8) and ordinary moral commitments can be accounted for;
(iii) the quasi-realist cannot plausibly claim that the generalization of (8) is a conceptual truth.

How plausible is Zangwill's argument? What about (i) and (iii)? I will now argue that Zangwill's argument for (i) is at best inconclusive, and that his argument for (iii) is utterly unconvincing.

Zangwill's argument for (i) goes as follows:

[I]s it the case that if someone makes a moral judgement then he believes or assumes that it is not the case that it is true because he thought it was? The answer to this ... is 'yes', for the following reason. It is part of making a moral judgement that it has a claim to correctness built into it. Call this the normativity of moral judgements. It is because of the aspiration to correctness in judgement that people sometimes disagree with the judgements of others and they sometimes express diffidence over their own. Disagreement and diffidence make no sense without such normativity. But then, given the normativity of moral judgements, it follows that it is part of making a moral judgement that one knows that there is a difference between making a judgement and making the right judgement. If so, one could not make a moral judgement without knowing that thinking something so doesn't make it so. For if I know that my judgement can be incorrect then I know that it is not the case that if I make a judgement then it is correct. (1994: 214)

This argument – from normativity to mind-independence – is unconvincing. To see this, note that we have the mind-dependence of moral goodness if we have the following:

It is an empirical truth that if we judge that X is good, then X is good.

But this is consistent with retaining the normativity of moral judgement: all that is required for the normativity of moral judgement is that it be *conceptually possible* for a moral judgement to be incorrect. If Zangwill required, for the normativity of some species of judgement, the stronger claim that it be empirically possible for judgements of that species to be incorrect, it would follow that we could never have judgements concerning areas in which we are, as a matter of fact, infallible. Thus, one could respect the normativity of moral judgement whilst holding that facts about moral goodness are empirically dependent upon our moral judgements. The normativity of moral judgement, then, does not by itself entail the mind-independence of moral facts. So the claim that mind-independence has some conceptual status is as yet unsupported. Of course, if one assumed that (8) and the like have conceptual status, one could derive them from the normativity of moral judgement: but whether they are conceptual truths is just the point at issue, so such an assumption would simply beg the question against the quasi-realist.

So Zangwill has no good argument to the effect that moral mind-independence is a conceptual truth. Suppose, however, that he did succeed in establishing the conceptual status of mind-independence claims. Why couldn't a quasi-realist accommodate this? Zangwill's argument to the effect that a quasi-realist cannot view the generalization of (8) as a conceptual truth goes as follows:

> [Blackburn] says that a person who asserts mind-independence expresses a (second-order) moral attitude, and thus the mind-independence negated conditionals [(8)–(11)] state a substantive moral truth. The argument against this is this: if mind-independence is a substantive truth, then it cannot be a conceptual truth. For substantive moral truths are eminently controversial, and if so they are unlikely candidates for conceptual truths. (1994: 213)

But this is just an unargued application of Moore's COQA in its crudest form! As such, it depends on the manifestly implausible assumption that there cannot be such a thing as a substantive (i.e., informative and potentially controversial) conceptual analysis (see 2.3, objection 2). Since it depends on this implausible assumption, Zangwill's argument for (iii) is unconvincing. Thus, Zangwill's objection to Blackburn's account of how the quasi-realist can secure the mind-independence of morals is a failure.

Let's pause for a moment to take stock. The first four problems that I raised for emotivism in the previous chapter were: the problem of implied error, the Frege-Geach problem, the 'schizoid attitude' problem and the problem of mind-dependence. We have just seen how Blackburn tries to deal with the problem of mind-dependence, and in the sections prior to this we saw how Blackburn's response to the Frege-Geach problem helped solve the problem of implied error. But what of the problem of the schizoid attitude? How can we take our moral commitments seriously when we realize, in our moments of philosophical lucidity, that there is no realm of distinctively moral facts to ground them? Blackburn thinks that quasi-realism can assuage this worry by showing how we can 'earn our right to talk of moral truth, while recognizing fully the subjective sources of our judgements inside our own attitudes, needs, desires, and natures' (1984: 197).

At this stage, it is important to be clear about the precise scope of the quasi-realist project. Blackburn's project could be taken to be that of showing how we could earn the right to speak *as if* moral commitments were capable of truth or falsity. This project could be described as the project of *modest* quasi-realism, and sits easily with the projectivist core of the quasi-realist enterprise: projectivism tells us that moral commitments are not in fact truth-apt, that moral judgements don't express beliefs, that there is no such thing as a moral fact, while quasi-realism earns us the right to speak *as if* moral commitments are truth-apt, *as if* moral judgements express beliefs, *as if* there are such things as moral facts.

Blackburn now goes on, in responding to the problem of the schizoid attitude, to pursue a more ambitious project: that of earning the right to notions of truth and falsity which are genuinely applicable to moral discourse:

> Why not regard ourselves as having *constructed* a notion of moral truth? If we have done so, we can happily say that moral judgements are true or false, only not think that we have sold out to realism when we do so. (1984: 196)

Call this the project of *ambitious* quasi-realism. That Blackburn is committed to the ambitious project is even clearer from his more recent writings. For example, in a question-and-answer session reproduced as an appendix in Blackburn (1998a) we have:

> Q: Aren't you really trying to defend our right to talk 'as if' there were moral truths, although in your view *there aren't any really*?
> A: No, no, no. I do not say that we can talk as if kicking dogs were wrong, when 'really' it isn't wrong. I say that it is wrong (so it is true that it is wrong, so it is really true that it is wrong, so this is an example of a moral truth, so there are moral truths). (1993a: 319)[15]

It is to this ambitious quasi-realism – the project of earning the right to use the notions of truth or falsity in application to moral commitments, as opposed to merely earning the right to think of them as if they are true or false – that we turn our attention in the sections which follow.[16]

4.8 Ambitious Quasi-Realism and the Construction of Moral Truth

Modest quasi-realism concedes that there is no such thing as truth in morality, or moral belief, or the truth-conditions of moral sentences, but attempts to earn, on a purely projectivist basis, our right to speak and think *as if* there is truth in morality, moral truth-conditions and so on. According to *ambitious quasi-realism*, there really is such a thing as moral truth, but it is to be explained on a purely projectivist basis: according to ambitious quasi-realism, we can *construct* a notion of moral truth using purely projectivist materials. Blackburn thinks that this project of constructing moral truth, if it is successful, will help to allay the fear of the 'schizoid attitude':

> To show that these fears have no intellectual justification means develop-
> ing a concept of moral truth out of the materials to hand: seeing how,
> given attitudes, given constraints upon them, given a notion of improve-
> ment and of possible fault in any sensibility including our own, we can
> construct a notion of moral truth. (1984: 198)

The problem of the schizoid attitude was as follows: how can we take our moral commitments seriously if they are just expressions of attitude, with no realm of distinctively moral facts underlying or grounding them? Blackburn's thought is that the grounding can be achieved in ways that do not involve the assumption that there is such a realm of moral facts. Specifically, he thinks that we can provide a grounding for our attitudes by considering the constraints that our natures and desires themselves place on the formation of attitudes:

> Just as the senses constrain what we can believe about the empirical
> world, so our natures and desires, needs and pleasures, constrain what
> we can admire and commend, tolerate and work for. There are not
> so many livable, unfragmented, developed, consistent, and coherent
> systems of attitude. (1984: 197)

We can use the constraints our natures and desires place upon our attitudes to construct a notion of moral truth, and in constructing this notion we will come to appreciate that we have all the grounding for our moral commitments that we could wish for – and all the grounding we require to see that the schizoid attitude to our own attitudes is not forced upon us by projectivism.

How does ambitious quasi-realism go about constructing a notion of moral truth? The first thing to note is that Blackburn's solution to the Frege-Geach problem and the problem of mind-independence provide us with the following ideas: (a) the notions of *coherence* and *consistency* as they apply to our moral sensibilities, and (b) the notions of *improvement* and *deterioration* as they apply to our moral sensibilities (at the very least, sensibilities can improve as they get more consistent or coherent, deteriorate as they veer towards inconsistency and incoherence).

Blackburn's thought is that the quasi-realist can use this notion of improvement to construct the notion of moral truth. We first of all define the notion of a *best possible set of attitudes*. This is the set of attitudes 'which would result from taking all possible opportunities for improvement of attitude' (1984: 198), using the notion of improvement mentioned above. So, take your current set of attitudes, and imagine them improved to such an extent that no further improvement was even possible. Then call the resulting set M*. Blackburn's suggestion is that we then define truth for moral commitments in the following way:

Attitudinal Truth: a given commitment or attitude m is true if and only if m is a member of M*.

The true moral commitments are those which express attitudes which are members of the best possible set of attitudes.

Having defined truth in this way, Blackburn immediately considers an obvious line of objection to his definition. The concept of truth has certain features, and it is not obvious that the notion delivered by Blackburn's definition can share them. For example, one such feature is that *truth is single*: if P is true, then not-P cannot also be true. But suppose that there is more than one best possible set of attitudes, that there is more than one way in which our current sensibilities can improve:

> Certainly there is improvement and deterioration. But why should not improving sensibilities diverge in various ways? An imperfect sensibility might take any of several different trajectories as it evolves into something better. We might imagine a tree. Here each node (point at which there is branching) marks a place where equally admirable but diverging opinion is possible. And so there is no unique M* on which the progress of opinion is sighted. (1984: 198–9)

It might then be the case that one commitment is a member of one such best possible set while a contrary commitment is a member of another such set. Blackburn's definition would then yield the conclusion that each of these commitments is true. But, the objection goes, no definition of truth can allow such a possibility: 'so there is no truth, since the definition lapses' (1984: 199). So Blackburn's definition cannot form the basis of an adequate definition of truth.

Blackburn's response to this is to argue against the idea that there can be two equally admirable sensibilities or sets of attitudes which nevertheless contain commitments which conflict with each other. His strategy (inspired by Hume 1742) is to suggest that whenever we have the appearance of such a situation, closer inspection will reveal that that appearance can be explained away. Think of an apparent case in which we have equally admirable sensibilities, neither of which can be improved, but which contain divergent commitments: Jean is a big fan of eighteenth-century music, and she thinks that Mozart's *The Marriage of Figaro* is the greatest opera ever written, while Lesley prefers nineteenth-century music, and thinks that Wagner's *Tristan and Isolde* is the best opera ever written. Jean and Lesley think very highly of each other: Jean thinks that Lesley has a musical ear which is just as sensitive as her own, and vice versa. Also, all of their friends – some of them quite musically accomplished themselves – agree that Jean and Lesley are on a par in terms of aesthetic sensitivity and so on. In addition, suppose that we couldn't find anyone with more refined aesthetic sensitivity than Jean and Lesley to adjudicate their apparent dispute. So we appear to have the following situation (Let **J** stand for Jean's sensibility and **L** stand for Lesley's sensibility):

(12) **J** contains the attitude expressed by the commitment 'Mozart's *The Marriage of Figaro* is the greatest opera ever written'.

(13) **L** contains the attitude expressed by the commitment 'Wagner's *Tristan and Isolde* is the greatest opera ever written'.

(14) There is no possible improvement on either **J** or **L**.

This is exactly the sort of situation which posed the threat to Blackburn's definition of truth. So what does Blackburn have to say about it? Blackburn suggests that (14) is false: there *is* a way of improving both **J** and **L**. Imagine you are Jean. You hold that Mozart's *Figaro* is the greatest opera ever written. But you also know and respect Lesley, and take her to be your equal so far as musical appreciation goes, and you know that she holds that Wagner's *Tristan* is the best opera ever written. Isn't the right conclusion for you to draw that your sensibility, and Lesley's sensibility, can *both* be improved by explicitly taking into account the fact that each of you has these opinions about *Figaro* and *Tristan*? The improved sensibility will be one which contains, not a simplistic claim like '*Figaro* is better than *Tristan*', or '*Tristan* is better than *Figaro*', but a more refined judgement along the lines of '*Figaro* and *Tristan* are operas of equal merit, although they exemplify the paradigm aspects of different types of opera in distinct periods in musical history.' Isn't a sensibility which contains the attitude expressed by this commitment an improvement on both **J** and **L**? Blackburn argues that it is, so that we have to jettison (14) in the triad above, and that this saves his definition from the worry that it may not respect the fact that truth is single:

> In practice evidence that there is a node is just treated as a signal that the truth is not yet finally argued, and it goes into discussions as part of the evidence. We are constrained to argue and practise as though the truth is single, and this constraint is defensible in spite of the apparent possibility of the tree structure. (1984: 201)[17]

4.9 McDowell on Projection and Truth in Ethics

In his 1987 'Projectivism and Truth in Ethics' (McDowell 1998, Essay 8), John McDowell raises three interconnected problems for Blackburn's quasi-realist project. In this section I'll outline two of those problems, and then argue that they fail to damage quasi-realism. I will deal with McDowell's third objection in chapter 10.

First, though, I'll note one important respect in which McDowell does quasi-realism a service. This concerns an objection raised against the quasi-realist project by Crispin Wright:

> The goal of the quasi-realist is to explain how *all* the features of some problematic region of discourse that might inspire a realist construal of it can be harmonised with projectivism. But if this program succeeds, and provides inter alia – as Blackburn himself anticipates – an account of what appear to be ascriptions of truth and falsity to statements in the region, then we shall wind up – running the connection between truth and assertion in the opposite direction – with a rehabilitation of the notion that such statements rank as assertions, with truth-conditions, after all. Blackburn's quasi-realist thus confronts a rather obvious dilemma. Either his program fails – in which case he does not, after all, explain how the projectivism that inspires it can satisfactorily account for the linguistic practices in question – or it succeeds, in which case it makes good all the things the projectivist started out wanting to deny: that the discourse in question is genuinely assertoric, aimed at truth, and so on. (1988b: 35; also 1985: 318–19)[18]

McDowell points out that Blackburn has a ready answer to the charge that a fully successful projectivist quasi-realism would be self-defeating in this way. The projectivist rejects any *unearned* appeal to the notion of truth, as applicable to what appear to be moral judgements: any position which relies on such an unearned appeal simply helps itself to the notion of ethical truth, the correlative notion of moral fact, and the idea of a special cognitive faculty via whose exercise we access facts of that sort. Such a position is little better than the Moorean non-naturalism criticized in chapter 3 above. What the quasi-realist provides, if successful, is an *earned* right to the notions of truth, fact and so on: we earn the right to the notion of moral truth by showing how the propositional surface of moral discourse can be justified in advance of postulating a realm of distinctively moral facts, on a purely attitudinal or projectivist basis. As McDowell puts it, 'The point about the application of the notion of truth that quasi-realism is supposed to make available is that we do not merely help ourselves to it, but work for it' (1998: 153).

Having helped Blackburn see off the charge that the quasi-realist project is self-defeating, McDowell proceeds to develop some objections of his own. McDowell writes:

> The point of the image of projection is to explain certain seeming features of reality as reflections of our subjective responses to a world which really contains no such features. Now this explanatory direction seems to require a corresponding priority, in the order of understanding, between the projected response and the apparent feature: we ought to be able to focus our thought on the response without needing to exploit the concept of the apparent feature that is supposed to result from projecting the response. (1998: 157)[19]

McDowell thinks that in some cases, there may well be the sort of explanatory priority of response to apparent feature necessary for the plausibility of projectivism. For example, consider feelings of *disgust* and *nausea*: 'we can plausibly suppose that these are self-contained psychological items, conceptualizable without any need to appeal to any projected properties of disgustingness or nauseatingness' (1998: 157). You can describe the subjective response characteristic of nausea without having to use the concept of nausea: the subjective response can be described otherwise than as a response to the presence in the world of the property of being nauseating. But McDowell wonders whether there is a similar sort of explanatory priority in the interesting cases, such as ethics, and he suggests that comedy provides an example where priority of response to projected feature fails:

> What exactly is it that we are to conceive as projected onto the world so as to give rise to our idea that things are funny? 'An inclination to laugh' is not a satisfactory answer: projecting an inclination to laugh would not necessarily yield an apparent instance of the comic, since laughter can signal, for instance, embarrassment just as well as amusement. Perhaps the right response cannot be identified except as amusement; and perhaps amusement cannot be understood except as finding something comic. If this is correct, there is a serious question whether we can really *explain* the idea of something's being comic as a *projection* of that response ... Surely it undermines a projective account of a concept if we cannot home in on the subjective state whose projection is supposed to result in

the seeming feature of reality in question without the aid of the concept of that feature, the concept that was to be projectively explained. (1998: 158)

If the same is true in the ethical case, projectivism about morals will founder upon the same difficulty.

This objection is closely connected with a second point McDowell makes about the quasi-realist project. That project, as we have seen, consists in attempting to earn the right to the notion of truth in morals on a purely projectivist basis, without postulating a realm of distinctively moral facts. What materials are we allowed to invoke, by quasi-realist lights, in this attempt? McDowell suggests that just as projectivism requires that the psychological state which projects a given feature on to the naturalistically described world be characterizable independently of using the concept of that very feature:

> A serious projective quasi-realism about the comic would construct a conception of what it is for things to be really funny on the basis of principles for ranking senses of humour that would have to be established from outside the propensity to find things funny. (1998: 160)

McDowell takes this to involve an impossible task, that of earning the right to the idea of truth as applied to judgements about morals or comedy:

> . . . from an initial position in which all such verdicts or judgements are suspended at once, as in the projectivist picture of a range of responses to a world that does not contain values or instances of the comic. (1998: 163)

I will now argue that these objections fail to damage quasi-realism.

First, the objection concerning the required explanatory priority of sentiment to projected feature. McDowell says that, for the projectivist quasi-realist project to be possible we need to be able to:

> focus our thought on the response without needing to exploit the concept of the apparent feature that is supposed to result from projecting the response. (1998: 157)

In this context, the quasi-realist is engaged on an essentially *explanatory* task: he is trying to explain the nature of moral judgement by characterizing the sentiment which he is taking moral judgements, *ab initio*, to express. If we have to use the concepts definitive of moral judgement, in attempting to characterize the sentiments moral judgements are taken to express, this explanatory ambition will be frustrated by circularity: in effect, we will be taking for granted the very thing that we are hoping to explain. The quasi-realist will thus accept McDowell's constraint on the identification of the sentiment which the projectivist takes to be 'spread' on the world.[20] But what are McDowell's grounds for thinking that the constraint cannot be satisfied? In the case of humour, McDowell provides absolutely no argument to the effect that the constraint cannot be satisfied, and merely asserts that:

> Perhaps the right response cannot be identified except as amusement; and perhaps amusement cannot be understood except as finding something comic. (1988: 158)

Well, perhaps; but, then again, perhaps not. This is clearly not a question that can be settled from the armchair. Can psychology provide us, in naturalistic terms, with some characterization of the sentiment of amusement? Or, in the ethical case, can psychology provide us, in naturalistic terms, with some characterization of distinctively ethical sentiments? McDowell's argument at best points to an explanatory space which the quasi-realist realizes that he has to fill. It seems to me (as we'll see shortly) that Blackburn does not quite succeed in attempting to fill the relevant space, but in the next chapter we'll see that Gibbard, in introducing the idea that *guilt* and *impartial anger* can be viewed as distinctively moral sentiments, comes much closer to achieving a non-circular account of moral sentiment. Whether Gibbard's account works may well be an open question, but the crucial point is simply that McDowell has so far provided no argument, let alone a knock-down argument, against the thought that the quasi-realist can avail himself of a substantial naturalistic explanation of the nature of ethical sentiment.[21]

That deals, at least provisionally, with McDowell's first point. Note, before we leave it, that the quote above from McDowell 1998 (at 157) would be better expressed as:

> The point of the image of projection is to explain certain features of reality as reflections of our subjective responses to a world which should not be assumed, *ab initio*, to contain such features.

There is nothing merely 'seeming' about the features of reality the quasi-realist views us as projecting on the world.[22]

The quasi-realist can also reply to McDowell's second point. Recall that McDowell sees the quasi-realist, in his attempt to earn the right to the notion of truth in morals or comedy, as constrained to do so whilst relying on no particular verdicts concerning morality or humour. McDowell seems to think that since the quasi-realist is constrained not to use evaluative or comic language in characterizing the sentiments distinctive of morals and comedy, he must also be constrained not to use, as his starting point in attempting to earn the right to the notion of truth as applicable to moral judgement, some distinctively ethical claim or a claim about the humour of a situation or sensibility. But this is based on a mistake. The quasi-realist accepted the constraint of non-circularity above because he was engaged there on an essentially *explanatory* enterprise: that of providing some naturalistic story about the nature of the sentiments allegedly expressed by moral judgements. But in attempting to earn the right to the notion of truth in ethics, the quasi-realist is no longer engaged on this sort of explanatory project: rather, in this context, the quasi-realist is engaged on an essentially *justificatory* exercise. The project is now that of *justifying* the use of the notion of truth in ethical discourse, and of justifying the idea that some ethical verdicts are actually true. In this exercise, the quasi-realist, like McDowell himself, needn't be constrained to begin from a standpoint on which all of his ethical views are suspended. The idea would be to start with some ethical claims (which may themselves subsequently come to be rejected), and *work out* to a notion of ethical truth. The quasi-realist may thus concede that the 'impossible task' is indeed impossible, but claim that in the justificatory part of his story about morals he is not committed to executing that sort of task. That this is so is shown, very clearly, by the fact that Blackburn does allow distinctively ethical judgements themselves to play a role in the ranking of ethical sensibilities:

> [N]ot all such sensibilities are admirable. Some are coarse, insensitive, some are plain horrendous, some are conservative and inflexible, others fickle and unreliable. (1984: 192)

In judging that a particular sensibility is 'plain horrendous', or that its fickleness means that it deserves censure, one is thereby relying upon a particular ethical claim. This is even clearer in the following passage:

> It is not at all surprising that a fickle function – one which has an apparently random element through time, or across similar cases – is one which we cannot readily endorse or identify with. Partly this is a question of the purpose of moralizing, which must at least partly be social. A fickle sensibility is going to be difficult to teach, and since it matters to me that others can come to share and endorse my moral outlook, I shall seek to render it consistent. *But partly it arises simply from the value of justice. When I react to like cases differently I risk doing an injustice to the one which is admired the least, and one of our common values is that we should be able to defend ourselves against such a charge.* (1981: 180, emphasis added)

Blackburn does not need – and does not try – to earn the right to a notion of truth in morals from an initial standpoint in which all ethical claims are suspended. So he does not need to attempt the 'impossible task'.[23]

The distinction between the explanatory and justificatory facets of quasi-realism, used in response to McDowell's second objection, can also be invoked to rebut a related objection, nicely developed by Iain Law (Law 1996).[24] This objection goes as follows. An essential part of Blackburn's story is that our moral sensibilities themselves can be fit objects of approval or disapproval: the notion of improvement which we obtain from this is an essential component in Blackburn's definition of what it is for an attitude to be true. But does Blackburn have any right to the notion that sensibilities can *improve* or *deteriorate*, rather than merely *change*? The answer to this depends on the nature of the standards by reference to which we 'rank' sensibilities. If we were allowed to appeal to *moral* standards in this process of ranking, we could perhaps obtain a notion of genuine improvement or deterioration: but Law suggests that this option is not available to Blackburn's quasi-realist at this point, since the whole point of the ambitious quasi-realist project 'is to arrive at such a standard: the ideal set of moral attitudes, M*' (Law 1996: 192). But, if the quasi-realist is not allowed to appeal to moral standards, what can he appeal to? Law suggests that 'the most obvious answer available to the quasi-realist is that other attitudes are inferior just insofar as they clash with my attitudes' (1996: 190). This would allow us to obtain a notion of improvement: a given set of attitudes improves insofar as it changes to fit or cohere with my current attitudes. *But, Law claims, this is unsatisfactory, because it seems to obliterate the possibility that my own current moral sensibility or set of attitudes might itself improve in the future.* Any change in my current sensibility will be ipso facto a deterioration: so the notion of improvement appears to have no application to my own moral sensibility.

It should be clear that this objection, too, relies on a misreading of the quasi-realist project and the constraints under which it operates. Law writes: 'Nothing that Blackburn has said suggests that he has some moral standard in mind against which all sensibilities including our own can be measured to see if they need improvement. How could he?' (1996: 192). This misfires in at least two ways. First, Blackburn does not need a standard against which all moral sentiments and sensibilities can be ranked; it would be enough, for the quasi-realist project, to find for *each* sentiment or sensibility, *some* standard against which it can be ranked. Of course, given these materials Blackburn then attempts to construct a notion of moral truth and thereby to delineate some overarching standard: but that is the result of the process of constructing moral truth, not some assumption which has to be made in order for the process to get under way. Second, as we saw above, there is nothing in the quasi-realist project to stop Blackburn appealing to particular ethical claims in the attempt to criticize moral sentiments and sensibilities and thereby justify the thought that moral judgements can be true. Indeed, as I showed above, this is what Blackburn actually does. Again, this means that the present objection to the quasi-realist fails: Blackburn is not attempting to construct a notion of truth appropriate for morals from a starting point in which all moral judgements are suspended. He can use some particular moral claims, whilst acknowledging their fallibility, and use them to trace out some working notions of deterioration and improvement: sensibilities will improve or deteriorate insofar as they match or clash with the attitudes used to get the process of constructing moral truth under way. No starting point, and no notion of improvement or deterioration, is sacrosanct: but there is nothing in this to prevent these notions from being employed in the construction of moral truth.

4.10 Quasi-Realism and the Moral Attitude Problem

At the end of the previous chapter, the ethical emotivist appeared to have no plausible response to what I called the 'moral attitude problem': what sort of sentiment, emotion or feeling is expressed by a moral judgement? I will now finish this chapter with a discussion of the quasi-realist's prospects for giving a satisfactory answer to this problem. Since the quasi-realist does not want to claim that moral judgements express non-cognitive attitudes rather than beliefs, and wants instead to earn the notion of moral belief by starting from an attitudinal base, the moral attitude problem, as faced by quasi-realism, has to be reformulated slightly. Accordingly, the problem can be framed as: give a characterization of the type of attitude assumed, *ab initio*, to be expressed by a moral judgement.

I will examine three possible answers which the quasi-realist might give to this question, and argue that none of them is satisfactory.

Emotional ascent

Blackburn writes:

> Suppose you become angry at someone's behaviour. I may become angry at you for being angry, and I may express this by saying it is none of your business. Perhaps it was a private matter. At any rate, it is not a moral issue. Suppose, on the other hand, I feel your anger or feel 'at one' with you for so reacting. It may stop there. But I may also feel strongly disposed to encourage others to share the same anger. By then I am clearly treating the matter as one of public concern, something like a moral issue. (1998: 9)

The quasi-realist thus attempts to avoid the reapplication of the OQA to the emotivist analysis of moral judgement (as in 3.6) by claiming that moral judgements can be assumed *ab initio* to express complex common-or-garden sentiments.[25] Again, let's represent a non-cognitive feeling of approval towards x by H!(x), and a non-cognitive feeling of disapproval of x by B!(x). Perhaps the aesthetic judgement that the *Missa Solemnis* is beautiful expresses H!(*Missa Solemnis*), while the judgement that murder is wrong expresses the complex sentiment: B!(murder) & H! (Everyone has the attitude B!(murder)). That is to say, when I judge that x is morally good, I am expressing approval of x *and* approval of everyone else approving of x. But this won't work (and, even if it did, it would still leave us with no account of the difference between aesthetic judgements and judgements of gustatory taste). The idea is this. $B!_M$(murder) =df B!(murder) & H!(Everyone has the attitude B!(murder)), where the subscript 'M' represents the fact that the complex attitude is intended to be definitive of a moral attitude and '&' is taken to conjoin commitments. But when I judge that murder is morally wrong, for example, I express a non-cognitive sentiment towards murder, and I approve of everyone sharing that *same type* of non-cognitive sentiment: it wouldn't be enough, for example, for others to find murder merely aesthetically displeasing. So what the quasi-realist really needs is rather $B!_M$(murder) =df B!(murder) & H!(Everyone has the attitude $B!_M$(murder)). And of course this is hopeless. As it stands, it is circular, and if we try to avoid the circularity by reapplying the move, we get an infinite regress: B!(murder) & H!(Everyone has the attitude: B!(murder) & H!(Everyone has the attitude: B!(murder) & H! (Everyone . . .))), and so on. No coherent account of the complex sentiment allegedly expressed by a moral judgement is forthcoming.

Thus, Blackburn's 'emotional ascent' style account of the moral attitude does not work.

Stable sentiment

Blackburn writes:

> [I]f we imagine the general field of an agent's concerns, his or her values might be regarded as those concerns that he or she is also concerned to preserve. (1998a: 67)

Might this be adapted to give us a plausible account of the non-cognitive attitude expressed by a moral judgement? The idea would be that we could define the moral attitude in the following way:

$$H!_M (x) =df (H!(x) \& H! (\text{stability of } [H!(x)])).$$

But this won't work either. For one thing, it falls prey to the OQA, as reconstructed in 3.6.

(15) There is a conceptual link between judging that Jones has judged that x is good (bad) and expecting Jones to be disposed, *ceteris paribus*, to demand that you share his non-cognitive sentiments towards x.

(16) Competent and reflective speakers of English are convinced that they are able to imagine clear-headed (and otherwise psychologically healthy beings) who judge that Jones expresses the sentiment $H!_M(x)$, but who fail to expect Jones to be disposed, *ceteris paribus*, to demand that they share this non-cognitive sentiment towards x.

The beings imagined may genuinely wonder whether Jones is expressing aesthetic, or some other form of, approval or disapproval.

(17) If there were no conceptual link between judging that Jones has expressed $H!_M(x)$ and expecting Jones to be disposed, *ceteris paribus*, to demand that you share this non-cognitive sentiment towards x, we would expect competent and reflective speakers of English to have the conviction described in (16).

So:

(18) Unless there is some other explanation of the conviction described in (16), we are entitled to conclude that there is no conceptual link between judging that Jones has expressed $H!_M(x)$ and expecting Jones to demand that you share this non-cognitive sentiment towards x.

So:

(19) Unless there is some other explanation of the conviction described in (16), we are entitled to conclude that the judgement that Jones has judged that x is good is not identical to the judgement that Jones has expressed $H!_M(x)$.

So:

(20) Unless there is some other explanation of the conviction described in (16), we are entitled to conclude that judging that x is good (bad) cannot be analysed in terms of the expression of $H!_M(x)$.

Moreover, this suggestion faces a circularity problem similar to that developed above against the 'emotional ascent' idea. The definition would be satisfied even if I approved of x and approved of my *aesthetic* approval of x remaining stable. What I approve of being stable is the moral sentiment *itself*. So the definition would have to come out rather as:

$$H!_M(x) = df\ (H!(x)\ and\ H!(stability\ of\ [H_M!(x)])).$$

Again, the circularity of this is evident. Again, no coherent account of the non-cognitive sentiment expressed by a moral judgement has been provided.

Higher-order sentiment

Perhaps the quasi-realist could view moral attitude as expressive of, say, second-order sentiment.[26] In other words:

$$H!_M(x) = H!([H!(x)])$$

That is to say, the judgement that honesty is morally good could be taken to be identical with the attitude of approving that one approves of honesty. An analogue of this proposal is criticized by Michael Smith as follows:

> [W]hy identify valuing with second-order desiring? Why not third-order, or fourth-order, or ... ? The question is a difficult one indeed for those proposing the reduction. For each such identification looks to be as plausible as any other. And if each is as plausible as any other then all such identifications are equally implausible. For any identification would require an arbitrary choice between levels. Therefore no plausible reduction has been effected at all. (Smith 1994a: 146)[27]

The objection, transposed, would be that there is no non-arbitrary way of deciding between second-order approval, third-order approval (approval of one's approval of one's approval ...), fourth-order approval, ... nth-order approval and so on; hence there is no level m at which mth-level approval can be taken to be the attitude expressed by a moral judgement.

However, I think that this objection fails. There is a non-arbitrary way of selecting between levels, by citing facts about what sorts of questions – at given levels – we are, as a matter of contingent fact, able to entertain. Suppose, as is plausible, that competent adult speakers of English are able to 'get their heads' around the question: do I approve of my approval of x?: and also, as is plausible (in my case at least), that they cannot 'get their heads around' the question: do I approve of my approval of my approval of x? Why doesn't this provide us with a non-arbitrary way of selecting second-order – as opposed to some higher-order – level of approval as that which is expressed by moral judgements?

If there is no answer to this question, Smith's objection to the proposal fails. But there is another objection looming, again stemming from an application of the OQA to the non-cognitivist analysis of moral judgement. The quasi-realist may be able to identify value judgements with second-order approval, but it looks as though this is not sufficient to capture what is distinctive about judgements of *moral* value. To see this, note that we can simply reapply the version of the OQA which put pressure on the 'stable sentiments' suggestion:

(21) There is a conceptual link between judging that Jones has judged that x is good (bad) and expecting Jones to be disposed, *ceteris paribus*, to demand that you share his non-cognitive sentiments towards x.

(22) Competent and reflective speakers of English are convinced that they are able to imagine clear-headed (and otherwise psychologically healthy beings) who judge that Jones expresses the sentiment H!([H!(x)]), but who fail to expect Jones to be disposed, *ceteris paribus*, to demand that they share this non-cognitive sentiment towards x.

The beings imagined may genuinely wonder whether Jones is expressing aesthetic, or some other form, of approval or disapproval.

(23) If there were no conceptual link between judging that Jones has expressed H!([H!(x)]) and expecting Jones to be disposed, *ceteris paribus*, to demand that you share this non-cognitive sentiment towards x, we would expect competent and reflective speakers of English to have the conviction described in (22).

So:

(24) Unless there is some other explanation of the conviction described in (22), we are entitled to conclude that there is no conceptual link between judging that Jones has expressed H!([H!(x)]) and expecting Jones to demand that you share this non-cognitive sentiment towards x.

So:

(25) Unless there is some other explanation of the conviction described in (22), we are entitled to conclude that the judgement that Jones has judged that x is good is not identical to the judgement that Jones has expressed H!([H!(x)]).

So:

(26) Unless there is some other explanation of the conviction described
      in (22), we are entitled to conclude that judging that x is good
      cannot be analysed in terms of the expression of H!([H!(x)]).

Again, the proposed account of moral sentiment fails to convince.

How damaging is the quasi-realist's failure to respond adequately to
the moral attitude problem? Blackburn, in his earlier writings, clearly
views this as a problem of some importance. At various places he refers
to this as a 'juicy issue', a solution to which 'is required to establish
projectivism' (1984: 189); and as the 'central remaining task for the
metaphysic of ethics' (1993a: 129). In his more recent writings he takes
a more deflationary view of the matter:

> Analytical philosophers demand definitions, but I do not think it is prof-
> itable to seek a strict 'definition' of the moral attitude here. Practical life
> comes in many flavours, and there is no one place on the staircase that
> identifies a precise point, before which we are not in the sphere of the
> ethical, and after which we are. (1998a: 13–14)

But this is weak: the point is not that we don't have a 'strict' definition of the notion of moral attitude, or a vague sense of the boundary
between moral and non-moral attitudes, but that we have *no* definition
of the notion of a moral attitude, and not *even* a vague sense of what the
boundary between moral and non-moral attitudes consists in.[28]

Thus, if what I have argued in this chapter is correct, the quasi-
realist has at least the beginnings of replies to the four problems which
plagued emotivism: the problem of implied error, the Frege-Geach
problem, the problem of mind-dependence and (via the construction of
moral truth) the problem of the schizoid attitude. But, until the moral
attitude problem is solved, the quasi-realist position will not fully
satisfy those who seek a metaethical theory with a plausible psychology of morals.

4.11 Further Reading

The key texts by Blackburn here are: Blackburn (1984, especially chapters 5–6, 1993a, especially essays 1, 3, and 6–11, and 1998a, especially
chapters 1–4). Blackburn (1996) is a useful, short account of what the
quasi-realist project is not. Blackburn (1981 and 1993b) are also worth
consulting. For good critical discussion of quasi-realism, see Wright
(1985, 1988b, and 1992, chapter 1); and Hale (1986, 1993a, and 1993b).
John McDowell's writings on the issue of ethical non-cognitivism are

demanding, but well worth the effort. See McDowell (1998, especially essays 6–10). For useful commentary on Blackburn's attempt to evade the Frege-Geach problem, see Brighouse (1990), Zangwill (1992), and Van Roojen (1996). A superbly clear commentary can be found in Kolbel (1997 and 2002, chapter 4). For discussion of issues relating to what I have called the 'moral attitude problem', see Smith (2001 and 2002). For a useful exchange on quasi-realism and relativism, see Blackburn (1999) and Kirchin (2000). Other interesting exchanges include those between Harcourt (2005) and Ridge (2006b), and between Egan (2007) and Blackburn (2009). Schroeder (2010) will give the reader a good sense of Blackburn's contribution to the non-cognitivist tradition: see in particular chapters 6 and 7.

An interesting issue, not discussed here, is how minimalism about truth and truth-aptitude impacts upon the quasi-realist project. For discussion of this issue, see Smith (1994b, c); Divers and Miller (1994, 1995); Jackson, Oppy and Smith (1994); Wright (1998); Blackburn (1998b); and Cowie (2009). For an overview, and more suggestions for further reading, see Miller (2012a).

5

Gibbard's Norm-Expressivism

5.1 Norm-Expressivism Introduced

I now move on to consider the version of non-cognitivism about morals that has been developed by the contemporary American philosopher Allan Gibbard: *Norm-Expressivism*. Recall that non-cognitivism is the view that moral judgements do not express beliefs, but rather serve to express some non-cognitive, non-truth-assessable, mental state. Gibbard's theory is non-cognitivist in this sense: according to Gibbard, a moral judgement *expresses an agent's acceptance of norms*. In the first instance we can think of norms as rules, so that Gibbard's view is that moral judgements express an agent's acceptance of rules.

Gibbard thinks that moral questions are questions about the rationality of certain types of sentiment. An act is morally wrong if and only if it is rational for the agent who performed the action to feel *guilty* about having done it, and for other people to feel *angry* or *resentful* at him for having done it.[1] Consider Jones's stealing the exam questions from his tutor's desk. On Gibbard's analysis this is morally wrong if and only if it is rational for Jones to feel guilty at having taken the exam questions, and for the rest of us to feel angry at his having done so.

At first glance this might not look much like a non-cognitivist account of morality: haven't we just given necessary and sufficient conditions for the moral wrongness of an act? And don't these necessary and sufficient conditions amount to *truth-conditions* for the claim that the act is morally wrong? This would be inconsistent with the non-cognitivist claim that ascriptions of moral wrongness don't *have* truth-conditions. But in fact this appearance is misleading, for the non-cognitivist aspect of Gibbard's theory is contained in his analysis of *rationality*: Gibbard is first and foremost a non-cognitivist about rationality. To say that X is rational is not to ascribe a property to X, to utter a truth-conditional statement about X; rather, it is to *express accept-ance* of a system of norms which permits X. Thus, to say that murder is wrong is to say that it is rational for someone who commits a murder to feel guilt at having done so, and for the rest of us to feel angry at his having done so. To say that it is rational for someone who commits a murder to feel guilty at having done so is to express one's acceptance of a system of norms which permits whoever commits a murder to feel guilt at having done so; to say that it is rational for the rest of us to feel angry at the murderer is to express one's acceptance of a system of norms which permits the feeling of anger to be directed towards mur-derers.[2] *Questions about morality get analysed as questions about rationality; rationality gets a non-cognitivist analysis; so moral judgements themselves turn out to be non-cognitive.*

Gibbard's development of the norm-expressivist theory is very rich and very complicated, utilizing materials from psychology, sociol-ogy, anthropology, philosophy of mind and evolutionary biology. I am going to look in detail only at one aspect of his overall theory, his attempt to provide a non-cognitivist solution to the Frege-Geach problem.

5.2 The Frege-Geach Problem Revisited

A good way to approach Gibbard's attempted solution of the Frege-Geach problem is to view it as an attempt to solve the problem in a way that is in principle superior to Blackburn's 1984 quasi-realist solu-tion. So first of all I'll briefly recap on the Frege-Geach problem, and then show that Blackburn's 1984 solution apparently fails to satisfy a very general constraint on attempted solutions, a constraint which Gibbard's norm-expressivist analysis is explicitly designed to satisfy.

Let's develop the Frege-Geach problem in a slightly different way from that adopted in the previous two chapters. Non-cognitivism is in part a view about the semantic function of sentences formed by using a normative operator such as 'It is wrong that . . .'. According to emotiv-ism, for instance, the semantic function of 'It is wrong that Jones stole the money' is to express a feeling of disapproval towards Jones's stealing the money. In this sentence the normative operator 'It is wrong that . . .' is said to have *widest scope*. Technically, this means that the smallest gram-matical unit in which this occurrence of the normative operator occurs is the *entire sentence*. But there are also sentences in which the normative operator has narrow scope: an example would be 'If it is wrong to steal, then it is wrong to get little brother to steal'. The normative operator 'It is wrong . . .' does not have widest scope in this sentence because the small-est grammatical unit in which it occurs is *less* than the entire sentence: it is 'It is wrong to steal'. In 'If it is wrong to steal, then it is wrong to get little brother to steal', the logical operator *If . . . then . . .* has widest scope: the smallest grammatical unit in which it occurs is the entire sentence. The Frege-Geach problem for non-cognitivism can then be formulated as follows. We can perhaps view sentences in which normative moral operators have widest scope as having an expressive semantic function. But it is very implausible to view occurrences of moral operators which have only narrow scope as having the same sort of function. In 'If abortion is wrong, then it ought not to be performed', or 'Hank believes that abortion is wrong', the meaning of the sentence as a whole does not appear to be a function of attitudes towards abortion. This suggests that moral operators such as 'It is wrong . . .' or 'It is right . . .' are systematically *ambiguous*, depending on whether they have wide or narrow scope in the sentences in which they appear. If the non-cognitivist wants to avoid postulating ambiguities where intuitively there are none, he must respond to this charge: he must show how moral operators can appear, with the same meaning, in statements in which they have wide scope and in statements in which they have narrow scope. That is to say, the non-cognitivist must give a *uniform* account of the meanings of moral operators.[3]

Recall, briefly, the structure of Blackburn's 1984 response to this problem. The reason we have to avoid postulating the ambiguity mentioned above is that if we don't, certain intuitively valid inferences will be rendered invalid, for example, moral *modus ponens*:

(1) Lying is wrong.
(2) If lying is wrong, then getting little brother to lie is wrong.

Therefore:

(3) Getting little brother to lie is wrong.

The first appearance of the sentence 'lying is wrong' will have a different semantic function (and a fortiori, different meaning) from the second occurrence, so that the argument will commit a fallacy of equivocation. Blackburn's 1984 response is to give an expressive account of what we are doing when we utter 'If lying is wrong, then getting little brother to lie is wrong': we are expressing our disapproval of moral sensibilities which combine disapproval of lying with lack of disapproval of getting little brother to lie. This then secures the validity of moral *modus ponens*: in the example above, someone who accepts the premises but not the conclusion possesses a combination of attitudes of which he himself disapproves, so that in that sense he is inconsistent.

Put on one side the question of whether this is sufficient to capture the validity of moral *modus ponens*, and ask instead: how would Blackburn account for the validity of a common-or-garden (i.e., non-moral) example of *modus ponens*? For example:

(4) It is raining outside.
(5) If it is raining outside, then the streets are wet.

So:

(6) The streets are wet.

Presumably, Blackburn will here just give the standard account, in terms of the impossibility of the premises being true while the conclusion is false. He can do this, because it is no part of his brief to deny cognitivism about sentences such as 'It is raining outside' – the utterance of this can be assumed straightforwardly to express the truth-assessable belief that it is raining outside.

Note what Blackburn has done here. *He has given one account of what the validity of moral* modus ponens *consists in, and a different account of what the validity of non-moral* modus ponens *consists in.* This stems from the fact that he assigns different semantic functions to 'if . . . then . . .', depending on whether or not the sentences embedded within it contain occurrences of moral or normative operators. If they do contain moral operators, then we give an expressivist account of the conditional as expressing a higher-order sentiment; if they don't, then we just give the standard account (truth-functional, or whatever). *Blackburn's account seems to entail that occurrences of 'If . . . then . . .' are systematically ambiguous, depending on whether or not they embed sentences containing moral operators.*

Why does this matter? Well, the postulation of this ambiguity may not lead to the same sort of problem as the ambiguity in sentences in which moral terms have widest scope: no obviously valid arguments are rendered invalid, since we do (we're assuming) have an account of what the validity of moral *modus ponens* consists in. The objection is that it is ad hoc to postulate an ambiguity between occurrences of 'If . . . then . . .', as it embeds or fails to embed sentences containing occurrences of normative operators. The only reason why the ambiguity is postulated appears to be that it saves quasi-realism from an objection. But if you are going to postulate an ambiguity where intuitively there is none, there had better be some *independent* reason for doing so. Note that this objection will apply even if the details of Blackburn's solution to the problem are unimpeachable. In order to avoid this charge of postulating ad hoc ambiguities, the non-cognitivist must give a *uniform* account of the logical operators, and, correspondingly, a *uniform* account of the validity of inferences in which those logical operators figure.[4]

This is what Gibbard sets out to do: in that sense he is trying to give a solution to the Frege-Geach problem which is superior to Blackburn's, insofar as it avoids postulating ad hoc ambiguities and attempts to give a uniform account of the logical operators and the patterns of inference in which they figure. Gibbard's strategy is to give a completely *general* account of the meanings of the logical operators, and of the forms of inference in which they figure. The truth-functional account of non-moral *modus ponens* will be seen to be a special case of this general account, a special case which results when the *if . . . then . . .* operator does not embed sentences containing moral operators; and the case of moral *modus ponens* will also be seen to be a special case of this more general account, the special case which results when the *if . . . then . . .* operator does embed sentences containing moral operators. *Crucially, in Gibbard's account the explanations (of 'if . . . then . . .' and the validity of* modus ponens*) in each case exemplify a shared general pattern, so that there is no implication of systematic ambiguity.*

5.3 Gibbard's Solution to the Frege-Geach Problem

Gibbard's project is thus to give a uniform account of the meaning of the logical operators and thus a uniform account of the validity of inferences involving sentences which feature those operators. He wants to give a general account which entails as a special case the standard account of validity given for arguments which feature no moral vocabulary, but which *also* entails as a special case an account of the validity of arguments which do contain moral vocabulary, such as moral *modus ponens*. I'll work towards his general account by considering the standard account of validity for arguments all of whose sentences receive a straightforwardly cognitivist interpretation.

According to the standard account, an argument is valid if its conclusion follows from its premises. And the conclusion follows from the premises when it is impossible for those premises to be true and the conclusion to be false. Thus arguments of the form

(7) $P \to Q$,
(8) P

therefore

(9) Q

are valid because it is impossible for both $P \to Q$ and P to be true and yet for Q to be false. And arguments of the form

(10) $Q \to P$
(11) P

therefore

(12) Q

are invalid because it is possible for both premises to be true yet for the conclusion to be false (e.g., with Q false, and P true).

As we saw earlier (4.2), one way to explain the notions of possibility and impossibility is via the notion of possible worlds. A statement P is said to be possible if there is some possible world – some logically consistent state of affairs – in which P is true; likewise a statement is said to be impossible if there are no possible worlds in which P is true; and a statement is said to be necessarily true if it is true in all possible worlds. Thus we can explain the standard account of validity as follows: *an argument is valid if there are no possible worlds in which all of its premises are true and its conclusion is false.*

Gibbard tries to provide a more general account of validity for all types of arguments, be they moral or non-moral, of which the account just outlined is a special case. In order to do this, he develops the notion of a *factual-normative world*, symbolized <w, n>, intended to play the role in the more general account played in the standard account by possible worlds. What is a factual normative world? Gibbard explains this as follows:

> Imagine a goddess Hera who is entirely coherent and completely opinionated both normatively and factually. She suffers no factual uncertainty; there is a completely determinate way she thinks the world to be. She likewise lacks all normative uncertainty; there is a complete system of general norms that she accepts. She is consistent in her factual and normative beliefs, and accepts everything descriptive and normative that follows from the things she accepts. Together, w and n constitute a completely opinionated credal-normative state, a factual normative world <w, n>. (1990: 95)

What Gibbard calls 'a completely determinate way Hera thinks the world to be' is just the notion of a possible world that is used in the standard account of validity. The other notion involved in Gibbard's explanation of a factual-normative world is the notion of a *system of norms*:

> A person's normative judgements all told on a given matter will typically depend on his acceptance of more than one norm, and the norms he accepts may weigh in opposing directions. . . . Our normative judgements thus depend not on a single norm, but on a plurality of norms that we accept as having some force, and on the ways we take some of these norms to outweigh or override others. (1990: 86–7)

Our normative judgements are the result of a complex interaction between many different norms. Thus, I may judge that smoking in confined public places is bad, despite accepting a norm which says that people should be allowed to freely pursue whatever gives them pleasure – because I also accept a norm which says that people should not be allowed to unnecessarily endanger the health of others, and because I take the latter norm to outweigh the former. The essentials about systems of norms are set out in the following quote:

> What matters about a system of norms is what it requires and what it permits in various conceivable circumstances. We can characterize any system N of norms by a family of basic predicates 'N-forbidden', 'N-optional', and 'N-required'. Here 'N-forbidden' simply means 'forbidden by system of norms N', and likewise for its siblings. Other predicates can be constructed from these basic ones; in particular 'N-permitted' will mean 'either N-optional or N-required'. (1990: 87)

Thus, if we take N to be the Ten Commandments, coveting your neighbour's wife is N-forbidden, telling the truth is N-required, playing cricket is N-optional, and so on. We'll see that it is important for Gibbard's purposes that these predicates are themselves genuinely descriptive: unlike moral predicates, these predicates do actually stand for genuine properties, and the sentences in which they are ascribed are truth-evaluable:

> These predicates are descriptive rather than normative: whether a thing, say, is N-permitted will be a matter of fact. It might be N-permitted without being rational, for the system N might have little to recommend it. People who agree on the facts will agree on what is N-permitted and what is not, even if they disagree normatively – even if, for instance, one accepts N and the other does not. (1990: 87)

Thus it is a purely factual matter whether, for example, the system of norms constituted by the Ten Commandments forbids adultery, or permits smoking, or whatever.

We need one more piece of detail before seeing how Gibbard puts this machinery into action: the system of norms which features in the explanation of a factual-normative world is said to be *complete*. Gibbard characterizes completeness as follows:

> We can call a system complete if N-forbidden, N-optional, and N-required trichotomize the possibilities: if on every occasion, actual or hypothetical, each alternative is either N-forbidden, N-optional, or N-required. (1990: 88)

With this on board we can go back to the notion of a factual-normative world, <w, n>. Gibbard writes:

Together, w and n entail a normative judgement for every occasion. They entail, for instance, whether or not it is rational for Antony to give battle. Hera is not at all uncertain what Antony's subjective circumstances are, and she is not at all undecided what norms to apply or how to weigh them against each other. She applies the norms she accepts to Antony's subjective circumstances as she thinks them to be, and comes to one of three definite conclusions: that for Antony, giving battle is rationally required, that it is rationally optional, or that it is irrational. (1990: 95)

Gibbard now defines the notion of a particular normative judgement *holding* in a factual-normative world <w, n>. Let's use the judgement that x is rational as an example. Corresponding to the normative predicate 'rational' there will be a purely descriptive predicate, namely, 'N-permitted', or 'permitted by system of norms N'. This is the predicate which, as Gibbard puts it, *N-corresponds* to the normative predicate. To say that the normative judgement 'x is rational' holds in the factual-normative world <w, n> is to say that the purely descriptive judgement 'x is N-permitted' is true in the possible world w. *In general, a normative judgement S holds at a factual-normative world <w, n> if and only if S*, the judgement which results from S by replacing all of its normative predicates with the descriptive predicates which N-correspond to them, is true in the possible world w.*

Gibbard can now define a general notion of validity, which applies even to arguments whose constituent sentences contain normative or moral vocabulary: *an argument is valid iff every factual-normative world at which the premises hold is a factual-normative world at which the conclusion holds.*

Let's consider an example, using our old warhorse.

(1) Lying is wrong.
(2) If lying is wrong, then getting little brother to lie is wrong.

So:

(3) Getting little brother to lie is wrong.

Remember that for Gibbard this amounts to:

(1a) It is rational to feel anger at acts of lying.
(2a) If it is rational to feel anger at acts of lying, then it is rational to feel anger towards anyone who gets your little brother to lie.

So:

(3a) It is rational to feel anger towards anyone who gets your little brother to lie.

What, on Gibbard's account, does the validity of this argument consist in? It consists in the fact that there are no factual-normative worlds <w, n> at which the premises hold but at which the conclusion fails to hold. To see this consider the argument:

(1b) Feeling anger at liars is N-permitted.
(2b) If feeling anger at liars is N-permitted, then feeling anger towards anyone who gets your little brother to lie is N-permitted.

So:

(3b) Feeling anger towards anyone who gets your little brother to lie is N-permitted.

There are no possible worlds in which the premises of this argument are true and the conclusion is false. So the argument from (1b) and (2b) to (3b) is valid. So the argument from (1a) and (2a) to (3a) is valid. So, finally, the moral *modus ponens* argument from (1) and (2) to (3) is valid.

It is important to note that the validity of a common-or-garden example of *modus ponens*, one whose sentences contain no moral or normative vocabulary, can be accounted for as a special case of the above structure. Consider again:

(4) It is raining.
(5) If it is raining, then the streets are wet.

So:

(6) The streets are wet.

Since there are no normative predicates involved in 'It is raining', the notion of this holding at a factual-normative world <w, n> just reduces to the notion of its being true at the possible world w. So in this case Gibbard's theory yields the result that the argument is valid because there are no possible worlds in which (1) and (2) are both true yet in which (3) is false. Thus, the general account of validity given by Gibbard, when applied to common-or-garden cases like that above, yields the result that the argument is valid if and only if there are no possible worlds w in which all of its premises are true and yet its conclusion is false. The standard account of validity is thus a special case of Gibbard's account. Gibbard can claim then that, unlike Blackburn, he can give an account of what the validity of *modus ponens* consists in which is uniform across the moral and non-moral cases. So he can evade the charge of postulating ad hoc ambiguities in the logical operators.

5.4 Comments and Objections

(a) Blackburn's objections

Blackburn notes that there is a constraint which applies to any non-cognitivist theory of morals:

> A solution to the Frege-Geach problem must explain, and make legitimate, the propositional surface [of moral discourse]. But it must do this without invoking properties of evaluative discourse that go beyond the expressivist starting point. The constraint is quite delicate. For example it would not be met if we simply invoked the fact that evaluative judgements can be negated: negation is itself in need of a theory – it is itself part of the propositional surface, and the wrong side of the Fregean abyss. The constraint would not be met if we allowed ourselves a notion of consistency and inconsistency, since that too is on the wrong side. All these notions must be built, if they can be, on the more primitive basis. (1992a: 948)

Blackburn claims that Gibbard's norm-expressivism violates this constraint. The first worry is about Gibbard's notion of a *system of norms*. As Blackburn puts it: 'Norms are described as outweighing or over-riding others, and systems disagree' (1992a: 948), and in developing his solution to the Frege-Geach problem Gibbard uses the notion of *consistency* of normative beliefs in characterizing the notion of a 'completely opinionated credal-normative state' (Gibbard 1990: 95; see the quote above). Blackburn worries that Gibbard at this point has not done anything to earn the right to use the notion of disagreement or inconsistency as applied to relationships between systems of norms. Blackburn's second worry echoes an objection raised against his own quasi-realism by Hale and Wright (see 4.4 above): that the notion of inconsistency which it uses to underpin the validity of moral *modus ponens* is not sufficient to convict someone who endorses its premises but denies its conclusion of some *logical* failing. At best, such a person is convicted of a *moral* failing. Consider an inference whose constituent sentences contain moral vocabulary:

(13) Either Freddy behaved badly or Jane did.
(14) Freddy did not behave badly.

So:

(15) Jane behaved badly.

What can Gibbard say about someone who accepts the premises, but who is happy to tolerate Jane's behaviour? Blackburn writes:

> What do we say to someone who refuses to hear the wrong combination as ruled out by logic? If we accept (p v q) and rule out p, naturally we must accept q. But that is already describing our state of mind propositionally. If we take the more expressivist descriptions – I express acceptance of a system allowing Freddy's behaviour, and I stand ready to oppose an indefinite combination of systems that allows both their behaviours – it will not be so apparent why it is a defect of *logic* in me also to tolerate Jane. It might be a defect more like that of being fickle, or impractical. The dilemma seems to be that if states of mind are each described in their own functional terms we lose a logical conception of what is wrong with their combination, whereas to describe them propositionally is already to draw material from across the Fregean abyss. (1992a: 950)

Blackburn thus questions whether Gibbard really has given a *uniform* account of what the validity of common-or-garden *modus ponens* and moral *modus ponens* consists in.[5]

(b) Ambiguity and logical operators

In 5.2, I outlined one line of argument that would provide a motivation for Gibbard's attempt to solve the Frege-Geach problem: the argument was that Blackburn's 1984 quasi-realist solution to the Frege-Geach problem, if it worked at all, did so only at the cost of postulating an ad hoc ambiguity between different occurrences of logical operators, such as the conditional. But one might wonder whether Blackburn's solution to the Frege-Geach problem really does entail that occurrences of 'If . . . then . . .' are systematically ambiguous, depending on whether or not they embed sentences containing moral vocabulary. It is important to be clear on the difference between the charge that Blackburn's account, if otherwise successful,[6] leads to the postulation of ad hoc ambiguities between different occurrences of 'If . . . then . . .', and the worry about equivocation between the premises of a moral *modus ponens* which is in essence the Frege-Geach problem. In response to the latter worry, Blackburn develops an account of indirect contexts which is intended to capture, inter alia, the validity of the moral *modus ponens* argument. Obviously, in developing this account, Blackburn cannot assume that his solution to the Frege-Geach problem is otherwise successful, for the account in question is an attempt to solve that very problem. However, since the former charge concerns *what is postulated by an otherwise successful solution to the Frege-Geach problem*, Blackburn is entitled, in responding to *this* charge, to assume that his account of indirect contexts is otherwise successful. The question is precisely whether, *if* that account is otherwise successful, it postulates an ad hoc ambiguity. Blackburn should grant that the ambiguity, if postulated by what is assumed to be an otherwise successful account of indirect contexts, is ad hoc, but *deny* that an otherwise successful account of indirect contexts postulates such an ambiguity. How can Blackburn deny this? Well, suppose that Blackburn's account of indirect contexts is otherwise successful. Since the objection concerns what follows from this assumption, it is perfectly legitimate for Blackburn to make it himself in responding to the charge. Then Blackburn can claim – so long as the replies to distinct objections to quasi-realism, such as those discussed in chapter 4, are plausible – to have constructed on an attitudinal basis, the right to the notion of truth in ethics, and the right to the idea that ethical judgements are truth-conditional. But, with this much on board, Blackburn has a ready answer to the further charge that his account postulates ambiguities between different occurrences of the logical operators. He can argue that since his account of indirect contexts is assumed to be otherwise successful, the meanings of the logical operators are constant across the moral and non-moral cases: since the otherwise successful account of indirect contexts yields truth-conditions for moral statements, the meaning of the conditional operator, for example, can be assumed to be the same regardless of whether its constituents do or do not embed moral vocabulary. Blackburn does not assign different occurrences of the conditional different semantic functions, depending on whether or not their constituents contain moral vocabulary; rather, he gives different accounts for each of *identical* semantic functions.[7] Two hammers may have been made in different ways from different materials, but it does not necessarily follow from this that they have different functional roles.

If this is right, then the motivation for seeking an account of indirect contexts, such as Gibbard's, in preference to Blackburn's 1984 account, is at the very least somewhat diminished. And this point would be strengthened if Blackburn is correct in his claim, outlined above, that Gibbard's account of indirect contexts faces essentially the same objection as levelled by Hale and Wright against his own 1984.

(c) Mind-independence

Does Gibbard's norm-expressivism make morals mind-dependent in some questionable way? Gibbard's answer to this question is essentially the same as Blackburn's (see Gibbard 1992: 164–6). Take the judgement that bullying is wrong. I express my acceptance of a norm which prohibits bullying. But if I thought bullying was OK, would it be OK? Gibbard answers no: mind-independence can be captured by the norm-expressivist in terms of my acceptance of a higher-order norm which prohibits letting first-order norms vary with thought, taste and inclination. Someone who rejects this higher-order norm is guilty of a moral transgression. Gibbard's reply to the problem of mind-independence is thus as plausible or implausible as Blackburn's (see 4.7).

(d) Gibbard and the moral attitude problem

The emotivist faced the following problem: what non-cognitive feeling or sentiment is expressed by a moral judgement? And Blackburn's quasi-realist faced the analogous problem: what non-cognitive attitude are moral judgements assumed, *ab initio*, to express? This problem – the moral attitude problem – arises for Gibbard in a slightly less direct fashion (see 1990: chapter 7). According to Gibbard, the judgement that murder is wrong expresses acceptance of a system of norms that requires one to feel *guilty* at having committed murder or to be *angry* at someone else if they have committed murder. So guilt and anger are distinctively moral sentiments in the sense that it is in virtue of governing them that a given system of norms counts as a system of moral norms, and a judgement which expresses acceptance of those norms counts as a moral judgement. Now Gibbard must answer the challenge: explain guilt and anger otherwise than as 'those feelings governed by the sorts of norms acceptance of which is expressed by moral judgements'.

Can this be done? Why would it be a problem for Gibbard if it couldn't? If it couldn't, we would have no non-trivial answer to the question: what are the distinctively moral sentiments governed by the norms acceptance of which is expressed by moral judgements? In effect, we would have only the trivial answer: 'those sentiments, whatever they are, that are governed by the norms acceptance of which is expressed by moral judgements'. This is no answer at all.

Gibbard's response to this worry is measured. In chapter 7 of his 1990, he raises some worries about *judgemental theories of emotion*. According to these, emotions such as *anger* are explained in terms of moral judgement rather than vice versa; so, if they were plausible, Gibbard's strategy of explaining moral judgement in terms of emotions would be short-circuited. But Gibbard argues that judgemental theories are anyway implausible: amongst other worries, there is the worry that 'it is not even true that anger requires a judgement of wrong – at least in any informative sense. I can feel angry at you and yet think it makes no sense to do so; I can think that really you have acted as you should' (1990: 130). Gibbard then argues that the competing hypotheses about the nature of the emotions – *adaptive syndrome theories* (1990: 131–42) and *attributional theories* (1990: 141–50) – are both consistent with the main tenets of norm-expressivism.[8]

(e) Norm-expressivism and the normativity of norms

According to Gibbard, predicates like 'N-permitted', 'N-required', and so on, are purely *descriptive* (in other words, non-normative) predicates.

It is a matter of fact whether a given course of action is N-permitted or N-optional or N-required. Now predicates like 'N-permitted', and so on, concern the relationship between a system of norms and courses of action which comply or fail to comply with them. Another way of putting this is to say that they concern the relationship between rules and courses of action which follow or fail to follow them. *But many philosophers think that this itself is a normative matter.* Rules do not tell us how we will behave: they tell us how we *ought* to behave (see Kripke 1982 and the papers in Miller and Wright 2002 for more on this idea). Now it is the normativity of morals which inclines Gibbard towards a non-cognitivist account of moral judgement (1990: chapter 1). So, given that rules or norms are *themselves* normative, the question arises as to how Gibbard can avoid having to give an expressivist account of rule-following, and thus treat predicates such as N-permitted and so on as normative rather than purely descriptive. Investigating this question is beyond the scope of this chapter, but we can at least pose a number of related questions to which the norm-expressivist owes us answers:

(1) Can Gibbard consistently treat 'N-permitted' and so on as purely descriptive?[9]
(2) If the answer to (1) is negative, can he consistently avoid having to embrace an expressivist account of rule-following?
(3) How plausible is expressivism about rule-following?
(4) Can expressivism about rule-following be plugged into Gibbard's theory in a way that conserves his attempt to solve the Frege-Geach problem?[10]

(f) Commitments and plans

In chapter 3 of his 2003 book, *Thinking How To Live*, Gibbard expresses the view that the 1990 solution to the Frege-Geach problem outlined above is 'a good solution' (Gibbard 2003: 42), although he concedes that it can look 'contrived and gruesome'.

Gibbard discusses the Frege-Geach problem in his 2003 by focusing on the following example:

(16) Either packing is now the thing to do, or by now it's too late to catch the train anyway;
(17) It's not even now too late to catch the train; thus,
(18) Packing is now the thing to do.

where the conclusion (18) – which is also the first disjunct of (16) – expresses a decision. Given that it expresses a decision we face the familiar question:

> How ... do we explain the disjunction (16)? Not just any explanation will do: a satisfactory explanation must explain the apparent validity of Holmes's argument. It must explain why this validity seems of a piece with the validity of plain arguments of fact. (2003: 42)

Gibbard views normative judgements in terms of plans and commitments to plans; moreover, 'The inferential import of a state of mind, we can try saying, is a matter of the commitments one takes on in reaching that state of mind' (2003: 45). So what plan does Holmes commit himself to in accepting (16)? And how does this feed into an account of the validity of the argument from (16) and (17) to (18)? Gibbard writes:

> If Holmes accepts (16), he rules out the following: coming both (i) to reject its being too late to catch the train and (ii) to reject deciding to pack. With (17), he rejects its being too late to catch the train. He has thus ruled out rejecting deciding to pack. (2003: 45)

The argument is valid since it would be 'inconsistent for me to accept the premises and reject the conclusion: I would be doing what I had ruled out doing' (ibid.), and Gibbard claims that the account applies equally to cases where only descriptive claims are involved. Consider:

(19) Either I am in Adelaide or I am in Dunedin;
(20) I'm not in Dunedin; so,
(21) I am in Adelaide.

In accepting (19) I rule out the following: coming both (i) to reject the belief that I am in Adelaide and (ii) to reject the belief that I am in Dunedin. So if I accept the premises and reject the conclusion I would have a belief set that I had committed myself not to having.

However, in the case of the argument from (19) and (20) to (21), we can say that accepting the premises and rejecting the conclusion would involve a straightforwardly inconsistent set of beliefs, so although accepting the premises and rejecting the conclusion would involve me having a belief set I planned not to have, that is not the fundamental failing to which I am prey. And, in the case of the argument from (16) and (17) to (18), the story offered by Gibbard appears to be open to the worry of Blackburn's that we outlined in section (a) above. On this account, someone who accepts the premises but rejects the conclusion of the logically valid argument from (16) and (17) to (18) does something that he has planned not to do. But, as Blackburn suggests, we might wonder whether this is strong enough to capture the idea of a *logical* mistake: it looks more like being fickle or impractical.[11]

5.5 Further Reading

The central text here is Gibbard (1990, especially chapters 1, 3, 5, 7 and 8, though the book is better read in its entirety). For good discussions of Gibbard's norm-expressivism, see Blackburn (1992a), Carson (1992), Hill (1992), and Railton (1992). Gibbard replies to these critics in his 1992. Another useful exchange between Gibbard and a critic can be found in Sinnott-Armstrong (1993) and Gibbard (1993). Also useful are Blackburn (1992b), Horwich (1993), Sturgeon (1995), Wedgwood (1997), and Yang (2009). Horwich (1993) should be read in conjunction with the reading on minimalism suggested at the end of the previous chapter.

Gibbard develops the theory of his 1990 further in Gibbard (2003). In particular, the notion of norm-acceptance is developed via the notions of planning and commitment to plans (with other notions in play above developed accordingly, for example, 'factual-normative worlds' become 'fact-plan worlds'). For a helpful discussion of Gibbard's views generally, see Schroeder (2010: chapter 7).

6

Mackie's 'Error-Theory', the Argument from Queerness and Moral Fictionalism

6.1 Introduction

In the previous three chapters I have been looking at *non-cognitivist* theories of moral judgement. Non-cognitivism can be viewed as the conjunction of the following two claims: (a) a claim about the *semantics* of moral discourse, that moral sentences are not truth-apt; (b) a claim about the *psychological* states expressed by moral judgements, that moral judgements do not express beliefs, but rather some non-cognitive sentiment or inclination.[1] I now move on to look at cognitivist accounts of morals: theories which claim that moral judgements are apt for assessment in terms of truth and falsity, and that moral judgements do express representational psychological states like beliefs. The first cognitivist theory which I'll consider is John Mackie's *error-theory* of morals. I'll also discuss Richard Joyce's 'revolutionary fictionalism', and in an appendix I briefly discuss Mark Kalderon's non-error-theoretic 'hermeneutic fictionalism'.

6.2 Error-Theories, Cognitivism and the Rejection of Moral Realism

An error-theory about a particular region of discourse is the claim that the positive, atomic sentences of that discourse are *systematically and uniformly false*. Thus, an error-theory about moral discourse would claim that ascriptions of moral qualities to acts, objects and events, are systematically and uniformly false.[2] This is clearly a significant departure from common sense: ordinarily we would say that *some* such sentences are false, but that others are true. According to the error-theory, this is a mistake. How might one argue for such a radical thesis?

The clearest way to view Mackie's argument for the error-theory is as a conjunction of a conceptual claim with an ontological claim (Smith 1994a: 63–6; Joyce 2001: 42). The *conceptual* claim is that our concept of a moral fact is a concept of an *objectively prescriptive* fact, or, equivalently, that our concept of a moral property is a concept of an objectively prescriptive quality (I'll explain this notion in the next section). The *ontological* claim is simply that there *are* no objectively prescriptive facts or properties. The conclusion is that there is nothing in the world answering to our moral concepts, no facts or properties which render moral judgements true. Our moral judgements are all of them false. We can thus construe the error-theory as follows:

Conceptual/semantic/psychological claim: moral sentences have truth-conditions, the obtaining of which would require the existence of objectively and categorically prescriptive facts; moral judgements express beliefs, whose truth would require the existence of objectively and categorically prescriptive facts.
Ontological claim: There are no objectively and categorically prescriptive facts.

The error-theory is thus a *cognitivist* view of morals, but *not* (in virtue of the ontological claim) a version of moral realism.

6.3 An Example of an Error-Theory: Locke on Colour

Before looking at Mackie's arguments for the conceptual claim and the ontological claim, let's look briefly at the error-theory which plausibly provides a model for Mackie's views on morals: Locke's error-theory concerning the secondary qualities, as developed in *An Essay Concerning Human Understanding* (Locke 1689). Let's focus on the case of colour. One way of reconstructing Locke's position on colour is as follows.[3] First of all, we draw a distinction between categorical and dispositional properties.

DISP: *A dispositional property is a property the ascription of which to an object is true, if it is true, in virtue of the truth of a counterfactual conditional.*

A counterfactual conditional is a sentence which claims that such and such would happen were some contrary-to-fact condition actually to obtain: for example, if I had been born English, I would have tried to cover it up. Thus brittleness is plausibly a dispositional property because an ascription of brittleness to an object is true, if it is true, in virtue of the truth of something like the following counterfactual conditional: if the object were dropped from a moderate height or struck with moderate force, then it would shatter. A categorical property is simply a property which is not dispositional in this sense: in other words

CAT: *A categorical property is a property the truth of an ascription of which to an object does not consist in the truth of some counterfactual conditional.*

Thus, triangularity is plausibly an example of a categorical property because 'x is triangular' is true, if it is true, in virtue of x's being a planar figure with three sides and internal angles adding up to 180 degrees – and there seems to be no mention of a counterfactual conditional in this.[4]

Using this distinction, we can now frame Locke's argument for an error-theory about colours as consisting of the following pair of claims: the *conceptual/phenomenological* claim that our concept of redness is a concept of a categorical property, or that redness presents itself to us in experience as a categorical property; and the *ontological* claim that there actually is no categorical property of redness instantiated in the world.

What is the argument for the conceptual/phenomenological claim? Well, just think about how dispositional properties present themselves to you in experience (Boghossian and Velleman 1989). Take a dispositional property, like the property the sleeping cat has to wake up and scratch itself when you switch the lights on. The cat isn't actually scratching itself in the dark: it starts to scratch itself when you flip the light switch. Is our experience of redness like our experience of the property we ascribe to the cat? It seems not: when we walk into a dark room and switch on the lights, the colours of the objects in the room do not appear to *come on*. We do not think that the table only starts to become brown when we switch the lights on: we think that it is brown even in the dark and that switching on the lights merely serves to *reveal* (as opposed to *activate*) its brownness. As Boghossian and Velleman put it:

> The dispelling of darkness looks like the drawing of a curtain from the colours of objects no less than the objects themselves. If colours looked like dispositions . . . when the light was extinguished, the colours would not look as if they were being concealed or shrouded in the ensuing darkness: rather, they would look as if they were becoming dormant, like the cat returning to sleep. But colours do not look like that; or not, at least, to us. (1989: 86)

If this is correct (and I'll say more on this below), *our concept of redness is a concept of a categorical property.* Alternatively, *colours-as-we-see-them, colours as they present themselves to us in experience, are categorical.*

That is an argument for the conceptual claim. But what is the argument for the ontological claim? The ontological claim is that there is no categorical property of redness in the world. The argument for this is that we cannot find a categorical property of redness in the world: what property could this be? The only property of redness actually in the world is a dispositional property: the property of being disposed to look red to normal observers in normal perceptual conditions. Thus, colours-as-we-see-them are categorical; but there are no categorical colour properties in the world; thus, there are no colours-as-we-see-them in the world; so our ascriptions of colours-as-we-see-them to objects in the world are systematically and uniformly false.

So there are two main ways in which we might try to avoid the error-theory about colours: we could either deny the conceptual claim or we could deny the ontological claim. We could deny the conceptual claim by claiming that our concept of redness actually is the concept of a dispositional property, perhaps the concept of being disposed to look red to normal observers in standard conditions of illumination. Since some objects are so disposed, it would follow that there are some objects which possess redness as we conceive it, or redness-as-it-appears-to-us. Some ascriptions of our concept of redness to objects would then be true, so that the error-theory would be avoided. At the very least, this sort of reply to the error-theory, a *dispositionalist reply*, would have to respond to the claim that it was at odds with the *phenomenology* of colour experience. On the other hand, we could concede the conceptual/phenomenological claim and deny the error-theorist's ontological claim by claiming that there is a categorical property of redness in the world, perhaps some complex physical property, such as that of possessing a particular spectral reflectance profile, or whatever. But this type of response faces many problems: for one thing, it is still going to face problems about the phenomenology of colour experience. When I see a red object I do not see it as possessing some complex physical property: this sort of reply seems to focus on the wrong sort of property from the phenomenological point of view. Correlatively, it also seems false that our concept of red is the concept of this type of categorical property: the claim that the truth-conditions of ascriptions of red have the form 'x is red iff x is N', where N is some complex physical property, is at odds with what we would judge about the extension of the concept redness in various counterfactual circumstances. For instance, what would we say if it turned out, as a matter of fact, that there was no underlying physical property N possessed by all of the things which look red to normal observers in standard conditions of illumination? If 'x is red iff x is N' is correct as a description of our conceptual practice, we would say that we had discovered that there are no red things. But we wouldn't say this: we would still say that there are lots of red things, although the concept of redness does not pick out an interesting physical kind.

It seems to me that the best hope for a cognitivist response to the error-theory about colours is to adopt some form of dispositionalist account of our colour concepts, and then attempt to neutralize the claim that this is at odds with the phenomenology of colour experience. I'll return to this in due course.

6.4 Mackie's Conceptual Claim

Mackie's conceptual claim is that our concept of a moral requirement is the concept of an objectively, categorically prescriptive requirement. What does this mean? To say that moral requirements are *prescriptive* is to say that they tell us how we *ought* to act, to say that they give us *reasons* for acting. Thus, to say that something is morally good is to say that we ought to pursue it, that we have reason to pursue it. To say that something is morally bad is to say that we ought not to pursue it, that we have reason not to pursue it. To say that moral requirements are *categorically* prescriptive is to say that these reasons are categorical in the sense of Kant's categorical imperatives.[5] The reasons for action that moral requirements furnish are not contingent upon the possession of desires or wants on the part of the agent to whom they are addressed: I cannot release myself from the requirement imposed by the claim that torturing the innocent is wrong by citing some desire or inclination that I have. This contrasts, for example, with the requirement imposed by the claim that perpetual lateness at work is likely to result in one losing one's job: I can release myself from the requirement imposed by this claim by citing my desire to lose my job. Reasons for action which are contingent in this way on desires and inclinations are furnished by what Kant (1785) called *hypothetical* imperatives.

So our concept of a moral requirement is a concept of a categorically prescriptive requirement. But Mackie claims further that our concept of a moral requirement is a concept of an *objectively*, categorically prescriptive requirement. What does it mean to say that a requirement is *objective*? Mackie says a lot of different-sounding things about this, and the following is by no means a comprehensive list (references are to chapter 1 of Mackie 1973). To call a requirement objective is to say that it can be an object of *knowledge* (24, 31, 33), that it can be *true or false* (26, 33), that it can be *perceived* (31, 33), that it can be *recognized* (42), that it is *prior to and independent of* our preferences and choices (30, 43), that it is a source of authority *external* to our preferences and choices (32, 34, 43), that it is *part of the fabric of the world* (12), that it *backs up and validates* some of our preferences and choices (22), that it is capable of being *simply true* (30) or *valid as a matter of general logic* (30), that it is *not constituted by our choosing or deciding to think in a certain way* (30), that it is *extra-mental* (23), that it is something of which we can be *aware* (38), that it is something that can be *introspected* (39), that it is something that can *figure as a premise in an explanatory hypothesis or inference* (39), and so on. Mackie plainly does not take these to be individually necessary: facts about subatomic particles, for example, may qualify as objective in virtue of figuring in explanatory hypotheses even though they cannot be objects of perceptual acquaintance. But his intention is plain enough: these are the sorts of conditions whose satisfaction by a fact renders it objective as opposed to subjective.[6] Mackie's conceptual claim about morality is thus that our concept of a moral requirement is a concept of a fact which is objective in at least some of the senses just listed, while his ontological claim will be that the world does not contain any facts which are both candidates for being moral facts and yet which play even some of the roles distinctive of objective facts.[7]

6.5 The Argument from Queerness

Having argued that our concept of a moral fact is a concept of an objectively and categorically prescriptive requirement, Mackie goes on to argue that there are no such things as objectively and categorically prescriptive requirements (henceforth, 'objective values'). His reasons for claiming this are primarily *metaphysical* and *epistemological*.[8] The metaphysical problem with objective values concerns 'the metaphysical peculiarity of the supposed objective values, in that they would have to be intrinsically action-guiding and motivating' (49). The epistemological problem concerns 'the difficulty of accounting for our knowledge of value entities or features and of their links with the features on which they would be consequential' (49).

Expounding the metaphysical part of the argument from queerness, Mackie writes: 'If there were objective values, then they would be entities or relations of a very strange sort, utterly different from anything else in the universe' (38). What is so strange about them? Mackie says that Plato's Forms (and, for that matter, Moore's non-natural qualities) give us a 'dramatic picture' of what objective values would be, if there were any:

> The Form of the Good is such that knowledge of it provides the knower with both a direction and an overriding motive; something's being good both tells the person who knows this to pursue it and makes him pursue it. An objective good would be sought by anyone who was acquainted with it, not because of any contingent fact that this person, or every person, is so constituted that he desires this end, but just because the end has to-be-pursuedness somehow built into it. Similarly, if there were objective principles of right and wrong, any wrong (possible) course of action would have not-to-be-doneness somehow built into it. Or we should have something like Clarke's necessary relations of fitness

between situations and actions, so that a situation would have a demand
for such-and-such an action somehow built into it. (40)[9]

The obtaining of a moral state of affairs would be the obtaining of a
situation 'with a demand for such and such an action somehow built
into it'; the states of affairs which we find in the world do not have such
demands built into them, they are 'normatively inert', as it were. Thus,
the world contains no moral states of affairs, situations which consist in
the instantiation of a moral quality.

Mackie now backs this metaphysical argument up with an epistemological argument:

> If we were aware [of objective values], it would have to be by some
> special faculty of moral perception or intuition, utterly different from
> our ways of knowing everything else. These points were recognized by
> Moore when he spoke of non-natural qualities, and by the intuitionists in
> their talk about a 'faculty of moral intuition'. Intuitionism has long been
> out of favour, and it is indeed easy to point out its implausibilties. What
> is not so often stressed, but is more important, is that the central thesis
> of intuitionism is one to which any objectivist view of values is in the
> end committed: intuitionism merely makes unpalatably plain what other
> forms of objectivism wrap up. (38)

In short, our ordinary conceptions of how we might come into cognitive contact with states of affairs, and thereby acquire knowledge of
them, cannot cope with the idea that the states of affairs are objective
values. So we are forced to expand that ordinary conception to include
forms of moral perception and intuition. But these are completely
unexplanatory: they are really just placeholders for our capacity to
form correct moral judgements (see 3.3 above).

6.6 Wright's Objection to the Error-Theory

Mackie concludes that since our ordinary moral judgements presuppose the existence of objective values, when in fact no such things exist,
they are systematically and uniformly false. This is Mackie's 'error-theory' of moral judgement, or 'moral scepticism', as he sometimes calls it:

> [O]rdinary moral judgements involve a claim to objectivity which both
> non-cognitive and naturalist analyses fail to capture. Moral scepticism
> must, therefore, take the form of an error-theory, admitting that a belief
> in objective values is built into ordinary moral thought and language, but
> holding that this ingrained belief is false. (1973: 48–9)

There are two main ways in which one might respond to Mackie's
argument for the error-theory: *directly*, via contesting one of its prem-

ises or inferences, or *indirectly*, pointing to some internal tension within the error-theory itself.

In this section I shall consider an indirect argument against the error-theory, developed in recent writings by Crispin Wright.

Mackie claims that the error-theory of moral judgement is a second-order theory, which does not necessarily have implications for the first-order practice of making moral judgements (1973: 16). Wright's argument against the error-theory takes off with the forceful presentation of the opposing suspicion:

> The great discomfort with [Mackie's] view is that, unless more is said, it simply relegates moral discourse to bad faith. Whatever we may once have thought, as soon as philosophy has taught us that the world is unsuited to confer truth on any of our claims about what is right, or wrong, or obligatory, etc., the reasonable response ought surely to be to forgo the right to making any such claims . . . If it is of the essence of moral judgement to aim at the truth, and if philosophy teaches us that there is no moral truth to hit, how are we supposed to take ourselves seriously in thinking the way we do about any issue which we regard as of major moral importance? (1996: 2; see also 1992: 9)[10]

Wright realizes that the error-theorist is likely to have some sort of story to tell about the point of moral discourse, about 'some norm of appraisal *besides* truth, at which its statements can be seen as aimed, and which they can satisfy' (1996: 2). And Mackie has such a story: the point of moral discourse is – to simplify – to secure the benefits of social cooperation (1973: chapter 5 *passim*; Joyce 2001: 8.0). Suppose we can extract from this story some subsidiary norm distinct from truth, which governs the practice of forming moral judgements. Then, for example, 'Honesty is obligatory' and 'Dishonesty is permissible', although both *false*, will not be on a par in point of their contribution to the satisfaction of the subsidiary norm: if accepted widely enough, the former will arguably facilitate the satisfaction of the subsidiary norm, while the latter will frustrate it. Wright questions whether Mackie's moral sceptic can plausibly combine such a story about the benefits of the practice of moral judgement with the central negative claim of the error-theory:

> [I]f, among the welter of falsehoods which we enunciate in moral discourse, there is a good distinction to be drawn between those which are acceptable in the light of some such subsidiary norm and those which are not – a distinction which actually informs ordinary discussion and criticism of moral claims – then why insist on construing *truth* for moral discourse in terms which motivate a charge of global error, rather than explicate it in terms of the satisfaction of the putative subsidiary norm, whatever it is? The question may have a good answer. The error-theorist may be able to argue that the superstition that he finds in ordinary moral thought goes too deep to permit any construction of moral truth which

avoids it to be acceptable as an account of *moral* truth. But I do not know
of promising argument in that direction. (1996: 3; see also 1992: 10)

Wright thus argues that even if we concede to the error-theorist that
his original scepticism about moral truth is well-founded, the error-
theorist's own positive proposal will be inherently unstable.

6.7 Joyce's Revolutionary Moral Fictionalism

Although he does not mention Wright explicitly, it is possible to read
the fictionalist position sketched in Richard Joyce's *The Myth of Morality*
(2001; see also 2005) as incorporating a response to Wright's indirect
argument against Mackie's error-theory. In this section I will sketch
Joyce's view, show how it provides a reply to Wright's objection, and
then venture some criticisms of Joyce's fictionalist position.

At the beginning of this chapter (in 6.1) – and indeed throughout
the rest of this book – we have been making the following assumption:
a factualist view of the semantics of moral statements goes hand in
hand with a cognitivist account of the psychological state expressed
by a moral judgement. That is to say, an account of moral statements
that sees them as truth-apt goes hand in hand with an account of moral
judgements that sees them as expressing beliefs: for example, if the
statement 'murder is wrong' has the truth-condition *that murder is
wrong*, the utterance of 'murder is wrong' will as a matter of convention
express the belief that murder is wrong. In similar fashion, a non-
factualist account of the semantics of 'murder is wrong' on which it has
no truth-condition will go hand in hand with a non-cognitivist view
according to which the utterance conventionally expresses a desire or
some other mental state not capable of being true or false. However,
it is possible to keep issues about the semantics of moral statements
sharply separate from issues about the psychological states conventionally expressed when they are uttered. This is how Joyce prefers to see
matters. He writes:

> The view that our moral judgements are neither true nor false is often
> equated with the metaethical position known as 'noncognitivism' . . .
> However, I prefer to understand noncognitivism not in terms of truth
> values, but in terms of assertion. Assertion is not a semantic category; it
> is, rather, a purpose to which a sentence may be put: one and the same
> sentence may on some occasions be asserted, on other occasions not
> asserted. The question then is not whether 'a is F' *is* an assertion, but
> whether it is typically used assertorically. (Joyce 2001: 8)

Given this, it would be possible to view moral statements as having
a factualist semantics according to which they have truth-conditions,

but simultaneously hold that they are not typically used to express beliefs that those truth-conditions obtain. Perhaps moral statements have truth-conditions, but they are typically used not to assert that those truth-conditions obtain, but to *pretend to assert* or *make-believe* that they obtain. ('Bilbo Baggins lived in Hobbiton' has the truth-condition that Bilbo Baggins lived in Hobbiton, but when I utter it in the course of reading aloud from *Lord of the Rings* I am not asserting that Bilbo Baggins lived in Hobbiton, but engaging in make-believe that he did.)[11] A certain kind of moral fictionalist – a so-called 'hermeneutic' moral fictionalist – would hold that something like this is an accurate description of our actual moral practice. Since on this view ordinary moral practice is not aiming at moral truth, it incorporates no error of the sort identified by Mackie. It is important to note that this is *not* the type of moral fictionalism proposed by Joyce. Joyce argues that our moral practice as it currently stands is accurately described in factualist and cognitivist terms: moral statements have truth-conditions and they are typically used to make assertions and express moral beliefs. However, for reasons broadly similar to those proposed by Mackie, these assertions and the beliefs they express are systematically and uniformly false. Joyce thus accepts that the error-theory provides an accurate description of our actual moral discourse. A fictionalist position, on which moral statements have truth-conditions but are not used to make assertions or express moral beliefs, is recommended as a *revision* of our current moral practice. This type of view, because it proposes that a fictionalist view be adopted as a revision rather than a description of our actual moral practice, is called a 'revolutionary' form of moral fictionalism.[12]

How does Joyce's revolutionary brand of fictionalism – which incorporates an error-theory of actual moral practice – reply to the objection of Wright's outlined in the previous section? Joyce's view of the 'subsidiary norm' is roughly the same as Mackie's: although all positive, atomic moral judgements are false, some of them are such that their general acceptance allows us as a group to obtain the benefits of social cooperation and thereby the material benefits such cooperation helps us obtain. Joyce attempts to block Wright's argument by challenging his remark:

> The error-theorist may be able to argue that the superstition that he finds in ordinary moral thought goes too deep to permit any construction of moral truth which avoids it to be acceptable as an account of *moral* truth. But I do not know of promising argument in that direction.

The element of superstition in ordinary moral thought identified by Mackie – the categoricity of moral norms – is according to Joyce a 'non-negotiable' part of ordinary moral thought:

[I]f we were to eliminate categorical imperatives and all that imply them from the discourse, whatever remained would no longer be recognizable as – could not play the role of – a *moral* discourse. Any system of values that leaves out categorical imperatives will lack the authority that we expect of morality, and any set of prescriptions failing to underwrite this authority simply does not count as a 'morality' at all. (Joyce 2001: 176–7)

Joyce argues persuasively that our everyday moral assessments of people and actions are insensitive to their desires and interests. For example, in morally condemning a murderer, the force of our condemnation is independent of considerations relating to the murderer's desires – our moral condemnation stands irrespective of these, and irrespective of whether or not the act of murdering frustrates the desires and interests of the murderer. Imagine a murderer who genuinely desired to be caught and punished: the fact that the murderer's desires are satisfied by the act of murdering does nothing to spare him our moral condemnation. Wright would need to argue that this aspect of our moral practice is 'negotiable' – that it could be dispensed with while leaving us with a recognizably moral practice: Joyce's claim that this is not possible strikes me as convincing. At any rate, the onus is now on a proponent of Wright's objection to Mackie to show that categoricity is a dispensable feature of ordinary moral judgement.

How, then, having reached the conclusion that ordinary moral practice trades in assertions or beliefs that are systematically and uniformly false, does Joyce propose to assuage the worry that our participation in this practice constitutes 'bad faith'? According to Joyce, there are four main ways in which we may react to the discovery that there are no moral facts, no moral 'oughts' that apply to people irrespective of their desires or interests.

First, we could simply decide to continue as before, more or less ignoring the conclusion of the argument for the error-theory. Joyce holds that this option is 'beyond contention' (2005: 299). He writes:

Even if we somehow could carry on believing in [moral propositions], surely we should not, for any recommendation in favour of having false beliefs while, at some level, knowing that they are false, is unlikely to be good advice . . . [S]urely to embark on such a course is likely to bring negative consequences. (2005: 287, 299)

Joyce subscribes to the doxastic policy that one ought to believe that p if and only if p is true (2005: 303–4), and this doxastic policy – 'concordant with *critical inquiry*' – is the best policy in practical terms for any group of agents.[13] Even if we could somehow put the conclusion of the error-theory out of our minds and continue to believe in moral propositions, in doing so we would sacrifice the value of critical inquiry, an outcome that Joyce describes as 'disastrous' (2005: 299).

Second, we philosophers could opt for 'propagandism': being open amongst ourselves about the falsity of moral judgements but 'keeping it quiet and encouraging the hoi polloi to continue with their sincere (false) moral beliefs' (2005: 299). Joyce gives this possible option short shrift, noting that it amounts to the 'promulgation of manipulative lies' (ibid.). Clearly, any moral distaste the error-theorist may feel towards this option is not to the point at this juncture in the story, since the statement that we ought not to propagate manipulative lies is, according to Joyce's error-theorist, false. Joyce clearly realizes this and instead rejects this option on the grounds that it would 'lead ultimately to no good'. Helping to promulgate such misplaced belief in a fabricated fiction would produce social confusion and a lack of confidence in normal belief-forming mechanisms. Deception on such a massive scale threatens to produce a society of epistemological wrecks.[14]

With the first and second options off the table, only two possibilities remain: we either do away with moral discourse altogether, or we decide to continue using it despite knowing that moral statements are uniformly false. In order to justify the latter 'fictionalist' response over the former eliminativist response, Joyce needs to identify the respects in which moral discourse is instrumentally valuable, and then argue that in terms of instrumental value, the fictionalist response fares better than eliminativism. As noted above, when we identified the 'subsidiary norm' sought after by Wright, the value of moral judgements resides in the way that acceptable moral judgements facilitate social cooperation and thereby help to secure the benefits that flow from it. So why not simply do away with moral discourse altogether and replace it with a discourse explicitly framed in terms of the prudential benefits of social cooperation? According to Joyce, this is inadvisable because of the role that moral thinking plays in countering 'akratic sabotage', the temptation to sacrifice long-term profit (which is 'distant and faint') for immediate and alluring short-term profit. Suppose that on finding a wallet stuffed with cash in the department corridor I judge that it is in my long-term self-interest to hand the wallet in to security rather than pocket the money: weakness of will, accidie, demoralization, and so on, may lead me to rationalize my opting for the short-term benefit of taking the money. The practical function of moral judgement, in Joyce's view, is to short-circuit tendencies to rationalize in this manner:

> [A]n important value of moral beliefs is that they function . . . to supplement and reinforce the outputs of prudential reasoning. When a person believes that the valued action is morally required – that it must be performed whether he likes it or not – then the possibilities for rationalization diminish. If the person believes the action to be required by an authority from which he cannot escape, if he imbues it with a 'must-be-doneness' (the categorical element of morality that Mackie found so troublesome), if he believes that in not performing he will not merely

frustrate himself, but will become more reprehensible and deserving of disapprobation – then he is more likely to perform the action. The distinctive value of categorical imperatives is that they silence calculation, which is a valuable thing when interfering forces can so easily hijack our prudential calculations. In this manner, moral beliefs function to bolster self-control against practical irrationality. (2005: 301)

Given this, the key question is whether we can avoid some of the costs of giving up moral thinking, and retain some of its benefits, while taking an attitude towards moral propositions that falls short of belief: in other words, can we avoid the costs and retain some of the benefits by going moral fictionalist, by treating morality as a 'useful fiction'?

Before trying to answer this question, we need more information about what it is to be a moral fictionalist. Joyce writes:

> [T]o take a fictionalist stance towards a discourse is to believe that the discourse entails or embodies a theory that is false (such that there is no error-free revisionary theory available), but to carry on employing the discourse, at least in many contexts, as if this were not the case, because it is *useful* to do so. (2001: 185)

Suppose that we philosophers, perhaps fully persuaded by Mackie's arguments against objective prescriptivity and categoricity, embrace an error-theory of moral judgement. Suppose also that outside the philosophy seminar room we choose to carry on our moral practice much as we did before we were persuaded by the Mackie-style arguments. Given that 'to make a fiction of p is to "accept" p while disbelieving p' (2001: 189), can we describe ourselves as moral fictionalists?

Key to Joyce's strategy here is his notion of 'critical contexts': these are contexts in which we are at our most 'undistracted, reflective, and critical' (2005: 290). They are contexts in which we give serious consideration to robust types of scepticism, contexts in which we scrutinize the assumptions we make in everyday life (in a way in which our thinking in everyday life does not scrutinize and challenge the assumptions we make when we are engaged in critical thinking). Subject to the proviso that an agent has actually occupied a critical context in which he has denied the propositions of theory T, even if in non-critical contexts he accepts them, he does not in so accepting them express beliefs in the propositions of T: rather he pretends to believe them, or engages in a make-believe with respect to them: in short, he treats T as a fiction. Such is the position of Joyce's error-theorist: in the philosophy seminar room – the critical context par excellence – he rejects the propositions of morality as false, but outside of the seminar room he engages in moral practice as before, feeling guilty when he doesn't do what he thinks he ought, and telling Jones that he ought to have handed back the wallet, irrespective of whether doing so was in line with Jones's desires and interests.

As noted above, Joyce is not claiming that the situation our error-theorist finds himself in – using moral discourse but not believing it – is an accurate description of the moral practice of normal, unphilosophical people. Rather 'it is being put forward as a change that a group can make in its attitude towards a faulty discourse' (2001: 186). But *should* the group make that change? Clearly, the 'should' here is not a moral 'should': what is being asked is whether it might be good from an instrumental point of view for people generally (i.e., not just 'philosophers of a revisionary temperament') to take up the attitude of Joyce's error-theorist.

How can engaging in an analogue of make-believe, or pretending to assert the propositions of morality, have the kind of practical force (and therefore the kind of practical benefits) associated with genuine moral belief? Joyce argues that we are familiar with this kind of phenomenon from our engagement with literary fiction: 'watching movies, reading novels, or simply engaging one's imagination can produce real episodes of fear, sadness, disgust, anger, and so on' (2005: 302). But how can make-believing a proposition I know to be false have a steady influence on my behaviour in the way that straightforwardly moral beliefs are supposed to? Suppose I have the sort of metabolism that would – given my diet and fondness for alcohol – result in my gaining more weight than I'd like unless I take regular exercise. I find it hard to get up at 6 a.m., and the last time I tried an exercise regime it petered out after a few weeks because I too often gave in to the temptation to get back into my warm bed for a bit more sleep. Fully aware of what happened last time, and slightly aghast at my expanding waistline, I decide to subject myself to the following rule: no matter what, you *must* get up at 6 a.m. and follow the exercise regime. Now consider the proposition P: Alex ought to get up at 6 every morning, without exception, and follow the exercise regime, otherwise he will put on weight at an unacceptable rate. Now, let's suppose, as is plausible, that in order to avoid putting on weight I do not have to do this every day: it would be enough if I did it (say) three days a week. When I'm thinking fully critically about the issue, I am aware of this: so I know that proposition P is false. Nonetheless, for pragmatic reasons, I decide to 'accept' P and organize my routine as if P were true. So, on frosty mornings when my bed looks so inviting and my wife asks me to go back to bed, I tell her: I can't, I must get up and go out for my morning run. In this sort of case, although I don't believe P (I've judged at least once in a critical context that P is false and I'm still disposed to judge it false were I to occupy a critical context again), and make-believe that P, my taking up the attitude of make-believe towards P acts as a bulwark against weakness of will and helps prevent 'akratic sabotage'. I can get the benefits of genuinely believing that P is true, even though I *don't* believe that P is true but adopt a fictionalist attitude towards P instead.

This is essentially the approach to morality advocated by the revolutionary fictionalist, although the element of conscious choice in the example above is likely to be lacking in the moral case. Strategies for combating weakness of will such as that above are what Joyce calls 'precommitments'. In the moral case, precommitments to acting morally are most likely put in place, when they are, by parents, and in almost all cases will involve the inculcation of belief. However, there is nothing to stop the clear-headed thinker from hanging on to the precommitments as useful fictions once he has become convinced that the idea of categorical obligations is philosophically troubling. This is effectively the course of action prescribed by Joyce's revolutionary fictionalist.

Before moving on to look at possible problems for revolutionary fictionalism, it is worth pausing to note that although the position that the moral fictionalist urges us to adopt is, as noted at the start of this section, at once both factualist and non-cognitivist, the non-cognitivist element of the view does not leave it open to the Frege-Geach problem that caused so much trouble for earlier forms of non-cognitivism. Since the sentences 'Murder is wrong' and 'Getting little brother to murder people is wrong' both have truth-conditions, the validity of the argument

(1) Murder is wrong.
(2) If murder is wrong, then getting little brother to murder people is wrong.

Therefore

(3) Getting little brother to murder people is wrong

can be accounted for in the standard way, in terms of the joint satisfaction of the truth-conditions of (1) and (2) being logically inconsistent with the obtaining of the truth-condition of (3). The fact that after the revolutionary fictionalist prescription has been adopted, the sentence 'Murder is wrong' is usually used, not to assert that its truth-condition obtains, but rather in some non-assertoric way, does nothing to render the argument from (1) and (2) to (3) guilty of a fallacy of equivocation.[15]

How plausible is the revolutionary fictionalist view explored by Joyce? In the remainder of this section, I'll venture some tentative criticisms. As we saw above, according to Joyce, to take a fictionalist stance towards a proposition p 'is to "accept" p while disbelieving p' (2001: 189), and 'To make a fiction of some thesis T is to be disposed to assent to T in certain circumstances without believing T' (2001: 199). Consider a philosopher – let's call him 'Boyce' – who has spent many an hour in his study and in the philosophy seminar room, thinking about Mackie's argument from queerness and discussing it with his colleagues, and has come to be convinced that our positive, atomic moral judgements are systematically and uniformly false. Outside of the study and the seminar room, though, Boyce is a model of moral probity. On finding a wallet stuffed with cash left on a table in the staff canteen, Boyce's judgement that it would be wrong not to hand it in to security silences any temptations he might have felt to pocket the cash, and even when it causes him minor inconvenience, his judgement that it would be wrong not to keep a promise without good reason silences any inclinations he might have to break the promise. Boyce thus judges in a 'critical context' that 'It is obligatory to hand back the wallet' and 'It is obligatory not to break a promise just because it is inconvenient' are false, even though in less critical contexts he would say that they are both true. Despite these latter cases, according to Joyce, Boyce *really* believes that both moral statements are false, in virtue of what he is disposed to say about them in the philosophy classroom. However, there is surely something unsatisfactory about the general principle underlying this description of Boyce's doxastic stance: that if Boyce is disposed to assent to p in a critical context, it follows that even when he 'accepts' p in less critical contexts, he actually disbelieves it. This principle is unsatisfactory because it appears to rule out as impossible a situation that seems eminently possible: that an agent believes one thing in a critical context but believes the opposite in less than critical contexts. After all, it is a commonplace that sometimes, at least, a person's beliefs can vary from context to context: indeed, this has to be the case if there is to be such a thing as doxastic progress, of what an agent really believes gradually evolving in the direction of the truth. If we are going to characterize what an agent believes in terms of her dispositions to assent to or dissent from propositions, what an agent believes in a context C (even what they 'really' believe in that context) has to be determined by how they are disposed to assent or dissent *in that context*. Since Boyce is disposed to assent to 'It is obligatory to hand back the wallet' in the context where he is buying his lunch in the staff canteen, that is what he believes in that context, even though he believes something altogether different when he gives his seminar on metaethics later in the week. That in the staff canteen context Boyce believes that it is obligatory to hand back the wallet also fits much better with the common-sense description of the situation: as Joyce himself admits, 'at the moment of utterance it doesn't *seem* to [Boyce] as if he is participating in an act of pretence' (2005: 291–2). Unless more is said, the natural thing to say here is that the best explanation for it seeming so to Boyce in this context is that it is so. Thus, because of its neglect of the fact that beliefs (even 'real' beliefs) can change from context to context, Joyce's description of what it is to take up a fictionalist stance towards a theory or type of proposition is, at best, seriously incomplete.[16] The idea that 'what a person believes [*in a particular context*] cannot be simply read off her actions, speech and thought [*in that context*]' (2001: 192, emphases added) seems wedded to a notion of belief that transcends what the believer is disposed to say, think and do, and as such stands in need of elaboration and defence.

Perhaps the needed elaboration and defence can be provided. However, even putting the above worry on one side, the account faces additional problems. When we are concerned with what an agent really believes with respect to a moral proposition, the true test is not what they say in the philosophy classroom, but what they are disposed to do in a context where in practical terms *it actually matters*. Indeed, the optimal situation in the moral case is where it not only matters, but also where acting in accord with the 'correct' moral judgement is in some conflict with the agent's short-term interests (or perceived short-term interests). Let's suppose that Boyce is heavily in debt and needs to pay back £100 by 2 p.m. in order to avoid his car being repossessed – yet on finding the money on the table (and, we may suppose, in a position where he can simply pocket it with impunity), Boyce judges that it is obligatory to hand it in and indeed goes ahead and does so. Are we really to hold that because of what he says during his seminar on Mackie, Boyce does not really believe that it is obligatory to hand in lost wallets? What is the basis for this account of the situation? At best, this description of Boyce's real moral beliefs seems ad hoc and gratuitous. And, in addition, the first problem we had with Joyce's account applies again: even if Boyce does believe one thing in the seminar room, the natural description of the situation is that he believes something else in the canteen scenario. Again, then, the way Joyce characterizes the predicament of the fictionalist fails to persuade.

A third problem concerns the nature of the 'revolution' advocated by the revolutionary fictionalist. As we saw above, the revolutionary fictionalist is fully committed to 'critical inquiry', the project of doing whatever one can to make sure one's beliefs are true. As Joyce writes:

> It is not merely that a stock of true beliefs is vastly more likely to be more helpful than a stock of false ones, but that the policy of aiming for the truth, of having and trying to satisfy a general (*de dicto*) desire for the truth – what we might simply call 'critical inquiry' – is the best doxastic policy around. Anything else, as Charles Peirce correctly insists, leads to 'a rapid deterioration of intellectual vigour'. (2001: 179)

It is this desire to avoid a 'deterioration of intellectual vigour' that drives the revolution urged by revolutionary fictionalism. Given that hanging on to our false moral beliefs would be bad policy on pragmatic as well as epistemic grounds, the best policy is for us to avoid false moral belief. By affirming the error-theory in the philosophy classroom and by acting at most 'as if' some moral beliefs were true outside of it, we avoid intellectual enervation, where – as Joyce points out explicitly – 'we' refers to 'users of the discourse, not philosophers of a revisionary temperament' (2001: 186).

The scope of the prescription urged on us by the revolutionary fictionalist is thus broad, extending as it does to all participants in moral discourse and not just philosophers. How seriously can we take the prescription? Given the potentially very negative upshot that according to the fictionalist is threatened by departing from 'critical inquiry', and given that the prescription that the fictionalist proposes applies to ordinary participants in moral practice, one would expect the revolutionary fictionalist to take practical steps towards implementing the prescription. Not to the extent, perhaps, of founding a campaigning movement dedicated to the error-theoretic cum fictionalist cause, but at least taking practical steps to advance its normative agenda. As far as one can see, though, error-theorists have taken no such steps. And Joyce himself pours cold water on the idea that any such practical steps would succeed: 'Do I really expect that ordinary speakers will adjust their attitude towards a problematic discourse? Of course not' (2005: 298). Can we take a prescription seriously when its proponents do nothing to persuade the majority of agents that fall under it that it merits serious attention? That they don't, and that they are calm in the face of the fact that ordinary agents would pay no attention anyway, suggests that the sense in which the prescription issued by revolutionary fictionalism is (in Joyce's words) 'radical' is a hollow one indeed.

6.8 Responding to the Argument from Queerness

Leaving revolutionary fictionalism behind, let's now explore the prospects for a direct response to the argument from queerness. First of all, let's try to get a little clearer on what viewing values as objectively and categorically prescriptive involves. Mackie is clearest on this in his discussion, quoted above, of the Platonic Form of the Good. Acquaintance with the Good provides an agent with both a 'direction' and a 'motive'. So an objectively and categorically prescriptive fact would tell an agent acquainted with it how he ought to act (it would direct him) and it would ensure that he actually was motivated so to act: it would have 'to-be-pursuedness' somehow built into it. Now Mackie's metaphysical argument is based on the thought that 'ordinary' states of affairs, states of affairs that we can unproblematically include in our catalogue of what there is, do not have these features. Take the fact that the table is rectangular, for instance. We are acquainted with this fact, but it apparently does not tell us how we ought to act (it does not direct us), let alone incline us to act in that way.

How plausible is this metaphysical point of Mackie's? I think Mackie is right when he says that 'the best move for the moral objectivist is not to evade the issue, but to look for companions in guilt' (39). If we could find states of affairs that we antecedently would be inclined to regard as philosophically unproblematic, but which possess features akin to those possessed by objectively and categorically prescriptive facts, the force of Mackie's argument would be significantly blunted.[17] Interestingly enough, an example is perhaps provided by one of the areas discussed in 6.3 as a candidate for another sort of error-theory: the case of *colour*. Let's note first of all that since 'ought implies can' (i.e., a normative requirement simply does not apply to an agent who cannot possibly comply with it), the believer in objective values is not going to say that anyone who becomes acquainted with an objective value will thereby be directed to act in a certain way and also be motivated to do so: a monkey, for example, will not be included in the scope of the normative requirement nor will he be motivated to act in the manner it prescribes. Thus, we are going to have to impose *some* conditions on the agent involved – the story about direction and motivation will only apply to *suitable* agents. Now what is a 'suitable' agent? Clearly, we cannot define suitable agents to be those who are properly directed and motivated by objective values, since that would simply trivialize the claim about direction and motivation. For the time being, let's take suitability to involve satisfying some condition C, to be spelled out in some non-trivial manner. Then, the claim that there are objective values will involve the claim that an agent, who satisfies condition C, will both be directed to act in a certain way and be motivated to act accordingly.

Now let's think about the case of *redness*. The fact that an object is red seems on the face of it to possess properties analogous to objective values. First of all, a suitable subject who becomes acquainted with that object will have a reason for judging that it is red and will also be inclined to see it as red. Mimicking Mackie, we might say that the fact that the object is red has to-be-seen-as-red somehow built into it. There is an *internal* connection between an object's being red and its being seen as red by a suitable subject, in the same way that there is an *internal* connection between an object's being objectively good and a suitable agent being motivated to pursue it.[18] (Note, though, that in this case also we will have to give some non-trivial characterization of what suitability consists in: we will come to this in due course.) Thus, if the metaphysical part of the argument from queerness is just that there don't appear to be any facts in the world which sustain the sort of internal connection to human activity which objective values would have, that argument is apparently weakened by the consideration that facts about colour also seem to possess this property. But surely we do not want to say that colours are metaphysically queer? It is more likely that there is something too restrictive about Mackie's philosophical conception of what sorts of fact the world can be assumed to contain.

Another, perhaps more controversial example, is supplied by facts about *humour*. The fact that a joke is funny also seems to possess properties analogous to those possessed by objective values. First of all, a suitable subject – someone with, inter alia, a sense of humour – who hears a funny joke will on the one hand have been provided with a reason for being amused by it, and on the other hand be disposed to find it amusing. The fact that a joke is funny has to-be-found-amusing somehow built into it. There is an internal connection between a joke's being funny and its being found amusing by a suitable agent. Again, we will need some non-trivial specification of what a suitable subject is, a specification other than as someone disposed to find funny jokes amusing.

How might we account for the internal connection between being red and being disposed to look red to a suitable subject in suitable circumstances? *One way to do this would be to say that our concept of redness is the concept of a disposition to appear red to suitable subjects in suitable circumstances.* How might we account for the internal connection between being funny and being disposed to amuse suitable subjects? *One way to do this would be to say that our concept of funny is the concept of a disposition to invoke amusement in suitable subjects.* This suggests that one way to begin responding to the argument from queerness would be to advance a dispositional theory of moral value: to claim that the concept of moral goodness is the concept of a disposition to be judged good by suitable agents in suitable circumstances. So one question we must ask is: how plausible is a dispositional account of moral value? Before doing so, we need to form some idea of the constraints dispositional accounts must satisfy in general in order to count as plausible. It will be easiest to do this if we concentrate on dispositionalism about colour.

6.9 Dispositionalism as a Response to the Error-Theory about Colour

Recall that the argument for the error-theory in the case of colours went as follows. Our concept of red is a concept of a categorical property (equivalently, the property red appears as a categorical property in colour experience; the phenomenology of redness presents it as categorical; red-as-we-see-it is a categorical property). But there is no categorical property of redness in the world: there are only dispositions objects have to appear red, and perhaps categorical physical properties underlying these dispositions, neither of which can plausibly be identified with the property of redness. Thus, nothing in the world possesses the property of redness-as-we-see-it.

One way to block this argument for the error-theory is to deny the first premise: to deny that our concept of redness is the concept of a categorical property. We could claim instead that our concept of redness is a concept of a dispositional property: the property of being disposed to appear red to normal observers in standard conditions.

Recall that the main objection to this was phenomenological: if our concept of red was the concept of a disposition, the colour of the phone on my desk would appear to *come on*, would appear to be *activated*, when I switch the lights on. But this is not how it appears: it appears to me to have been red all along and to have its redness *revealed* on switching on the lights (Boghossian and Velleman 1989). How good is this argument? It seems to me to be based on a misunderstanding. Objects do not cease to have dispositions when those dispositions are not actually being manifested: the brittle glass is still brittle even if it is never actually dropped or struck. So dispositionalism about colour is consistent with the claim that objects continue to possess their colours in the dark. We could take the manifestation of the disposition to reveal that the object had the disposition all along: for example, we could take the fact that the object appears red to us when we switch the lights on to reveal that it possessed even in the dark the disposition to look red, which, on the dispositionalist account, amounts to its being red in the dark.[19]

Perhaps we can get a better handle on the issue about phenomenology if we compare redness with *nausea*. Compare your experience of a red postbox with your experience of a piece of rotting meat. In the case of experiencing the postbox as red your attention is directed *outwards*, as Michael Smith puts it, 'away from the intrinsic character of the experience altogether and is focused instead on the object of our experience' (Smith 1993a: 244). However, in the case of experiencing the rotting meat as nauseating, your attention is largely directed *inwards*, and to the extent that your attention is directed outwards on to the object 'you fix on it merely as a cause of what is inwardly experientially salient' (ibid.). Where is the redness located? Out there on the object. Where is the nausea located? In here in my guts. To be sure, your attention will be focused outwards on the meat, but none of your outward attention will pick up on the nausea: all that your outward focused attention will pick up on will be the maggot-infestation, the purplish blush, the noisome stench, etc.[20] Smith summarizes this phenomenological fact as follows: the concept of redness, unlike the concept of nausea, is the concept of a property that is *there to be experienced*.

The question now is whether the dispositional account of redness can accommodate or explain this phenomenological fact. Smith suggests that it can: the specification of the suitable conditions in the colour account is actually quite rich, since they encapsulate a wealth of considerations that can be appealed to in order to correct any evidence we might have that a given object is red: bad lighting conditions, irradiation with red light, bad eyesight and so on. In the case of nausea, the 'suitable conditions' are actually very thin: there is no such rich set of considerations that can be appealed to – if something makes you feel sick, then it just is nauseating, and that is that. Thus the dispositional account can explain, in terms of the richness of the notion of suitable conditions, why our concept of red is, whereas our concept of nausea is not, the concept of something that is there to be experienced.

It thus looks as if the dispositional account can after all provide a plausible account of the phenomenology of colour experience. Now note that our fundamental moral concepts are, so far as the phenomenology goes, more like the concept of red than the concept of nausea: when we judge a murder to be wrong, our attention will be focused outwards, on aspects of the killing itself (see Smith 1993a: 242–7). This suggests that if we can provide a dispositional account of moral value we can respond to the metaphysical aspect of the argument from queerness and provide a plausible account of the phenomenology of moral experience at one stroke. But how plausible is a dispositional theory of moral value? And can it provide a response to the epistemological aspect of the argument from queerness? It is to these questions that I turn in the next chapter. Before that, though, some comments on 'hermeneutic fictionalism'.

6.10 Appendix: Kalderon's Hermeneutic Moral Fictionalism[21]

As we noted in 6.7, recent discussions of fictionalist accounts of moral judgement take off from the claim that views opposed to moral realism often run together psychological and semantic theses. In particular, non-cognitivist accounts that view moral judgements as expressing feelings, sentiments or desire-like states incorporate non-factualist accounts of moral language according to which moral predicates don't refer to properties and moral sentences don't represent distinctively moral states of affairs or express distinctively moral propositions. Like Joyce, Mark Kalderon uses this fact to open up space for a novel account of moral judgement: moral judgements are given a non-cognitivist treatment on which they express desire-like states, but this non-cognitivist view of moral judgement is allied with a *factualist* view according to which moral predicates stand for moral properties and moral sentences do represent distinctively moral states of affairs and express distinctively moral propositions.

However, whereas Joyce's revolutionary moral fictionalist sees our actual moral practice as both cognitivist and factualist, and therefore as massively in error, and recommends that we adopt non-cognitivist factualism as a revision of our actual practice, Kalderon's 'hermeneutic fictionalism' holds that non-cognitivist factualism is already an accurate *description* of our actual moral practice.[22]

Kalderon argues for hermeneutic moral fictionalism by (i) arguing in favour of non-cognitivism, (ii) arguing that non-factualism is 'hopeless on the grounds that it can never escape the lingering grip of the Frege-Geach problem' (Kalderon 2008b: 37), and (iii) sketching a positive account of how a non-cognitivist view of moral judgement can be joined to a factualist moral semantics. Kalderon's rich and ingenious account deserves a fuller discussion that can be attempted here: in this section I will limit myself to arguing against Kalderon's claim that hermeneutic moral fictionalism can secure the benefits of non-cognitivism whilst avoiding the Frege-Geach worries that undermine non-factualist moral semantics.

What is a participant in our moral discourse doing when he judges that abortion is wrong if not asserting that murder is wrong or expressing the belief that murder is wrong? According to fictionalism, we should view such a judgement as making a *quasi-assertion* rather than an assertion. There are various accounts of what a quasi-assertion might be. According to one such view, a 'metalinguistic view', moral judgements are akin to judgements about the content of a fiction. For example, if someone discussing Melville's *Moby Dick* utters 'Ahab went mad after his initial encounter with the White Whale',

> he is plausibly making an assertion about the content of [the book] *Moby Dick*: he is merely asserting that, according to *Moby Dick*, Ahab went mad after his initial encounter with the White Whale. (Kalderon 2005a: 121)

Likewise a moral fictionalist may hold that when a participant in moral discourse utters the sentence 'Murder is wrong', he is simply asserting that, according to prevailing moral norms, murder is wrong. This explains why the view is known as fictionalism, but it is important to note that this is not the kind of fictionalism proposed by Kalderon. A non-cognitivist holds that the utterance of a moral sentence does not express belief in a moral proposition: but this may be because the moral judgement expresses a belief in a non-moral proposition (as on the metalinguistic view just mentioned) or because the moral judgement fails to express belief in *any* proposition. Initially, at least, Kalderon appears to be advocating an instance of the latter 'non-assertion view' of quasi-assertion:

> [N]ot only is moral acceptance [moral judgement] noncognitive, but it centrally involves a certain affect, a desire in the directed attention sense. (Kalderon 2005a: 129)

We'll return to 'desire in the directed attention sense' shortly, but for now we should ask why Kalderon holds that hermeneutic fictionalism of this stripe avoids the Frege-Geach problem, and in so doing we'll take a stance on an exchange on this issue between Kalderon and Matti Eklund.

In order to obtain a clear view of the matter, we'll add a little to the description of the Frege-Geach problem outlined in chapters 3 and 4 above. Consider the argument:

(1) If lying is wrong, then getting little brother to lie is wrong.
(2) Lying is wrong.

So,

(3) Getting little brother to lie is wrong.

What problem does this pose for a standard view that weds non-cognitivism to a non-factualist moral semantics?

One problem – call it FG1 – is that for the argument to be logically valid premises (1) and (2) have to stand in a relation of *semantic entailment* to the conclusion (3). A cognitivist can capture this straightforwardly: since (1) and (2) both express propositions, the relation of semantic entailment holds in virtue of the fact that the propositions expressed by (1) and (2) semantically entail the proposition expressed by (3): if the former two propositions are true, then the conclusion must be true also. However, since the non-factualist holds that the premises and conclusion of the argument don't express propositions capable of having a truth-value, he needs an alternative account of the validity of the argument. This is far from straightforward: we need an account of the meaning of 'Lying is wrong' in (2) that can be used to account for its contribution – as the antecedent – to the meaning of the conditional (1), on pain of the argument being convicted of a fallacy of equivocation.

A second problem – call it FG2 – concerns, not the relationship between the *sentences* (1), (2) and (3), but between the states of mind of someone who uses those sentences in the course of an argument, conceived not as a set of sentences, but as a sequence of utterances or speech-acts. Again, a cognitivist has a straightforward account of the logical validity of an argument in which (1) and (2) figure as premises and (3) figures as conclusion: since the utterance of (2) expresses the belief that lying is wrong, and the utterance of (1) expresses the belief that if lying is wrong then getting little brother to lie is wrong, someone who has the beliefs expressed by the utterances of (1) and (2) but who rejects the belief that would be expressed by the utterance of (3) thereby has a *logically inconsistent* set of beliefs. Thus, a non-cognitivist owes us an alternative account of the states of mind of someone who accepts both (1) and (2) but rejects (3). This is far from straightforward for the non-cognitivist: because the utterance of (2) expresses a non-cognitive attitude, the contribution of 'Lying is wrong' as it appears in the antecedent of (1) to the state of mind expressed by (1) has to be given in terms of that non-cognitive attitude, on pain of convicting the argument of a fallacy of equivocation.

How does non-cognitivist non-factualism try to deal with FG1 and FG2? It seems to me that Blackburn, for example, attempts no direct answer to FG1. Rather, he attempts to provide an answer to FG2, feeds that in to an ambitious form of quasi-realism whose eventual conclusion is that moral sentences express moral propositions: once this ambitious form of quasi-realism has been vindicated, the quasi-realist can simply co-opt the standard cognitivist account of which moral sentences express moral propositions, thereby bypassing FG1.

With this much on board, we can ask whether Kalderon's hermeneutic fictionalism really does bypass the Frege-Geach problem in the way that he claims. Kalderon points out that since his view of moral semantics is straightforwardly factualist, there is no problem with FG1: 'there could be no problem about entailment – the fictionalist maintains that moral sentences have just the truth-conditional contents that the realist assigns to them, truth-conditional contents that unproblematically determine the relevant entailment relations' (Kalderon 2008c: 138). Matti Eklund, however, finds this response inadequate:

> [O]ne may reasonably worry that the envisaged fictionalist move doesn't in fact help at all with the Frege-Geach problem. For someone actually presenting an argument like this would be presenting a good argument. But for this to be so, what the arguer actually expresses by the premise sentence must provide good reason to accept what she actually expresses by the conclusion sentence. Since what the arguer actually expresses is, on the fictionalist view, different from what the sentences she utters semantically express, it is not sufficient for the fictionalist to point to how the sentences (1) and (2) when taken literally express propositions that entail the proposition expressed by the sentence (3) taken literally. Kalderon's moral fictionalist faces the problem of giving an account that respects the fact that the argument actually put forward is valid. But this seems not to be essentially different from the traditional non-cognitivist's problem of saying what the meanings of the relevant sentences are such that the impression that the argument is valid can be respected. (Eklund 2011: 4.6)

In effect, then, Eklund is pointing out that, although Kalderon has a reply to FG1, he still owes us a reply to FG2, and expresses the worry that Kalderon may find FG2 no easier than the standard forms of non-cognitivism that his hermeneutic fictionalism is supposed to supersede.

Does Kalderon have a convincing story to tell about FG2? It seems to me that he does not, and that if anything Eklund understates the problem Kalderon faces here. Suppose that an agent accepts premise (2) of the argument above. According to Kalderon, to such an agent 'there will seem to be a reason not to lie, and there will be a tendency for countervailing considerations to cease to be salient, and even where they are, there is a tendency for these to seem to be outweighed or even ruled out as reasons for doing otherwise' (2008b: 39). In the case of a judgement that such and such is right, a 'desire in the directed attention sense' is expressed, where 'A desire in the directed attention sense involves a tendency to focus on the object of desire as well as a tendency for the object of desire to appear in a favourable light' (2008c: 139). The same goes for a judgement of wrongness, with the light in which the object appears being instead unfavourable. Call the former a positive desire in the directed attention sense, the latter a negative desire in the directed attention sense. Thus, a speaker who accepts (2) has a negative desire in the directed attention sense towards lying. Likewise, a speaker who accepts (3) would have a negative desire in the directed attention sense towards getting little brother to lie, and a speaker who rejects (3) will fail to have that attitude.

What about the conditional premise (1)? Kalderon writes:

> It is natural to think of the attitude involved in accepting the conditional claim as a higher-order functional state that structures the speaker's affective sensibility – specifically, as the tendency to have the affect involved in accepting the consequent when having the affect involved in accepting the antecedent . . . It involves, as well, the endorsement of this affective sensibility. (2008b: 39)

Thus, an utterance of the conditional premise (1) expresses a positive desire in the directed attention sense towards affective sensibilities that combine negative desire in the directed attention sense towards lying with negative desire in the directed attention sense towards getting little brother to lie. It is this that gives Kalderon the ingredients for his reply to FG2. Of the speaker who accepts (1) and (2), he writes:

> It is reasonable, then, that, given these commitments, he should come to have the affective attitude towards getting his little brother to lie that is involved in accepting that it is wrong to get one's little brother to lie. Given the nature and content of these attitudes and how they bear on the configuration of a person's moral sensibility, the reasonableness of moral inference is prima facie plausible. (2008b: 40)

Eklund (2008: 709) notes the similarity between Kalderon's account and the account of moral *modus ponens* in Blackburn (1984). In fact, Kalderon's attempt to deal with FG2 suffers from the same problem levelled against Blackburn by Wright and Hale (see chapter 4 above). In Kalderon's account, the failing of someone who accepts (1) and

(2) but rejects (3) is a moral failing: they fail to have a combination of negative desires in the directed attention sense, a combination towards which they have a positive desire in the directed attention sense. Such a speaker violates the moral injunction 'Do what you hurrah!' Their failing is not the same as that of someone who accepts the premises but rejects the conclusion of a non-moral *modus ponens* argument. Kalderon therefore fails to secure the logical validity of an argument in which (1) and (2) are uttered as premises and (3) is uttered as conclusion, so he has not provided a satisfactory response to FG2.

Although Kalderon bypasses FG1, then, as far as FG2 goes, he is in no better position than standard non-factualist variants of non-cognitivism.

In fact, we can use the above to pose a further problem for Kalderon. Suppose that Jones utters 'Lying is wrong' and thereby makes a moral judgement, perhaps the moral judgement that lying is wrong. We can ask: what makes this a judgement with specifically *moral* content?

One answer might be that it is a moral judgement in virtue of the fact that 'wrong' stands for the moral property *being wrong*. However, there are at least two reasons why this answer is of no use to Kalderon. First, compositionality considerations apply not just to sentences considered as items with constituents that themselves have semantic properties, but also to utterances and uses of sentences: after all, compositionality is invoked to explain how I can understand a novel use of a sentence. As we saw above, Kalderon's moral fictionalist is committed to explaining the content of moral utterances in terms of the expression of 'desires in the directed attention sense'. So, if he invokes the idea that 'wrong' stands for a moral property to explain what gives a moral judgement its specifically moral content, his account of what makes for moral content will come apart from his account of how the contents of moral utterances are determined by the contents of their parts. This is problematic: we are surely entitled to expect that the determinants of moral content play a role in the story about how complex moral contents (i.e., the contents of utterances of complex moral sentences) are a function of the moral contents of their constituents. Second, since there is no mention of a non-cognitive attitude in the suggested account of what makes the moral judgement a *moral* judgement, it is unclear how Kalderon's brand of non-cognitivism can on this suggestion capture the idea that possession of a non-cognitive attitude of a certain sort is a constraint on being able to make a moral judgement in the first place. That is to say, it becomes unclear how Kalderon's moral fictionalist can be counted as a *motivational internalist*. Now, although Kalderon mentions motivational internalism at various points, he rather coyly avoids saying explicitly whether he accepts or rejects it. However, given the fact that motivational internalism is one of the traditional reasons why non-cognitivists are non-cognitivists, the result that moral fictionalism effectively loses its entitlement to motivational internalism would surely be an unwelcome outcome for Kalderon.[23]

Suppose, alternatively, that it is the fact that a 'desire in the directed attention sense' is expressed by Jones's utterance that makes his judgement a moral judgement. Then, there is certainly no problem about losing one's entitlement to motivational internalism. Nor is there a problem parallel to the problem the first suggestion faced with respect to compositionality: the determinant of the specifically moral content of the utterances – the desire in the directed attention sense – does play a direct role in the story about how the contents of utterances of complex sentences are determined by the contents of their constituents. However, the main problem mentioned above in connection with FG2 is thrown into sharper relief: the account of the workings of such compositionality is no more plausible than that attempted by the standard non-factualist brand of non-cognitivism.

Are there any other ways for Kalderon's moral fictionalist to account for what makes a moral judgement a judgement with specifically moral content? Up until now we have been treating Kalderon's moral fictionalist as a pure non-cognitivist, holding that a moral judgement expresses only a desire in the directed attention sense. However, perhaps this is an oversimplification. At some points Kalderon suggests that moral judgement might express both cognitive and non-cognitive states of mind. For example:

> Moral acceptance not only involves thoughts or perceptions with real content, a proposition that represents the morally salient facts about the relevant circumstance, but also crucially involves a phenomenologically vivid sense of the moral reasons apparently available in the circumstance as the real content represents it to be. Thus, *moral acceptance, according to the form of moral fictionalism argued for here, is a mixed case, involving as it does an amalgam of cognitive and noncognitive attitudes.* (2005a: 129, emphasis added)

Elsewhere, in the context of criticizing McDowell's 'disentangling' objection to non-cognitivism, Kalderon writes that on his view:

> [D]esire in the directed attention sense is a mixed state: it is a noncognitive attitude that involves thoughts and perceptions about the morally salient features of the circumstance. However, these attitudes are not distinct and so cannot be independently specified. (2005a: 49)

Now, perhaps viewing moral judgement as expressing such a 'mixed' state can help Kalderon deal with FG2: perhaps the state of mind of one who accepts the premises but rejects the conclusion of moral *modus ponens* will involve a straightforward inconsistency of belief. But it is unclear how this suggestion differs from the kind of anti-Humean

view espoused by McDowell himself, on which there are intrinsically
motivating beliefs. Again, given Kalderon's coyness with respect to
Humeanism this may not seem like a major problem: but as with our
comments above relating to motivational internalism, this would surely
mark a major departure from one of the traditional commitments of
non-cognitivism (which relies on motivational internalism combined
with a Humean view of motivation to generate a non-cognitivist
conclusion). Indeed, it would no longer be clear why Kalderon's hermeneutic moral fictionalism should count as a form of non-cognitivism
at all.[24]

   Thus, Kalderon's attempt to provide a form of fictionalism that
bypasses the Frege-Geach problem whilst speaking to the traditional
concerns of non-cognitivism faces some serious challenges.

6.11 Further Reading

The *locus classicus* here is Mackie (1973), especially chapters 1 and 5.
For Mackie's views on Locke on colour and primary and secondary
qualities, see Mackie (1976, chapter 1). For those unfamiliar with Locke,
a good introduction is Lowe (1995). For a difficult but rewarding
exchange centred around Mackie's work, see McDowell (1998, essay
7), and Blackburn (1993a, essay 8). For a superbly clear commentary
on this debate, see Smith (1993a) (and also Campbell 1993 and Smith
1993b). For Wright's views on Mackie, see his 1992 (chapter 1), the
opening pages of his 1996, and, for critical discussion, Miller (2002).
Discussion of error-theories has been stimulated in recent years by
Joyce's 'revolutionary fictionalism': see his 2001 and 2005. For another
form of revolutionary fictionalism, see Nolan, Restall and West (2005).
For an up-to-date critique of moral error-theory, see Suikkanen (2012),
and for a collection of articles on Mackie's error-theory see Kirchin and
Joyce (2010). For a helpful general survey of fictionalism, see Eklund
(2011).

   For hermeneutic moral fictionalism, see Kalderon's clear and elo-
quent 2005a, and also Kalderon (2008a, b, c). For criticism, see Eklund
(2008 and 2011), and the other papers in the 2008 *Philosophical Books*
symposium.

7

Judgement-Dependent Accounts of Moral Qualities

7.1 Introduction

In chapter 1, I distinguished between strong cognitivism and weak cognitivism. A *strong cognitivist* theory is one which holds that moral judgements (a) are truth-apt, and (b) can be the upshot of cognitively accessing the facts which render them true. A *weak cognitivist* theory is one which holds that moral judgements (a) are truth-apt, but (b) cannot be the upshot of cognitive access to moral properties and states of affairs. At the end of the previous chapter I had reached the following conclusion: if we could develop a dispositional theory of moral values, we might be able to answer the metaphysical aspect of Mackie's argument from queerness and at the same time provide a theory which was consistent with the phenomenology of moral experience. In this chapter I am going to look at one particular form a dispositional theory of moral qualities could take: a judgement-dependent (or 'best opinion') account, in a sense to be explained, of moral qualities. We shall see that *a judgement-dependent account is a weak cognitivist account*. Why is this important? It means that if we can give a plausible judgement-dependent account of moral qualities, we will have successfully responded to the *epistemological* aspect of Mackie's argument from queerness. If we view the formation of correct moral judgement as a way of putting oneself into cognitive contact with independent moral states of affairs, then, as Mackie says, we owe some account of the nature and workings of the cognitive faculty whereby the relevant sort of cognitive contact is achieved. Then, it seems but a short step to the postulation of an implausible intuitionist epistemology for moral facts. However, if we can give a weak cognitivist account of the epistemology of moral facts we can simply sidestep this problem: since a weak cognitivist account does not view the formation of correct moral judgements as the upshot of cognitive contact with moral states of affairs, there is no obligation to give an account of the nature and workings of the cognitive mechanisms whereby this contact is established, and thus no threat that we will need to postulate Moorean faculties of moral intuition. So what exactly is a judgement-dependent account of moral facts, and how can it provide a moral epistemology free from reliance on the notion of cognitive contact?

7.2 Judgement-Dependence and Judgement-Independence

I will begin by outlining Crispin Wright's conception of judgement-dependence and then give a brief account of its application in the cases of *shape* and *colour*. After that, I'll consider the prospects for a judgement-dependent account of moral value.

Suppose that we are considering a particular region of discourse D, and let 'F' be a representative central predicate of that discourse, a predicate that stands for the property of F-ness. Consider the opinions of the participants in that discourse, formed under conditions which are, for that discourse, *cognitively ideal*: call such opinions *best*, and the cognitively ideal conditions the *C-conditions*. Suppose we find that the best opinions formed by the practitioners co-vary with the facts about the instantiation of F-ness. Then, Wright suggests, there are two ways in which we might seek to explain this co-variance. On the one hand, we might take best opinions to be playing at most a *tracking* role: best opinions are just extremely good at *tracking*, or putting us into *cognitive contact* with, independently constituted truth-conferring states of affairs. In such a case, best opinions play merely an *extension-reflecting* role, serving merely to reflect the independently determined extensions of the central predicates of D. On the other hand, we might try to explain the co-variance of best opinion and fact by assigning to best opinions an altogether different sort of role. Rather than viewing best opinions as merely tracking the facts about the extensions of the central predicates of D, we can view them as themselves *determining those very extensions*. Best opinion, on this sort of view, does not serve merely to track independently constituted states of affairs which determine the extensions of the central predicates of D: rather, *best opinion serves to determine those extensions and so to play an extension-determining role.* When the co-variance of best opinion and the facts about the application of the central predicates of a region of discourse admits of this latter sort of explanation, the subject matter of that region is said to be *judgement-dependent*; when only the former sort of explanation is possible, the subject matter is said to be *judgement-independent*. (You can see why the judgement-dependent account of, for example, redness is going to count, broadly, as a version of a dispositional theory of redness: the claim that our concept of redness is the concept of a disposition to appear to normal observers in suitable circumstances gets cashed out as the claim that the extension of 'red' – the class of objects to which it can correctly be applied, the class of things that possess the property of redness – gets determined by our disposition to form opinions in cognitively ideal conditions. Likewise, it should be clear why a judgement-dependent account would be *anti-realist*: on the judgement-dependent account, judgements about redness are sometimes true, but their truth is constitutively tied to facts about human opinion.)[1]

How do we determine whether the subject matter of a region of discourse is judgement-dependent or judgement-independent? Wright's discussion proceeds by reference to what he terms *provisional equations*. These have the following form:

(PE) $(\forall x)\,(C \rightarrow (A$ suitable subject S judges that Fx iff Fx$))$

where 'C' denotes the conditions (the C-conditions) which are cognitively ideal for forming the judgement that x is F. The property of F-ness is then said to be judgement-dependent if and only if the provisional equation meets the following four conditions:

(1) The A Prioricity Condition: The provisional equation must be a priori true: there must be a priori co-variance of best opinions and truth.

The justification for this condition is that 'the truth, if it is true, that the extensions of [a class of concept] are constrained by . . . best opinion . . . ought to be available purely by analytic reflection on those concepts, and hence available as knowledge a priori' (Wright 1992: 117). This is because the thesis of judgement-dependence is the claim that, for the region of discourse concerned, best opinion is the *conceptual ground* of truth.

(2) The Substantiality Condition: The C-conditions must be specifiable *non-trivially*: they cannot simply be described as conditions under which the subject has 'whatever it takes' to form a true opinion concerning which things are F.

The justification for this condition is that, without it, any property will turn out to be judgement-dependent, since for any predicate 'G' it is going to be an a priori truth that our judgements about whether x is G, formed under conditions which have 'whatever it takes' to ensure their correctness, will co-vary with the facts about the instantiation of G-ness. We thus require this condition on pain of losing the distinction between judgement-dependent and judgement-independent subject matters altogether.

(3) The Independence Condition: The question as to whether the C-conditions obtain in a given instance must be logically independent of the class of truths for which we are attempting to give an extension-determining account: whether an opinion is best in a given case must not presuppose some logically prior determination of the extension of F.

The justification for this condition is that if we have to assume, say, certain facts about the extension of F in the specification of the conditions under which best opinions about F-ness are formed, then we cannot view best opinions as somehow constituting the facts about F-ness, since whether a given opinion is best would then presuppose some logically prior determination of the very facts claimed to be constituted by best opinions.

(4) The Extremal Condition: There must be no better way of accounting for the a priori co-variance: no better account, other than according best opinion an extension-determining role, of which the satisfaction of conditions (1), (2) and (3) above is a consequence.

The justification for this condition is that, without it, the conditions (1)–(3) above would be consistent with the thought that there are 'states of affairs in whose determination facts about the deliverances of best opinions are in no way implicated although there is, a priori, no possibility of their misrepresentation' (Wright 1992: 123).

When each of the conditions (1)–(4) can be shown to be satisfied, we can accord best opinion an extension-determining role. If these conditions cannot collectively be satisfied, best opinion can be assigned, at best, a merely extension-reflecting role.

I shall now consider whether, by the lights of the operational test just outlined, colour and shape fall out as judgement-dependent or judgement-independent.

7.3 Colours are Judgement-Dependent

What are the prospects for finding a provisional equation meeting the conditions (1)–(4) for ascriptions of colour to macroscopic material objects? Wright argues that we can give an account of the C-conditions, and of what it is for a subject to be suitable, in such a way that a *substantial* and a priori provisional equation, meeting the independence and extremal conditions, is true. In the case of red, for example, the provisional equation will be:

RED: $(\forall x)$ $(C \rightarrow$ (A suitable subject S judges that x is red if and only if x is red))

Wright suggests that the C-conditions in this case can be spelled out roughly as follows: 'S knows which object x is, and knowingly observes it in plain view in normal perceptual conditions; and is fully attentive to this observation; and is perceptually normal and is prey to no other cognitive disfunction; and is free from doubt about the satisfaction of any of these conditions' (Wright 1988a: 15). Crucially, normality can be given a statistical interpretation in this case. For example, the notion of normal perceptual function can be spelled out as: 'perceptual function of a kind, which is actually typical of human beings'. Likewise, normal perceptual conditions can be spelled out as: 'conditions of illumination like those which actually typically obtain at noon on a cloudy summer's day out of doors and out of shadow' (Wright 1988a: 16). When the C-conditions are spelled out in this way, it is plausible that RED holds a priori. Our knowledge that the conditions just described are optimal for the appraisal of ascriptions of colour is not a posteriori knowledge: someone who grasps the concept of red does not have to appeal to experience to find out that they are optimal. Moreover, the C-conditions thus specified plausibly satisfy the substantiality and independence conditions since these specifications are far from trivial, and in answering the question whether the C-conditions obtain there seems to be no implication of logically prior assumptions about the extension of 'red'. Since no better account appears to be available of why the conditions (1)–(3) hold in this case than that visually determined best opinion plays an extension-determining role, the extremal condition (4) also appears to be satisfied. The conclusion is thus that redness is judgement-dependent: best opinions about redness serve to determine the extension of the predicate 'red'. Or, in other words, a dispositional account of redness is plausible.

In the next section, I'll explain why, according to Wright, a dispositional account of shape is not plausible: why we cannot view facts about shape as being determined by best opinion.

7.4 Shapes are Not Judgement-Dependent

In the case of, for example, 'square', the provisional equation will be:

SQUARE: ($\forall$x) (C $\rightarrow$ (A suitable subject S judges that x is square if and only if x is square))

An initial account of the conditions that are optimal for the visual appraisal of shape might be given as follows: 'S knows which object x is, and knowingly observes it in plain view from a sufficient variety of conditions in normal perceptual conditions, and is fully attentive to these observations, and is perceptually normal and is prey to no other cognitive disfunction, and is free of doubt about the satisfaction of any of these conditions' (Wright 1988a: 17).

According to Wright, there are, however, two main reasons for thinking that the provisional equation SQUARE does not satisfy the conditions (1)–(4) on judgement-dependence.

The first reason why there is no such specification of the C-conditions in the shape case is that here a *number* of observations from different positions are required for a judgement to be optimal. (This is different from the colour case: since we do not have to correct for perspective when judging whether an object is red, say, a single observation suffices for optimal judgement.) If we appeal to square-appraising observations that take place at distinct times, we need to find some guarantee that no *change in shape* of the relevant object takes place in the intervals that separate observations – that is, we need to include among the C-conditions some proviso to the effect that the shape of the object in question is stable over the relevant period of time. But the inclusion of this proviso would call, in Wright's words,

> for some ingredient in the C-conditions of which it is an a priori consequence that whatever is true of x's shape at any time during the subject's observations is also true at any other time within the relevant period. Some independent determinant is therefore called for of what it *is* true to say about x's shape during that period – independent, that is, of the opinion formed by the subject. (1989: 248)

The fact that we have to be able to rely on is that at each time t during the period in which the observations are being made, x's shape is stable. But what is it that determines this fact? We cannot appeal here to best opinion since we are in the process of attempting to establish that best opinion determines the truth about shape. But, on the other hand, if what determines the fact of shape stability is something other than best opinion, then best opinion is no longer conceived as playing an extension-determining role. Thus, it seems that insofar as a temporal sequence of observations is required for optimal conditions of shape-judgement, the independence condition must be violated – whether a given opinion is best will presuppose a logically prior determination of the extensions of our shape predicates.

Moreover, even if we could avoid the problem of stability of shape over time by collating the relevant judgements about shape from different visual perspectives from a number of strategically positioned observers forming judgements at the same time, according to Wright a more fundamental problem undermines the suggestion that squareness is judgement-dependent. For, even if optimal conditions of appraisal can be specified in a way that avoids the problem about meeting the independence condition, Wright holds that the resultant provisional equation is bound to fail the condition of a prioricity. The problem is that there is another canonical bi-conditional concerning squareness that is uncontroversially a priori:

SQUARE*: ($\forall$x) (x is square if and only if (if the four sides and four interior angles of x were to be correctly measured, and no change were to take place in the shape or size of x during the process, then the sides would be determined to be equal in length, and the angles would be determined to be right angles)).

Wright now argues as follows. If the original provisional equation SQUARE also holds true a priori, then the result of substituting the right-hand side of SQUARE* into the right-hand side of SQUARE – call this result SQUARE** – should also be a true a priori bi-conditional.[2] Thus:

SQUARE**: ($\forall$x)(C $\rightarrow$ (A suitable subject S judges that x is square if and only if (if the four sides and four interior angles of x were to be correctly measured, and no change were to take place in the shape or size of x during the process, then the sides would be determined to be equal in length, and the angles would be determined to be right angles)).

But Square** is not a priori true. As Wright argues:

> It is not a priori true that our (best) judgements of approximate shape, made on the basis of predominately visual observations, usually 'pan out' when appraised in accordance with more refined operational techniques, where such are appropriate, of the kind the canonical biconditional illustrates. It is not a priori that the world in which we actually live allows reliable perceptual appraisal of approximate shape and is not, for example, a world in which the paths travelled by photons are subject to grossly distorting forces. (1988a: 20; also 1989: 249)

So, even if it is possible to formulate a provisional equation for squareness that satisfies the independence condition (perhaps by involving a number of observers who collaborate with each other), that equation will not be an a priori truth. Since these considerations exploit no special facts about squareness in particular, it follows that the extensions of shape predicates in general cannot be viewed as determined by best opinion: shape cannot be viewed as judgement-dependent, and a dispositional account of shape does not seem to be possible.

7.5 Moral Qualities are not Judgement-Dependent

Are moral qualities judgement-dependent? Consider as a typical moral predicate 'culpably insensitive'. Can we give an account of the cognitively ideal conditions for the appraisal of ascriptions of culpable insensitivity that will ensure that the relevant provisional equation satisfies the various conditions on judgement-dependence? That provisional equation will have the following form:

MORAL: $(\forall x)$ $(C \rightarrow$ (A suitable subject S judges that x is culpably insensitive if and only if x is culpably insensitive)).

Wright suggests the following rough characterization of the C-conditions (where Jones is the author of the putatively insensitive remark):

> S scrutinizes the motives, consequences, and, for Jones, foreseeable consequences in the context of the remark; and does this in a fashion which involves no error concerning non-moral fact or logic, and embraces all morally relevant considerations; S gives all this the fullest attention, and so is victim to no error or oversight concerning any relevant aspect of his/her deliberation; S is a morally-suitable subject – accepts the right moral principles, or has the right moral intuitions or sentiments, or whatever; S has no doubt about the satisfaction of any of these conditions. (Wright 1988a: 22–3)

A condition concerning moral suitability does indeed seem indispensable: S's judgement as to whether a particular action is culpably insensitive cannot be taken as a reliable guide to its moral status if S is himself, for instance, utterly insensitive, or prey to some other sort of moral deficiency. But we now have a clear problem relating to the satisfaction of the independence condition: even if this (rough) specification of the C-conditions plausibly renders MORAL a priori and 'not wholly insubstantial', *the appeal to the notion of moral suitability will lead to a violation of the independence condition.* Whether or not the C-conditions in MORAL obtain is not independent of the extension of moral concepts, for whether or not S is morally suitable is itself a substantive moral question. Michael Smith makes a similar point when he writes:

> Is there any answer [about what constitutes suitability in the moral case] that could plausibly hope to give the truth-conditions of ascriptions of value except the answer that [the 'suitable' subjects] are those who accept the correct moral principles and that conditions are 'suitable' when we can apply these principles without error? If not, then the idea that we have given any kind of *analysis* of value is simply a sham. (1993a: 247)[3]

The difficulties about the satisfaction of the independence condition noted by Wright and Smith suggest that a plausible judgement-dependent account of moral qualities, or a plausible dispositional account of moral value, are unlikely to be found. In fact, as I'll now suggest, even if we could find a dispositional theory of moral value that avoided the problems raised by Wright and Smith, it would not help assuage the fundamental worry underlying Mackie's argument from queerness.

7.6 Judgement-Dependence and Categoricity

Where does this leave us? A plausible dispositional or judgement-dependent account of value appeared to promise to solve both the epistemological and metaphysical aspects of Mackie's argument from queerness, and to provide some explanation of the phenomenology of moral experience. In the previous chapter we canvassed the idea that the kind of internal relationship between colour properties and idealized human response essayed in dispositional or judgement-dependent theories of colour might blunt the force of a Lockean error-theoretic argument against colour. This suggested that a dispositional or judgement-dependent theory of moral value might help blunt the force of Mackie's error-theoretic argument from queerness. In fact, though, this promise was always illusory. Unlike our colour concepts, our concept of a moral fact is the concept of a *categorical* reason for action. So moral facts, if such there be, must be capable of providing a reason for agents to act in a particular way independently of facts about their desires or affective make-up. That is to say, moral requirements apply to rational beings as such. But no matter how rational an agent is, they will not have a reason to judge that ripe cherries are red unless they have a desire to tell the truth, or some end which is served by applying the predicate 'red' to objects within its extension.[4] Moreover, in the colour and humour cases, suitability to judge goes well beyond what we might expect to find in rational beings as such: in one case we need certain specific visual equipment and in the other we need a 'sense of humour' which is more likely to be seen as an aspect of an agent's affective as opposed to rational make-up. So the internal relationship between property and response postulated in a dispositional or judgement-dependent theory of the kind familiar from the case of colour does not appear to be of the right kind to enable an analogous dispositional theory of moral value to successfully undermine the argument from queerness. So, even if we waive the problems surrounding the satisfaction of the independence condition, we do not have here a basis for a convincing rejoinder to the argument from queerness.[5]

Do the above conclusions – that a dispositional conception of moral value is implausible, and that in any case it wouldn't help to domesticate the notion of a categorical reason for action – mean that we have lost all hope of a convincing reply to the argument from queerness? In the next three chapters, I will look at a number of possible directions of response to this question. In chapter 8, I consider non-reductionist naturalistic cognitivism, as espoused by the 'Cornell Realists'. In chapter 9, I'll examine some reductionist versions of naturalistic cognitivism. In chapter 10, I'll examine contemporary non-naturalistic cognitivism, as defended in the writings of John McDowell.

7.7 Further Reading

Wright's notion of judgement-dependence has been discussed extensively in the recent literature. For Wright's views, see especially Wright (1988a, 1989, and the appendix to chapter 3 of Wright 1992). Wright's notion of judgement-dependence is only one of the vehicles available for developing dispositional theories of moral qualities. For alternatives, see the papers on 'Dispositional theories of value' by Michael Smith, David Lewis and Mark Johnston in the 1989 supplementary volume of *Proceedings of the Aristotelian Society*. For an exploration of the idea that Wright's judgement-dependent view of intention might help with some of the worries about a judgement-dependent view of moral qualities, see Hood (2010).

A notion closely related to Wright's notion of judgement-dependence is that of response-dependence. This notion too has received extensive discussion. See, in particular, Pettit (1991), Blackburn (1993c), Johnston (1993a, 1993b and 1998), the papers in Menzies (ed.) (1991), the papers collected in Casati and Tappollet (eds) (1998), and the papers collected in Menzies (ed.) (1998). For a useful overview of the different forms of response-dependence, see Gundersen (2007). For an attempt to apply the idea of judgement-dependence to the case of simple arithmetic, see Divers and Miller (1999). If, as Wright argues, moral anti-realism cannot be formulated in terms of a judgement-dependent account, how can it be formulated? For Wright's own answer to this question, see Wright (1992, in particular 199–201).

The issue about the relationship between cognitive access and judgement-dependence is more complicated than suggested by the opening paragraph of this chapter: in fact, a property's being judgement-dependent might be consistent with the idea that optimal judgements track or cognitively access the facts about its extension. See Miller (2012b, especially §2).

One philosopher not discussed in this book is Christine Korsgaard. For a discussion of whether her constructivism can be viewed as a kind of metaethical judgement-dependence view, see Surgener (2012). Other useful attempts to place Korsgaard in the context of metaethics can be found in Hussein and Shah (2006 and 2013).

8

Naturalism I – Cornell Realism

8.1 Introduction

A *strong cognitivist* theory is one which holds (a) that moral judgements are truth-apt, and (b) that making a correct moral judgement is a way of putting oneself into *cognitive contact* with some independently constituted state of affairs. A *weak cognitivist* theory is one which holds (a) that moral judgements are truth-apt, and (b) that making a correct moral judgement is *not* a way of putting oneself into cognitive contact with some independently constituted state of affairs. In the previous chapter I looked at a version of weak cognitivism, the 'best opinion' account of moral truth. In the next three chapters I will examine some contemporary versions of strong cognitivism. Recall that, in chapters 2 and 3, I have already discussed one strong cognitivist theory: Moorean Intuitionism. This was a version of non-naturalistic strong cognitivism, since moral qualities are held by Moorean intuitionism to be non-natural and causally inefficacious. I showed that this non-naturalistic version of strong cognitivism is very implausible and nowadays almost universally rejected. But what are the prospects for the development of a *naturalistic* version of strong cognitivism? There are two main forms such a theory could take. Let Natural properties (capital 'N') be the properties that form the subject matter of the natural and social sciences (including psychology but not ethics itself).[1] Then, a strong cognitivist theory could be *reductionist*, identifying moral properties with Natural properties, or it could be *non-reductionist*, claiming that moral properties are themselves irreducible natural properties in their own right (so that a full inventory of natural properties would include moral properties in addition to the Natural properties). Reductionist theories have been developed by Gilbert Harman (1975, 1977), Richard Brandt (1979), David Lewis (1989), Peter Railton (1986a, 1986b, 1989), and Frank

Jackson and Philip Pettit (1995). I will consider some reductionist views in the next chapter. In this chapter, I will focus on non-reductionist naturalistic cognitivism, mainly as developed by Nicholas Sturgeon (see his 1986a, 1986b, 1988, 1992; and also Boyd 1988, Brink 1989, and Sayre-McCord 1988). These philosophers have close connections with Cornell University, so the view is known as *Cornell Realism*.

Before introducing Cornell Realism, a few remarks on the distinction between reductionism and non-reductionism are in order. I will follow Darwall, Gibbard and Railton (1992: 174) in taking reductionism to cover theories which claim that moral vocabulary is analysable in terms of Natural vocabulary, or which claim that moral properties are identical to Natural properties as a matter of synthetic fact. Correspondingly, non-reductionist theories do not claim that there are any interesting analytic relationships between moral and Natural terms; nor that moral properties are identical to Natural properties as a matter of synthetic fact. As we'll see, non-reductionists claim instead that moral properties are *constituted by*, or *supervene upon*, or are *multiply realized by*, Natural properties: the view thus counts as a version of naturalism even though there is no straightforward reduction of the moral to the Natural. We can illustrate this by considering the moral property of *rightness*. We can imagine an indefinite number of ways in which actions can be morally right. Non-reductionist naturalistic cognitivists think that in *any one* example of moral rightness, the rightness can be identified with Natural properties (e.g., being the handing over of money, being the opening of a door for someone else, etc.). But they claim that across *all* morally right actions, there is no one Natural property or set of Natural properties that all such situations have in common and to which moral rightness can be reduced. As Darwall, Gibbard and Railton put it:

> [The Cornell Realists] have pursued analogies with natural and social science to argue that moral properties might be both irreducible and explanatorily efficacious. One might, for example, argue that various chemical or biological 'natural kinds' – acid, catalyst, gene, organism – are not obviously type reducible to the natural kinds of physics, and yet play a role in good scientific explanation. (1992: 169–70)

Likewise, functionalist theories in the philosophy of mind rejected any reduction of mental types, such as *being in pain*, to neurophysiological types, such as *being in a state of C-fibre stimulation*: since many organisms which do not *have* C-fibres can nevertheless be in pain, being in pain is a state which is multiply realized by neurophysiological types, even though there is no neurophysiological type to which it is reducible (see Burwood, Gilbert and Lennon 1999, chapter 2).[2] Cornell Realism makes similar claims about the relationship between moral types or properties and the Natural types or properties upon which they supervene.

8.2 Harman's Challenge

Perhaps the easiest way to get a handle on Cornell Realism is via consideration of a challenge posed against moral realism by Gilbert Harman (1977). The Cornell Realists argue that we can view moral properties and facts as part of the natural fabric of the world for the same reason that we can view, for example, physical, chemical or biological facts as part of the fabric of the natural world, namely, *that they pull their weight in explanatory theories.* In other words, the assumption is that we are justified in postulating a type of fact or property to the extent that it is required in our best overall explanatory picture of the world.[3] Thus, for example, physical facts play this sort of explanatory role. Consider the fact that a physicist believes that there is a proton in a given cloud chamber: this fact can be explained by the fact that there is actually a proton in the cloud chamber. Facts about protons can also enter into the explanation of other facts, not necessarily about belief: for example, the fact that there is a proton in the cloud chamber may explain why some of the electrons in the cloud chamber behave the way they do. So we are justified in including this fact in our inventory of what is out there in the natural world. Harman argues that moral facts and moral properties can never be assigned this sort of explanatory role, so that barring the reduction of such facts and properties to some independently respectable (i.e., explanatorily efficacious) Natural facts and properties, there is simply no justification for thinking that there are such things as moral facts and properties. Harman's challenge thus threatens us with a version of moral scepticism. We can view the Cornell Realists and Harman as arguing in the following ways:

Cornell Realism

(1) P is a real property if and only if P figures ineliminably in the best explanation of experience.
(2) Moral properties figure ineliminably in the best explanation of experience.

Therefore:

(3) Moral properties are real properties.

Harman

(1) P is a real property if and only if P figures ineliminably in the best explanation of experience.
(2a) Moral 'properties' do not figure ineliminably in the best explanation of experience.

Therefore:

(3a) Moral 'properties' are not real properties.

Moreover:

(4)   The judgement that a is P can be justified only if P is, in the above sense, a real property.

So:

(5)   Moral judgements are never justified.[4]

I'll proceed by outlining Harman's argument: the Cornell Realists' argument will then emerge in the form of Nicholas Sturgeon's reply to Harman.

Harman asks us to consider the example of someone who sees a group of hoodlums pouring petrol over and setting fire to a cat, and who immediately forms the belief that what the hoodlums are doing is wrong. Do we need to cite the wrongness of the hoodlums' action as part of the explanation of why the person involved forms the belief that what they are doing is wrong? Harman thinks not:

> You need to make assumptions about certain physical facts to explain the occurrence of the observations that support a scientific theory, but you do not seem to need to make assumptions about any moral facts to explain the occurrence of the so-called moral observations I have been talking about. In the moral case, it would seem that you need only make assumptions about the psychology or moral sensibility of the person making the moral observation. (1977: 6)[5]

Harman's claim is thus that physical facts earn their explanatory keep in a way that moral facts do not: whereas the best explanation of the physicist's forming the belief that a proton is present requires the assumption that there is a proton present, our explanation of the belief that what the hoodlums are doing is wrong does not need the assumption that what they are doing is wrong: all we need to advert to in this latter explanation are *Natural* facts about the hoodlums (e.g., that they are pouring gasoline on a cat, causing the cat extreme pain, etc.) and *Natural* facts about us (e.g., about our beliefs about good and bad, our upbringing, etc.). In eschewing reference to moral facts in this latter explanation, we suffer no explanatory *loss*.

8.3 Sturgeon's Reply to Harman

Reductionism and non-reductionism

Harman is willing to allow that Natural facts and properties can pull their weight in explanatory theories: accordingly, the only way he can envisage the postulation of moral facts and properties being justified is via some version of *reductionism*, via the provision of *reductive definitions* of moral terms in Naturalistic vocabulary. If a set of reductive definitions could be provided, then we might after all be able to avoid moral scepticism. Sturgeon, however, wants to argue that we can avoid moral scepticism without embracing any form of reductionism. That is, Sturgeon argues that we can be ethical naturalists *without* being ethical reductionists: moral predicates might not be translatable into, or even co-extensional with, Naturalistic predicates, but they might nevertheless stand for irreducible natural properties.[6]

The main problem with the thought that ethical naturalism requires ethical reductionism, according to Sturgeon, is the difficulty of spelling out the distinctive and privileged Naturalistic vocabulary in terms of which ethical language would have to be defined. There are two broad options: we might require that moral language be definable in terms of the language of *physics*, or we might require that moral language be definable in terms of the language of *biology, psychology and social theory*. Sturgeon has arguments against both suggestions.

Against requiring ethical terms to be defined in the language of physics
Sturgeon's first argument goes as follows:

> If there are (as there appear to be) any continuous physical parameters, then there are continuum many physical states of the world, but there are at most countably many predicates in any language, including that of even ideal physics; so there are more physical properties than there are physical expressions to represent them. Thus, although physicalism arguably entails that biological and psychological properties (and ethical properties, too, if there are any) are physical, nothing follows about whether we have any but biological, or psychological, or ethical terminology for representing these particular physical properties. (1988: 240)[7]

Against requiring ethical terms to be defined in biological, psychological or social terms
Sturgeon notes that reductionists have not usually required that the vocabulary of the area to be reduced be definable in terms of the language of physics. Instead it is usually assumed that:

> [T]here are a number of disciplines that we pretty well know to deal with a single natural world, for example, physics, biology, psychology,

and social theory; that it is a matter of no great concern whether any of *these* disciplines is reducible to some one of the others or to anything else; but that the test of whether ethical naturalism is true is whether ethics is reducible to some (nonmoral) combination of *them*. (1988: 241)

Sturgeon then argues that the imposition of this extra requirement on ethics is ill-motivated:

What rationale is there for holding ethics alone to this reductive test? Perhaps there would be one if ethics appeared in some salient respect strikingly dissimilar to these other disciplines: if, for example, Harman were right that whereas physics, biology, and the rest offer plausible explanations of many obviously natural facts, including facts about our beliefs and observations, ethics never does. Perhaps ethics could then plausibly be required to earn its place by some alternative route. But I shall of course argue that Harman is wrong about this alleged dissimilarity, and I take my argument to provide part of the defence required for a naturalistic but nonreductive view of ethics. (1988: 241)

It's not clear that Sturgeon is right. He writes as if the only possible source of relevant disanalogy between ethics and the other disciplines that he mentions would concern the explanatory potency of the facts and properties in which they trade. But, of course, there are other differences: what about the fact that moral properties and facts are *intrinsically action-guiding* (cf. chapter 6) or that ethics seems to be more prone to *irresolvable disagreement* than the other areas (cf. Railton 1993a: 281–3)? Sturgeon seems to think that citation of these features would be to enter another argument for moral scepticism, whereas Harman's challenge is supposed to be a free-standing and independent challenge in its own right: we could then only run Harman's sceptical challenge by presupposing the correctness of some other argument for moral scepticism, thereby rendering Harman's challenge otiose. But this is not pertinent at this point: in order to get a relevant disanalogy, all we need is the fact that ethics exhibits the feature concerned (e.g., action-guidingness or proneness to irresolvable disagreement); *we do not need the assumption that the presence of these features justifies a version of moral scepticism*. So Sturgeon's argument that ethical naturalism does not require ethical reductionism is not convincing as it stands.[8]

However, we can let this point go: the main test of whether ethical naturalism requires ethical reductionism in this sense will be whether a viable and more attractive version of non-reductionist ethical naturalism can be developed. It is to this question that I now turn.

Sturgeon's examples of explanatorily efficacious moral facts

(i) The Hitler example

Sturgeon argues (1988: 232) that the fact that Hitler was morally depraved explains (at least in part) why he instigated and oversaw the death of millions of persons; the fact that Hitler instigated and oversaw the death of millions of persons explains why I believe that Hitler was morally depraved. So the fact that Hitler was morally depraved explains (in part) why I believe that Hitler was morally depraved. (This style of explanation is an example of a general form of explanation, namely, explanation in terms of a person's *moral character*.)

(ii) The slavery example

In addition to examples which cite facts about moral character as part of an explanation, there are also examples where moral features of actions or institutions themselves appear to play a genuinely explanatory role:

> An interesting historical question is why vigorous and reasonably widespread moral opposition to slavery arose for the first time in the eighteenth and nineteenth centuries, even though slavery was a very old institution; and why this opposition arose primarily in Britain, France, and in French and English speaking North America, even though slavery existed throughout the New World. There is a standard answer to this question. It is that chattel slavery in British and French America, and then in the United States, was much worse than previous forms of slavery, and much worse than slavery in Latin America. . . . Equally good for my purpose would be the more limited thesis that explains the growth of antislavery sentiment in the United States, between the Revolution and the Civil War, in part by saying that slavery in the United States became a more oppressive institution during that time. The appeal in these standard explanations is straightforwardly to moral facts. (1988: 245; also Brink 1989: 195)

These examples suggest, according to Sturgeon, that the prospects for a satisfying response to Harman's challenge are much brighter than Harman leads us to believe. I'll evaluate Sturgeon's claim in due course.

Where Harman goes wrong

So where, according to Sturgeon, is the mistake in Harman's challenge? Let's compare the examples of the presence of the proton and the wrongness of the torching of the cat. Harman claims that the wrongness of the act of torching the cat is irrelevant to the explanation of why you believe that it is wrong. Now one way to test claims of explanatory relevance is by applying the *counterfactual test*: to say that a's being F is explanatorily relevant to b's being G is to say that if a had not been F, then b would not have been G (e.g., the striking of the match explains the occurrence of the explosion because if the match had not been struck the explosion would not have occurred). Now how do we get on when we apply this test to the case of the cat? Is it true to say that if the torching of the cat had not been wrong, we would not have believed that the hoodlum's act of torching the cat was wrong? As Sturgeon points out, this counterfactual conditional can be read in a number of different ways. The first thing to note is that we have a normative moral theory about the relationship between natural facts and moral facts: according to our moral theory, an act which possesses the non-moral property of *pointless, deliberate cruelty,*[9] say, or some of the other natural properties upon which moral properties supervene, also possesses the moral property of *wrongness.* Now suppose that this theory is correct. Then, in order for the action not to be wrong, it would have to have lacked the property of pointless, deliberate cruelty, or any of the other relevant natural properties upon which moral properties, according to our favoured normative moral theory, supervene. *Now, it seems simply false to say that if the act had lacked the property of pointless, deliberate cruelty, we would still have believed the action to be wrong.* So, on the assumption that our moral theory is roughly correct, it looks as if, by the counterfactual test, the wrongness of the action *is* in fact explanatorily relevant to our believing that it is wrong.

At this point, you may protest that we are surely not entitled to assume that our normative moral theory *is* roughly correct. But Sturgeon will reply that (a) if Harman requires the assumption that our moral theory is incorrect in order for his challenge to work, that challenge can never provide us with an independently plausible sceptical challenge to morality. We would need some other sceptical challenge to our favoured moral theory to be in place in order to establish Harman's sceptical conclusion: this would render Harman's sceptical challenge redundant; (b) if Harman is allowed this assumption, then we can also derive a sceptical conclusion about the explanatory relevance of *physical* facts and properties! Our physicist has a theory about what sorts of phenomena signal the presence of a proton: say, the presence of a vapour trail in a cloud chamber. Now suppose that this theory is correct. Then, if there hadn't been a proton present, there wouldn't have been a vapour trail, and if there hadn't been a vapour trail, the physicist would not have formed the belief that there is a proton present. So the presence of the proton is relevant in explaining why the physicist believes that there is a proton present. So far this is exactly the same as in the moral case. But suppose that the physicist's physical theory is mistaken: that it is false that the presence of a vapour trail signals the presence of a proton, that there could have been a vapour trail even in the absence of a proton. Then, if there had been no proton, there would still have been a vapour trail, and because of the physicist's allegiance to a mistaken physical theory, he would still have believed that a proton was present. *So, on the assumption that the physicist's theory is incorrect, we can also derive the conclusion that if there had been no proton, the physicist would still have believed that a proton is present. The presence of the proton would therefore be irrelevant, by the counterfactual test, to the explanation of the physicist's belief that a proton is present.* So, even if Harman were allowed to assume the incorrectness of our normative moral theory as part of his argument, this would not allow him to derive any sceptical conclusions that are specifically about morality. The sceptical conclusion would also apply to scientific theory, whereas Harman wants to establish that moral theory is problematic in a way in which scientific theory is not.

8.4 More on Harman and Sturgeon

In his later piece (1986), Harman attempts to reply to Sturgeon's claim that irreducible moral facts and properties can play a genuine role in explanations of our moral beliefs and natural facts.

Suppose Jane observes Albert torturing a cat. On the basis of this observation, she forms the belief that what Albert is doing is wrong. Sturgeon claims that it is sometimes legitimate to at least in part explain Jane's formation of this belief by citing the fact that the action is actually wrong. If the action hadn't been wrong, then it would not have possessed the feature of deliberate pointless cruelty, or one of the other relevant natural properties on which moral properties supervene; and if it hadn't possessed one of those properties, then Jane wouldn't have formed the belief that what Albert is doing is wrong. Sturgeon thus claims that by the counterfactual test the wrongness of the act is explanatorily relevant to the formation of Jane's belief. Harman objects:

> What is needed is some account of *how* the actual wrongness of Albert's action could help to explain Jane's disapproval of it. And we have to be able to believe in this account. We cannot just make something up, saying, for example, that the wrongness of the act affects the quality of the light reflected into Jane's eyes, causing her to react negatively. That would be an example of wrongness manifesting itself in the world in a way that could serve as evidence for and against certain moral claims, but it is not something we can believe in. (1986: 63)

Dworkin's comment is also relevant:

> The idea of a direct impact between moral properties and human beings supposes that the universe houses, among its numerous particles of energy and matter, some special particles – morons – whose energy and momentum establish fields that at once constitute the morality or immorality, or virtue or vice, of particular human acts and institutions and

also interact in some way with human nervous systems so as to make people aware of the morality or immorality or of the virtue or vice. (Dworkin 1996: 104)

These passages suggest that it is not enough to cite the *counterfactual dependence* of Jane's belief on the wrongness of Albert's action: in order for the wrongness of the action to have genuine explanatory relevance, we also need some account of *how it could be* that there is such a dependence, some account of the *mechanisms or processes* which underlie that dependence. Since we have no plausible story to tell about this in the moral case, we should conclude that unless moral properties and facts are reducible to Natural properties and facts, they have no genuine explanatory role. This point is developed further in another passage from Harman's counterattack, where he claims that the mere counterfactual dependence Sturgeon points to cannot justify the ascription of explanatory relevance to moral facts and properties, since even a *moral epiphenomenalist* – someone who explicitly *accepts* the *explanatory impotence* of moral facts and properties – could nevertheless accept the counterfactual dependence in question:

> A good and conclusive way to see that this sort of explanation is irrelevant to full empirical testing is to notice that a moral epiphenomenalist can accept the relevant counterfactual judgement without having to suppose that moral features of actions ever explain any nonmoral facts. A moral epiphenomenalist takes moral properties to be epiphenomenally supervenient on natural properties in the sense that the possession of moral properties is explained by possession of the relevant natural properties and nothing is influenced or explained by the possession of moral properties. (1986: 63)

Sturgeon himself explains this objection more clearly (before going on to respond to it):

> The moral epiphenomenalist who accepts the counterfactual about Hitler [if Hitler hadn't been morally depraved, then we wouldn't have believed that he was morally depraved] will understand it as follows. Hitler had certain *nonmoral* features that did two things: they *made it true* that he had another property, depravity, and they also *caused* him to behave in certain ways: but unlike these nonmoral properties, the depravity that supervened on them was causally inert, so it is a mistake to cite it in explanation of his behaviour. Still, in order for him not to be depraved he would have had to lack these nonmoral features; so, unless his behaviour was overdetermined, if he hadn't been depraved he would have acted differently. Similarly for Albert. There are features which make his action wrong, and which cause Jane to believe that it is wrong, but the *wrongness* of the action plays no causal role. (1986a: 74)[10]

Sturgeon's counter-reply to Harman's point falls into two parts: (a) he concedes that even a moral epiphenomenalist could accept that moral facts and properties pass the counterfactual test, but he goes on to argue (b) that this would only endanger the intuitive explanations in terms of them if moral epiphenomenalism were independently plausible. But we have no good reason to think that moral epiphenomenalism is independently plausible:

> If we are to take [moral epiphenomenalism] to be credible enough to take it seriously as a challenge to the view that we find (and should find) moral facts explanatory, we need to be given some *argument* for doing so. And the argument cannot be merely that this position represents a logical possibility; it must show moral epiphenomenalism to be credible enough to require independent rebuttal. (1986a: 74)

Thus, according to Sturgeon, the mere consistency of the moral epiphenomenalist position with acceptance of the counterfactual dependence in question is not by itself sufficient to cast doubt on the explanatory efficacy of moral facts and properties. And Sturgeon goes on to write:

> Since we find it plausible to attribute causal efficacy and explanatory relevance to moral facts, why should we not conclude, rather, that their supervenience on nonmoral facts is not 'epiphenomenal' at all, but is instead like the supervenience of biological facts on physical or chemical ones, or (on a physicalist view) of psychological facts on neurophysiological ones – a kind of 'causal constitution' of the supervening facts out of the more basic ones, which allows them a causal efficacy inherited from that of the facts out of which they are constituted? (1986a: 75)[11]

Sturgeon thinks that the only way to rebut this point would be to accept that all supervenient facts are epiphenomenal. He argues that this is implausible, since it would render biological, chemical and psychological facts and properties explanatorily impotent, and in any case could not serve Harman's purpose of establishing that moral facts and natural facts are not on a par when it comes to their role in explanations. But his reply to Harman strikes me as implausible for another reason. Sturgeon's original claim was that the counterfactual dependence of b's being G upon a's being F is *sufficient* to justify the idea that the property F is explanatorily relevant to b's being G: this is what allows him to argue that moral properties are explanatorily relevant. Harman's objection to this position *questions* this sufficiency claim. Harman's point is that if moral epiphenomenalism is *coherent* or *consistent* (as opposed to plausible), then the following combination is possible: acceptance of the counterfactual dependence of moral belief upon moral properties plus denial of the claim that moral properties are explanatorily relevant. And, if this is *possible*, Sturgeon's sufficiency claim is false. It follows that Sturgeon's reply to Harman is implausible as it stands: Sturgeon needs to *add* something to mere counterfactual dependence to get the conclusion that moral properties are genuinely explanatorily relevant. I'll investigate whether there is anything Sturgeon can add to counterfactual dependence to get this conclusion in the next section. Specifically, I will investigate whether a general account of the role played by second-order properties in explanation – 'program explanation', as developed by Frank Jackson and Philip Pettit in their 1990 – can be used by Sturgeon to bolster Cornell Realism against Harman's counterattack.

8.5 Program Explanation

What Sturgeon needs is a constructive account of how it can be that irreducible but supervenient facts and properties – whether in science or outside it – can figure in best explanations, explanations whose unavailability would result in some explanatory impoverishment. An interesting option for Sturgeon is to turn to the notion of 'program explanation' as developed by Jackson and Pettit. In this section I'll outline the idea of program explanation, and show how, prima facie at least, there may be 'moral' program explanations that have some claim to count as 'best'.

Jackson and Pettit identify four assumptions which together seem to imply that some of the non-moral properties we would ordinarily deem to be explanatorily potent are in fact explanatorily impotent. They argue that there are good reasons for the rejection of one of these assumptions, so that the explanatory potency of the properties in question can be saved.

The four assumptions in question are as follows (as stated in 1990: 108):

(1) A causal explanation of something must direct us to a *causally relevant* property as opposed to a *causally irrelevant* property of the factor it identifies as explanatory: a property relevant to the causal production of the effect explained.
(2) One way in which properties are causally relevant is by being *causally efficacious*. A causally efficacious property with regard to an effect is a property in virtue of whose instantiation, at least in part, the effect occurs; the instance of the property helps to produce the effect and does so because it is an instance of that property.
(3) A property F is not causally efficacious in the production of an effect e if the following sub-conditions are all fulfilled:
   (i)   there is a distinct property G such that F is efficacious in the production of e only if G is efficacious in its production;

(ii) the F-instance and the G-instance are not sequential causal factors;

(iii) the F-instance and the G-instance are not coordinate causal factors.

(4) The *only* way in which a property can be causally relevant to an effect is by being causally efficacious in its production.

The problem is that these four assumptions together conflict with some very strong intuitions about the role of certain properties in explanation. Jackson and Pettit give a number of examples from different areas, but here I will focus on just one of these. Suppose that we boil water in a closed glass container, and the water reaches such a temperature that the glass cracks. What explains why the glass cracks? Intuitively, we would want to be able to say that the glass cracks because of the temperature of the water: the temperature of the water is causally relevant to the cracking of the glass. However, assumptions (1)–(4) above imply that the temperature of the water is in fact *causally irrelevant* to the cracking of the glass. Jackson and Pettit spell out why as follows:

> Why did it crack? First answer: because of the temperature of the water. Second answer, in simplified form: because of the momentum of such and such a molecule (group of molecules) in striking such and such a molecular bond in the container surface. The temperature property was efficacious only if the momentum property was efficacious: hence 3(i). But the temperature of the water – an aggregate statistic – did not help to produce the momentum of the molecule in the way in which it, if efficacious, helped to produce the cracking: hence 3(ii). And neither did the temperature combine with the momentum to help in the same sense to produce the cracking: one could have predicted the cracking just from full information about the molecule and the relevant laws. Hence 3(iii). (1990: 110)

So, by assumption (3), the temperature of the water is not causally efficacious in the cracking of the glass. Whence, by (4), it is not causally relevant to the cracking of the glass! Jackson and Pettit respond to this intuitively puzzling result by rejecting assumption (4): there are ways of being causally relevant other than being causally efficacious. Even if a property is not causally efficacious, it can still *program for the existence* of a distinct, lower-level, property that *is* causally efficacious, and in that sense can be *causally relevant*. Jackson and Pettit explain this in general terms as follows:

> Although not efficacious itself, the temperature property was such that its realization ensured that there was an efficacious property in the offing: the property, we may presume, involving such and such molecules. The realization of the higher order property did not produce the cracking in

the manner of the lower order. But it meant that there would be a suitably efficacious property available, perhaps that involving such and such particular molecules, perhaps one involving others. And so the temperature was causally relevant to the cracking of the glass, under a perfectly relevant sense of relevance, though it was not efficacious. It did not do any work in producing the cracking of the glass – it was perfectly inert – but it had the relevance of ensuring that there would be some property there to exercise the efficacy required. (1990: composed from 114)

Why is the explanation the temperature property figures in called a *program explanation*?

> A useful metaphor for describing the role of the property is to say that its realization programs for the appearance of the productive property and, under a certain description, for the event produced. The analogy is with a computer program which ensures that certain things will happen – things satisfying certain descriptions – though all the work of producing those things goes on at a lower, mechanical level. (1990: 114)

Thus, the realization of the temperature property, though inefficacious, ensures the presence of some lower-order property – the property of such and such molecules having such and such momentum – which is efficacious in producing the cracking of the glass. Thus, the temperature property is causally relevant even though it is not causally efficacious.

But why are program explanations useful? Because:

> A program explanation of an event e may provide information which the corresponding process (i.e. lower-level, mechanical) explanation does not supply. Thus, it may be an explanation which the process explanation does not supersede . . . The momentum of a water molecule can crack a container without the water's being at boiling temperature. Thus, to know that the temperature is explanatory, programming for the result in question, is to have information which is not available from the corresponding process explanations. (1990: 116–17)

Jackson and Pettit elaborate further:

> A program explanation provides a different sort of information from that which is supplied by the corresponding process account and therefore a sort of information which someone in possession of the process account may lack. The process story tells us about how the history actually went: say that the momentum of such and such molecules was responsible for the cracking of the glass. A program explanation tells us about how that history might have been. It gives modal information about the history, telling us for example that in any relevantly similar situation, as in the original situation itself, the fact that the water was at boiling temperature means that there will be a property realized – that involving the momentum of particular molecules – which is sufficient in the circumstances

to produce the cracking of the glass. In the actual world it was this, that and the other molecule whose momentum led to the cracking of the glass but in possible worlds where their place is taken by other molecules, the cracking still occurs. (1990: 117)[12]

Can Sturgeon view the relationship between irreducible moral properties and the natural properties upon which they supervene as analogous to the relationship between, for example, the temperature property and the momentum property of the molecules? If so, he could then claim that moral properties are causally relevant even though they are not causally efficacious, since they can play a role in program explanations similar to the role played by the temperature property; and that not having these program explanations would constitute an explanatory loss, so they count, in the appropriate sense, as 'best'. This would allow Sturgeon the idea that irreducible moral properties might figure in best explanations without having to postulate the existence of Dworkin's 'morons'.

Let's investigate how this might work by going back to the example of Albert and Jane. Jane sees Albert torturing a cat and forms the belief that what Albert is doing is wrong. Is there an explanation of Jane's forming this belief in terms of the wrongness of Albert's act which can plausibly count as best? Albert's act had certain natural features – say, the feature of pouring gasoline on the cat's surface and the feature of applying a flame there – which made it true that Albert's act was wrong and which were causally efficacious in producing Jane's belief that what Albert did was wrong. (The natural features cited may themselves only be causally relevant if there are still lower-order natural properties that are causally efficacious, etc., but we can ignore this complication here.) Can we say that the explanation of Jane's forming the belief in terms of the wrongness of Albert's act is a program explanation? It looks like we can. Note first that the wrongness of Albert's act is causally inefficacious in the production of Jane's belief: the wrongness of Albert's act is efficacious in the production of Jane's belief only if some natural property or properties are efficacious, and the wrongness and the natural properties are neither sequential nor coordinate causal factors in the production of Jane's belief. But we can say that the wrongness programs for the existence of a lower-order natural property which is efficacious in the production of Jane's belief. Can we say that this program explanation is, in the relevant sense, best? It looks like we can: we can run analogues of the two points Jackson and Pettit made about the program explanation of the cracking of the glass in terms of there being some molecules having such and such momentum. Pouring gasoline over a cat and then igniting it can cause Jane to form the belief that what she has just seen is wrong even though it is not: think of the far-fetched case in which Albert's only option in saving the cat from an even worse fate than burning is to ignite it. Moreover, the program explanation provides us with modal information which the corresponding process explanation cannot impart: in possible worlds where the property of being ignited is replaced by other natural properties, for example, applying an electric current to the cat, Jane would still have formed the belief that what Albert did was wrong. Thus, we can mount a program explanation of the formation of Jane's belief in terms of the wrongness of Albert's act, such that the unavailability of that explanation would result in explanatory impoverishment. So the explanation is, in the relevant sense, best.

Prima facie, the same can be said of Sturgeon's other examples. Hitler's depravity programs for the existence of non-moral properties which are efficacious in the production of our belief that Hitler was depraved. In this case it is not clear that the analogue of Jackson and Pettit's first claim about the temperature/cracking case holds: are there possible worlds in which Hitler starts a world war and attempts to commit genocide, and yet in which he is not depraved? This seems unlikely.[13] But an analogue of their second point does appear to hold. The program explanation provides us with modal information that the corresponding process explanation fails to impart: in other possible worlds in which, say, Hitler does not start the Second World War and then attempt to commit genocide, but rather systematically ignites all of the cats in Europe, we would still have formed the belief that he was depraved. And an analogue of the first point would seem to be available in the case of explanations in terms of less extreme defects of moral character. My belief that Jones is a coward can be explained in terms of his being cowardly: this latter property programs for the existence of lower-order natural properties, such as his being unable to look anyone in the eye. There are possible worlds in which Jones has this property but in which he is simply shy rather than morally lacking (and the explanation also provides modal information: in other possible worlds where Jones bullies people who are in a weaker situation than himself but can nevertheless look me in the eye, I would still form the belief that he is a coward).

Likewise for the point about slavery. The claim is that widespread opposition to slavery arose when it did because slavery at that time was much worse than at other times: the property of being morally worse at the appropriate time programs for the existence of natural features which are causally efficacious in the production of more widespread opposition to slavery, features such as the harsher conditions suffered by the slaves. Again, the program explanation can impart information which would be lost in the corresponding process explanation. The conditions of the slaves could be harsher for reasons other than the fact that the institution is morally worse, and there are possible worlds in which the conditions of the slaves are less harsh, and yet in which more widespread opposition to slavery arises (perhaps because the slaves, though well fed and better treated, are put to a morally worse use).

Sayre-McCord provides us with some other cases in the same vein as those above. He writes:

> [C]ertain regularities – for instance, honesty's engendering trust or justice's commanding allegiance, or kindness's encouraging friendship – are real regularities that are unidentifiable and inexplicable except by appeal to moral properties. Indeed, many moral virtues (such as honesty, justice, kindness) and vices (such as greed, lechery, sadism) figure in this way in our best explanations of many natural regularities. Moral explanations allow us to isolate what it is about a person or an action or an institution that leads to its having the effects it does. And these explanations rely on moral concepts that identify characteristics common to people, actions, and institutions that are uncapturable with finer-grained or differently structured categories. (1988: 276)

In effect, Sayre-McCord is suggesting that we can provide program explanations of trust in terms of honesty, of allegiance in terms of justice, and of friendship in terms of kindness, and in addition that the unavailability of these explanations would entail an explanatory loss, so that they count, in the relevant sense, as best.

In 8.9 I will evaluate the proposal that program explanation might be utilized in this way in defence of Cornell Realism. Before doing that, I'll look at another possible line of defence, that suggested by David Wiggins's notion of a 'vindicatory explanation'.

8.6 Vindicatory Explanation

What is a vindicatory explanation? The idea is due to David Wiggins (see, e.g., his 1991), and has been developed somewhat by Crispin Wright (1992: chapter 5). In what follows I rely heavily on Wright's exposition and development of Wiggins.

Why might one conclude that the subject matter of a region of discourse cannot figure ineliminably in the best explanation of our experience? One straightforward way to this conclusion would be to construe the sort of explanation in question as *causal* explanation and then advert to the fact that the subject matter of the discourse is incapable of entering into any causal relations. An example would be mathematical discourse, if the subject matter of mathematics is conceived of as abstract and so incapable, by its very nature, of entering into causal relations. Wiggins suggests that this route to the conclusion can be blocked if we question whether the explanation concerned always has to be causal. As Wright puts it, Wiggins questions the claim that:

the belief that 'People think that P because P' can be an acceptable claim only where we may conceive of the fact, or state of affairs that P as situated in the causal swim . . . and thus as a potentially direct causal source of people's beliefs about it. (1992: 184)

Rather, we should ask whether an explanation of the following form – a 'vindicatory explanation' – is possible:

> For this, that and the other reason (here the explainer specifies these), there is really nothing else to think but that P; so it is a fact that P; so given the circumstances and given the subject's cognitive capacities and opportunities and given his access to what leaves nothing else to think but that P, no wonder he believes that P. (Wiggins 1991: 66)

As an example, he cites the following vindicatory explanation of his young son's and his classmates' belief that $7 + 5 = 12$:

> The best explanation of why they all believe this is not that they have learnt and taken on trust the one truth '$7 + 5 = 12$' but (I hope and believe this):
>
> (i) As can be shown by the use of the calculating rules (and could in the end be rigorously demonstrated) it is a fact that $7 + 5 = 12$. There is nothing else to think but that $7 + 5 = 12$.
> (ii) The best explanation of my son and his classmates' shared belief is that they are going by the calculating rule that shows that there is nothing else to think but that $7 + 5 = 12$. If there is nothing else to think, then no wonder that, if their beliefs are answerable to the calculating rules, they agree in the belief that $7 + 5 = 12$. (1991: 67–8)

According to Wright, the general form of a vindicatory explanation involves the following claims:

> First, it will be contended that procedures of assessment appropriate to the discipline in which P is expressed leave, when properly applied, no option but the verdict that P; second, it will be claimed that the relevant subjects belief that P is formed and guided by the application of these procedures. (1992: 185)

At this point it becomes moot whether the invocation of vindicatory explanation really can secure an explanatory claim of the form 'Wiggins's son thinks that $7 + 5 = 12$ because $7 + 5 = 12$'. It emerges that Wiggins is not really after an explanatory claim of this form, where the 'because' is that of some genre of non-causal explanation. Rather, in formulating a vindicatory explanation he is seeking a causal explanation, though one in which the explanans is not the fact that $7 + 5 = 12$. Wiggins himself puts the point as follows:

Vindicatory explanations are causal explanations but the causality that they invoke is not one that holds between minds and values or between minds and integers. That would be a gross misunderstanding of what is got across by the explanatory schema exemplified by 'There is nothing else to think but that $7+5=12$. So no wonder they think that $7+5=12$'. (1991: 80)

And Wright elaborates:

What is cited in the vindicatory explanation is not the fact that $7+5=12$, but the fact that, in the light of the proper application of relevant rules, there is nothing else but to think that $7+5=12$; which is to say that a duly careful and attentive application of the rules of assessment appropriate to the discipline leads ineluctably to the conclusion that one of its sentences commands assent. (1992: 187)

Given this, how can Wiggins earn the right to a claim like 'We think that Hitler was depraved because Hitler was depraved'? To see how this works, we have to do two things. First, show that we can mount a vindicatory explanation in this case. Second, show how we can get from the vindicatory explanation to the claim that we think that Hitler was depraved because he was depraved.

First, the vindicatory explanation. Arguably, the procedures of assessment appropriate to moral discourse leave, when properly applied, no option but the verdict that Hitler was depraved. Moreover, it is arguable that – for some of us at least – the belief that Hitler was depraved is formed and guided by the application of these procedures (though in this case, unlike controversial cases, the route from the procedures to the verdict will presumably be swift and unproblematic).

Now we can proceed to what Wright terms 'one straightforward extension' of the notion of vindicatory explanation. We can show that the procedures of assessment appropriate to moral discourse leave, when properly applied, no option but to think of Hitler's actions as depraved. Then, in Wright's words:

[I]t may happen that, in such cases, we are inclined to transfer the epithet from the situations generated to the source and so as to describe agents, for instance, as F or in cognate terms. (1992: 194)

Now we have an explanatory chain which runs from (i) Hitler's being depraved to (ii) his performing actions which the proper application of the procedures appropriate to moral discourse leave nothing to think but that those actions are depraved, to (iii) our responding to the proper application of these procedures by believing that Hitler's actions are depraved, to (iv) our regarding Hitler himself as depraved. Wright concludes:

> Such an extension, then, of the kind of explanation envisaged by Wiggins
> can provide a perfectly acceptable natural explanation of subjects' believ-
> ing that [Hitler is depraved] in terms of the very fact that he is. (1992: 194)

Thus, it may look as though Wiggins's notion of vindicatory explanation can be adopted by the Cornell Realists. I'll evaluate this idea in
8.10.

8.7 Copp on Explanation and Justification in Ethics

David Copp (1990) takes the views of the Cornell Realists to suggest
what he calls 'confirmation theory'. Copp identifies two theses as
central to confirmation theory:

> First, a moral code or set of moral standards, or a normative moral
> theory, is an empirical theory that is confirmed to the degree that it is
> useful in explaining phenomena and is part of our best overall explana-
> tory account of the world. And second, certain moral standards are well
> confirmed on this basis. (1990: 239)

Copp argues against these claims, claiming that, even if the properties it postulated contributed to our best explanatory account of the
world, this would have no tendency whatsoever to justify the claims –
involving those properties – to be found within that theory. This would
show that moral theory could not be an empirical theory along the lines
envisaged by confirmation theory, since an empirical theory is justified
to the extent that it contributes ineliminably to our best explanatory
account of the world. In order to show this, Copp imagines a sceptic,
specifically concerned with moral standards, as opposed to non-moral
norms and standards. This sceptic *concedes* that the properties desig-
nated by moral terms such as 'good' and 'right' figure in the right kind
of way in our best explanatory account of the world, but holds that 'no
moral standard is or could be justified' (1990: 244). If this is possible,
Copp argues, then Cornell Realism is threatened, since according to
confirmation theory moral standards are justified precisely to the
extent that the properties they invoke contribute to our best explanatory account of the world.

It will help here if we add some further steps to the Cornell Realist
argument that I outlined in 8.2. These steps are analogous to the
further steps, concerning justification, which appear in the argument
of Harman's against Cornell Realism outlined in that section. The argument for Cornell Realism would now, in its entirety, go as follows:

(1) P is a real property if and only if P figures ineliminably in the best
explanation of experience.

(2) Moral properties figure ineliminably in the best explanation of experience.

Therefore:

(3) Moral properties are real properties.

Moreover:

(4) If 'P' denotes a real property and x has that property, then the judgement that x is P is justified.

So:

(5) Moral judgements are sometimes justified.

Copp in effect challenges (4): if it is possible for a sceptic to accept that 'P' denotes a real property and yet reject the idea that the judgement that x is P is justified, (4) cannot be true, so the route to the conclusion (5) is blocked. First of all, Copp attempts to show this via analogies with explanations in legal theory and etiquette. He writes:

> Alan's being in prison is explained by his having been convicted of theft. Here we invoke legal conceptions to characterize the events that led to his incarceration. But the law is not an explanatory theory in the way that sociology is. Similarly, Brenda's behaviour at a concert may be explained by her rudeness. But standards of etiquette are not explanatory postulates. If they are justified at all, they are not justified on the basis of their explanatory utility. Neither legal standards nor standards of etiquette are justified on the basis of their explanatory success, yet there are both 'legal explanations' and 'etiquette explanations'. (1990: 246)

Second, he considers the concept of the *overman*, as found in Nietzsche. He writes:

> A Nietzschean might seek to explain Stalin's ruthless behaviour on the basis that he was an (approximation to the) overman. But this would be an ordinary psychological explanation . . . Psychology could even adopt the Nietzschean concept and postulate the existence of an 'overman' personality, but we would not be tempted in the least to accept Nietzschean morality on this basis. This is because we would not regard the explanatory utility of the concept as justifying any standard that treats being overmanlike as a virtue or ideal. (1990: 247–8)

Lastly, Copp runs a related argument with respect to utilitarianism:

> The sceptic can acknowledge that we are responding to the properties of things when we call things 'good' or 'bad' or 'right' or 'wrong'. Hence,

she should admit that there may be a 'natural' property which answers to the uses of the term 'good' in our moral discourse such as, perhaps, the property of *having maximal social utility*. But she would demand a non-question begging justification for a moral code which treats this property as the good by, for example, prescribing the pursuit of states of affairs with this property as opposed to other states of affairs that could be pursued ... an antiutilitarian could concede that the term 'right' as used in his community picks out the property *maximizes social utility*. He would not thereby be committed to utilitarianism, for it would not follow that a moral standard is justified that calls on us to maximize social utility. (1990: 251)

It seems to me, though, that Copp's arguments here miss their intended targets. Note that Copp is quite explicit in claiming that the sceptic who figures in the examples above is *not* just the amoralist, who agrees that things are good, bad and so on, but who claims to see no reason for acting in accordance with those judgements. Copp admits that the possibility of this sort of amoralist sceptic would not threaten the confirmation theorist 'unless it can be shown that externalism about the relation between morality and reasons or motivations to be moral is not a theoretically viable option' (1990: 245). Since the Cornell Realists are externalists (see 9.9), and think that a metaethical theory should leave the amoralist sceptic as a genuine possibility, establishing that such a sceptic is indeed possible will do nothing to harm Cornell Realism. *But this is in fact all that Copp manages to establish.* To see this, note the following passages where Copp makes some crucial concessions:

It is quite possible that any successful explanation ... tends to confirm some proposition. For example, if Alan's being in prison is explained by his having been convicted of theft, then there is such a thing as *being convicted of theft*. The success of the legal explanation confirms the existence of the corresponding legal system. However, it has no tendency to justify the legal system. Similarly, if Brenda's behaviour at the concert is explained by her being rude, then there must be such a thing as *being rude*. The success of the explanation tends to confirm the existence of the psychological trait of rudeness. However, it has no tendency to justify any norm that proscribes rude behaviour. (1990: 247)

And:

The explanatory utility of the concept [overman] would not undermine our conviction that there is no warranted norm which prescribes that we aspire to be overpeople. (1990: 248)

And finally:

An antiutilitarian could concede that the term 'right' as used in his community picks out the property *maximizes social utility*. He would not thereby be committed to utilitarianism, for it would not follow that a moral standard is justified that calls on us to maximize social utility. (1990: 251)

Note what has happened. In each of these cases, Copp's sceptic, in order to undermine step (4) in the Cornell Realist argument, is supposed to concede that the relevant property (having being convicted of theft, being rude, being an overman, maximizing social utlity) figures in the best explanatory account of the world, even though the judgements, that Alan has been convicted of theft, that Brenda is rude, that Stalin is an overman, are all unjustified. But this is not what happens. Copp's sceptic *concedes* that the judgements, that Alan has been convicted of theft, that Brenda is rude, that Stalin is an overman, are in fact justified, but *rejects* further claims linking the justifiability of these judgements to reasons for action. Thus, the sceptic agrees that Alan has been convicted of theft, but fails to see any reason why Alan should be incarcerated; agrees that Brenda has been rude, but rejects the idea that we have a reason not to be rude at concerts; agrees that Stalin is an overman, yet rejects the idea that this gives us a reason to emulate Stalin. In each case, what we have here is simply the sort of scepticism – illustrated by the amoralist – which Cornell Realism, as an externalist view, wishes to leave open as a genuine conceptual possibility. Copp thus fails to establish the possibility of the sort of sceptic which would threaten Cornell Realism.[14]

8.8 Moral Twin-Earth and the Revived Open-Question Argument

In this section, I want to consider the semantic claim that is at the heart of Cornell Realism, and introduce some arguments that might be developed against that semantic claim.

The Cornell Realists wish to view the semantics of fundamental moral terms, such as 'good', as similar to the semantics of natural kind terms, such as 'water' and 'gold', suggested in the work of Putnam (1975) and Kripke (1980).[15] I'll begin with a very rough sketch of what Putnam and Kripke say about natural kinds.

Perhaps the easiest way into the Kripke-Putnam account of the semantics of natural kind terms is via contrasting what they have to say about the semantics of, for example, 'gold' with the views espoused by the famous empiricist philosopher John Locke (1689). Locke distinguishes between the *nominal essence* and the *real essence* of a substance such as gold. The nominal essence of gold is the cluster of superficial qualities by which we typically recognize something to be a sample of gold: something along the lines of 'a yellow, shiny, hard substance, etc.'. The real essence of gold, on the other hand, is the hidden chemical structure which typically causes samples of gold to have the superficial qualities that figure in its nominal essence (in the case of gold, the real essence is having atomic no. 79). Among the claims Locke makes about real and nominal essence is the following: the meaning of a substance term like 'gold' is given by its nominal essence. Thus, for Locke:

x is gold if and only if x is a yellow, shiny, hard substance, etc.

But this cannot be right. If Locke were right in thinking that the meaning of 'gold' is given by its nominal essence, it would be impossible for there to be something which satisfied the nominal essence of gold but which didn't turn out to be really gold. But, of course, there can be something which is not really gold even though it satisfies the description of its nominal essence. In fact, there actually is such a thing: fool's gold or iron pyrites. Kripke and Putnam suggest that we should not take the description of gold's nominal essence to *give the meaning* of 'gold'; rather we should see that description as *fixing the reference* of the term 'gold'. The description fixes the reference via a clause such as the following:

GOLD: x is gold if and only if x is made of that stuff which is actually dominantly causally responsible for our perceptions of co-instantiations of yellowness, shininess, hardness, etc.

The stuff in question is that which has atomic number 79. Since a sample of iron pyrites doesn't have this atomic number, it doesn't count as a sample of gold.

The famous 'Twin-Earth' thought experiment is supposed to suggest that a similar semantic account should be given for 'water'. Twin-Earth is a planet in a distant part of the universe which is identical to Earth except for the fact that the stuff to which the Twin-Earthers apply the word 'water', although it has the same superficial characteristics as our water, has a completely different molecular structure, XYZ. Suppose an Earthling is transported to Twin-Earth, points to a sample of the clear, odourless liquid that falls from the sky in Twin-Wales, and says that the substance is water. Has he spoken truly? According to Putnam, our intuition is that he has not: since Earthers refer to H_2O by 'water', and the substance pointed to is XYZ, he has spoken falsely. Likewise, suppose an Earther and a Twin-Earther disagree about whether 'water' should be applied to some sample. Are they really disagreeing, or just talking at cross purposes? According to Putnam, our intuitions are that they are talking at cross purposes: since 'water' as used by the Earther refers to H_2O, while 'water' as used by the Twin-Earther refers to XYZ, there is no real disagreement. It would be like two speakers disagreeing about the location of the referent of 'Archie', where one of them uses the name to refer to a dog in Adelaide while the other uses the name to refer to a man (Archie Dover) in Glasgow. Putnam's claim is that these intuitions will be accounted for if we view the description 'clear, odourless liquid that falls from the sky, etc.' as fixing the reference of the Earthers' 'water' as follows:

WATER (Earth): x is water if and only if x is composed of that stuff which is actually dominantly causally responsible for Earthers' perceptions of wetness and the other features which figure in water's nominal essence.

Likewise for the Twin-Earther:

WATER (Twin-Earth): x is water if and only if x is composed of that stuff which is actually dominantly causally responsible for Twin-Earthers' perceptions of wetness and the other features which figure in water's nominal essence.

In the Earthers' case, it is H_2O which plays the appropriate causal role, whereas in the Twin-Earthers' it is XYZ. So the Twin-Earther refers to XYZ, and the Earther refers to H_2O, so that our intuitions about the Twin-Earth cases are accommodated.

According to the Cornell Realists, moral terms, such as 'good', denote natural kinds which are not reducible to any other kind, in much the same way that 'water' and 'gold' denote natural kinds. Terence Horgan and Mark Timmons (1990, 1992a, 1992b) have developed a sophisti-cated argument, based on a thought experiment concerning what they call 'moral Twin-Earth', which attempts to undermine the claim that the correct semantics for 'good' is similar to that for natural kind terms like 'water' and 'gold'.

Horgan and Timmons note that since the Cornell Realists do not claim that moral terms are synonymous with naturalistic predicates, Moore's OQA cannot even get started. Since 'H_2O' is not held to be synonymous with 'water', there is no reason to expect the question

(a) Is x, which is H_2O, water?

to be closed (where 'A question is open if and only if it is possible for someone to completely understand the question, and yet not know its answer; otherwise it is closed' (1992b: 155)). So the fact that:

(b) Is x, which is N, good?

is open, exerts no pressure on a version of naturalism which sees 'good' as standing in the same relation to 'N' as 'water' stands in to 'H_2O'. However, Horgan and Timmons develop a revised version of Moore's open-question argument, a version that is intended to apply to theories which view 'good' and 'N' as non-synonymous terms nevertheless denoting the same natural property.

Horgan and Timmons point out that although the question

(a) Is x, which is H_2O, water?

can be open even if the Kripke-Putnam account of the semantics of 'water' is correct, the following question must nevertheless be closed:

(c) Is x, which is composed of that stuff which is actually dominantly causally responsible for Earthers' perceptions of wetness and the other features which figure in water's nominal essence, water?

This is because, although the description which figures in water's nominal essence only fixes the reference of 'water', it does so via figuring in a more complex clause, that given on the right-hand side of WATER (Earth) which does give the meaning of 'water', as used by Earthers. This is of course no problem for the Kripke-Putnam style account of the semantics of 'water', since the claim that the meaning of 'water' as used by Earthers is given by WATER (Earth), and so the claim that (c) is closed, meshes perfectly with the relevant intuitions about the Twin-Earth scenario.

Suppose, then, that some analogue of WATER (Earth) and WATER (Twin-Earth) is true for the Earthers' term 'good'. This will be something like:

GOOD (Earth): x is good if and only if x possesses a property M
with the following causal role: its presence typically leads Earthers
to pursue things that they judge to be M: its presence typically leads
Earthers to encourage others to pursue things that they judge to be M;
judgements about the presence of M are accorded great, perhaps even
overriding, importance by Earthers, and so on.

Likewise for the Twin-Earthers' term 'good':

GOOD (Twin-Earth): x is good if and only if x possesses a property
M with the following causal role: its presence typically leads Twin-
Earthers to pursue things that they judge to be M: its presence
typically leads Twin-Earthers to encourage others to pursue things
that they judge to be M; judgements about the presence of M are

accorded great, perhaps even overriding, importance by Twin-Earthers, and so on.

Then we would expect to find that our intuitions about 'moral Twin-Earth' match those of the Twin-Earth experiment concerning 'water'. But what is moral Twin-Earth? Horgan and Timmons describe the twin planets in the moral case as follows:

> [Earthers'] uses of 'good' and 'right' are regulated by certain functional properties; and . . . as a matter of fact these are consequentalist properties whose functional essence is captured by some specific consequentialist normative theory . . . Tc (1992b: 163)

> Twin-Earthers' . . . uses of twin-moral terms are causally regulated by certain natural properties distinct from those that regulate [Earthian] moral discourse. The properties tracked by twin English moral terms are also functional properties, whose essence is functionally characterizable by means of a normative moral theory. But these are non-consequentialist moral properties, whose functional essence is captured by some specific deontological theory . . . Td. (1992b: 164)

Now suppose that an Earther goes to Twin-Earth and 'disagrees' with one of the locals about the application of 'good' to some type of act: the Earther says 'euthanasia is good', while the Twin-Earther says 'euthanasia is not good'. If GOOD (Earth) and GOOD (Twin-Earth) accurately capture the meanings of their respective uses of 'good', we ought to find ourselves with the intuition that there is no real disagreement between them, that they are talking at cross purposes. Horgan and Timmons point out, however, that our intuitions about this case point in the opposite direction:

> If [GOOD (Earth) and GOOD (Twin-Earth)] were true, then recognition of these differences [between the properties that play the relevant causal roles in GOOD (Earth) and GOOD (Twin-Earth)] ought to result in its seeming rather silly, to members of each group, to engage in inter-group debate about goodness – about whether it conforms to normative theory Tc or Td. . . . But such inter-theoretic group debate would surely strike both groups not as silly but as quite appropriate, because they would regard one another as differing in moral beliefs and moral theory, not in meaning. (1992b: 166)[16]

Thus, our intuitions are completely at odds with what we would expect if GOOD (Earth) and GOOD (Twin-Earth) were correct. Thus, this outcome constitutes 'strong empirical evidence' (1992b: 166) against GOOD (Earth) and GOOD (Twin-Earth), and against any metaethical theory, such as Cornell Realism, which incorporates them. Or, to put the point in another way: if the semantics of 'good', as used on Earth, is correctly given by GOOD (Earth), the question (c*) Is y, which has a property M such that its presence typically leads Earthers to pursue things that they judge to be M; its presence typically leads Earthers to encourage others to pursue things that they judge to be M; and judgements about the presence of M are accorded great, perhaps even overriding, importance by Earthers, and so on, good?

ought to be closed. But as the moral Twin-Earth thought experiment shows, (c*) is actually open (this is why Horgan and Timmons describe their argument as a 'revived' version of the open-question argument). So GOOD (Earth) cannot accurately describe the semantics of 'good', as used on Earth. Likewise for GOOD (Twin-Earth) and 'good', as used on Twin-Earth.

How plausible is this 'revived' OQA? Recall from chapter 2 that Moore's deployment of the OQA against definitional naturalism was undermined by Frankena's objection, to the effect that the argument simply begs the question against the definitional naturalist. Arguably, the revived open-question argument advanced by Horgan and Timmons falls prey to a similar type of objection. The Horgan and Timmons argument works only if our conviction that the question (c*) is open is well grounded, or, equivalently, that our intuitions about the moral Twin-Earth case are correct. But to make either of these assumptions is already to presuppose the falsity of the idea that the semantics of 'good' is given by the likes of GOOD (Earth) and GOOD (Twin-Earth). Thus, the Horgan and Timmons argument only works against the Cornell Realist account of the semantics of 'good' if it presupposes the falsity of that view, and so begs the question against it.

Recall, too, that although the Frankena objection shows that the OQA does not provide a knock-down objection to the definitional naturalist, there are modified versions of the argument, such as that suggested by Darwall, Gibbard and Railton, which merely pose a challenge to the definitional naturalist. This version of the argument begs no questions, since it relies only on the claim that we have the intuitions in question, not on the stronger claim that those intuitions are correct. Can we use an analogue of this weaker, but non-question-begging, version of the OQA to at least exert some leverage on the Cornell Realist account of the semantics of 'good'? I cannot pursue this interesting question here, but must leave it as an exercise for the reader.

8.9 Moral Program Explanation Evaluated

In 8.5 I outlined the idea that the notion of program explanation, as developed by Jackson and Pettit, might be used by Cornell Realism as a defence against Harman. In this section, I'll evaluate that idea.

I looked at four cases: the case of Albert, Jane and the wrongness of Albert's act; the case of Hitler's moral depravity; the case of slavery's being morally worse in a particular historical era; and the cases suggested by Sayre-McCord, honesty and trust, justice and allegiance, and kindness and friendship. I'll consider objections to some of these particular examples, then I'll go on to make some general comments about the application of the idea of program explanation to the moral case.

In order for the notion of program explanation to get a grip, two things need to be the case: first, there must be genuine regularities for the program explanation to explain; second, the program explanations must be, in the relevant sense, 'best'. Brian Leiter, in his 2001 paper, is sceptical about whether Sayre-McCord's examples can succeed on both of these counts. With respect to the first:

> Is 'honesty's engendering trust' a 'real regularity'? To the contrary, it seems honesty just as often engenders not trust, but annoyance, bitterness, or alienation; people, as is well-known, do not want those around them to be *too* honest. Indeed, someone who is too honest may often be thought untrustworthy, precisely because he or she cannot be expected to guard one's secrets and keep one's counsel. [Also] ... it seems that justice provokes opposition just as often as it produces allegiance: many people have little interest in just arrangements, and so resist them at every step. Furthermore, do we necessarily befriend the kindly, or do we simply appreciate them – or perhaps take advantage of them? (2001: 95)

It is not clear to me that this objection is compelling. What Leiter says about the 'regularities' offered by Sayre-McCord is fine so far as it goes, but why couldn't Sayre-McCord respond by narrowing the scope of the explanation, not (as Leiter anticipates (2001: 95, n.57)) by spelling out *ceteris paribus* clauses, but by using moral concepts in providing a fuller specification of the explanans and explananda? For example, although there may be no straightforward regularity between honesty and trust, there does seem to be a regularity between *appropriate* honesty and the trust of *good* people: plausibly, trust is engendered in morally virtuous people by appropriate levels of honesty; likewise, justice would seem to command allegiance *among the just*, and kindness encourage friendship *among the decent*. Does the use of moral concepts, such as 'appropriateness', 'goodness', 'justice' and 'decency', invalidate the relevant program explanations? The circularity would be fatal were the Cornell Realists attempting to provide a reductive analysis of moral vocabulary. But of course they are not. The real worry is that the appearance of moral concepts in this way renders the explanations utterly *trivial*. But it is not clear that the proffered explanations are actually trivial. They might be if the Cornell Realist had no account of justice other than 'that which commands allegiance among the just'. But the Cornell Realist will reply that he has a first-order normative theory about the nature of justice (the precise details of which are not relevant here). So long as he has such a theory he can pick out just arrangements and then determine whether there is an empirical regularity between them and the allegiance of the just. Likewise for the other cases. So it seems to me that if Leiter's first objection to Sayre-McCord is ultimately to be pressed home, at the very least some more work is required: specifically, an argument to the effect that the 'restricted' regularities picked out in part by the use of moral concepts admit of no non-trivial program explanation.

Leiter's second line of objection runs:

> Do we need moral facts to explain these putative regularities – or just the assumption that people who believe others are honest will trust them? In fact, surely the latter is a better explanation, for if there is a regularity here, it requires only the perception of honesty, rather than its actual presence. Perceived honesty should, it seems, engender trust as readily as real honesty, while making real honesty the basis of the regularity will leave out of the regularity's explanatory scope those cases where people trust those who only seem honest, but really are not. Similarly what people believe or perceive to be 'just' probably does engender allegiance, whereas the regularity collapses when we talk about real justice, which is often a threat to privileged groups. (2001: 96)

Leiter proposes here that (i) there is a regularity between beliefs in honesty and the formation of trust and (ii) the explanation 'trust is engendered by beliefs in honesty' is better than explanations which cite honesty itself. It is not clear to me that either of these claims is compelling. First, is there really a regularity between beliefs in honesty and the formation of trust? On the assumption that you cannot accurately describe yourself as trusting someone for whom you have contempt, and given that those who lack the appropriate moral virtues are likely to have contempt for those they believe to be honest, there appears to be no straightforward regularity of the sort alluded to by Leiter.[17] Second, why think that Leiter's explanation is better than 'trust in the virtuous is engendered by honesty'? If we had only the explanation proffered by Leiter we would be explanatorily impoverished: we would not know that there are two distinct ways in which trust can be engendered, on the one hand by honesty itself, and on the other by *mere* seeming honesty. The availability of the program explanation in terms of honesty itself would allow us to signal which of these distinct possibilities is actually the case. To be sure, the explanation of trust in terms of honesty itself won't explain the cases in which someone trusts someone simply because they seem honest. So there is something Leiter's explanation can do which the program explanation can't: but, as I pointed out, there is also something the program explanation can do which Leiter's cannot. Arguably, similar considerations apply to Leiter's comments concerning justice and allegiance. Among the vicious, a belief to the effect that something or someone is just is not likely to foster allegiance to that person or thing: it is more likely to foster an affectation of allegiance combined with disguised animosity. And discarding the program explanation would leave us unable to record the difference between cases in which justice itself, as opposed to mere seeming justice, is the ultimate explanation of the formation of allegiance.

Leiter also objects to Sturgeon's claim that we can explain why Hitler did what he did because he was depraved (and thereby explain our belief that he is depraved in terms of his actually being depraved). Leiter writes:

> My own feeling is that if I were seeking an explanation for Hitler's conduct and was offered the explanation 'He was morally depraved', I would take such an answer to be a bit of a joke: a repetition of the datum rather than an explanation. (2001: 94, n.53)

This does seem trivial, but it may be that Sturgeon hasn't chosen the best example to show how facts about character can enter into explanations. Take a less extreme case: Jones, say, is visibly rude to a guest speaker during a philosophy seminar, and leaves halfway through, slamming the door behind him. A new graduate student asks one of his colleagues for an explanation of this, and gets the reply 'because he is a rude, unpleasant man'. Is the explanation of Jones's behaviour in terms of a fact about his character vacuous? It seems not: it rules out the possibility that he behaved that way, perhaps because, although normally polite, he was suffering from unbearable stress or from the onset of a mental illness.[18] Suppose also that Smith believes that Jones is a rude, unpleasant individual. Can we give a 'best' program explanation of Smith's belief in terms of the fact that Jones is rude and unpleasant? That is, can we give a program explanation whose unavailability would result in an explanatory loss? It seems we can. The unavailability of the program explanation would result in our losing modal information to the effect that in nearby possible worlds in which Jones behaves himself during talks by visiting speakers, but in which he is abusive to his students, Smith still forms the belief that Jones is rude and unpleasant. This suggests that facts about character can play a role in program explanations whose unavailability would result in an explanatory loss.

What about Sturgeon's slavery example: the claim that widespread opposition to slavery arose when it did because slavery at that time was much worse than at other times? I outlined earlier how one might make a case for the claim that a 'best' program explanation could be mounted here. Leiter doubts that any useful explanation in terms of slavery's being morally worse can be given. Leiter criticizes Brink's idea (1989:

187) – essentially the same as Sturgeon's – that political instability and social protest in pre-1990 South Africa can be explained in terms of the fact that racial oppression existed in South Africa over the relevant period. Leiter has two criticisms of the Brink-Sturgeon claim. First, he doubts whether the explanatory statement is even true. He does this by using Carl Hempel's 'predictability' requirement on explanation:

> Any rationally acceptable answer to the question 'Why did X occur?' must offer information which shows that X was to be expected – if not definitely … then at least with reasonable probability. (Hempel 1965: 369, quoted in Leiter 2001 at 96–7)

But the fact that a particular society is racially oppressive seems to have no 'cash value' when it comes to prediction:

> Racial oppression existed *for decades* in South Africa without the signifi-cant political unrest and social protest that finally marked the collapse of apartheid. Racial oppression in the American South was similar; it existed for nearly a hundred years after the Civil War with only episodic and ineffectual resistance. From the standpoint of the historian, then, what exactly is the 'distinct and privileged' explanatory role of racial oppression? What predictions, if any, follow from knowing that a society is racially oppressive? Does it not seem, instead, that we have to turn precisely to the particular lower-order social, economic, and political facts to really explain why social protest arose against racial oppression at the times it actually did? (2001: 97)

In addition, even if such an explanation were plausible, it would still be unclear whether it was better than an alternative explanation in which the work is done by the claim 'that people believe racial oppression to be unjust, regardless of whether it really is unjust' (2001: 97). Thus, Leiter is sceptical as to whether the slavery example can do any work for the Cornell Realist.

Initially, Leiter's objection seems quite powerful, though he perhaps slightly overstates the case: one would not expect racial oppression to lead to social unrest *instantaneously*, in the way that the temperature of the glass leads to its cracking. So the fact that it took decades for social unrest to develop is neither here nor there. But it does seem prima facie plausible to claim that there is not a sufficient regularity here to merit a program explanation. However, Leiter effectively undermines this prima facie claim himself when he says that 'we have to turn precisely to the particular lower-order social, economic, and political facts to really explain why social protest arose against racial oppression at the times it actually did' (2001: 97). Given this, and given that racial oppression programs for the existence of a set of social, economic and political facts of this kind, it will follow that there will be a regularity which after all ensures that we can give a program explanation of social unrest in terms of racial oppression. And, as shown earlier, we will be able to make out a case for the claim that the unavailability of this explanation would result in an explanatory loss, so that it counts as best.[19]

Thus, the objections raised by critics such as Leiter against the particular examples proffered by sympathizers of Cornell Realism can perhaps be assuaged by application of the notion of program explanation along the lines I have suggested. But now I'll suggest that program explanation ultimately does *not* afford Cornell Realism a way of entering irreducible moral facts into our ontological inventory.

The main problem which the invocation of program explanation faces in this context is as follows. The question we are considering is whether higher-level properties of a certain sort can earn their ontological rights by figuring in 'best' program explanations. We can dramatize the question by imagining ourselves to have unlimited epistemic access to the facts about the distribution of lower-level properties and then asking whether program explanation can be invoked to justify the inclusion of the relevant higher-level properties in our ontology. The answer appears to be negative. In all of the cases in which I have argued that program explanations are available and are 'best', their being 'best' – such that the lack thereof results in an explanatory loss – is a direct consequence of some *epistemic limitation* of ours vis-à-vis facts about lower-level properties.[20] Take the case of the temperature and the glass, which I have used as a model for the application of program explanation to the moral cases. Recall that the program explanation is 'best' because it conveys the following information, not conveyed by process explanations: (i) that the water is at boiling temperature, and (ii) that the glass would still crack in relevantly similar possible worlds.

Note first that (i) is actually not relevant in the cases where we are concerned with whether program explanation can confer ontological rights. If we *assume* that there is a fact about the temperature of the molecules, knowledge of which would be lost given the unavailability of a program explanation, then we are already assuming what we set out to prove: namely, that there are higher-order facts and properties of the relevant kind. To assume that not being aware of P constitutes an epistemic limitation is already to assume that P is a fact. 'Epistemic limitations' of this kind simply are not relevant in contexts in which we are attempting to earn ontological rights for P-type facts.

Thus the program explanation which explains the glass's cracking in terms of its temperature would be 'best' only for someone who lacked information of type (ii). But, presumably, when we are in the business of asking about which properties earn their ontological rights, we should be concerned with what properties would figure in the world as seen from a viewpoint in which all such epistemic limitations were transcended. Thus, the question to ask in this context is not whether the unavailability of program explanation would be 'best' for creatures in some limited epistemic predicament vis-à-vis lower-level properties, but rather whether God – someone with no such limitations – would suffer an explanatory loss if deprived of the relevant program explanations.[21] Given that God knows all of the facts about the relevant process explanations and the modal information about how things would go in relevantly similar possible worlds, it is clear that he would not. How, then, could program explanation earn ontological rights for higher-order properties? Likewise, if we assume that God knows all of the naturalistic explanations of moral beliefs,[22] as well as modal information about how things would go in relevantly similar possible worlds, it is clear that the unavailability of program explanations would not result in his suffering an explanatory loss.[23] Thus, program explanations which invoke moral facts and properties do not count as best for God; thus, they do not count as best in the right sort of way for their availability to earn ontological rights for the higher-order properties in which they trade.[24]

I suggest, then, that program explanation cannot be invoked in such a way as to underpin the Cornell Realist's claim that irreducible moral properties can earn their ontological rights by figuring in our best explanatory account of the world. In the next section, I return to the question of whether the notion of vindicatory explanation can be put to good use on behalf of Cornell Realism.

8.10 Vindicatory Explanation Evaluated

In 8.6, I outlined the idea that a vindicatory explanation of our believing that Hitler was depraved might be mounted in terms of his being depraved. But the important question, of course, is whether the relevant vindicatory explanations are 'best'. An explanation is best if not having it would result in a genuine explanatory loss. An explanation will not be best if there is another and 'better' explanation of the same phenomena. So, in order to evaluate the idea that a vindicatory explanation of moral beliefs is best, we need to have some idea of what features make one explanation better than another. We can extract some intuitively plausible suggestions on this from Thagard (1978).[25] Thagard identifies two virtues which theoretical explanations can possess, *consilience* and *simplicity*. Consilience is explained as follows: 'one theory is more consilient than another if it explains more classes of facts than the other does' (Thagard 1978: 79). Consilience thus corresponds, approximately, to what Crispin Wright terms *wide cosmological role*:

> Let the *width of cosmological role* of the subject matter of a discourse be measured by the extent to which citing the kinds of states of affairs with

which it deals is potentially contributive to the explanation of things other than, or other than via, our being in attitudinal states which take such states of affairs as objects. (1992: 196)

Simplicity is a measure, not of what gets explained, but of what does the explaining. One explanation is simpler than another if it explains at least as much whilst making fewer assumptions, without invoking a wider range of types of states of affairs to do the explanatory work. How do considerations of consilience and simplicity combine to determine whether one explanation is better than another? There are various possibilities, including the following: if E1 and E2 are alike in point of consilience and E1 is simpler than E2, then E1 is the better explanation; if E1 and E2 are alike in point of simplicity and E2 explains more types of things than E1, then E2 is better than E1; if E1 is simpler than E2 *and* E1 explains more types of things than E2, then E1 is clearly better than E2. It is this last possibility that concerns us here. We can argue that naturalistic explanations of moral beliefs are clearly better than vindicatory explanations in virtue of instantiating this possibility. I'll show first that vindicatory explanations score really badly in point of consilience and width of cosmological role. Since naturalistic explanations are clearly simpler than vindicatory explanations, since moral facts and states of affairs do not figure among the explanatory factors they invoke, it will follow that so long as the states of affairs invoked in naturalistic explanations explain at least some things other than moral beliefs, they – the naturalistic explanations – will count as better than vindicatory explanations. Vindicatory explanations will thus fail to earn ontological rights for irreducible moral properties and states of affairs.

Wright makes out a compelling case for the claim that moral facts and states of affairs have maximally narrow cosmological role. He invites us to compare the property of wetness, as possessed by some rocks, with the property of wrongness, as possessed by, say, the hoodlums' actions:

Reference to the wetness of the rocks can, uncontroversially, contribute towards explaining at least four kinds of thing:
(1) My perceiving, and hence believing, that the rocks are wet.
(2) A small (prelinguistic) child's interests in his hands after he has touched the rocks.
(3) My slipping and falling.
(4) The abundance of lichen growing on them.
The wetness of the rocks can be ascribed, that is, each of four kinds of consequence: cognitive effects, precognitive-sensuous effects, effects on us as physically interactive agents, and certain brute effects on inanimate organisms and matter. By contrast, the wrongness of that act, although citing it may feature in a vindicatory explanation of my moral

disapproval of the action, and hence of the further effects on the world which my disapproval may generate, would seem to have no part to play in the *direct* (propositional-attitude unmediated) explanation of any effects of the latter three sorts: precognitive sensuous, interactive, and brute. (1992: 197)

Thus, since naturalistic explanations of moral beliefs are clearly simpler than vindicatory explanations, all we need show to conclude that naturalistic explanations are better is that the states of affairs invoked in naturalistic explanations do not have this maximally narrow cosmological role. And, unsurprisingly, it turns out that they don't:

[T]he mechanisms employed by naturalistic explanations explain much more than ... moral beliefs and observations ... This should hardly be surprising: after all, naturalistic explanations were generally proffered as accounts of other phenomena first; only later did they find application in the moral cases. For example, the causal mechanisms underlying Freudian explanations work to explain not only morality, but also various neuroses as well as the psychopathologies of everyday life. The application of evolutionary explanation to moral phenomena is a relatively recent and sometimes contentious matter; by contrast, evolutionary accounts of physiological characteristics, social phenomena, and other things abound, and many are now well-established. (Leiter 2001: 88)

Of course, at this stage one could mount a defence of Cornell Realism by arguing that the naturalistic explanations, in terms of lower-order natural facts, are no good as explanations. Such an argument is unlikely to succeed, but more importantly this suggestion is in a sense simply not to the point, since the Cornell Realists have no desire to undermine these naturalistic styles of explanation: they want to argue that even *given* the availability of the relevant sort of naturalistic explanation, irreducible moral properties can still earn their ontological rights by figuring in 'best' moral explanations.

Thus, I conclude that moral vindicatory explanations are highly unlikely to count as best. The Cornell Realist cannot use the notion of vindicatory explanation to establish (2) or to see off Harman's (2a). Given that the same held true of the attempt to use the notion of program explanation to these ends, we can say that the Cornell Realist argument for moral realism, and the Cornell Realist defence of moral realism against Harman's challenge, both fail. In the next chapter I move on to consider some versions of reductionist naturalistic cognitivism.

8.11 Further Reading

The best way into the debate is via the Harman-Sturgeon dialectic: Harman (1977, chapters 1 and 2, 1986); Sturgeon (1986a, 1986b, 1988, 1991, 1992, 2006a, 2006b). For more on the Cornell Realist side, see Brink (1989), Boyd (1988), and Sayre-McCord (1988). For commentary on the debate see Blackburn (1991, 1993a, essay 11), Cohen (1997), Copp (1990), Dworkin (1996), the papers by Leiter and Svavarsdottir in Leiter (ed.) (2001b), Quinn (1986) and Snare (1984). Leiter (2001a) provides a useful overview of the debate, as well as some interesting arguments against Cornell Realism. Wright (1992, chapter 5) is indispensable for anyone wishing to get a clear picture of the issues. For program explanation, see Jackson and Pettit (1990) and the other papers in the 'Psychological and Social Explanation' section of Jackson, Pettit and Smith (2004). For further debate about the argument of 8.9, see Nelson (2006), Miller (2009), Bloomfield (2009) and Field (2010). For vindicatory explanation, see Wiggins (1991), Wright (1992, chapter 5), and Wiggins (1996). The 'moral Twin-Earth' arguments can be found in Horgan and Timmons (1990, 1992a, 1992b and 2000). For reactions, see Gampel (1997), Copp (2000) and Merli (2002). Harman's recent work on moral character is also relevant: see Harman (1999), Athanassoulis (2000), Harman (2000). For a useful little guide to recent work on moral explanation, see Majors (2007), and for an excellent paper broadly consonant with the line on moral explanation defended in this chapter, see Sinclair (2011).

9

Naturalism II – Reductionism

In the previous chapter, I discussed one important type of contemporary cognitivist naturalism, that defended by the Cornell Realists. In this chapter, I move on to consider some other contemporary versions of cognitivist naturalism: Railton's reductionism, and the reductionism implied by 'network-style analyses' of the sort proposed by Frank Jackson and Philip Pettit. I will begin with a brief account of the nature of Railton's naturalism, followed by an account of how his naturalism differs from that of the Cornell Realists. I will then outline his theory of non-moral value, before explaining how it provides the foundation for his account of moral rightness. I will then consider some of the main objections that have been levelled against Railton's position. I then provide an outline of 'network-style' reductionism, and attempt to assess some objections that have recently been levelled against it. Inter alia, I discuss two important debates in moral psychology, between internalism and externalism, and Rationalism and Anti-Rationalism.

9.1 Methodological Naturalism and Substantive Naturalism

Railton distinguishes between two different types of naturalism, which he calls *methodological naturalism* and *substantive naturalism*. Railton characterizes methodological naturalism as follows:

> Methodological naturalism holds that philosophy does not possess a distinctive, a priori method able to yield substantive truths that, in principle, are not subject to any sort of empirical test, Instead, a methodological naturalist believes that philosophy should proceed *a posteriori*, in tandem

with – perhaps as a particularly abstract and general part of – the broadly empirical inquiry carried on in the natural and social sciences. (1989: 155–6)

And:

A methodological naturalist is someone who adopts an a posteriori, explanatory approach to an area of human practice, such as epistemology, semantics, or ethics. (1993b: 315)

Whereas methodological naturalism is a view about *method*, substantive naturalism is a view about *substance*:

Substantive naturalism is . . . a view about philosophical conclusions. A substantive naturalist advances a philosophical account of some domain of human language or practice that provides an interpretation of its central concepts in terms amenable to empirical inquiry. (1989: 156)

And:

A substantive naturalist is someone who proposes a semantic interpretation of the concepts in some area of practice or discourse in terms of properties or relations that would 'pull their weight' within empirical science. (1993b: 315)

Methodological naturalism and substantive naturalism are distinct positions. Suppose one argued, on a priori grounds, that 'good' could be analysed as, say, 'contributing overall to the greatest happiness of the greatest number'. This is the sort of analytic naturalism that was the main target of Moore's OQA. On this view, 'good' would be interpreted as standing for a property, the property of contributing overall to the greatest happiness of the greatest number, which figures in an empirical science (psychology). Since the grounds for this interpretation of 'good' would be courtesy of an a priori *philosophical analysis*, this would be an example of a view that was substantively naturalist but *not* methodologically naturalist.

Alternatively, one could be a methodological naturalist whilst rejecting any form of substantive naturalism. One could start by adopting an a posteriori, explanatory approach to moral discourse, and conclude that the best account of moral judgement is *non-cognitivist*. Since predicates such as 'good' would, on such a non-cognitivist account, not be interpreted as standing for any sort of property, a fortiori they would not be interpreted as standing for properties that 'pull their weight' in empirical science. We might even combine methodological naturalism with the denial of substantive naturalism by combining methodological naturalism with substantive non-naturalism. According to this sort of view, 'good', and the like, stand for *sui generis* non-natural properties that do not pull their weight in empirical theory.

Finally, one might embrace *both* methodological naturalism and substantive naturalism. In fact, this is what Railton proposes. He makes it clear that it is his commitment to methodological naturalism which is the more fundamental of the two (1989: 156, 1993b: 316). So what does Railton's methodological naturalism consist in, and how might it lead to a form of substantive naturalism? The answer to this question lies in what Railton calls the 'generic stratagem of naturalistic realism'. This is:

> . . . to postulate a realm of facts in virtue of the contribution they would make to the *a posteriori* explanation of features of our experience. (1986a: 171–2)

The postulation of this realm of facts proceeds via a *reforming definition*: we propose, for example, that 'right' be interpreted as standing for some naturalistic property N, and then investigate whether N contributes to the *a posteriori* explanation of features of our experience. There is no suggestion that 'right', as actually used by speakers of English, stands for or means N. The fact that the question 'Is an x which is N also right?' strikes us as open may jeopardize this interpretation of 'good' construed as a piece of descriptive analysis, but the 'definition' offered here 'is revisable, as well as revisionist, and must earn its place by facilitating the construction of worthwhile theories' (1989: 157). Thus, 'our naturalist's central claims are, at bottom, synthetic rather than analytic' (ibid.). Thus, Railton's methodological naturalism consists in his proposing a reforming definition of moral concepts, a definition which must be vindicated by the capacity of the reforming definition to contribute to the a posteriori explanation of features of our experience. Whether or not a reforming definition is ultimately acceptable is an a posteriori matter.[1]

9.2 Hegemonic and Non-Hegemonic Naturalism

We'll return to the question of Railton's reforming definition and its explanatory value in due course. First, though, we can see how Railton would dispel one potential line of criticism. This will afford us more than one way of contrasting Railton's naturalism with that of the Cornell Realists.

Railton points out that the methodological naturalism which he adopts might in principle lead to the view that moral properties are simultaneously natural and *sui generis*, that they are *irreducible* natural properties which, though supervenient upon Natural properties (in the sense defined in the previous chapter), are able to pull their weight in empirical explanations in their own right. That is, methodological naturalism might in principle lead to the non-reductionist naturalism of the Cornell Realists discussed in the previous chapter. Railton makes it clear, though, that he prefers a form of *reductionist naturalism* to the non-reductionist naturalism of the Cornell Realists:

> [M]y naturalist ... entertains a reductionist hypothesis, a synthetic identification of the property of moral value with a complex non-moral property. He does so because he believes the identification can contribute to our understanding of morality and its place in our world – including such matters as semantic and epistemic access to moral properties – while preserving important features of the normative role of moral value. (1993b: 317)

Does it follow that Railton's naturalism, since reductionist, is motivated by some 'hegemonic' view, according to which the world contains only natural properties, or by some 'scientistic' view, according to which the world contains only the properties dealt with in the sciences and that 'everything worth knowing or saying about the world and our place in it . . . belongs to scientific theory' (1989: 159)? Railton is emphatic that his brand of naturalism is neither 'hegemonic' nor 'scientistic':

> It can be informative to find a reduction basis for a range of properties R within a range of properties S, even without any claim to the effect that S is utterly comprehensive. A reduction of R to S could none the less tell us about the place of R in the world, and would be of special interest if there existed a well-developed theory of properties of kind S, or if properties of kind S were less problematic in some way than those of kind R seemed (before the reduction) to be. (1993b: 318)

Neither is Railton's reductionist naturalist committed to a 'test of reality' of the sort criticized by Thomas Nagel when he writes:

> . . . it begs the question to assume that this [scientific] sort of explanatory necessity is the test of reality for values . . . To assume that only what has to be included in the best causal theory of the world is real is to assume that there are no irreducibly normative truths. (quoted at Railton 1989: 160)

Railton's naturalism is 'non-hegemonic': he does not presuppose in advance of a posteriori inquiry some 'test of reality', the capacity to meet which will determine the fate of a particular region of human practice. There is thus no scope for Nagel's charge of question-begging to be levelled at Railton's naturalist.

In the previous chapter, we saw how the debate between Harman and the Cornell Realists turned on the assumption, common to both, that the question of the reality of moral properties turns on the question whether moral properties figure ineliminably in the best explanation of experience. Railton, though he seeks to show that properties with the normative role of moral properties can also have a genuine explanatory role, does not assume that explanatory potency provides a sufficient condition for the reality of a species of property.[2] We can thus point to two differences between the naturalism of Railton and the naturalism of the Cornell Realists. First, whereas the Cornell Realists hold the *non-reductionist* view that moral properties are natural, irreducible and *sui generis* properties which play an explanatory role within empirical theorizing in their own right, Railton holds the *reductionist* view that moral properties are reducible to complex Natural properties, via a synthetic property identity delivered courtesy of an empirically justifiable reforming definition. Second, whereas some at least of the Cornell Realists flirt with the idea that inference to the best explanation provides a license for a realistic treatment of an area of human practice, Railton's program does not rely on inference to the best explanation.

9.3 Varieties of Revisionism

We have seen that Railton's project proceeds via a reforming definition of moral terms like 'right' in terms of a complex naturalistic property N. There is no claim to the effect that this is a descriptively adequate account of the meaning of 'right'. Thus, there is no claim to the effect that the judgement that x is right is, as a matter of fact, equivalent in meaning to the judgement that x is N. Rather, the idea is that we revise our understanding of 'right' so that the two judgements coincide in meaning. (Again, since the revision has to be justified on a posteriori grounds, the question whether the two judgements ought to be viewed as coinciding in meaning turns out to be an a posteriori matter also.) Suppose that the reforming definition turns out to be empirically justifiable. Then Railton's account implies that the content of everyday judgements concerning moral rightness has to be revised in terms that invoke the naturalistic property N. Railton is thus a revisionist about the content of everyday moral judgements. Call this *surface-content revisionism*. However, there is another sense of 'revisionism', under which Railton comes out as a non-revisionist. This concerns the underlying semantics of a discourse. As we've noted before, the surface syntax of moral discourse suggests that its underlying semantics is to be given straightforwardly in terms of facts and truth-conditions, and that sincere utterances of moral statements straightforwardly express truth-assessable states like beliefs. As we saw in previous chapters, non-cognitivists are revisionists about the underlying semantics of moral discourse: the correct semantics for moral discourse is not that suggested by the surface syntax of the discourse. Call this type of revisionism *underlying-semantics revisionism*. Although Railton is a surface-content revisionist, he is an underlying-semantics *non*-revisionist: on his account, moral statements have truth-conditions, and express cognitive states such as beliefs that are straightforwardly truth-assessable. Railton's revisionism is thus the mirror-image of the revisionism of the non-cognitivist: whereas the non-cognitivist revises the underlying semantics of moral discourse whilst attempting to conserve the contents of everyday moral judgements, Railton proposes to conserve the underlying semantics whilst trying to justify the revision of the contents of everyday moral judgements on methodologically naturalist grounds.

We can now see some other contrasts between Railton's naturalism and the naturalism of the Cornell Realists. Since the Cornell Realists eschew any attempt to analyse moral predicates in naturalistic terms and also do not propose any reforming definitions of moral language, their theory is non-revisionist along *both* of the dimensions mentioned above: the semantics of moral discourse is as its surface syntax suggests, so that there is no commitment to underlying-semantics revisionism, and the content of everyday moral judgements is conserved, so that there is no commitment to surface-content revisionism.

9.4 Tolerable Revisionism and Vindicative Reductionism

Does the surface-content revisionism implicit in Railton's theory lead to the abandonment of moral concepts such as *right* and *good*? This depends on the nature of the reduction effected by the relevant reforming definitions. A reduction of one set of phenomena to another can be either *vindicative* or *eliminative* (1989: 160–1; 1993b: 317). As an example of the latter, Railton cites the case of 'polywater', which in the late 1960s was thought to be a peculiar form of water. However, it turned out that polywater was nothing over and above ordinary water which, due to improperly cleaned laboratory equipment, contained a number of impurities. The conclusion drawn was that there was no such thing as polywater: the reduction of polywater to water-containing-some-impurities-from-improperly-washed-glassware was eliminative. The revisionism implicit in the account of polywater in terms of ordinary water with impurities in fact amounts to an *abandonment* of the concept of polywater, since one of the things that goes by the board in the revision – the idea that polywater is a compound distinct from ordinary water – would have to be retained if the revision was to be, as Railton puts it, 'tolerable':

> Revisionism may reach a point where it becomes more perspicacious to
> say that a concept has been abandoned, rather than revised. No sharp
> line separates tolerable revisionism and outright abandonment, but if
> our naturalist wishes to make his case compelling, he must show that his
> account of . . . [good] is a rather clear case of tolerable revision, at worst.
> (1989: 159)

Sometimes, a reduction leaves enough intact to ensure that the
revision is 'tolerable'. Railton points out that the reduction of water to
H_2O is of this nature. This is revisionary of our prior concept of water,
since it entailed that a substance which was thought to be one of the
fundamental elements out of which the things in the natural world are
composed is itself a compound of more fundamental elements. But it
is nevertheless vindicative: 'the successful reduction of water to H_2O
reinforces, rather than impugns, our sense that there really is water'
(1989: 161). Will the reduction of moral rightness to natural property
N be vindicative rather than eliminative? Railton's hope is that it will
be vindicative. It will be so if it can be shown (a) that facts about N can
play a genuine role in the explanation of features of our experience
and (b) that N is a property which 'through identifiable psychological
processes, could engage people motivationally in the ways characteristic of moral properties' (1993b: 317). In other words, Railton's
reductionist proposal about morality will be vindicative rather than
eliminative if and only if it constitutes 'a plausible synthesis of the
empirical and the normative' with respect to moral properties (1986a:
163).

9.5 Railton's Realist Account of Non-Moral Value

Railton's moral realism flows from his realist account of non-moral
value, where this is 'the notion of something being desirable for
someone, or good for him' (1986a: 173).

When I judge that something – a foodstuff, a course of medicine, or a
kind of life – is valuable or desirable, what am I judging? According to
Hobbes, if I judge that something is desirable I am in effect judging that
I desire it.[3] In a way, we could view Hobbes as proposing a crude type
of reforming definition of 'is desirable for x' as *is desired by x*. Since this
is a reforming definition, it cannot be undermined simply by applying
an a priori test like the open-question argument, and noting that of
something which is desired by x, it is always an open question whether
it is desirable for x. Rather, we must ask whether the notion of desire
can play both an explanatory role and the normative role associated
with the notion of desirableness. Railton points out that Hobbes's suggestion falls down on the latter requirement:

[Hobbes's] theory is deeply unsatisfactory, since it seems incapable of capturing important elements of the critical and self-critical character of value judgements. On this theory one can, of course, criticize any particular current desire on the grounds that it ill fits with other, more numerous or more powerful desires on one's part, or (if it is an instrumental desire) on the grounds that it is the result of a miscalculation with the information one has. But this hardly exhausts the range of assessment. Sometimes we wish to raise questions about the intrinsic desirability of the things that are now the main focus of our desires, even after any mistakes in calculation have been corrected. This appears to be a specific function of the vocabulary of goodness and badness, as distinct from the vocabulary of desire and aversion. (1986b: 11)

Or:

My [actual desires] frequently reflect ignorance, confusion, or lack of consideration, as hindsight attests. The fact that I am now so constituted that I desire something which, had I better knowledge of it, I would wish I had never sought, does not seem to recommend it to me as part of my good. (1986a: 173)

One way to avoid the sort of objection which Railton here raises against Hobbes would be to make what is desirable for a person a matter of what they would desire were they free of ignorance, confusion and so on. So how about the following: X is desirable for a person A if and only if A would, if fully and vividly informed and ideally rational, desire X. This would arguably capture the elements of the critical and self-critical character of value judgements that were missing from Hobbes's account of the desirable. Yet, as Railton points out, this characterization does not seem quite right. A map would be desirable for Joe, a philosopher lost in the heart of one of Chicago's slums. Yet his fully informed and ideally rational self would not desire to have a map were he in Joe's shoes, since he is already assumed to possess full factual information, which will include information about the geography of Chicago. In general:

A fully informed and rational individual would . . . have no use or desire for psychological strategies suited to circumstances of limited knowledge and rationality; but he would no doubt want his incompletely informed and imperfectly rational actual self to develop and deploy such strategies. (1986b: 16)[4]

This suggests that what is desirable for a person in a given set of circumstances be characterized not in terms of what his ideal self would desire were he to be placed in those circumstances, but rather in terms of what his ideal self *would want his non-ideal self to want* in those circumstances. Even if Joe's ideally rational and fully informed self would have no use for a map were he to find himself stranded in Cabrini Green, he would presumably want his actual self to form a desire for such a map were he in the same position. Thus, the proposal that Railton makes is:

> [A]n individual's good consists in what he would want himself to want, or to pursue, were he to contemplate his present situation from a standpoint fully and vividly informed about himself and his circumstances, and entirely free of cognitive error or lapses of instrumental rationality. (1986b: 16)

It is important to note that this is intended to be a non-circular and reductionist construal of a person's good: 'full information' here means only full *descriptive* information, and cannot include, for example, information about what is desirable for the individual concerned. Likewise, 'fully rational' means 'free from defects of *instrumental* rationality'. Reason here is not conceived of as dictating particular ends, but merely as facilitating the pursuit of ends which are antecedently assumed. This is evident in:

> Give to an actual individual A unqualified cognitive and imaginative powers, and full factual and nomological information about his physical and psychological constitution, capacities, circumstances, history, and so on. A will have become A+, who has complete and vivid knowledge of himself and his environment, and whose instrumental rationality is in no way defective. We now ask A+ to tell not what *he* currently wants, but what he would want his non-idealized self A to want – or, more generally, to seek – were he to find himself in the actual condition and circumstances of A. (1986a: 173–4)

Call this the 'full-information analysis' of what is good for a person. In order to see whether this analysis can underwrite a plausible form of naturalistic realism about a person's non-moral good, we must do two things. First, we must show that the notion thus defined can play a role in the explanation of aspects of our experience; and, second, we must show that the notion thus defined is capable of playing the normative role appropriate for facts about a person's good.

Railton notes that in order for the 'generic stratagem of naturalistic realism' to work in any case, the reality postulated in order to explain the relevant features of our experience must possess the following two characteristics:

(1) independence: it exists and has certain determinate features independent of whether we think it exists or has those features, independent, even, of whether we have good reason to think this;
(2) feedback: it is such – and we are such – that we are able to interact with it, and this interaction exerts the relevant sort of shaping influence or control upon our perceptions, thought, and action. (1986a: 172)

I will now illustrate the sorts of explanatory uses to which non-moral value, on his characterization, can be put, and then show how facts about non-moral goodness, on his characterization, possess features (1) and (2) above. I will then proceed to the question of normative role.

Railton gives the example of Lonnie, who finds himself miserable and lethargic on his travels in a foreign country. Lonnie finds himself with a desire for a glass of milk (1986a: 174–5). Unknown to Lonnie, his lethargy and feeling of ill-being is due to the fact that he is seriously dehydrated. Moreover, drinking the milk will actually make him feel worse, since milk is hard to digest, and will thus put further strains on his already suffering body. What is desirable for Lonnie in these circumstances? According to Railton's characterization, it is what Lonnie+ – Lonnie idealized to possess full factual information and full instrumental rationality – would want himself to want were he in Lonnie's shoes. Given that Lonnie+ knows the cause of Lonnie's malaise, and knows that drinking milk will only make things worse, Lonnie+ will want the actual, non-ideal Lonnie to lose his desire for milk and acquire instead a desire for clear, rehydrating liquids. Thus, water is desirable for Lonnie in these circumstances. Suppose that Lonnie goes ahead and drinks the milk, and ends up feeling worse as predicted. Now compare Lonnie with Tad (1986a: 178). Tad is in a similar set of circumstances, but unlike Lonnie he actually does have a desire for clear, rehydrating liquids. Tad+, we can suppose, would want his actual, non-ideal self to have a desire for clear rehydrating liquids in these sorts of circumstances. Tad goes ahead and satisfies his desire by drinking lots of water. Railton suggests that we can invoke the notion of non-moral good to explain the difference between the subsequent fortunes of Lonnie and Tad: Lonnie feels worse because his actual wants are out of step with what was desirable for him, while Tad feels better because his wants are in line with what is desirable for him. *We can thus use the notion of non-moral good to explain how satisfactory Lonnie and Tad find aspects of their lives.* In addition, if Tad's having the desire for water is not merely fortuitous, but is perhaps the result of self-discipline or training, we can say that Tad feels better because he knows what is good for him (whereas Lonnie doesn't feel better because he doesn't know what is good for him).[5]

Do the facts about what is good for Lonnie and Tad satisfy the independence condition (1) above? According to Railton's characterization, what is desirable for Lonnie in the given circumstances is constituted by what Lonnie+ would want Lonnie to want were he to step into his shoes. But the fact represented by the counterfactual *if Lonnie were fully informed and ideally rational, he would want his non-ideal self to form a desire for water* is not simply true in its own right; it is true in virtue of some other set of facts. What facts are these? Well, upon what does Lonnie+

base his decision as to what he would want Lonnie to want? Railton suggests:

> facts about Lonnie's circumstances and constitution, which determine, among other things, his existing tastes and his ability to acquire certain new tastes, the consequences of continued dehydration, the effects and availability of various sorts of liquids, and so on. (1986a: 175)

Railton suggests that *these* are the facts in virtue of which it is desirable that Lonnie should drink clear, rehydrating liquids. Thus, in general, what a fully informed and ideally rational person would want his non-ideal and less than fully informed self to want is at most an *indicator* of what is desirable for the latter; the truth-condition for the claim that such and such is desirable for a person is given by the reduction basis for the counterfactual concerning what his ideal self would want his non-ideal self to want. Now we can see why the independence claim (1) holds: the facts in the reduction basis all exist and have the features they have independently of whether we think they exist or have those features, independently, even, of whether we have good reason to think that they exist and have those features.[6] And note that in these explanations we cannot simply replace the reference to Lonnie's good with some claim about what Lonnie *believed* his good to be. Even if Lonnie had self-consciously believed that drinking milk in the given circumstances was part of his good, we would still have been able to explain why things subsequently turned out as they did in terms of the fact that drinking milk in those circumstances was not part of his good (1986a: 179, 1986b: 26).

How about the feedback condition (2)? How do the facts in question interact with us, and how does this interaction shape and control our perceptions, thoughts and action? Answering this question allows Railton to illustrate another explanatory role played by the notion of a person's non-moral good, in the explanation of the *evolution* of one's desires. This account of how the feedback condition is satisfied proceeds via what Railton terms the 'wants/interests mechanism':

> [T]he wants/interests mechanism ... permits individuals to achieve self-conscious and unselfconscious learning about their interests through experience. In the simplest sorts of cases, trial and error leads to the selective retention of wants that are satisfiable and lead to satisfactory results for the agent. (1986a: 179)

Go back to Lonnie, and suppose that after he gives in to his desire for a glass of milk, restless and unable to sleep, he goes for a walk to a local all-night store in search of some milk. To his dismay, they have run out, and there will be no delivery of fresh supplies until the morning. The storekeeper, recognizing his Scottish accent, offers him a couple of bottles of Irn Bru. Lonnie, although he has no desire for Irn Bru, buys the bottles since there is nothing better on offer. He takes them back to his room, and drinks both of them before falling asleep. Lonnie wakes up in the morning feeling a bit better and, recalling that there will be a fresh supply of milk on sale at the store, goes out with the intention of buying some. When he gets to the store, however, the fact of his feeling better, which he associates unconsciously with the drinking of the Irn Bru, leads him to buy a couple more bottles of Irn Bru rather than the milk. He drinks those too, feels his sense of well-being grow, and then, via a similar process, buys a few more bottles of Irn Bru during the day. What is the effect of this on Lonnie's desires? Whereas Lonnie started out with the desire for milk, the wants/interests mechanism, via pleasant associations with the things that are actually desirable for him, may lead him when he finds himself in similar circumstances in the future to lose the desire for milk and form the desire for rehydrating fluids instead. Thus, *facts about what is desirable for Lonnie may explain why his desiderative profile evolved in the way that we have supposed.*[7]

Railton suggests tentatively that these sorts of explanations may support some qualified predictions (1986a: 182, 1986b: 28–9). First, since a person's good is determined by what *her* fully informed and ideally rational self would want her to want given her actual circumstances, we would expect that, *ceteris paribus*, an individual will generally be a better judge of what is good for her than other people; second, that one's knowledge of one's good should increase as one's informational base increases with experience; third, since an agent's ideal self will take into account what her non-ideal self *is like* as well as her *actual circumstances*, we would expect that people with 'similar personal and social characteristics' will tend, in similar circumstances, to have similar values; and, fourth, what is good for one person will tend to approach what is good for another 'in those areas of life where individuals are most alike in other regards (for example, at the level of basic motives), and where trial-and-error mechanisms can be expected to work well (for example, where esoteric knowledge is not required)' (1986a: 182). Railton is cautious about claiming that these predictions are correct, but notes that 'it may be to their credit that they accord with widely held views' (1986a: 183).

Railton's examples show how facts that constitute what is desirable for Lonnie can play a genuine role in the explanation of features of our experience. What about the normative role of non-moral goodness? Can the facts that on Railton's account constitute non-moral goodness play this role? What is this role? Railton writes:

> It does seem to me to capture an important feature of the concept of intrinsic value to say that what is intrinsically valuable for a person must have a connection with what he would find in some degree compelling

or attractive, at least if he were rational and aware. It would be an intolerably alienated conception of someone's good to imagine that it might fail in any such way to engage him. (1986b: 9)

And:

It is essential to the concept of intrinsic goodness that nothing can be of intrinsic value unless it has a necessary connection to the grounds of action. . . . . . [W]e simply could not make sense of a claim that something is someone's intrinsic good if that thing could not afford that person positive grounds for action. An account of intrinsic good that purports to be no more than tolerably revisionist must . . . capture this truism. (1989: 171)

Railton calls this view *internalism about intrinsic non-moral value*.[8] Does Railton's account of the facts which constitute a person's non-moral good preserve this internalism? Railton argues, via an example, that it does, as a matter of psychological necessity. Consider Beth, a successful and happy accountant, who has a strong desire to become a writer. Beth's desire leads her to give up the accounting job (when she has saved enough to live on), though she finds it very difficult to put in the hours at her desk, and the things that she does manage to write fail to impress editors and publishers. The main reason for this is – though at this stage it is not apparent to Beth – that she has neither the skill nor the temperament to be a writer. These facts concerning skill, temperament, and the suitability of Beth for alternative pursuits such as accounting, will form the reduction base for the facts about how desirable the writer's life is for Beth. Plausibly, if Beth were ideally rational and fully informed about such facts, she would desire that her non-ideal self lose the desire to become a writer. If Beth knew Beth+'s view on this matter, what would the effect be? It might have the effect of sapping the strength of Beth's desire to become a writer, though 'desires being what they are' (1986a: 177), Beth's desire to become a writer may remain as strong as it was. But in this latter case:

[I]t is natural to expect that her desire that this desire be effective will become more tentative, and that some contrary desires will emerge. (1986b: 13)

And:

If one were to become genuinely and vividly convinced that one's desire for X is in this sense not supported by full reflection upon the facts, [it is natural to expect that one] would feel this to count against acting upon the desire. (1986a: 177–8)

Railton then provides an explanation of why this expectation is natural:

> Partly because it is natural to care about whether one is happy and whether one's desires are satisfied. . . . [The actual] Beth has every reason to believe that her [idealized] self takes these concerns to heart, since the [idealized] Beth is contemplating what she would want to pursue were she actually to [find herself in the shoes of the actual Beth]. Moreover, the [actual] Beth also has reason to believe that her [idealized] self is better situated than she to know what would most satisfy Beth's desires [in the circumstances in which Beth actually finds herself.] (1986b: 13–14)

In general:

> Although fuller information about how one's actual desires will fare in the world may not always contribute to the satisfaction of those desires – one may know too much – the advice of someone who has this fuller information, and also has the deepest sort of identification with one's fate, is bound to have some commending force. (1986b: 14)

Thus, the facts which on Railton's account constitute non-moral value will have the normative force which facts about non-moral value, truistically, have to possess.[9]

Thus, Railton claims that the facts which on his account constitute non-moral value can simultaneously play an explanatory role with respect to features of our experience *and* capture the normative role which facts about non-moral value are ordinarily thought to possess. Thus, Railton claims that his reduction of non-moral value is vindicative and not eliminativist.

One might worry that Railton's reductionism about non-moral goodness conflicts with his claim that non-moral goodness can play a genuine role in the explanation of features of our experience. If what is good for a person reduces to the facts which constitute what her ideal self would want her to want in her actual circumstances, isn't all the explanatory work being done by the facts in the reduction base and not by the facts about what is good for her? Railton is short with such objections. In the relevant respects, the reductionist account of non-moral value is on a par with the reduction of water to H_2O, and:

> Because the form of the reduction of water to H_2O is that of an identification, it makes no sense to ask of a causal role assigned to water (as in 'This erosion was caused by water') whether the causal work is 'really' being done by water or by H_2O. There can be no competition here: the causal work is done by water; the causal work is done by H_2O. In a similar way, if a naturalist in value theory identifies value with a – possibly complex – descriptive property, then it would make no sense to ask of a causal role assigned to value (as in 'He gave that up because he discovered that it was no good for him') whether the causal work is 'really' being done

by value or by its reduction basis. The causal work is done by value; the causal work is done by the reduction basis. (1989: 161; see also 1986a: 183–4, 1993b: 327, n.19)

I'll finish this exposition of Railton's reductionist account of non-moral value with some remarks on the nature of Railton's internalism about intrinsic non-moral value (see above). This can be broken down into two separate theses:

(RIa) If X is intrinsically valuable for Jones, then *ceteris paribus* Jones has a reason to pursue X.
(RIb) If Jones has a reason to pursue X, then *ceteris paribus* Jones will be motivated to pursue X.

which together give us:

(RI) If X is intrinsically valuable for Jones, then *ceteris paribus* Jones will be motivated to pursue X.

Now suppose that one accepted a *Humean* or *instrumental* conception of rationality, according to which 'there are no substantive ends or activities . . . that all rational beings as such have a reason to pursue, regardless of their contingent desires' (1986b: 8; see also 10.4 below). It then might appear that we are forced in the direction of an error-theory about non-moral value. Suppose that X is intrinsically valuable for Jones, and that Jones is a rational agent. Then consider another rational agent, Wilkes. Since Jones, a rational agent, has a reason to pursue X, it follows that Wilkes has a reason to pursue X. But we have said nothing about Jones's contingent desires or ends. So it looks as though Wilkes must have a reason to pursue X, independent of his contingent desires and ends. This is precisely what the instrumental conception of rationality denies. So, our original assumption – that Jones has a reason to pursue X – must be rejected. Since that followed from the claim that X was intrinsically valuable for X, this claim must be rejected too. An error-theory about intrinsic non-moral value looms (1986b: 8–9).

Railton blocks this argument by identifying and rejecting a suppressed premise. The premise in question is what Railton terms *value absolutism*: the view that:

In order for something to be intrinsically valuable for a particular person, that something must induce a resonance in any arbitrarily different rational being. (1986b: 9; see also 1989: 171–2)

Railton suggests that intrinsic non-moral goodness might be viewed as similar to *nutritiveness*. What is a nutrient for a particular type of organism depends in part upon the nature of organisms of that type: cow's milk nourishes infant cows and many humans, but there are organisms for whom cow's milk is not a nutrient, since they lack the enzymes necessary to digest it properly. So:

> There is . . . no such thing as an absolute nutrient, that is, something that would be nutritious for all possible organisms. There is only relational nutritiveness: substance S is a nutrient for organisms of type T. (1986b: 10)[10]

Does this compromise realism about nutritiveness? Does it follow from this that we must be *relativists* about nutritiveness, and deny that there are objective facts about what is a nutrient for what? Railton takes pains to distinguish relationalism of this sort from relativism:

> Heaviness, for example, is a relational concept; nothing is absolutely heavy. But the two-place predicate 'X is heavier than Y' has an objectively determinate extension. (1986b: 11)

Railton suggests that we view the notion of non-moral goodness in a similar way:

> [W]e might say that although there is no such thing as absolute goodness – that which is good in and of itself, irrespective of what and whom it might be good *for* or the good *of* – there may be relational goodness. (1986b: 10)

And here too relationalism does not imply relativism:

> Although a relational conception of value denies the existence of absolute good, it may yield an objectively determinate two place predicate 'X is part of Y's good'. (1986b: 11)

In rejecting value absolutism, then, Railton is able to combine his internalism about non-moral goodness with an instrumentalist conception of rationality, without being pushed in the direction of an error-theory about non-moral value.

We'll now see how Railton uses this theory of non-moral goodness to defend a form of naturalistic moral realism.

9.6 Railton's Account of Moral Rightness

Railton now goes on to use the reductionist, 'full-information' analysis of non-moral value to define a notion of moral rightness. The strategy here is broadly similar to that provided for non-moral value. First, a reforming definition of moral rightness is proposed. Then, it is argued that the notion thus defined can play a genuine explanatory role with respect to features of our experience, and that it can also be viewed as possessing the central normative characteristics required of a notion of moral rightness.

In order to formulate his reforming definition of moral rightness, Railton requires the notion of *a social point of view*. He works towards capturing this notion by considering what is distinctive of moral norms as opposed to non-moral criteria of assessment:

> Moral evaluation seems to be concerned most centrally with the assess-ment of conduct or character where the interests of more than one individual are at stake. . . . [it] assesses actions or outcomes in a peculiar way: the interests of the strongest or most prestigious party do not always prevail, purely prudential reasons may be subordinated, and so on. More generally, moral resolutions are thought to be determined by criteria of choice that are *non-indexical* and in some sense *comprehensive*. This has led a number of philosophers to seek to capture the special character of moral evaluation by identifying a *moral point of view* that is impartial, but equally concerned with all those potentially affected. (1986a: 189)

So:

> [M]oral norms reflect a certain kind of rationality, rationality not from the point of view of any particular individual, but from what might be called a social point of view. (1986a: 190)

Railton now considers an idealization of the notion of social rationality. This is

> . . . what would be rationally approved of were the interests of all poten-tially affected individuals counted equally under circumstances of full and vivid information. (1986a: 190)

This idealization provides the key to the reforming definition of 'moral rightness':

> *x is morally right if and only if x would be approved of by an ideally instru-mentally rational and fully informed agent considering the question 'How best to maximize the amount of non-moral goodness?' from a social point of view in which the interests of all potentially affected individuals were counted equally.*

In short, moral rightness is a matter of 'what is instrumentally rational from a social point of view' (1986a: 200).

As with the notion of non-moral value, Railton adopts – though more tentatively – the 'generic stratagem of naturalistic realism'. The first part of this stratagem involves delineating an explanatory role for the notion of rationality from the social point of view. Go back to Lonnie and imagine that the next time he finds himself tired and washed out in a foreign country, he actually does go ahead and give in to his desire for glasses of milk. Just as we can explain Lonnie's consequent malaise in terms of his not doing what he would desire himself to do were he to contemplate his situation from a viewpoint of full information and ideal instrumental rationality (i.e., drinking lots of clear liquids), we can explain *social dissatisfaction* or *social unrest* in terms of a *society's* not doing what is instrumentally rational from a social point of view:

> Just as an individual who significantly discounts some of his interests will be liable to certain sorts of dissatisfaction, so will a social arrangement – for example, a form of production, a social or political hierarchy, etc. – that departs from social rationality by significantly discounting the interests of a particular group that have a potential for dissatisfaction and unrest. (1986a: 191)

Just as had Lonnie believed that drinking milk was in his interests he would still have experienced the malaise, so too a society which departs from social rationality might experience social unrest even though it collectively believes that its present arrangements are socially rational:

> [D]iscontent may arise because a society departs from social rationality, but not as a result of a belief that this is the case. Suppose that a given society is believed by all constituents to be just. This belief may help to stabilize it, but if in fact the interests of certain groups are being discounted, there will be a potential for unrest that may manifest itself in various ways – in alienation, loss of morale, decline in the effectiveness of authority, and so on – well before any changes in belief about the society's justness occur, and that will help explain why members of certain groups come to believe it to be unjust, if in fact they do. (1986a: 192)

Recall that in the case of non-moral good there was a feedback mechanism that could sometimes be invoked to explain why an individual's desires evolved in the direction of what is actually in his interest: the unpleasantness of Lonnie's malaise might contribute to his losing the desire for milk the next time he is in the relevant sorts of circumstances, and acquiring instead the desire for water or some other clear liquid. Although Railton explicitly admits that the working of the mechanism in the social case is not as straightforward as the working of the analogous mechanism in the individual case, and that the scope for the influence of distorting factors is much greater in the case of the former (see especially 1986a: 194–6), he thinks that it may sometimes be able to explain the evolution of social structures in terms of the notion of social rationality:

The potential for unrest that exists when the interests of a group are discounted is potential for pressure from that group – and its allies – to accord fuller recognition to their interests in social decision-making and in the socially-instilled norms that govern individual decision making. It therefore is pressure to push the resolution of conflicts further in the direction required by social rationality, since it is pressure to give fuller weight to the interests of more of those affected. (1986a: 193)

Although there are also examples where the influence of distorting factors prevent or stall the evolution of social structures in the direction of social rationality – the late arrival and longevity of New World plantation slavery, for example – Railton suggests that there are at least some cases which do appear to exemplify a general trend towards rationality from a social point of view: the downfall of the system of feudal estates, the weakening of restrictions on religious practices, moves in the direction of universal suffrage, for instance. Moreover, he tentatively suggests that there are some trends in the evolution of moral norms that appear to bear out the predictions of his theory of social rationality:

Generality

Over the span of history, through processes that have involved numerous reversals, people have accumulated into larger social units – from the familial band to the tribe to the 'people' to the nation-state – and the scope of moral categories has enlarged to follow these expanding boundaries. (1986a: 197)

Humanization

Whereas in the past, moral norms have been viewed as variously supernatural in origin ('grounded in the will or character of a deity') or as flowing from reason or conscience in ways that are at most only fortuitously connected with human well-being, and though vestiges of these views survive in contemporary philosophical theory:

It is typical of almost the entire range of such theory, and of much of contemporary moral discourse [i.e. informed moral thinking in scientifically advanced societies], to make some sort of intrinsic connection between normative principles and effects on human interests. (1986a: 198)

Patterns of variation

What sorts of features would be likely to interfere with a general trend in the direction of social rationality? Social rationality concerns what would be rationally approved of by a fully informed and ideally rational agent considering the question 'How best to realize the maximal amount of non-moral goodness?', whilst counting equally the interests of all potentially affected individuals. So we would expect disagreement and strife to be minimal on matters where there is large-scale uniformity so far as the interests of all potentially affected individuals are concerned, where almost everyone has the capacity to infringe upon those interests, where the advantages of following a certain set of norms is clear and where a person's following those norms is likely to encourage others to do likewise. Railton suggests that this is in fact what we find. There is widespread agreement and hence a venerable and stable set of social norms 'to do with prohibitions of aggression and theft, and of the violation of promises' (1986a: 198). This is in marked contrast to cases where the above features are not exhibited, cases which concern:

> such matters as social hierarchy – for example, the permissibility of slavery, of authoritarian government, of caste or gender inequalities – and social responsibility – for example, what is the nature of our individual or collective obligation to promote the well-being of unrelated others? (1986a: 198–9)

Railton suggests, then, that his theory can explain why in cases such as these there is/was little 'early or stable approximation to social rationality' (1986a: 198).

Having argued that instrumental rationality from a social point of view has a genuine explanatory role, Railton must now argue that it has the right sort of normative force to serve as the content of a working notion of moral rightness. We can work towards Railton's views on this by seeing how he reacts to an argument which appears to push the naturalistic cognitivist in the direction of an error-theory. Suppose one thought that our concept of a moral fact is a concept of a reason for action. Call this claim about our concept of a moral fact *rationalism* (see also 9.10 below). Then we ask: what sort of reason? One cannot release oneself from a moral obligation simply by pointing out that it does not sit well with one's goals or desires. This is the familiar point that moral 'oughts' are *categorical* (Kant 1785). Suppose I want to get to Barry Island by 10 a.m. and there is a train leaving from Cardiff Central that will get me there by 9.55 a.m. Then it is true to say that I ought to catch the train. However, suppose I lose the desire to get to Barry Island by 10 a.m. Then it is no longer the case that I ought to catch the train. This sort of 'ought' is *hypothetical*: a change in my desires can exempt me from its scope. Moral 'oughts', by contrast, are categorical. Suppose I pass an old woman lying bleeding in the street. Then it is true that I ought to help her. The key point is that I cannot exempt myself from the scope of this obligation by pointing to some feature of my desires.[11]

Even if I do not *want* to come to her aid and phone for an ambulance, it is still the case that I ought to. Thus, if our concept of a moral fact is a concept of a reason for action, it is a concept of a *categorical* reason for action. Call this claim *the categoricity of moral reasons*. If we put rationalism and the categoricity of moral reasons together, we get what we can call *absolutism* about moral value. Thus, if an activity is morally good, rationalism entails that we have a reason to engage in that activity, and the categoricity of moral reasons entails that all rational beings, independent of their contingent inclinations, have a reason to engage in that activity. Thus:

rationalism plus the categoricity of moral reasons entails absolutism about moral value

where absolutism about moral value is the view that if x is morally good, then all rational beings, independent of their contingent inclinations, have a reason to pursue x. What if one accepts a *Humean* or *Instrumental Theory of Rationality* in addition to absolutism about moral value? Recall that, according to this, 'there are no substantive ends or activities . . . that all rational beings as such have a reason to pursue, regardless of their contingent desires' (1986b: 8). Given this, it follows from rationalism and the categoricity of moral reasons that moral judgements are systematically and uniformly false: by rationalism, for a judgement that x is morally good to be true there has to be a reason to pursue x, by the categoricity of moral reasons this must be a reason that all rational beings have to pursue x independently of their contingent desires, but by the instrumental view of rationality there are no such reasons. The combination of rationalism plus categoricity plus instrumentalism together entails an *error-theory* of moral judgement. Railton avoids committing himself to embracing an error-theory by rejecting rationalism: if our concept of a moral fact is not a concept of a reason for action, then categoricity (which just says that *if* our concept of a moral fact is a concept of a reason for action, then the reason provided is categorical) and instrumentalism *by themselves* will not lead to the error-theory.[12] Railton is thus an *anti-rationalist*:

> [On] the present account rational motivation is not a precondition of moral obligation. For example, it could truthfully be said that I ought to be more generous even though greater generosity would not help me to promote my existing ends, or even to satisfy my objective interests. This could be so because what it would be morally right for me to do depends upon what is rational from a point of view that includes, but is not exhausted by, my own. (1986a: 201)

Railton explains how this anti-rationalism is compatible with a sensible view of the normative force of moral facts by means of an analogy with logical 'oughts'. Plausibly, I ought not to believe both a proposition P and some other proposition or propositions that entail its negation, not-P. But can it be said that simply in virtue of the truth of this 'ought' statement I have a reason to seek out and rectify all logical contradictions from my belief set? Think of the amount of intellectual effort this would require: I'd have to check my existing belief set for consistency (no easy matter) and ensure that every time I acquired a new belief it was consistent with my pre-existing belief set. Railton suggests that this would be like someone leaving 'his home in suburban New Jersey to hunt alligators in the Okefonekee on the off-chance that he might one day find himself stranded and unarmed in the backwaters of southeast Georgia' (1986a: 202). It is enough to capture the force of the fact that I ought not to believe both a proposition and some other proposition that entails its negation that logical contradictions are necessarily false whilst logical inferences are truth-preserving and that 'we are often concerned with whether our thinking is warranted in a sense that is more intimately connected with its truth-conduciveness than with its instrumentality to our peculiar personal goals' (1986a: 202). Thus, it is enough that logical facts, as it were, can sometimes provide us with reasons for action, in cases where it matters to our ends. If a contradiction 'rears its head in practice', then I may indeed have a reason to sort out the tangle this leads to in my belief system, but there is no need to think that this provides all rational agents, independent of their contingent desires, with a reason for rooting out every contradiction buried deep in their belief systems. The same sort of thing holds for moral rightness construed as instrumental rationality from a social point of view:

> [W]e may say that moral evaluation is not subjective or arbitrary, and that good, general grounds are available for following moral 'oughts', namely, that moral conduct is rational from an impartial point of view. Since in public discourse and private reflection we are often concerned with whether our conduct is justifiable from a general rather than merely personal standpoint, it therefore is far from arbitrary that we attach so much importance to morality as a standard of criticism and self-criticism. (1986a: 202)

Thus, we can account for the importance of moral facts without seeing morality 'as something that it cannot be, as "rationally compelling no matter what one's ends"'. Rather, 'we should ask how we might change the ways we live so that moral conduct would more regularly be rational given the ends we actually will have' (1986a: 204). I'll now consider some objections that have been raised against Railton's naturalistic programme.

9.7 Wiggins on Substantive Naturalism

On the face of it, it seems that there is simply no scope for the application of an OQA against the sort of substantive naturalism defended by Railton. It doesn't follow from the fact that 'water' and 'H_2O' pick out the same property that the question 'Is this x, which is H_2O, water?' is conceptually closed, since 'water' and 'H_2O' can pick out the same property even though they are not synonymous or equivalent in meaning. So the fact that, for any natural property N, the question 'Is this x which is N also good?' is conceptually open doesn't show that the property of goodness cannot be identical to N. However, David Wiggins, himself an ethical non-naturalist, has argued that there is a descendant of the OQA which does threaten even non-analytic versions of substantive naturalism:

> Once they are put on to a proper basis, Moore's objections [to naturalism] will reach further (I shall argue) than 'definitional naturalism'. (1993b: 330)

I will now attempt to reconstruct Wiggins's argument in such a way that its flaws are apparent. Wiggins argues as follows (see his 1993b: 329–33, and also 1992a: 644–6). We imagine that V is a value property, X a natural property, and we begin by supposing that these are identical.

(I) $V = X$.
(II)   A property is natural if some predicate which presents it either 'pulls its weight' in an experimental science or is definable in terms of such (otherwise it is non-natural) (1992b: 330).
(III)   V must have been presented to us under a predicate with the right kind of sense to express a valuational interest (see 1993b: 332).
(IV)   X can be presented to us under a predicate with the right kind of sense to express an interest in explanation and prediction (from (II) and the assumption that X is a natural property). (1993b: 332, 1992a: 645)
(V)   There corresponds to the property V some particular function from objects to truth-values, the V-function (1993b: 332, 1992a: 646).
(VI)   There corresponds to the property X some particular function from objects to truth-values, the X-function (1993b: 332, 1992a: 646).[13]
(VII)   The X-function matches the V-function exactly (from (I), (V), (VI)).
(VIII)   The X-function projects the valuational interest non-accidentally

faithfully into the future and across any other cases that could arise (from (VII); 1993b: 332, 1992a: 646).

(IX)   The valuational interest is not the same as the interest in explanation and prediction, since:

> In the case of an ethical or aesthetic interest, the only way to characterize that kind of interest is by reference to the proper response to the value in question. In its original or pure form, the proper response, whatever else it is, will be a response of engagement. More specifically, this will not be the response of merely believing item x to have the value V but the response of *finding* V in x. In the second place, this response will be keyed not to the question whether everyone reacts in such and such a way to item x *qua* possessed of V but to the question whether one is oneself to concur in this reaction. (1993b: 311)

So:

(X)   It is difficult to see how the X-function could project *both* the interest in explanation and prediction and the valuational interest non-accidentally faithfully into the future and across any other cases that could arise.

> What is required is a function from objects to truth-values that will faithfully and systematically mimic the [V]-function over *indefinitely many new cases*. If the claim that that can be a physical function is to be substantially made out, then the function itself must be explainable or specifiable in physical terms, that is terms that pull their weight in the experimental sciences. It is because I do not see how that is possible that I see myself as justified in speaking not only of the non-natural *senses* of predicates but also, on the level of reference, of *concepts* or *properties* that are non-natural. (1992a: 646)

So:

(XI)   It is difficult to see how it could be the case that V = X.

Wiggins's argument strikes me as unconvincing. My two principal claims are: (a) that Wiggins's argument is straightforwardly question-begging as directed against a naturalist of Railton's stripe, and (b) that Wiggins's position is not only, as advertised, *anti-scientistic* (1993a: 304), but also profoundly *anti-scientific*.

The key to getting clear on the question-begging nature of Wiggins's argument lies in the fact that Railton's *substantive* naturalism is grounded in his *methodological* naturalism. Recall that methodological naturalism with respect to a given area of human practice is the view that we have to take an a posteriori and explanatory approach to that area. This means that the identity $V = X$ is put forward as a proposal to be justified or rejected on the same sorts of grounds as a posteriori, explanatory hypotheses generally are: that it has explanatory value in our attempt at understanding the area of practice in question. This is stressed so clearly by Railton that it is difficult to see how Wiggins could have missed it:

> The naturalistic definitions should permit the evaluative concepts to participate in their own right in genuinely empirical theories. Part of this consists in showing that we have appropriate epistemic access to these concepts. Part, too . . . consists in showing that generalizations employing these concepts, among others, can figure in potentially explanatory accounts . . . [We must] also show that the empirical theories constructed with the help of these definitions are reasonably good theories, that is, theories for which we have substantial evidence and which provide plausible explanations. (1986a: 205)

When Wiggins requires that it be 'substantially made out' how there could be a function which presents both an interest in explanation and prediction and a valuational interest non-accidentally faithfully into the future, he is in effect asking for some a priori demonstration that this sort of thing is possible. Given that he is not satisfied with the naturalist's answer 'Because we have good empirical grounds for thinking that $V = X'$, what else could he be requiring? Why, given empirical evidence to the effect that $V = X$, should we require some a priori demonstration of how it could be that the relevant function presents two different interests non-accidentally into the future? Wiggins, in imposing this requirement, and in refusing to meet Railton's position by evaluating its empirical credentials, effectively begs the question against his methodologically naturalist brand of substantive naturalism.[14]

There are other ways of bringing out this point. When Wiggins writes 'In the case of an ethical or aesthetic interest, the only way to characterize that kind of interest is by reference to the proper response to the value in question', and then proceeds to argue that the response is radically different from the sort of response via which an interest in explanation and prediction has to be characterized, all he establishes is that the *responses* distinctive of evaluation are different from the *responses* distinctive of scientific enquiry. *But the non-analytic naturalist already explicitly concedes that much.* The non-analytic naturalist explicitly points out that the responses distinctive of evaluation, evaluative judgements, are different in content from the responses distinctive of scientific enquiry – naturalistic judgements. He points this out, because he points out that on his account 'good' and 'N' are not synonymous or analytically equivalent. So, pointing out that the responses distinctive of evaluative enquiry are different from the responses distinctive of scientific enquiry will have no force against Railton's naturalist, unless

Wiggins makes the assumption that non-synonymous predicates cannot denote the same property. In this context, this adds up to the assumption that the only sort of naturalism there can be is definitional or analytic naturalism. Wiggins's argument thus presupposes that non-analytic naturalism is a non-starter. Since that is precisely what he is attempting to establish, his argument begs the question against the non-analytic naturalist.

Wiggins represents himself as an opponent of *scientism*, not as an opponent of science. Scientism, as I understand it, is the view that the methods, concepts and ontological categories of natural science are the only ones that matter so far as we are concerned with serious enquiry, and not, say, idle pastimes or 'colourful emoting'.[15] Someone opposed to scientism would – lest they be accused of harking back to a medieval, pre-scientific worldview – represent themselves as challenging only the allocation to natural science of some foundational status concerning matters outside the strictly demarcated boundaries of natural science itself. Thus, the philosopher opposed to scientism will argue that he is opposed only to science having imperialist aspirations with respect to other, non-scientific, areas of human practice, and not opposed to science's sovereignty over scientific matters themselves.

I will now argue that Wiggins's argument against Railton's naturalism, if sound, will also undermine a scientific reduction as well entrenched as water = H_2O. I take it that this will be enough to establish that (a) Wiggins is himself committed to opposing science as well as scientism, and that (b) his argument against Railton can have no force whatsoever for anyone not prepared to advocate subscribing to a medieval, pre-scientific worldview.

Just as Wiggins distinguishes between evaluative properties and natural properties, we can mount a similar distinction between what I will call practical properties and natural properties. *A practical property is a property that can be presented to us under a predicate with the right kind of sense to express an interest in satisfying one's desires.* Now we can run an argument analogous to the argument which Wiggins uses against the non-analytic ethical naturalist. So, imagine that WATER is a practical property and that H_2O is a scientific property, and suppose that they are identical:

(Ia)   WATER = H_2O.
(IIa)   A property is natural if some predicate that presents it either pulls its weight in an experimental science or is definable in terms of such. Otherwise, it is non-natural.
(IIIa)   WATER must have been presented to us under a predicate with the right kind of sense to express a practical interest.
(IVa) H_2O can be presented to us under a predicate with the right kind of sense to express an interest in explanation and prediction.

(Va)   There corresponds to the property WATER some particular function from objects to truth-values, the WATER-function.

(VIa)   There corresponds to the property H_2O some particular function from objects to truth-values, the H_2O-function.

(VIIa)   The H_2O-function from objects to truth-values matches the WATER-function exactly.

(VIIIa) The H_2O-function projects the practical interest non-accidentally faithfully into the future and across any other cases that could arise.

(IXa)   The practical interest is not the same as the interest in explanation and prediction. Since:

In the case of a practical interest, the only way to characterize that kind of interest is by reference to the proper response to the practical property in question. In its original or pure form, the proper response, whatever else it is, will be a response of *activity*. More specifically, this will not be the response of merely believing an item x to have the practical property, but the response of desiring to *do* something with x *qua* the bearer of that property, given one's overall scheme of wants, needs and goals. In the second place, this response will be keyed not to the question whether everyone reacts in such and such a way to item x *qua* possessed of the practical property, but to the question: what, given one's overall scheme of wants, goals and needs, should one do with x?

(Xa)   It is difficult to see how the H_2O-function could project both the interest in explanation and prediction and the practical interest non-accidentally faithfully into the future and across any other cases that could arise.

So:

(XIa)   It is difficult to see how it could be the case that WATER $= H_2O$.

It is important to note the following three points about this argument. First, I am not claiming that this argument is a good argument: if an argument can be shown to establish a priori that WATER isn't H_2O, that suffices as a *reductio* of the argument. Second, that Wiggins's original argument begs the question can be seen even more clearly now that we have the present argument on the table. Presumably, the chemist who claims that WATER $= H_2O$ will question why some a priori demonstration is required of how it could be that a single function projects both a practical interest and an interest in explanation and prediction non-accidentally faithfully into the future. He will reply that he is not giving an a priori argument for the claim of property identity, but is proposing that it is a well-grounded empirical and a posteriori hypothesis. In pressing for an a priori justification, the argument above is effectively assuming that the position the chemist attempts to occupy cannot be occupied. Third, this point can be pressed home in another way. The non-analytic naturalist explicitly concedes that judgements about water are not equivalent in content to judgements about H_2O, since he explicitly stresses that 'water' and 'H_2O' are not synonymous or analytically equivalent. Thus, in proceeding from the claim that the responses distinctive of practical engagement with the world are different from the responses distinctive of scientific enquiry, to the claim that 'water' isn't H_2O, the argument above simply passes over the possibility that 'water' and 'H_2O' might denote the same property even though they are non-synonymous. So the argument begs the question. By parity of reasoning, so does Wiggins's argument against Railton's ethical naturalist.

I submit, then, that if Wiggins's argument against non-analytic ethical naturalism is sound, he is committed not only to rejecting scientism, but to rejecting a well-entrenched scientific identity such as $WATER = H_2O$. Like anyone not prepared to return to a medieval, pre-scientific worldview, I take this as a *reductio* of Wiggins's argument against non-analytic ethical naturalism. If Wiggins believes that there is a significant difference between the argument from (I) to (XI) and the argument from (Ia) to (XIa), or that I have misunderstood his original argument, the onus is on him to point out the difference or correct the misunderstanding.

I conclude that Wiggins's argument against non-analytic ethical naturalism is a failure.

9.8 Problems for the Full-Information Analysis of Non-Moral Value

According to Railton's 'full-information' analysis of non-moral value or well-being, what is non-morally good for a person Lyn is what Lyn would want herself to want were she to contemplate her actual situation vividly and from a standpoint of full factual information and ideal instrumental rationality. In this section, I will deal with four powerful-sounding objections that have been developed by David Sobel in his 'Full Information Accounts of Well-Being'.[16]

Suppose we were considering the question: what kind of life is non-morally best for Lyn? According to Railton's analysis, the answer to this question is: the kind of life that Lyn would want herself to want were she to contemplate her actual situation from a standpoint of full factual information and ideal instrumental rationality. Sobel's main criticisms of the full-information analysis take off from the fact that in many cases first-hand experience of what it is like to lead a kind of life is necessary if one is to form an accurate impression of what it is really like to lead that kind of life:

> [F]ull appreciation of a possibly valuable aspect of one's life requires 'getting into the skin of the part' ... often one cannot fully appreciate, or be sure that one does fully appreciate, the value of an experience to oneself without having that experience. (1994: 797)

How can the full-information analysis accommodate this fact? Sobel suggests that the best available option would be for the analysis to adopt what he calls the 'experiential model', where:

> This model would have it that it is the same agent who experiences first-hand each type of life they might live. (1994: 801)

Sobel distinguishes between two forms which the experiential model might assume. This first of these is the 'serial' version, in which:

> [O]ur ideal self is expected to achieve full information by acquiring firsthand knowledge of what one of the lives we could live would be like, retaining this knowledge, and moving on to experience the next kind of life we could lead. I will call this acquiring full information incremen-tally. (1994: 801)

The main problem for the serial version is that having the experiences necessary to appreciate what one kind of life is like may *distort* one's appreciation of what an alternative kind of life is really like. This is a problem because on the full-information analysis Lyn's fully informed and ideally rational self contemplates a number of different kinds of life that Lyn, her actual self, could lead and then selects one (or maybe some) of them as the kind of life that is non-morally best for her actual self. But if the experiences necessary to form an accurate impression of what it would be like to live one kind of life distort one's impression of what it would be like to live a life of some alternative kind, it is hard to see why the actual Lyn should take the verdict of the ideally rational and fully informed Lyn as normatively compelling: why take her verdict on the latter kind of life as authoritative or even reliable when it is based on a potentially distorted impression of what it would be like to lead that kind of life? Sobel illustrates the worry with a number of examples, including that of 'an Amish person who does not know what other options society holds for her':

> The experience of such a person could differ significantly from the experience of the same person who did have knowledge of many other options that society offers ... [T]o be able to claim that one knows what it is like to lead such a life one must experience what it would be like to

be in those shoes (explicitly not what it would be like to be in those shoes with the accumulated knowledge of what it would be like to have lived a multitude of alternative sorts of lives). Attempting to give the idealized agent direct experience with what it would be like to be such an Amish person, while this agent has the knowledge of what it would be like to live many significantly different sorts of lives, will in many cases be impossible. (1994: 801)

The serial version of the experiential model could avoid this problem if there was a straightforward way of ordering the lives that Lyn could potentially lead from most naive, as it were, to most sophisticated. Then having the experiences required to appreciate accurately what it would be like to live a kind of life at the nth place in the series could not distort one's idealized self's impression of what it would be like to live a kind of life at the n+1th or higher place in the series. But, of course, the idea that there could be such a straightforward way of ordering kinds of lives is highly implausible. The relative 'naivety' or 'sophistication' of kinds of lives does not extend along a single dimension: along one dimension (perhaps that relating to one's sexual development), the life of a nun devoting her life to the study of Aquinas is more naive than the life of a waitress successfully chasing only carnal pleasures in between stints at the restaurant, but it is easy to see that there are other dimensions (perhaps those relating to intellectual development) along which the latter kind of life is more naive than the former. So the fact that 'Providing us with experiential information can alter our ability to experience certain types of lives' (1994: 802) scuppers the serial version of the experiential model.

Sobel now considers a version of the experiential model that is designed to avoid the objection outlined above. He calls this the 'amnesia version', and describes it as follows:

> [According to the amnesia version] [t]he agent must have an experience of what some life would be like, then forget this and be ready to learn what some other life would be like without the latter process being affected by its position in the series. Then at the end of the learning and forgetting process we would have to remove (serially or all at once) each instance of amnesia while, on some views, adding factual information and immunity to blunders of instrumental rationality somewhere along the way. (1994: 805)

Sobel now raises four problems for the amnesia version of the experiential model, some of which ((b) and (c)) are specific to the amnesia version, some of which ((a) and (d)) apply to any form of the experiential model. I will now outline the four problems, and show that in each case the amnesia version of the experiential model has the resources to neutralize the problem.

Problem (a)

Sobel calls this the problem of 'too many voices':

> [W]e need more than just firsthand experience with all the lives we
> could lead. For the purposes of the full-information account we need a
> perspective whose preferences between the lives in question accurately
> determine their value to the agent. But now a problem arises. Our actual
> evaluative perspective changes over time. We can therefore expect that
> we would respond differently to factual and experiential knowledge at
> different times in our future. Thus we do not have a single informed
> perspective to deal with, but several. And each will offer occasionally
> conflicting assessments of where the agent's well-being lies. How are we
> to render univocal this discordant chorus such that value commensura-
> tion can be accomplished? (1994: 805)

Sobel considers three replies: that we construct a non-ad hoc method of
weighting the preferences of various idealized selves, that we construct
a temporally privileged vantage point such that preferences formed
from that vantage point determine what constitutes one's overall
well-being, that we argue that idealized selves will have identical
preferences simply in virtue of being fully informed and prey to no
lapses of instrumental rationality. In each case, Sobel argues that the
reply fails. I will not consider Sobel's worries about these replies, since
I will develop a response to the problem of too many voices, which is
independent of each of them.

Problem (b)

Sobel expresses this as follows:

> [I]t would surely take much very complicated research to have anything
> to say about the question of the similarity of the experience and a later
> sudden recollection of it in cases in which the evaluative perspectives
> held at the time of the original experience differs significantly from that
> held by the person who is suddenly remembering. (1994: 807)

Problem (c)

How could we have any confidence in the verdict expressed by our
idealized self when the temporary and controllable amnesia is cured,
given that:

> [T]here is no way of estimating the psychological shock of experiencing
> such a large number of instances of amnesia and loss of amnesia to our
> idealized selves. The full-information theorist cannot simply stipulate
> that the idealized agent remains sane throughout this process. (1994: 807)

Finally:

Problem (d)

How could we have any confidence in the verdict expressed by our idealized self when:

> [T]he idealized agent might, after having experienced what it is like to be so nearly perfect in understanding, come to think of her actual self as we might think of ourselves after a serious brain injury (i.e., better off dead). (1994: 807)

I'll now develop responses to each of these problems.

Response to Problem (a)

Recall that Railton's full-information analysis of well-being has to be such that it can be fed into his characterization of moral rightness: x is right if and only if it produces at least as large a sum total or average of individual non-moral value as any other available x where the interests of all affected parties are treated impartially and equally. In order to use this sort of characterization of moral rightness to, for example, settle some matter of public policy, we require some means of commensurating the interests of one individual with those of another: we need to be able to carry out some *interpersonal* comparison of interests. Jones prefers quiet and solitude, whilst Smith prefers company and entertainment: when we come to decide on whether some act or policy is morally right, how do we weight Jones's preference against Smith's? This is a problem for Railton's characterization of moral rightness. Sobel in effect suggests that a similar, and possibly more difficult, worry is lurking within Railton's account of a *single* individual's well-being. Since evaluative perspectives change over time, it may be that Lyn's non-moral good between time t and time t* consists in Q, yet between t* and t** consists in R. How do we weight Lyn's preference between t and t* against her preference between t* and t**? If we cannot do this, it looks as though the idea of Lyn's overall well-being or non-moral good is a chimera. So the account founders upon a problem of *intra*personal commensurability of non-moral value even before we get to the stage where we have to consider the problem of *inter*personal commensurability.

I suggest that the defender of the full-information analysis can deal with the worry about intrapersonal, cross-temporal commensurability as follows. Let Jones+ stand for Jones, idealized to possess full factual information and perfect instrumental rationality. Let JONES stand for Jones's self at some time t in the future, and let JONES+ stand for

JONES, idealized to possess full factual information and perfect instrumental rationality. As I see it, there are two types of case to consider. In case A, Jones+ wants Jones to want Q, JONES+ wants JONES to want R, where Q and R are 'compatible' in the sense that Jones's pursuing Q does not undermine or rule out JONES'S pursuing R. In this sort of case we can just take Jones's non-moral good to consist in the pursuit of Q up to time t and in the pursuit of R thereafter. This will make the calculation of Jones's overall non-moral good more complex, to be sure, but I don't see that it introduces any difficulties of principle. Case B is more problematic. Here, Jones+ wants Jones to want Q, JONES+ wants JONES to want R, where Q and R are '*in*compatible' in the sense that Jones's pursuing Q *does* undermine or rule out JONES'S pursuing R. As it stands, this is a problem for the full-information account because we have no way of telling whether the non-moral good for Jones consists in his having Q up to time t and not having R thereafter, or whether it consists in his not having Q up to time t but having R thereafter. Since we don't want to assume that either Jones+ or JONES+ occupies some privileged vantage point, this question appears unanswerable. However, I will now argue that this situation, which on the face of it appears possible, is in fact impossible.

Case B is impossible because of the assumption that Jones+ and JONES+ are both fully informed and ideal in point of instrumental rationality. Jones+, because he is fully informed, can be assumed to know both that JONES+ will want JONES to want R, that Jones's pursuing Q will undermine or rule out JONES's pursuing R, and that JONES is his own future self. But how can Jones+, if he possesses ideal instrumental rationality, want himself to pursue a course of action that will frustrate the satisfaction of his own future interests? Jones+, to retain his claim to ideal instrumental rationality, must either revise what he wants Jones to want, or take steps to ensure that Jones does not develop into someone whose idealized self wants him to want R. Which of these he chooses will be an evaluative judgement about non-moral value along with the rest, but either way, we will not have a case B-type scenario. So there will be no difficulty of principle for the full-information analysis.

We can see that this sort of move won't deal with the problem of interpersonal commensurability, and this will explain why the problem of interpersonal commensurability is more of a problem for Railton's account of moral rightness than the problem of intrapersonal commensurability is for his account of an individual's non-moral good. Suppose we tried to make an analogous move in the interpersonal case, and suppose for ease of exposition that all of the action occurs at the same point in time. Let Jones+ stand for Jones, idealized to possess full factual information and perfect instrumental rationality, and let Smith+ stand for the corresponding idealization of Smith. As before, A-type scenarios present no problem of principle: we take the non-moral good of Jones to consist in Q, the non-moral good of Smith to consist in R. This will make the calculation of overall or average utility more difficult than it would be if the same thing or pursuit were desirable for both of them, but again it introduces no difficulty of principle: the overall non-moral good is achieved by maximizing Q for Smith and R for Jones. However, B-type scenarios do now appear to present a difficulty of principle. Jones+ wants Jones to want Q, Smith+ wants Smith to want R, and Jones's pursuing Q will undermine or rule out Smith's pursuing R. In this case we cannot argue as we did before that one or the other must lack full-instrumental rationality: there appears to be no lapse in instrumental rationality in Jones+'s wanting Jones to want something the pursuit of which will frustrate Smith's obtaining what is in his interest, because Jones and Smith, unlike Jones and JONES, are not temporal slices *of the same self.*

Sobel writes, of problem (a):

> This problem strikes me as worse than the traditional worries about the interpersonal comparability of utility since some version of existence-internalism [the view, for a given value V, that an agent will, at least when idealized, be motivated to pursue V] looks more irresistible in the case of an agent's own well-being than in the case of moral value. That is, we might think one need not find motivating, even after idealization, the fact that an act promotes the aggregate of individuals' interests. But this manoeuvre seems unavailable in the case of an agent's own good. Hence the constraints on resolving intrapersonal comparisons of utility appear even more severe than those in the case of interpersonal value. (1994: 806)

I have argued that this claim is unwarranted. Railton, in the full-information analysis of non-moral value, faces no problem about intrapersonal comparisons of utility in addition to the problem of interpersonal commensurability which he already faces in the analysis of moral rightness. Problem (a) for Railton's full-information analysis of non-moral value is thus neutralized.[17]

Response to Problem (b)

This problem is specific to the amnesia version of the experiential model. Lyn+ has first-hand experience of all the lives that Lyn could possibly lead, As she moves from life L1 to life L2 she temporarily 'forgets' the experiences that were necessary for forming an accurate impression of what it would be like to lead life L1, and so on. Then, at the end of this process she recovers all of the experiental knowledge she has forgotten and chooses the life she would want her actual self to want. Problem (b) arises because there seems to be no guarantee that the evaluative perspective+ occupied by the idealized agent is the same at the initial stage and the recovery stage, and so no guarantee that the experience of, say, L1 at the recovery stage will match the experience of L1 at the initial stage.

I suggest that Sobel's problem (b) arises only if we take a very naive view of what is involved in the idealized agent's wanting her actual self to want to pursue one of the kinds of life possible for her. First of all, it is not, as Sobel implies, a *temporal* process at all. We already have to idealize Lyn+ so that she possesses full factual information and flawless instrumental rationality, and given that there are presumably at least a countably infinite number of lives possible for Lyn, Lyn+ must be capable of carrying out an infinitary task. Given this amount of idealization already, it adds little if anything to idealize further and require that Lyn carry out *infinitely quickly* the process of moving from L1, L2, . . . to the stage where the forgotten experiential knowledge is recovered, and selecting from among L1, L2, ... There is thus no scope for the sort of *change over time* of Lyn+'s evaluative perspective as there is with everyday, non-idealized agents. Of course, the question now arises whether we can have any confidence in what Lyn+ decides with this amount of idealization and after undergoing an infinitely quick process. But this simply takes us on to problem (c).

Response to Problem (c)

Like problem (b), problem (c) is specific to the amnesia version of the experiential model. What assurance do we have that Lyn+, with the huge amount of idealization of her actual self required to select from among the lives possible for her, will not simply go mad as a result? As Sobel puts it, we cannot simply *stipulate* that Lyn+ remains sane given this massive idealization. I think there are a number of things the full-information theorist can say in response to this worry. First of all, Sobel himself speaks of the 'psychological shock' Lyn+ might experience as a result of undergoing the idealization and then having all of the stored pieces of experiential knowledge instantaneously restored. But notice that we would normally reserve the term 'shock' to describe the effect of *unexpected* occurrences or events upon an agent. Note, further, that Lyn+ can be assumed to know exactly what sort of process she is to undergo and what, in general terms, to expect at the end of it. Because she possesses full factual information Lyn's expectations match what will happen to her. So the scope for psychological shock would be correspondingly limited. Second, undergoing an extreme process might normally drive one insane because of psychological or physical limitations. If I had a perfect capacity to blot out what is happening in my immediate vicinity, even a trainload of loudmouthed merchant bankers would not unsettle my reason. Given that Lyn+ will have a number of such unbounded capacities, we would expect her to emerge unscathed and sane when the stored experiental knowledge is recovered and brought to consciousness. Third, and most importantly, problem (c) seems to depend on a faulty assumption to the effect that 'we can't have reason to accept that a generalization defined for idealized conditions is lawful unless we can specify the counterfactuals which would be true if the idealized conditions were to obtain' (Fodor 1990: 94). To be sure, no one can be certain how Lyn would behave were she to possess full factual information, perfect instrumental rationality, and all of the various unbounded physical and cognitive-psychological capacities required by the idealization. But:

> God only knows what would happen if molecules and containers actually met the conditions specified by the ideal gas laws (molecules are perfectly elastic; containers are infinitely impermeable; etc.); for all *I* know, if any of these things were true, the world would come to an end ... But it's not required, in order that the ideal gas laws should be in scientific good repute, that we know anything like all of what would happen if there really were ideal gasses. All that's required is that we know (e.g.) that if there were ideal gasses, then, ceteris paribus, their volume would vary inversely with the pressure upon them. And *that* counterfactual *the theory itself tells us is true.* (Fodor 1990: 94–5)

Likewise, the fact that we don't know exactly what would happen if the conditions for the idealization of Lyn were realized needn't prevent us from claiming that, if she were thus idealized, she would want her actual self to want the action that is in her actual self's best interests. Mimicking Fodor, we might say that *that* counterfactual *Railton's theory itself tells us is true.* The main difference is that Railton's theory is (as he would be the first to admit) much less empirically confirmed than the ideal gas laws. Of course, it is open to Sobel to argue that Railton's theory is not empirically well confirmed. But that would be to broach a different sort of objection altogether.[18]

Response to Problem (d)

This problem can be quickly dispatched (as Sobel notes, it is not specific to the amnesia version of the experiential model). Why do we require Lyn+ to require full factual information and perfect instrumental rationality? We require this because it is a fact that people often mistake what is in their interests because they lack certain factual information, or because of some defect in instrumental rationality. By the same token, people can mistake what is in their interests because they base their estimate not on intrinsic facts about their situation, but on facts about their condition relative to others. The patient recovering after horrifying brain surgery forms the desire to kill himself as a result of comparing his position with that of his previously healthy self:

someone attempting to dissuade him would naturally get him to focus on his intrinsic state and his genuine prospects for a full recovery and to give up comparing his current situation with that of his former self or other, more healthy people. Thus it would be entirely natural and non-arbitrary to add a clause to the full-information analysis of non-moral value that Lyn+'s verdict about what is good for Lyn not be due to 'the only relatively degraded condition of [Lyn] compared to [Lyn+]'. If there is a deeper reason to outlaw the addition of a clause along these lines, the onus is on Sobel to provide it.

In conclusion it seems to me that none of the objections Sobel presses against the full-information analysis of non-moral value ultimately damage it. Of course, there may be many other objections that can be levelled against the full-information analysis, but we will not pursue those in the present chapter.

9.9 Internalism and Externalism in Moral Psychology

I have referred in passing to the debate between internalist and externalist views of moral motivation (e.g., 1.8, 2.4, 3.3, 8.8), the Humean and Anti-Humean theories of motivation (e.g., 1.8, 4.2, 9.5, 9.6), and rationalist and anti-rationalist conceptions of moral facts (9.6). Before the end of the book, I will have a little to say about each of these debates. In this section I concentrate on the debate between internalists and externalists, in 9.10 I consider the debate between rationalists and their opponents, and in 10.4 I look at the debate between Humean and Anti-Humean Theories of Motivation. Each of these debates has generated a vast amount of literature, much of it very difficult, and even a basic treatment of any of them would probably require a book at least as long as the present one. So my approach in these sections will be minimalist. I will attempt to evaluate just one argument for or against one of the sides in each of the various debates. The arguments I will consider are those developed by one of the leading contemporary metaethicists, Michael Smith, in his 1994a. In this section I will discuss Smith's argument for internalism about moral motivation, in 9.10 I will consider his argument in favour of moral rationalism, and in 10.4 I will examine his argument in favour of Humean Theories of Motivation.

A good way of setting the scene here is to consider what Smith terms 'The Moral Problem'. According to Smith, the problem is that the following three propositions are individually plausible, but apparently inconsistent:

(1) Moral judgements express beliefs.
(2) Moral judgements have a necessary connection with being motivated.

(3) Motivation is a matter of having, inter alia, suitable (and independently intelligible) desires.[19]

When I judge that buying *The Big Issue* is right I express the belief that buying *The Big Issue* is right. Prior to philosophical reflection, that seems a natural thing to say: hence the plausibility of (1). What about (2)? Well, when someone sincerely utters an evaluative sentence like 'Buying *The Big Issue* is right' we typically know that, other things being equal, they will be motivated to buy *The Big Issue*, or will be willing, other things being equal, to purchase a copy when invited to do so by a street vendor. It seems plausible to think that this is not an accident, but is a necessary or conceptual fact about moral judgement: hence the plausibility of (2). What about (3)? Well, very roughly, the justification for this might run as follows. Beliefs cannot produce actions all by themselves. Beliefs tell us how the world is. So, although beliefs tell us of lots of ways in which the world could be changed in order to make it different, they do not tell us how it is to be changed. Similarly, desires cannot produce actions all by themselves. Desires tell us how the world is to be. So, although desires tell us of lots of ways in which the world should be changed, because they don't tell us of the way the world actually is, they don't tell us whether or how the world has to be changed in order to be the way they tell us that it should be. So beliefs cannot on their own motivate someone to act. And neither can desires. But beliefs and desires together can produce action: the desire tells us how the world is to be, and the belief tells us whether and how we are to change the world in order to make it that way. Hence the plausibility of (3).

In fact, (1) is simply a statement of a form of *cognitivism*, (2) is a statement of *internalism* about moral motivation, and (3) is a statement of the *Humean theory of motivation*. Smith argues that there is a prima facie tension between (1), (2) and (3). Why might we worry that (1), (2) and (3) are inconsistent? Well, take the case of a moral evaluation like 'Buying *The Big Issue* is right'. This, when uttered sincerely, expresses the belief that buying *The Big Issue* is right. And that belief itself is capable of motivating me to act in a certain way: I know that someone who believes that buying *The Big Issue* is right will, other things being equal, be motivated to buy copies of *The Big Issue*. But this then contradicts (3): believing that buying *The Big Issue* is right can motivate the person to act even in the absence of a suitable desire. I do not need to know anything about the person's desires in order to work out how, other things being equal, he is disposed to act when he sincerely utters 'Buying *The Big Issue* is right'.

So there appears to be a prima facie tension between (1), (2) and (3). This is what Smith calls 'The Moral Problem'. How can we deal with this tension?

According to Smith, there are at least three main ways of attempting to deal with it:

Externalism
Externalism holds that (1), (2) and (3) are actually inconsistent. It retains (1) and (3) by giving up (2). Moral judgements have no necessary or conceptual connection with motivation: rather, the connection is at most contingent and external. The Cornell Realists (chapter 8) and Railton's reductionism (this chapter) provide examples of externalist cognitivists.

Anti-Humeanism
This also holds that (1), (2) and (3) are inconsistent. But it preserves (1) and (2) by giving up (3): it rejects the Humean Theory of Motivation that requires both (independently intelligible) beliefs and (independently intelligible) desires to be present in order for action to be motivated. Moral beliefs can and do motivate people to act in the absence of (independently intelligible) desires. Contemporary non-naturalists such as John McDowell advocate Anti-Humean theories of motivation. I will return to Anti-Humeanism in 10.4.

Non-Cognitivism
This follows externalism and Anti-Humeanism in holding that (1), (2) and (3) are inconsistent. But it preserves (2) and (3) by giving up (1). When I sincerely utter 'Buying *The Big Issue* is right', I'm not expressing a belief at all. I'm doing something altogether different: I am not asserting that such and such is the case or attempting to report that a certain fact obtains in the world. Rather, I am expressing a desire, or some other non-cognitive attitude. So the non-cognitivist gives up (1). And so there is no need to give up either (2) or (3). Moral judgements can certainly retain a necessary connection with motivation, because someone who makes a moral judgement is expressing a desire. And likewise there is no denial of the Humean claim that requires motivation to be, inter alia, a matter of possessing suitable desires. I have already discussed non-cognitivist theories in chapters 3, 4, 5 and 6 (6.10).

In the rest of this section I'll consider an argument that Michael Smith develops in favour of internalism (or 'the practicality requirement' as Smith sometimes calls it).[20] The brand of internalism favoured by Smith himself is that the following is a conceptual truth (1994a: 61):

If an agent judges that it is right for her to G in circumstances C, then either she is motivated to G in C or she is practically irrational.

In other words, there is a conceptual connection between moral judgement and the will, but a *defeasible* one. For example, if Jones judges that it is right to give to famine relief, then, as a matter of conceptual necessity, he will be motivated to give to famine relief, just as long as he is not suffering from some form of practical irrationality, such as weakness of will, apathy, despair or the like (1994a: 120). Before considering the argument Smith develops in favour of this form of internalism, it is worth pausing to compare it with a stronger form of internalism which Smith rejects. According to this stronger form, the connection between moral judgement and motivation is captured by the following claim:

If an agent judges that it is right for her to G in circumstances C, then she is motivated to G in C.

According to this form of internalism, the relationship between moral judgement and the will is an *indefeasible* one. Smith thinks that this claim is too strong:

> It commits us to denying that, for example, weakness of the will and the like may defeat an agent's moral motivations while leaving her appreciation of her moral reasons intact. (1994a: 61)

Smith's worry about the stronger form of internalism appears to be a reasonable one. Nevertheless, we can question whether Smith is in a position to offer his weaker form of internalism as an alternative. In particular, we can question whether Smith has so much as even *formulated* a coherent alternative. The internalist thesis, although it is a *conceptual* claim, is not intended to be an entirely *trivial* claim. That is, the internalist thesis must be formulable in such a way that some substantial debate will be possible as to its truth. The problem is that, as formulated by Smith, the weaker internalist thesis faces a very real danger of lapsing into triviality. In order to avoid the lapse into triviality, Smith requires some substantial characterization of 'practically rational'. When Smith talks about what practical rationality involves, though, he typically characterizes it as freedom from 'weakness of will, apathy, despair, or the like' (1994a: 120). But, unless more is said, the phrase 'or the like' seems to amount to some condition along the lines of 'and of any other condition which is such as to frustrate the connection between moral judgement and motivation'. And, of course, if the condition is read in this way the weak internalist thesis comes out as the wholly insubstantial:

If an agent judges that it is right for her to G in circumstances C and she is free of any condition which is such as to frustrate the connection between moral judgement and motivation, then she is motivated to G in C.

This is entirely trivial: so trivial that it could not serve as the focus for any sort of genuine philosophical debate. So it seems to me that although the stronger of the two internalist theses is, as Smith claims, unreasonable, Smith is not yet entitled to a weaker form of internalism: without a characterization of 'practically rational' which does not simply trivialize the thesis, it looks as though Smith has not even got as far as formulating a weaker alternative to the strong internalist thesis, let alone providing a compelling argument in favour of that alternative.[21]

However, in what follows, I imagine that this worry has been adequately dealt with, and that Smith has provided some suitably non-trivializing account of practical rationality. Smith's argument for his preferred form of internalism goes as follows. It is a 'striking fact' that there is a certain sort of *reliable connection* between the formation of moral judgement and the motivation to act as that judgement prescribes in the *good and strong-willed person*.[22] This is manifested in the fact that in the good, strong-willed, and otherwise practically rational person, 'a *change in motivation* follows reliably in the wake of *a change in moral judgement*' (1994a: 71). Internalism is to be preferred to externalism because it alone can provide a plausible explanation of this striking fact.

As an example of this reliable connection, consider two agents engaged in an argument about some fundamental moral issue: Jill believes that it is wrong to eat meat, whereas James believes that meat-eating is morally permissible. Suppose, for the sake of argument, that James is a good, strong-willed and otherwise practically rational person. Suppose also that Jill succeeds in convincing James that meat-eating is morally impermissible, so that he comes to revise his moral judgement about this issue. Given this, what will happen to James's motives? Clearly, they will change: they will 'fall in line behind [his] newly arrived at moral judgements' (1994a: 72). Whereas James previously lacked the motivation to avoid eating meat, to persuade others to refrain from doing so, and so on, he will now be so motivated.

Smith suggests that there are only two possible ways in which we might try to explain this fact about the reliable connection between James's moral judgements and his motivation to act. One possible explanation is provided by the internalist account of moral motivation: the reliable connection between judgement and motivation 'follows directly from the content of moral judgement itself' (1994a: 72). Smith writes:

> Since those who defend [internalism] think that it is in the nature of a moral judgement that an agent who judges it right to G in circumstances C is motivated to G, at least absent weakness of will or some other such psychological failure, they will insist that it comes as no surprise that in

a strong-willed person a change of moral motivation follows in the wake
of a change in moral judgement. For that is just a direct consequence of
[internalism]. (Ibid.)

In other words, according to internalism, it is a conceptual constraint on
forming a judgement with the content *that meat-eating is impermissible*,
that you are, if you are a good and strong-willed person, motivated to
act accordingly. This explains why James, who *ex hypothesi* revises his
moral scheme to include a judgement with that content, and who is *ex
hypothesi* good and strong-willed, undergoes a corresponding change
in his motivational states.

The other possible explanation is an externalist one: the reliable
connection in question 'is to be explained *externally*: it follows from the
content of the motivational dispositions possessed by the good and
strong-willed person' (ibid.). Since the externalist does not view the
possession of a suitable motivational state as a constraint on the mere
formation of a moral judgement, he will have to look elsewhere for an
explanation of the reliable connection between moral judgement and
motivation in the good and strong-willed person. And if the explanatory weight is not carried by constraints on the good and strong-willed
person's formation of judgements with moral content, it will have to be
carried by some fact about the good and strong-willed person himself:
and what fact could this be except a fact about the content of his moral
motivation? Smith's claim is now that the externalist cannot provide
a plausible account of what the content of this moral motivation is. In
short, the only motivational content capable of explaining why changes
of motivation reliably track revisions in moral judgement 'is a motivation to do the right thing, where this is now read *de dicto* and not *de re*.
At bottom, the externalist will have to say, having this self-consciously
moral motive is what makes me a good person' (1994: 74).[23] Suppose
Jones has the motive to do the right thing, where this is read *de dicto*.
When he revises his judgement about the permissibility of meat-eating,
he forms the judgement that not eating meat is the right thing to do. So
it is not surprising that he acquires the motive to avoid eating meat: this
follows from the interaction between his new moral judgement and his
self-consciously moral motive.

Smith objects to this externalist explanation of the reliable connection
in question because it attributes the *wrong content* to the motivational
disposition possessed by the good and strong-willed person and, in so
doing, it 'elevates a moral fetish into the one and only moral virtue'
(1994a: 76). And:

Good people care non-derivatively about honesty, the weal and woe of
their children and friends, the well-being of their children and friends,
people getting what they deserve, justice, equality, and the like, not just

one thing: doing what they believe to be right, where this is read *de dicto* and not *de re*. Indeed, commonsense tells us that being so motivated is a fetish or a moral vice, not the one and only moral virtue. (1994a: 75)

Smith suggests that this objection to externalism is similar to an objection raised by Bernard Williams against ethical views that emphasize impartiality. Suppose a man sees two people drowning in the sea. One of them is his wife; the other is a complete stranger. What would move a morally good person to action in this kind of situation? Smith, expounding Williams's argument, writes:

Many moral philosophers think that, even in such a case, a morally good person would be moved by impartial concern; that this man's motivating thought would have to be, at best, 'that it was his wife, and that in situations like this kind it is permissible to save one's wife'. But, Williams objects, this is surely wrong. It provides the husband with 'one thought too many'. . . . [C]onsider matters from the wife's perspective. She would quite rightly hope that her husband's 'motivating thought, fully spelled out' is that the person he saved was *his wife*. If any further motivation were required then that would simply indicate that he doesn't have the feelings of direct love and concern for her that she rightly wants and expects. He would be alienated from her, treating her as in relevant respects just like a stranger; though, of course, a stranger that he is especially well placed to benefit. (1994a: 75)[24]

Smith points out that although his argument against the externalist is parallel to Williams's argument, it is also *stronger*: the argument against the externalist, unlike Williams's argument, does not require an assumption to the effect that partial values such as love and friendship can figure in an ethical system:

[T]he objection in this case is simply that, in taking it that a good person is motivated to do what she believes right, where this is read *de dicto* and not *de re*, externalists too provide the morally good person with 'one thought too many'. They alienate her from the ends at which morality properly aims. Just as it is constitutive of being a good lover that you have direct concern for the person you love, so it is constitutive of being a morally good person that you have direct concern for what you think is right, where this is read *de re* and not *de dicto*. This is something that must be conceded even by those moral philosophers who think that the only right course of action is one of impartiality. (1994a: 76)

Thus, externalism cannot explain the reliable connection between moral judgement and motivation in the good and strong-willed person without attributing a wholly implausible motivational disposition to him, without crediting him with 'one thought too many'. The internalist explanation of the reliable connection labours under no such difficulty, so internalism is preferable. This is Smith's argument in favour of internalism about moral motivation.

I will now argue that Smith's argument is inconclusive, and that it appears to undermine the version of internalism he favours as much as the externalism that he rejects. Smith's argument actually calls for a radical overhaul of the notion of moral judgement, and it is simply unclear, for all that Smith has said so far, whether an internalist or externalist view of moral judgement will emerge as victorious after that overhaul.

Suppose that George is a good and strong-willed person, and that George judges that it is right to be honest, or that honesty is right. The externalist, on Smith's reading, must attribute to George the following overarching and non-derivative desire: the desire to do what he believes to be right. From this non-derivative desire and the moral belief that it is right to be honest, George acquires the *derivative* desire to be honest. According to Smith, this is at odds with how we think a person such as George should be described: a person like George should possess a *non-derivative* desire to be honest, not derive that desire from some other non-derivative desire to do what he judges to be good, on pain of 'moral fetishism'. But it seems to me that unless more is said, Smith's internalist story about someone like George would be open to a similar charge. According to Smith's internalist, if George judges that honesty is right, it follows, as a matter of conceptual necessity, that George will be motivated to be honest. Now note that on this account George's motivation to be honest is still derived: not, to be sure, from his belief that it would be right to be honest in conjunction with an overarching non-derivative desire to do the right thing, but from the belief that it would be right to be honest *itself*. According to the internalist, that George has the relevant motivational state is entailed by his judging that it would be right to be honest, and if P entails Q it seems correct to say that Q is derived from P. Indeed, that George's motivational state is derived follows directly from the datum which Smith claims the internalist can plausibly explain: if George's motivational states are sensitive to his moral beliefs in the sense that a change in motivation follows reliably in the wake of a change in moral belief, it seems right to describe this fact by saying that the relevant motivational states of George are derived from his moral beliefs. Thus, even the internalist cannot see George's desire to be honest as non-derivative, since even on the internalist account it is derived from the belief that it would be right to be honest. Thus, unless more is said, if the externalist account leaves George looking like a moral fetishist, so does the internalist account.[25]

In a later exposition of the argument for internalism, Smith switches from talk of derivative and non-derivative desires to instrumental and non-instrumental desires. Could this switch neutralize the worry just developed? Smith writes:

[According] to externalists, [morally perfect people] must have as their primary source of moral motivation a desire to do the right thing. Thus, even though they believe it is right to, say, look after the well-being of their family and friends, and even though this belief is, let's assume, true, they do not desire non-instrumentally to look after the well-being of their family and friends. Their desire to look after the well-being of their family and friends is only an instrumental desire because it must have been derived from their non-instrumental desire to do the right thing together with their true means-end belief that they can do the right thing by looking after the well-being of their family and friends. (1996a: 182)

It may be that Smith thinks he can block the application of his argument to his own internalist position in the following way. Suppose one defined an instrumental desire as a desire which is derived from another desire together with a means–end belief. Then, for the externalist, the desire to be honest is indeed an instrumental desire: it is derived from the desire to do the right thing together with the means–end belief that being honest is a way of doing the right thing. But, Smith may argue, this does not hold of the internalist. To be sure, the presence of the belief that it is right to be honest entails that the morally perfect person will have a desire to be honest, but since in this case the motivational state is derived from a belief *alone*, not a belief in conjunction with some other desire, even though the morally perfect person's desire to be honest is in a sense 'derivative' it is still non-instrumental. And it is this which marks out the difference between the internalist and the externalist: the externalist attributes an instrumental desire to be honest to the morally perfect person, whereas the internalist attributes a non-instrumental desire to be honest to them.

However, it seems to me that this is not sufficient to see off the worry. We can see why by considering again Williams's example of the drowning wife. The wife's complaint, remember, was that if the husband required, in addition to the belief that the woman drowning was his wife, some additional thought to the effect that in these sorts of cases it is permissible to save one's wife, the husband would have 'one thought too many'. The wife's worry is that there is some aspect of her husband's psychology, in addition to the belief that the woman drowning is his wife, to which his motivation to save the drowning woman is sensitive: if he didn't believe that in cases such as this it is permissible to save one's wife, he would lack the motivation to jump in and save her. Now, the woman's complaint is that there is some aspect of the husband's psychology, in addition to the belief that the woman drowning is his wife, to which his motivation to jump in and save her is sensitive, where, crucially, it doesn't matter whether or not the other aspect of the husband's psychology is a desire or whatever. All the woman needs to form a basis for her complaint is that there *is* such an aspect of her husband's psychology, not some story about what *sort* of aspect that is. Transposing this back into the case considered by Smith, what happens? Even if, on the definition of 'instrumental' that I proffered on behalf of Smith, it turns out that the morally perfect person's desire to be honest is 'non-instrumental', it is still sensitive to some other aspect of the morally perfect person's psychology, namely, the belief that it is right to be honest.[26] As in the case of the husband with 'one thought too many', this is enough to merit the charge that the psychology of the morally perfect person has been misdescribed: in the morally perfect person, the motivation to be honest would be sensitive to no such aspect.

Thus, as things stand, the internalist is in no better shape than the externalist. What Smith's argument shows, if carried to its logical conclusion, is that if we think of the morally virtuous person as forming beliefs or judgements to the effect that it is right to be honest, it is right to be concerned with the well-being of one's friends and family and so on, then we get an analogue of Williams's 'one thought too many' objection. What this seems to imply is that on pain of misdescribing the psychology of the morally perfect person, we have to view such a person not as making judgements to the effect that, for example, it is right to be honest, but as having non-derivative concerns for the things which are, as a matter of fact, examples of honesty. The notion of *moral judgement* appears to drop out of the picture altogether. But Smith sets up the internalist and externalist positions, and the debate between them, in terms of that very notion. So, unless much more is said, we cannot be sure that the internalist position is so much as formulable, let alone capable of being established by an argument such as Smith's. To put matters another way, if Smith's argument is successful it undermines the very basis for the internalist–externalist debate as Smith conceives it. If Smith's argument is unsuccessful, externalism as he conceives it is left intact. Either way, there is no compelling argument for the internalist thesis as formulated by Smith.

9.10 Rationalism and Anti-Rationalism

In 9.6, I defined *rationalism* as the view that our concept of a moral fact is a concept of a reason for action, and the *categoricity of moral reasons* as the view that if our concept of a moral fact is a concept of a reason for action, then it is a concept of a categorical reason for action, a reason for any rational agent irrespective of their contingent desires and inclinations. We saw that although Railton, for example, accepts the conditional claim embodied in the categoricity of moral reasons, he rejects rationalism: he denies that our concept of a moral fact is a concept of a reason for action. Moral facts may provide agents with reasons for action, but only in virtue of some facts about the contingent goals and desires of the agent concerned and not as a matter of conceptual necessity. Smith argues, against Railton, that our concept of a moral fact is a concept of a categorical reason for action. In this section, I will attempt to show that Smith's arguments in favour of this claim are unconvincing.

Before doing so, it might be good to make a few remarks in the interests of avoiding terminological confusion. Smith is not consistent in his use of the term 'rationalism'. For example, he characterizes rationalism as the view that our concept of a moral fact is a concept of a reason for action (1994a: 62), while later (e.g., 1994a: 85) he characterizes it as the view that our concept of a moral fact is a concept of a *categorical* reason for action. Since I have already used 'rationalism' in accord with the first of Smith's uses, as the view that our concept of a moral fact is a concept of a reason for action, I will reserve 'Rationalism' (capital 'R') for the view that our concept of a moral fact is a concept of a categorical reason for action. Rationalism, thus understood, is the conjunction of rationalism with the categoricity of moral reasons. This conjunction plainly entails rationalism, so if Smith's arguments in favour of Rationalism are cogent, Railton's anti-rationalism will be undermined.

It is worth noting, too, that rationalism entails internalism, but not vice versa (Smith 1994a: 62). Suppose that rationalism is true: that our concept of a moral fact is a concept of a reason for action. Suppose that Lyn judges that it is right for her to G in C. Then, by the rationalist claim, she judges that she has a reason to G in C. Platitudinously, Lyn will have a reason to G in C just in case she would be motivated to G in C were she rational. Thus, Lyn judges that she would be motivated to G in C if she were rational. Now if she fails to be motivated to G in C she is irrational 'by her own lights' (1994a: 62). Thus, if Lyn judges that it is right for her to G in C then, unless she is practically irrational, she will be motivated to G in C. And this last claim is just a statement of the internalist thesis discussed above. Since Rationalism entails rationalism, and rationalism entails internalism, Rationalism entails internalism.

Smith points out that although rationalism entails internalism, the converse implication does not hold. Non-cognitivists and expressivists accept internalism, but they hold that our concept of a moral requirement is not a concept of a reason for action. According to non-cognitivists, 'rational agents may . . . differ in their moral judgements . . . without being in any way subject to rational criticism' (1994a: 86). It will be important to bear this in mind when we come to evaluate Smith's case for Rationalism.

Smith's first argument for Rationalism is set out in the following passage:

Moral requirements apply to rational agents as such. But it is a conceptual truth that if agents are morally required to act in a certain way then we expect them to act in that way. Being rational, as such, must therefore suffice to ground our expectation that rational agents will do what they are morally required to do. But how could this be so? It could be so only if we think of the moral requirements that apply to agents as themselves categorical requirements of rationality or reason. For the only thing we can legitimately expect of rational agents as such is that they do what they are rationally required to do. (1994a: 85)

Smith is aware that 'expect' here is ambiguous. To 'expect' an agent to do something could be either to believe that they *ought to* or *should* do that thing or to believe that they *will* do that thing. Call the former reading the *normative* reading of 'should' and the latter the *descriptive* reading of 'should'. Smith makes it clear that it is the latter of the two senses of 'expect' that is relevant here. Do we really expect that rational agents *will* do what they are morally required to do? Smith realizes that this is apt to sound unconvincing and therefore provides an argument for the claim based on the weaker internalist claim that he has already established (although I claimed in the previous section that Smith's argument for internalism is unconvincing, let's forget my claim and grant Smith his internalism for the sake of argument). It follows from internalism that 'we certainly expect rational agents to do what they *judge* themselves to be morally required to do' (1994a: 86). Smith imagines an objection to the effect that this is as far as we can go:

[The objection runs] . . . even if, other things being equal, rational agents will do what they judge themselves morally required to do, the argument provides us with no reason to think that rational agents will all come up with the same judgements about what they are morally required to do. . . . But if agents may differ in their moral judgements without being subject to rational criticism, then it cannot be that their judgements are about what they are required to do by the categorical requirements of rationality. (1994a: 86)

And, indeed, this is the sort of objection that a non-cognitivist or expressivist anti-Rationalist is likely to make (as well as a Railton-style anti-Rationalist who is granting Smith internalism for the sake of argument). But Smith argues that the objection 'backfires':

It is a platitude that our moral judgements at least purport to be objective . . . Thus if A says 'It is right to G in circumstances C' and B says 'It is not right to G in circumstances C' then we take it that A and B *disagree*. And that means, in turn, that we can fault at least one of A's and B's judgements from the rational point of view, for it is false. (1994a: 86)

And then it follows that:

[W]e do expect *rational* agents to do what they are morally required to do, not just what they judge themselves to be morally required to do. For we can and do expect rational agents to judge *truly*; we expect them to *converge* in their judgements about what it is right to do. Our concept of a moral requirement thus turns out to be the concept of a categorical requirement of rationality after all. (1994a: 86–7)

However, it seems to me that this argument of Smith's simply begs the question against the anti-Rationalist. The crucial step is the one where Smith assumes that the *falsity* of a *moral* judgement implies that the judgement in question can be faulted from the rational point of view: the non-cognitivist, for example, holds that from the fact that Lyn's *moral* judgement is false, nothing whatsoever follows to the effect that Lyn is irrational. Thus, in assuming that falsity in moral judgements is a mark of irrationality, Smith is simply assuming the very thing he is trying to establish: that our concept of a moral fact is a concept of a categorical requirement of reason.[27] Alternatively, all Smith is entitled to say is that we assume rational agents to judge truly on *rational* matters: to say that we assume that rational agents judge truly on moral matters is simply to assume exactly what the anti-Rationalist denies, namely, that moral matters are matters of reason. Again, Smith's argument clearly begs the question.

In addition to the argument I've just discussed, Smith provides another argument for rationalism. Smith starts out from the datum 'that we approve and disapprove of what people do when moral matters are at stake' (1994a: 87). He then claims that 'it makes sense to say that I disapprove of your behaviour only if we presuppose that you are to take account of that fact in deciding what to do' (1994a: 88). The rest of the argument is contained in the following passage:

[D]isapproval of those who do not do what they are morally required to do presupposes the legitimacy of our expectation that they will act otherwise; it presupposes that, as we see it, their decision is a bad one in terms of the commonly acknowledged standards by which their decisions are to be judged. But what provides grounds for the legitimacy of this expectation? . . . What grounds the expectation is the mere fact that people are rational agents. Being rational suffices to ground the expectation that people will do what they are morally required to do. Given that moral approval and disapproval are ubiquitous, the truth of the rationalists' conceptual claim thus seems to be entailed by the fact that the preconditions of moral approval and disapproval are satisfied. (1994a: 89–90)

This argument seems to me to be vitiated by an equivocation very much like the one on 'should' which Smith himself earlier warned us against. According to Smith, disapproving of a liar, for example, can only take place given 'the legitimacy of our expectation that they will act otherwise'. But it seems to me that this is only plausible if 'expectation' is given the normative, rather than descriptive, reading we distinguished between earlier. Otherwise, it would not be possible for me to morally disapprove of Arnold, who I know to be an inveterate and habitual liar. What needs to be presupposed in order for my disapproval of Arnold to make sense is not the legitimacy of my expectation that he *will* act otherwise than lying (I have no such expectation), but simply the legitimacy of my belief that he *ought not to* lie. Smith more or less concedes this himself when he speaks of the presupposition as holding that 'their decision is a *bad* one in terms of the *commonly acknowledged standards* by which their decisions are to be judged' (emphases added). All the anti-Rationalist requires in order to satisfy the preconditions of moral approval and disapproval are legitimate moral 'oughts': and since the anti-Rationalist thinks our concept of a moral requirement, of a moral 'ought', is not a concept of a reason for action, the anti-Rationalist can reply that for all that Smith has managed to show, the anti-Rationalist too can claim that the preconditions for moral approval and disapproval can be satisfied. And, of course, if Smith assumes that the mere legitimacy of moral 'oughts' entails that our concept of a moral requirement is a concept of a reason for action, this argument, like the previous one, will simply beg the question against the anti-Rationalist.

It seems to me, then, that Smith's arguments in favour of Rationalism, and by implication rationalism, fail to establish their intended conclusions.

9.11 Analytic Moral Functionalism and Smith's 'Permutation Problem'[28]

Earlier in the chapter, we saw that Railton's ethical reductionism is surface-content revisionist but non-revisionist with respect to the underlying semantics of moral discourse. Railton, although he proposes a definition of 'morally right', proposes it as a reforming definition the plausibility of which is to be determined on a posteriori grounds. In other words, Railton's ethical reductionism does not claim to discern any analytic connections between moral predicates and naturalistic predicates as they are actually used in, say, English. I'll now look briefly at another form of ethical reductionism, a form which is like Railton's in being non-revisionist about the underlying semantics of moral discourse, but unlike Railton's in also being non-revisionist about the surface-content of moral judgements. The form of ethical reductionism in question is *analytic moral functionalism*. The main proponents of analytic moral functionalism in the recent literature have been Frank Jackson and Philip Pettit.[29]

Analytic moral functionalism, as the name implies, is in the business of discerning analytic connections between moral predicates and naturalistic predicates, but it does not do so by attempting to find some naturalistic predicates synonymous with moral predicates. Rather, it attempts to do so by providing what Michael Smith has termed a 'network-style analysis' of the content of moral judgements.

Network-style analyses of a set of concepts take off from a particular view of the nature of conceptual analysis, nicely outlined by Smith. Suppose, for example, that we are in the business of giving an analysis of the content of judgements about colours: our judgements about red, blue, orange and so on. Smith suggests (i) that there are all sorts of *platitudes* about colours, and (ii) that 'an analysis of a concept is successful just in case it gives us knowledge of all and only the platitudes [relevant to mastery of that concept]' (1994a: 31). A platitude is relevant to the mastery of a term when it captures the inferential and judgemental dispositions vis-à-vis the term of those who have mastery of it. Platitudes, in the relevant sense, are thus a priori, and:

> Since an analysis of the concept of being red should tell us everything there is to know a priori about what it is for something to be red, it follows that an analysis should give us knowledge of all the relevant platitudes about redness . . . . accordingly, we might suppose, an analysis is itself simply constituted by, or derived from, a long conjunction of these platitudes. (1994a: 31)

In the case of colour terms, for example, the platitudes will include: (a) platitudes about the way colour terms are *learned* by linking them with features of the world, for example, 'To teach someone what the word for red means say the word for red whilst showing them some red things'; (b) platitudes which connect colour *experiences* with colours, for example, 'Redness causes us, under certain circumstances, to have experiences of redness'; (c) *corrective* platitudes, for example, 'To see something's colour, look at it in daylight'; and (d) platitudes about *similarity relations* between colours, for example, 'Red is more similar to orange than to yellow', 'Orange is more similar to yellow than to blue', and so on.

A proposed analysis of the content of colour judgements will thus be inadequate to the extent that it fails to capture this set of platitudes, the set of judgements and inferences licensed by our mastery of colour concepts themselves. And likewise for any proposed analysis of the content of moral judgements: just as there are platitudes surrounding our use of colour terms, there are also platitudes surrounding our use of moral terms, and any proposed account of moral judgement will be inadequate insofar as it fails to capture these platitudes. According to Smith (1994a: 39–41), the platitudes surrounding our use of moral terms include platitudes concerning *practicality* (e.g., 'If someone judges her

A-ing to be right, then, other things being equal, she will be disposed to A'), *objectivity* (e.g., 'When Les says that A-ing is right, and Lyn says that A-ing is not right, then at most one of Les and Lyn is correct'), *supervenience* (e.g., 'Acts with the same ordinary everyday features must have the same moral features as well'), *substance* (e.g., 'Right acts are in some way expressive of equal concern and respect'), and *procedure* (e.g., 'We try to discover what acts are right by employing something like the method of "reflective equilibrium"').

How, then, does a network-style analysis of a discourse attempt to capture the platitudes surrounding the terms distinctive of that discourse? I will illustrate this by following Smith and showing how a network-style analysis of the contents of our colour judgements attempts to capture all and only the platitudes surrounding our use of colour terms (the same method would be used in a network-style analysis of moral discourse).

Roughly, a network-style analysis of the contents of colour judgements follows the method developed by David Lewis for providing definitions of theoretical vocabulary (Lewis 1970, 1972; see also Ramsey 1931). As noted above, a network-style analysis takes off from the fact of there being a large range of platitudes about the colours, platitudes such as 'redness causes us, under certain circumstances, to have experiences of redness', 'red is more similar to orange than to blue', and so on. Lewis shows how we can obtain an analysis of the concept of being red from this range of platitudes. We first of all run through the various platitudes and rewrite them so that the references to colours appear in property-name style. So the two platitudes mentioned above would be rewritten as 'the property of being red causes us, under certain circumstances, to have experiences of the property of redness', 'the property of being red is more similar to the property of being orange than it is to the property of being blue'. Having done that for all of the colours, we go on to represent the result of conjoining the totality of platitudes as a relational predicate 'T' true of all the various colour properties. That is, the conjunction will be represented by $T[r\ g\ b \ldots]$, where 'r', 'g' and so on stand for the properties of being red, green and so on. Having done this, we remove the property-names of the various colours and replace them with free variables so that we get $T[x\ y\ z \ldots]$. So, if the platitudes are 'the property of redness causes us, under certain conditions, to have experiences of the property of redness' and 'the property of redness is more similar to the property of orangeness than the property of blueness' and .... then, $T(x, y, z)$ will be '(x causes us, under certain conditions, to have experiences of x) & (x is more similar to y than z) & ...'. Then, if there actually are colours, there is a unique set of properties related to the world and to each other in exactly the way that the conjunction of platitudes says there are. In other words, if there actually are colours then it is true that:

∃x ∃y ∃z . . . {T[x y z . . .] & ((∀x*)(∀y*)(∀z*) . . . T[x* y* z* . . .] iff (x=x*, y=y*, z=z* . . .))}.

Then the property of being red can be defined in the following manner: the property of being red is the x such that:

∃y ∃z . . . {T[x y z . . .] & ((∀x*)(∀y*)(∀z*) . . . T[x* y* z*. . .] iff (x=x*, y=y*, z=z* . . .))}.

This is a *reductive analysis* of redness: it defines it in purely non-colour vocabulary, since no colour vocabulary appears on the right-hand side of the definition.

Smith raises the following objection against this network-style analysis of redness. Think again about the platitudes in the case of, for example, red, orange and yellow. Then, for the property of being red, we shall have: 'the property of being red causes objects to look red to normal perceivers under standard conditions', 'the property of being red is more similar to the property of being orange than it is to the property of being yellow', and so on. For the property of being orange, we shall have: 'the property of being orange causes objects to look orange to normal perceivers under standard conditions', 'the property of being orange is more similar to the property of being yellow than it is to the property of being green', and so on. For the property of being yellow, we shall have: 'the property of being yellow causes objects to look yellow to normal perceivers under standard conditions', 'the property of being yellow is more similar to the property of being green than it is to the property of being blue', and so on. But now when we go through the Lewis-style procedure we sketched above, we get the following definitions of the properties of being red, orange and yellow:

the property of being red *is* the x such that: ∃y ∃z . . . objects' having x causes them to look x to normal perceivers under standard conditions, and x is more similar to y than it is to z . . . & . . . (uniqueness).

the property of being orange *is* the y such that: ∃z ∃u . . . objects having y causes them to look y to normal perceivers under standard conditions, and y is more similar to z than it is to u . . . & . . . (uniqueness).

the property of being yellow *is* the z such that: ∃v ∃w . . . objects having z causes them to look z to normal perceivers under standard conditions, and z is more similar to v than it is to w . . . & . . . (uniqueness).

If this is correct, then the proponent of the network-style analysis will have a problem: there will be no way of distinguishing, on his definitions, between the properties of being red, being orange, and being yellow. As Smith puts it:

> The network of relations specified by the definitions on each right-hand side . . . is the *very same* network of relations in each case . . . Network-style analyses of the various colours therefore lose a priori information about the *differences* between colours. (1998: 96)

This shows that the success of a network-style analysis depends upon the truth of an assumption, an assumption which is actually false in the colour case:

> The assumption is that, when we strip out all mention of the terms we want analysed from a statement of the relevant platitudes there will still be enough left in the way of relational information to guarantee that there is a unique realisation of the network of relations just in case the concepts we are analysing really are instantiated. (1994a: 48)

Since network-style analyses of the colours are susceptible to this 'permutation problem', as Smith calls it, they are inadequate as analyses of our colour terms.

But why are network analyses of the various colours susceptible to a permutation problem? Smith points to two main features of the colour case that allow a permutation problem to develop. He writes:

> [The permutation problem] arises because, first, we acquire mastery of colour terms inter alia by being presented with paradigms of the colours and by having our use of particular colour terms directly 'hooked up' with the particular colours these terms pick out, and because, second, as a consequence, the platitudes surrounding our use of colour terms therefore form an extremely tight-knit and interconnected group. The permutation problem arises because our colour concepts are not defined in terms of enough in the way of relations between colours and things that are not themselves colours – or, at any rate, things that are not themselves characterized in terms of colours. (1994a: 55)

Smith then suggests that the features of the colour case which allowed a permutation problem to develop are also present in the moral case:

> Our moral concepts are just like our colour concepts in this regard . . . We learn all our normative concepts, our moral concepts included, inter alia by being presented with paradigms. (Ibid.)

Smith's conclusion is that because of this similarity between our colour concepts and our moral concepts, it is highly unlikely that a successful network-style analysis of the contents of our moral judgements is possible.

9.12 A Reply to the Permutation Problem

Is there any way a defender of network-style analyses can reply to the permutation problem? Smith thinks not:

> Suppose the best theory of colour tells us that the colour wheel is not perfectly symmetrical – that, say, reds and blues have a feature that the other colours don't have. Might we use that feature of the reds and blues to solve the permutation problem? As is perhaps evident, the answer depends on whether it is plausible to suppose that it is a priori that reds and blues have the feature in question. My own view is that though it may be discovered that the reds and blues have a feature that the other colours don't have, it would be at best an *a posteriori* truth that this is so. (1998: 97, n.5)

The examples which Smith considers appear to bear this out:

> Claims like 'Red is the colour of blood', 'Yellow is the colour of a new born chicken', and the like, are certainly widely believed to be true, and in that sense they are indeed platitudes. But, unfortunately, being widely believed to be true is neither necessary nor sufficient for being platitudes in the relevant sense. Platitudes, in the relevant sense, have a prima facie a priori status because they constitute the description of the judgements and inferences we make in virtue of being masters of colour concepts. But claims like 'Red is the colour of blood', 'Yellow is the colour of a new born chicken', and the rest, are at best widely believed a posteriori truths about the colours. We therefore cannot use them to enrich our definitions of the colours. (1998: 96–7)[30]

In response, I will now argue that there are at least two arguments which plausibly establish that there are a priori asymmetries between the colours, asymmetries which allow us to dissolve the permutation problem without introducing considerations from outwith the rich set of a priori truths surrounding colour discourse.

First, I argue that, contra Smith, it is not at all clear that there are no colour platitudes which characterize our colour concepts in terms of things which are not themselves colours. If that is right, then the case of colour will not serve Smith as a model from which he can extrapolate his claim that if a set of concepts is largely interdefined, then network analysis of it will be afflicted by the permutation problem. Second, I argue that, in any case, the permutation problem would not arise in the colour case even if colour concepts were interdefined to the extent that Smith thinks they are. If that is right, then it shows that the fact that set of concepts is largely interdefined shows nothing about whether the permutation problem arises in connection with it. So Smith's argument against network-style analyses of moral concepts would be blocked

To the first argument: as we saw above, Smith assumes that any colour 'platitudes' which characterize our colour concepts in terms of things which are not themselves colours will have to be at best a posteriori, and therefore useless from the point of view of responding to the permutation problem (i.e., not platitudes in the relevant sense). But this seems to me to be unduly pessimistic. Indeed, Smith's assumption will be false so long as colour terms enter, in a different way, into the stories about how the referents of non-colour terms get fixed. And this does in fact appear to be the case. Take the case of natural-kind terms, for example. The standard Kripke-Putnam story about how the reference of 'gold' gets fixed, for example, has it that gold is whatever sort of physical stuff is dominantly causally responsible for our perceptions of co-instantiations of yellowness, shininess, lustrousness and so on.[31] Since this is a story about reference-fixing, the following will be true a priori:

(1) x is gold if and only if x is composed of whatever physical stuff is dominantly causally responsible for our perceptions of co-instantiations of yellowness, malleability, lustrousness, etc.

Given that this is a priori true, we can add it to the list of platitudes about yellowness, and following the procedure described in the previous section, we can reach a reductive definition along the following lines:

the property of being yellow *is* the x such that: $\exists v \; \exists w \ldots$ objects having x causes them to look x to normal perceivers under standard conditions, and x is more similar to v than it is to w ... & ... & u is gold if and only if u is composed of whatever physical stuff is dominantly causally responsible for our perceptions of co-instantiations of x, malleability, lustrousness, etc. ... & ... (uniqueness).

Note, first, that since we are not here in the business of giving a reductive analysis of substance terms, or other non-colour terms, we do not have to replace the occurrences of 'gold', 'malleability', and so on, with variables. And note, second, that this immediately suggests that the permutation problem is dissolved. For it will not be true, let alone a priori true, that:

(1*) x is gold if and only if x is composed of whatever physical stuff is dominantly causally responsible for our perceptions of co-instantiations of redness, malleability, lustrousness, etc.

or:

(1**) x is gold if and only if x is composed of whatever physical
stuff is dominantly causally responsible for our perceptions of
co-instantiations of orangeness, malleability, lustrousness, etc.

Thus, the reductive analysis of 'yellow' is distinguished – and distinguished a priori – from the reductive definitions of 'red' and 'orange'.
Given that the permutation problem can be dissolved in this way, by
referring even to only one reference-fixing story about a non-colour
term, such as a natural-kind term, and given that it is highly plausible
that colour terms enter in *all sorts* of diverse ways into reference-fixing
stories about other natural-kind terms, and other non-colour terms, it
would be utterly incredible if a permutation problem remains for the
network-style analysis of our colour terms.

That concludes my first argument against the claim that a permutation problem afflicts the network style of analysis of colour terms. That
argument purported to establish that we can establish a priori asymmetries between the colours on the basis of truths relating colours to
various non-colours. I now proceed to my second argument, in which
I suggest that the permutation argument would not arise in the colour
case even if colour terms were interdefined to the extent that Smith
thinks they are. A permutation problem arises in connection with a
given set of concepts only if there are at least two members of the set
which are indistinguishable once all mention of the relevant terms is
removed from a statement of the relevant platitudes. But the appearance that this condition is satisfied in the colour case disappears once
account is taken of two kinds of platitude – overlooked by Smith – *both
of which concern relations between colours.*

First, the platitudes which concern relations between colours are not
limited to those which specify their similarity relations, for there are
also platitudes which reflect the fact that some colours are phenomenologically composite whilst others are not.[32] Thus, it is platitudinous
that orange is both reddish and yellowish and that purple is both
reddish and bluish, and similarly for every other phenomenologically composite hue. And it is also platitudinous that none of the four
so-called pure hues – pure red, pure yellow, pure green and pure
blue – is composite in this way. So, once all mention of colour terms
is removed from a statement of the colour platitudes, there will be
sufficient information remaining to distinguish every pure hue from
every impure hue. Second, the platitudes which concern similarity
relations between colours are not limited to those which state simply
that colour *A* is more similar to colour *B* than to colour *C*, etc. For there
are also platitudes which reflect our dispositions to make *more finely
grained* judgements as to the respective degrees of similarity between

colours. *And since the results of psychometric experiments designed to gauge these relations purport to reflect our dispositions to make judgements about the respective degrees of similarity between colours, we can, in accordance with Smith's criteria for platitudinousness, look to the results of such experiments to ascertain the details of such platitudes.* Now, as far as the relations between the pure hues are concerned, what is of particular importance here is that the results of these experiments suggest that no two pure hues are as similar as pure green and pure blue, and that no two pure hues are as dissimilar as pure red and pure blue (Ekman 1954; Shepard 1962; Indow and Ohsumi 1972) (see Figure 9.1).

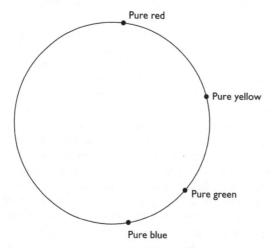

Figure 9.1   Colour wheel for pure hues (*after Indow and Ohsumi 1972*)

This entails that each of the pure hues has a network of platitudinous degree-of-similarity relations to the others, which is not isomorphic with that had by any of the others. In which case, once all mention of colour terms is removed from a statement of the colour platitudes, there *will* be sufficient information remaining to distinguish each pure hue from every other pure hue. Furthermore, this result is also important in connection with the relations had by the impure hues. For there will also be platitudes about the respective degrees of similarity between the impure hues and the pure hues. And given that each of the pure hues has a network of degree-of-similarity relations to the other pure hues, which is not isomorphic with that had by any other pure hue, it follows that each of the impure hues has a network of degree-of-similarity relations to the other impure hues, which is not isomorphic with that had by any of the other impure hues. So, once all mention of colour terms is removed from a statement of the colour platitudes, there *will* be sufficient information remaining to distinguish each impure hue from every other impure hue. To repeat: each pure hue will be distinguishable from each other pure hue in virtue of the platitudes which describe our dispositions to make more finely grained judgements about degrees of similarity; each pure hue will be distinguishable from each impure hue in virtue of the platitudes about compositeness and pureness; and we can then distinguish each impure hue from every other impure hue in virtue of the different relations they sustain to the pure hues. *In sum, then, even if all the colour platitudes concern relations between colours, it will still be the case that once all mention of colour terms is removed from a statement of the colour platitudes, there will be sufficient information remaining to distinguish every colour from every other.*

What is the relevance of my two arguments to the possibility of network-style analyses of our moral terms? Recall that Smith argues as follows: the very features (i.e., that (i) 'we acquire mastery of colour terms inter alia by being presented with paradigms of the colours and by having our use of particular colour terms directly "hooked up" with the particular colours these terms pick out', and that (ii) 'the platitudes surrounding our use of colour terms therefore form an extremely tight-knit and interconnected group') that generate the permutation problem in the colour case are also present in the moral case (since 'our moral concepts are just like our colour concepts in this regard'). This suggests, according to Smith, that any attempt to provide a network-style analysis of moral terms will fall prey to a permutation problem. I have argued above that *despite* the fact that colour terms exhibit the features (i) and (ii), it does *not* follow that a permutation problem arises. This shows that for all Smith has shown, the permutation problem needn't arise in the moral case either. My conclusion is thus that Smith's argument against network-style analyses of the contents of moral judgements is a failure.

9.13 Conclusion

I have examined two forms of contemporary naturalistic reductionism concerning moral judgements: Railton's reductionism about moral rightness, and the analytic moral functionalism of Jackson and Pettit. I have argued that Railton can see off Wiggins's 'Moorean' argument against his substantive naturalism, and that the attack mounted by Sobel against his account of non-moral value can be repulsed. I have argued that Smith's 'permutation problem' can be dealt with by analytic moral functionalism. As far as this chapter is concerned, then, ethical reductionism emerges in relatively good shape. However, this is only the beginning of a study of ethical reductionism, and no doubt many problems and difficulties remain to be faced.[33]

9.14 Further Reading

Railton's papers are generally clear and accessible: see his 1986a, 1986b, 1989, 1993a, 1993b, 1995, 1996a, and 1996b. Many of Railton's key papers are collected in his 2003. Also relevant are Brandt (1979), Velleman (1988), and Rosati (1995a, 1995b). Those wishing to follow up the various threads in Railton's account of non-moral value could start with Sobel (1994) and follow up the works he refers to in his footnotes. For an illuminating discussion of the empirical parts of Railton's programme, see Rosenberg (1990). For the debate between internalism and externalism, Smith (1994a, chapter 3) is the best place to start. Smith (1996b) is also useful. For criticism and discussion of Smith's argument in favour of internalism, see Miller (1996), Smith (1996a), Stratton-Lake (1998 and 1999), and Dreier (2000). For a clear statement of an externalist position, see Brink (1989). For analytic moral functionalism, see Jackson (1992), Jackson and Pettit (1995), and Jackson (1998). For criticism, see Zangwill (1997), the papers collected in Ravenscroft (ed.) (2009), and Miller (2011). Smith's permutation problem is developed in Smith (1994a, chapter 2), and Smith (1998). See also Smith's collected papers (2004). For a paper that argues against Rationalism, see Morgan (2006).

10

Contemporary Non-Naturalism – McDowell's Moral Realism

In chapter 9, I looked at a non-reductionist form of strong cognitivism, the naturalistic strong cognitivism of Cornell Realism. In this chapter, I will discuss another form of non-reductionist strong cognitivism, the non-naturalist moral realism of John McDowell. In 10.1, I discuss and reject McDowell's 'disentangling' objection to non-cognitivism, and attempt to tie this in with the remarks concerning the 'contaminated response' objection which I made in 4.9 and with the response I developed in 9.7 to Wiggins's argument against substantive naturalism. In 10.2, I consider and reject the suggestion that metaphysical and epistemological worries about non-naturalism can be assuaged by McDowell's notions of *Bildung* and 'second nature'. In 10.3, I reconstruct McDowell's view that we can be genuinely receptive to non-naturalistic moral states of affairs and properties without simply lapsing back into the implausible intuitionistic non-naturalism of Moore and his followers. It will emerge that there is a clear gap in this non-naturalistic strategy. In 10.4, I will consider McDowell's 'Anti-Humean' Theory of Motivation. In 10.5, I consider and reject McDowell's claim that a naturalistic version of non-cognitivism, such as Blackburn's quasi-realism, has to be motivated by an insidious 'scientism'. Overall, then, I will conclude that McDowell's objections to his non-cognitivist competitors are unsuccessful, and that there are serious problems with the non-naturalistic brand of cognitivism he advocates as an alternative.

10.1 'Disentangling' and the Argument Against Non-Cognitivism

In this section, I will consider the 'Disentangling' objection McDowell develops against non-cognitivism in his 'Non-Cognitivism and Rule-

Following'. McDowell argues that non-cognitivism makes a number of interconnected claims, which for convenience I will label as follows:

DISENTANGLING: '. . . when we feel impelled to ascribe value to something, what is actually happening can be disentangled into two components. Competence with an evaluative concept involves, first, a sensitivity to an aspect of the world as it really is . . . and, second, a propensity to a certain attitude – a non-cognitive state that constitutes the special perspective from which items in the world seem to be endowed with the value in question' (McDowell 1998: 200–1).

SHAPEFULNESS: '. . . evaluative classifications correspond to kinds into which things can in principle be seen to fall independently of an evaluative outlook' (1998: 216).

GENUINE: 'A genuine feature of the world . . . is a feature that is there anyway, independently of anyone's value experience being as it is' (1998: 201). That is, only kinds into which things can in principle be seen to fall from outwith an evaluative perspective are genuine.

McDowell argues as follows:

(i)   DISENTANGLING presupposes SHAPEFULNESS: the rejection of SHAPEFULNESS, and with it DISENTANGLING, would leave the non-cognitivist unable to view uses of evaluative language as genuine instances of concept-application (as opposed to mere 'sounding off').
(ii)   SHAPEFULNESS is undermined by some Wittgensteinian arguments concerning rule-following.
(iii) GENUINE records 'a prejudice, without intrinsic plausibility' (1998: 217), which depends on an unmotivated scientism.

I will now proceed as follows. I will concede (ii), that SHAPEFULNESS, in the sense in which McDowell intends it, is undermined by the arguments concerning rule-following. I will then argue that there is a version of DISENTANGLING which can survive the rejection of SHAPEFULNESS, so that the non-cognitivist can simply agree with McDowell about the upshot of the rule-following considerations, without damaging his right to the idea that our uses of evaluative language are genuine instances of concept-application. Inter alia, I will consider the thought that the non-cognitivist cannot disown SHAPEFULNESS because of his commitment to GENUINE. I will suggest that the non-cognitivist simply has no need for GENUINE, so he can disown SHAPEFULNESS with impunity. Overall, McDowell's 'Disentangling' argument emerges as a failure.

I will begin by rehearsing McDowell's argument against SHAPEFULNESS (1998: 203–12). Since I am going to concede, on behalf of the non-cognitivist, that this argument is convincing, I can afford to be brief. The non-cognitivist wishes to view our uses of evaluative language, spoken or written, not as mere 'sounding off', but as genuine instances of concept application, as a practice of 'going on *doing the same thing'* (1998: 201). McDowell argues against one conception of what 'going on doing the same thing' amounts to, a conception that is a more general version of the SHAPEFULNESS assumption. The conception in question is summarized as follows, in application to any sort of practice of concept-application:

> What counts as doing the same thing, within the practice in question, is fixed by its rules. The rules mark out rails along which correct activity within the practice must run. These rails are there anyway, independently of the responses and reactions a propensity to which one acquires when one learns the practice itself; or, to put the idea less metaphorically, it is in principle discernible, from a standpoint independent of the responses that characterize a participant in the practice, that a series of correct moves in the practice is really a case of going on doing the same thing. (1998: 203)

We can see here the connection with the notion of shapefulness that McDowell is attempting to undermine. To say that 'evaluative classifications correspond to kinds into which things can in principle be seen to fall independently of an evaluative outlook' is, in terms of the less metaphorical formulation in the above passage, to say that it is in principle discernible, from a standpoint independent of the responses that characterize a participant in moral practice, that a series of correct applications of (say) 'good' is really a case of going on doing the same. Thus, undermining the thesis which McDowell here formulates less metaphorically, would in effect undermine SHAPEFULNESS.

So what is wrong with the thesis in question? McDowell argues that the notion of understanding how to apply a concept which the thesis presupposes is useless, and illustrates this with respect to the example of understanding a simple rule, 'Add 2', for continuing the series 2, 4, 6, 8, ... According to the thesis, a competent rule-follower's understanding of how to continue the series correctly is constituted by his grasp of an item which is graspable independently of the responses and reactions – the brute inclinations to 'go on in the same way' – that are characteristic of human mathematical practice. Such an item could be either an *explicit formulation* of the rule for continuing the series, or if (as is likely in less simple examples) the rule resists codification and cannot be explicitly formulated, a *universal*. But even in the simple case where there is an explicit formulation of the rule, the account of what constitutes understanding is inadequate. Someone with none of the brute inclinations to go on in the same way that characterize mathematical practice will need to *interpret* the rule in order to proceed to the next member of the series. And now a dilemma opens up. There are many ways in which an explicit formulation of a rule can be interpreted. Suppose that in the formulation of the rule 'Add 2', 'add' is interpreted as 'quadd', where quadding one number to another is defined by: x quus $2 = x + 2$ (if $x \leq 998$), x quus $2 = x + 4$ (if $x > 998$). Then the rule-follower, in correctly writing down the series, will proceed, not with 998, 1,000, 1,002, 1,004, 1,006, . . . but with 998, 1,000, 1,004, 1,008, . . .:

> The evidence we have at any point for the presence of the pictured state is compatible with the supposition that, on some future occasion for its exercise, the behaviour elicited by the occasion will diverge from what we would count as correct, and not simply because of a mistake. (1998: 205)

Someone could interpret the rule 'Add 2' and yet not mean what a competent follower of the rule means by it. Thus, if a state of interpreting the rule is to constitute genuinely understanding it, it must be a state of *correctly interpreting* the rule. But what is it to be able to correctly interpret a rule? Either we conceive of 'correctly interpret' as simply a notational variant of 'understand', in which case no constitutive account of understanding has been provided, or we conceive of correct interpretation as itself involving grasp of an item which is graspable independently of the relevant inclinations, in which case the problem simply re-emerges: any interpretation is itself subject to deviant interpretations analogous to the 'quus'-like interpretation in the case of the original formulation of the rule.

McDowell proposes to avoid this dilemma by refusing to accept the assumption that led to it. Contrary to that assumption, a competent rule-follower's understanding of how to continue the series correctly is not constituted by his grasp of an item which is graspable independently of reactions characteristic of human mathematical practice. Rather, nothing keeps the competent rule-follower's expansion of the series in line except the reactions he acquires in the course of being taught the rule. Put on one side the worry that since 'there is nothing that keeps our practices in line except the reactions and responses we learn in learning them' (1998: 207) there are simply insufficient materials to hand to ground genuine rule-following as opposed to a mere 'congruence of subjectivities'. Even if that worry is justified (and McDowell argues that it isn't), McDowell's attack on the notion of understanding tied to SHAPEFULNESS and the idea that 'it is in principle discernible, from a standpoint independent of the responses that characterize a participant in the practice, that a series of correct moves in the practice is really a case of going on doing the same thing' seems cogent. At any rate, I will assume that that is so. The question is:

what implications does the rejection of SHAPEFULNESS have for the plausibility of ethical non-cognitivism?

Why does McDowell take the rejection of SHAPEFULNESS to count as an insurmountable problem for the non-cognitivist who does not wish to see uses of evaluative language as mere 'sounding off'? There are at least two sets of considerations in the air here, and we would do well to separate them. First, there is the point, already mentioned above, that McDowell takes the non-cognitivist who wishes to see our uses of evaluative language as genuine instances of concept-application to be committed to DISENTANGLING. Recall the formulations from above:

DISENTANGLING: '. . . when we feel impelled to ascribe value to something, what is actually happening can be disentangled into two components. Competence with an evaluative concept involves, first, a sensitivity to an aspect of the world as it really is . . . and, second, a propensity to a certain attitude – a non-cognitive state that constitutes the special perspective from which items in the world seem to be endowed with the value in question.' (McDowell 1998: 200–1)

SHAPEFULNESS: '. . . evaluative classifications correspond to kinds into which things can in principle be seen to fall independently of an evaluative outlook' (1998: 216).

If we cannot identify a genuine aspect of the world as that to which the non-cognitive element in moral judgement is sensitive, it is doubtful whether we can view the repeated tokenings of evaluative language as instances of 'going on in the same way'. All we would have would be expressions of non-cognitive sentiment directed at a heterogeneous collection of items: not enough to ground a conceptual practice. (Put GENUINE on one side for the moment; I will return to that in due course.) Now, if SHAPEFULNESS is rejected, it appears that this is in fact the case: there will not be a genuine kind towards which the non-cognitive element in moral judgement can be viewed as sensitive. McDowell makes it clear that, according to him, the non-cognitivist does not have the option of disowning SHAPEFULNESS. He can do so only at a price:

[T]hat of making it problematic whether evaluative language is close enough to the usual paradigms of concept-application to count as expressive of judgements at all (as opposed to a kind of sounding off). Failing the assumption, there need be no genuine same thing (by the non-cognitivist's lights) to which the successive occurrences of the non-cognitive extra are responses. Of course the items to which the term in question is applied have, as something genuinely in common, the fact that they elicit the non-cognitive extra (the attitude, if that is what it is). But that is not a property to which the attitude can coherently be seen as a response. The attitude can see itself as going on in the same way, then, only by falling into a peculiarly grotesque form of the alleged illusion: projecting itself onto the objects, and then mistaking the projection for something it finds and responds to in them. So it seems that, if it disowns the assumption, non-cognitivism must regard the attitude as something that is simply felt (causally, perhaps, but not rationally explicable); and uses of evaluative language seem appropriately assimilated to certain sorts of exclamation, rather than to the paradigm cases of concept-application. (1998: 217)

The second of the two sorts of consideration I mentioned above is as follows. As we saw in chapter 4, an essential tool in the quasi-realist's philosophical kit is the notion of an *ethical sensibility*. Recall that the idea that we can direct attitudes of approval and disapproval upon ethical sensibilities as well as acts or states of affairs was an essential component in, for example, the quasi-realist's attempted solutions to the Frege-Geach problem and the problem of mind-dependence. And an ethical sensibility, as characterized by Blackburn, is analogous to an 'input–output function':

We can usefully compare the ethical agent to a device whose function is to take certain inputs and deliver certain outputs. The *input* to the system is a representation, for instance of an action, or a situation, or a character, as being of a certain type, as having certain properties. The *output*, we are saying, is a certain attitude, or a pressure on attitudes, or a favouring of policies, choices, and actions. Such a device is a function from input to output: an ethical sensibility. (1998: 5)

The problem for the non-cognitivist is clear. If SHAPEFULNESS is rejected, and DISENTANGLING along with it, the non-cognitivist will apparently be unable to distinguish input from output to an ethical sensibility. If there is no separating input from output, the whole notion of an ethical sensibility goes by the board, and the non-cognitivist will be deprived of an essential philosophical tool.

So: is the non-cognitivist really prey to the sorts of objection that McDowell raises? I will argue that the non-cognitivist can blunt the force of McDowell's argument. Specifically, I will argue that there is a version of the 'disentangling' thesis that survives the rejection of SHAPEFULNESS, and that this alternative version of the disentangling thesis can serve the non-cognitivist's needs.

According to the SHAPEFULNESS thesis, 'evaluative classifications correspond to kinds into which things can in principle be seen to fall independently of an evaluative outlook' (1998: 216). Why can't the non-cognitivist simply disown this thesis, and accept that evaluative classifications correspond to kinds into which things can in principle be seen to fall only from *within* an evaluative perspective? In order to answer this question, it is important to be clear about how precisely

McDowell reads SHAPEFULNESS. We can make progress on this by examining carefully some of McDowell's formulations (in fact these are of DISENTANGLING, but the formulations carry over easily to the formulation of SHAPEFULNESS):

> If the disentangling manoeuvre is always possible, that implies that the extension of the associated term, as it would be used by someone who belonged to the community, could be mastered independently of the special concerns that, in the community, would show themselves in emulation of actions seen as falling under the concept. (1998: 201)

> One could know which actions the term would be applied to, so that one would be able to predict applications and withholdings of it in new cases – not merely without oneself sharing the community's admiration . . . but without even embarking on an attempt to make sense of their admiration. (1998: 201–2)

And in the context of pointing out that the supervenience of the evaluative characteristics of a situation or act on its non-evaluative characteristics is not sufficient to deliver the DISENTANGLING thesis, McDowell describes the corresponding version of SHAPEFULNESS as follows:

> The set of items to which a supervening [evaluative] term is correctly applied . . . constitutes a kind recognizable as such at the [non-evaluative] level supervened upon. (1998: 202)

> However long a list we give of items to which a supervening term applies, described in terms of the level supervened upon, there is a way, expressible at the level supervened upon, of grouping just such items together. (1998: 202)[1]

I will suggest that McDowell's argument appears to undermine non-cognitivism only because in formulations such as the above he carelessly glosses over the Fregean distinction between *Sinn* and *Bedeutung* or, as I shall describe it, between sense and semantic value.[2] I'll call someone with no experience of the relevant 'special concerns' an *outsider*. In the first of the four passages just quoted, McDowell speaks of an outsider 'mastering the extension' of an evaluative concept. In order to keep the Fregean distinction sharply in focus, I'll talk of a speaker grasping the *sense* of an evaluative *predicate*. What is it, in Fregean terms, for a speaker to grasp that a group of items falls within the extension of a predicate? Since, for Frege, linguistic understanding is a matter of grasping items at the level of sense, not at the level of semantic value, and since extensions are items at the level of semantic value, what this involves is a speaker grasping the sense of a predicate which has the relevant extension as its semantic value.[3] Given this clarification, what the DISENTANGLING thesis amounts to is the requirement that for any evaluative predicate E there is a non-evaluative predicate E* *equivalent in sense* to E, so that grasp of the sense E, in virtue of being grasp of the sense E*, allows an outsider (who grasps the sense of E*) to acquire a capacity to competently apply E to new cases. Again, that McDowell's argument concerns items at the level of sense, at the level of items grasp of which constitutes linguistic understanding, is clear from the following passage in which he formulates the conclusion of his argument against DISENTANGLING:

> There need be no possibility of mastering, in a way that would enable one to go on to new cases, a term that is to function at the level supervened upon, but is to group together exactly the items to which competent users would apply the supervening term. (1998: 202)

It seems plausible that the disentangling thesis, thus construed, is indeed undermined by the rule-following considerations. Or at least, I'll now suggest, the non-cognitivist can quite cheerfully concede that this is the case. The non-cognitivist can agree that a competent user of evaluative language will not be able to isolate, *merely by a priori conceptual reflection*, the non-evaluative kind into which fall all and only items to which the evaluative predicate can correctly be applied. But he will point out that this precludes the possibility of the evaluative term standing for a non-evaluative kind *only on the assumption that co-referring expressions must be synonymous*. That is, the non-cognitivist can concede that for the evaluative predicate E there is no non-evaluative predicate E* with the same sense as E, such that mastery of the sense of E* (*ex hypothesi* available to an outsider) will confer mastery of the sense of E. But he can point out that it is possible for E and E* to denote the same kind (property, function, extension), even though they are non-equivalent in sense: the idea that non-synonymous predicates can co-refer is a familiar one in contemporary philosophy, as the example of 'water' and 'H$_2$O' displays. Thus, the non-cognitivist can suggest that on McDowell's reading, the disentangling thesis amounts to:

DISENTANGLING*. . . when we feel impelled to ascribe value to something, what is actually happening can be disentangled into two components. Competence with an evaluative concept involves, first, a sensitivity to an aspect of the world as it really is . . . and, second, a propensity to a certain attitude – a non-cognitive state that constitutes the special perspective from which items in the world seem to be endowed with the value in question. *The aspect of the world to which competent users are sensitive can be isolated purely by conceptual a priori reflection on the meaning of the evaluative term.*

This is the disentangling thesis which McDowell (I am conceding) successfully attacks, and which cannot survive McDowell's attack on SHAPEFULNESS. But the non-cognitivist can suggest an alternative disentangling thesis, a thesis which survives the rejection of SHAPEFULNESS:

DISENTANGLING**. . . . when we feel impelled to ascribe value to something, what is actually happening can be disentangled into two components. Competence with an evaluative concept involves, first, a sensitivity to an aspect of the world as it really is . . . and, second, a propensity to a certain attitude – a non-cognitive state that constitutes the special perspective from which items in the world seem to be endowed with the value in question. The aspect of the world to which competent users are sensitive *cannot* be isolated purely by conceptual a priori reflection on the meaning of the evaluative term: *if there is such an aspect of the world it will be isolatable only by substantive moral theorizing.*

That this is the version of the disentangling thesis which the non-cognitivist will prefer should come as no surprise. Recall Blackburn's remark:

> It does not seem a matter of conceptual or logical necessity that any given total natural state of a thing gives it some particular moral property. For to tell which moral quality results from a given natural state means using standards whose correctness cannot be shown by conceptual means alone. It means moralizing, and bad people moralize badly, but need not be confused. (1984: 184)

And recall also his remark on ethical sensibilities as input–output functions:

> [N]either input [n]or output is fixed by any kind of definition or linguistic convention. They are malleable, and change with the importance we attach to things and to our reactions to things. (1998: 103)

It seems to me, then, that although McDowell's 'rule-following' argument is successful in its own terms, targeted as it is on DISENTANGLING*, it simply fails to connect with its intended target. I will now make four comments related to the argument I've just developed.

First, McDowell may respond that there is a reading of SHAPEFULNESS on which its rejection does undermine DISENTANGLING** as opposed to DISENTANGLING* and thus does cause problems for the non-cognitivist. To see this, take again the formulation of SHAPEFULNESS which McDowell provides in the context of his remarks about supervenience:

The set of items to which a supervening [evaluative] term is correctly applied . . . constitutes a kind recognizable as such at the [non-evaluative] level supervened upon. (1998: 202)

Focusing on the 'as such', I have read this as:

The set of items to which a supervening [evaluative] term is correctly applied . . . constitutes a kind recognizable *as a kind containing all and only those items to which the supervening item can correctly be applied* at the [non-evaluative] level supervened upon.

Call this the *intensional* reading of SHAPEFULNESS. I have agreed that on this reading SHAPEFULNESS is indeed undermined by McDowell's argument, but have suggested that the rejection of SHAPEFULNESS thus read leaves DISENTANGLING** intact, and so fails to damage the non-cognitivist. However, McDowell may suggest that there is another reading of SHAPEFULNESS which runs:

The set of items to which a supervening [evaluative] term is correctly applied . . . constitutes a kind recognizable *as a kind* at the [non-evaluative] level supervened upon.

Call this the *extensional* reading of SHAPEFULNESS. Now the rejection of this thesis would clearly undermine DISENTANGLING**. The falsity of this thesis would guarantee that even a non-evaluative predicate E* *non-equivalent* in sense to the evaluative predicate E could not be viewed as itself standing for a kind: it would thus guarantee that E and E* could not be non-synonymous yet co-referring. But the crucial point to appreciate is that, on the extensional reading, SHAPEFULNESS cannot be undermined by McDowell's rule-following argument. For one thing, as I showed above, the arguments McDowell uses concern a competent speaker's grasp of the *sense* of an evaluative predicate and not the *semantic value* of that predicate. McDowell's arguments simply function at the wrong level to damage the extensional reading of SHAPEFULNESS. Perhaps McDowell has another argument against the extensional reading, but it is clear that such an argument cannot be extracted from the rule-following considerations: a rule of application is, after all, *grasped* by someone who knows how to correctly continue a series, and thus is analogous to the sense of a predicate. As it stands, the argument provides no grounds for concluding anything about the nature of the semantic value (property, extension, function) of an evaluative predicate. Thus, the rejection of the extensional reading of SHAPEFULNESS would damage the non-cognitivist, but fails to do so because when we move to the extensional reading the rule-following arguments simply no longer apply.

Second, there are interesting parallels between the flaws in

McDowell's rule-following objection to non-cognitivism and his 'contaminated response' objection to quasi-realism (4.9). Recall that the latter failed to damage quasi-realism on the grounds that McDowell confused an explanatory dimension of the quasi-realist project with a purely justificatory dimension: and, as a result, his claim that there could be no suitable characterization of the sentiments claimed by quasi-realism to be distinctive of moral judgement failed because it (a) presupposed, a priori, that an a posteriori discipline such as psychology could not come up with an adequate form of such characterization, and (b) presupposed that finding such a characterization would involve being able to justify ethical claims from within some standpoint in which all ethical judgements were initially suspended. The parallel with McDowell's objection to the non-cognitivist's 'disentangling' thesis should be clear. That objection turned on an argument to the effect that for any evaluative term there is no way to isolate, via purely conceptual a priori reflection, the naturalistic aspect of the world to which competent uses of that term are sensitive. The reply I developed for the non-cognitivist was that this would not be a problem, since there was never any assumption that the naturalistic feature in question could be discerned by conceptual means alone. This would be an a posteriori matter, or at best a substantively (as opposed to purely conceptually) a priori matter. Like the 'contaminated response' objection, McDowell's objection presupposed, courtesy of a purely conceptual a priori argument, an answer to a question which the non-cognitivist presupposes is answerable only a posteriori or substantively a priori. Moreover, the 'contaminated response' objection actually reappears as a component of the argument against disentangling: since isolating the relevant naturalistic feature involves disentangling sensitivity to that feature from the attitude expressed, McDowell is again presupposing on a priori grounds that a certain answer to an a posteriori question cannot be produced by empirical psychology (namely, that a particular type of attitude can be disentangled from sensitivity to the relevant naturalistic feature).[4]

Third, there is an even clearer parallel with the flaw identified in the argument of Wiggins against substantive naturalistic cognitivism (9.7).[5] Wiggins's argument turned on the unargued assumption that an evaluative predicate could not pick out a naturalistic property even though there was no naturalistic predicate with which it was analytically equivalent. Wiggins was presupposing, a priori, the unfeasibility of a particular project whose success the substantive naturalist takes to be an a posteriori matter. Thus, there is a common flaw in the arguments developed by Wiggins and McDowell against naturalistic metaethical theories: they presuppose, on purely conceptual a priori grounds, particular answers to questions which the naturalist deems to be answerable only a posteriori or as a matter of *substantively* a priori moral theorizing.

Fourth, recall that McDowell attributes the following assumption to non-cognitivism:

GENUINE: 'A genuine feature of the world . . . is a feature that is there anyway, independently of anyone's value experience being as it is' (1998: 201). In other words, only kinds into which things can in principle be seen to fall from outwith an evaluative perspective are genuine.

McDowell then suggests that this records 'a prejudice, without intrinsic plausibility' (1998: 217). It might seem that the strategy I advocated above for the non-cognitivist – namely, disowning SHAPEFULNESS, and using the assumption DISENTANGLING** to ground both the idea that uses of evaluative language constitute genuine patterns of concept-application and the idea of an ethical sensibility as an input–output function – is not available to the non-cognitivist since he is committed to GENUINE. Given GENUINE, it follows that the naturalistic feature mentioned in DISENTANGLING** is not a *genuine* feature of the world: so how could sensitivity to it mark out a pattern of genuine concept-application?

There are at least two things we can say in reply.

First, we can point out that the non-cognitivist who commits himself only to DISENTANGLING**, and the weaker, extensional reading of SHAPEFULNESS, should be committed at most to a weaker reading of GENUINE which meshes with the extensional reading of SHAPEFULNESS and 'disentangling' construed as DISENTANGLING**. Since neither DISENTANGLING** nor the extensional reading of SHAPEFULNESS is jeopardized by McDowell's reading of the rule-following considerations, what is the problem with GENUINE if read correspondingly? McDowell has suggested that on the stronger reading of GENUINE – corresponding to the intensional reading of SHAPEFULNESS and to DISENTANGLING* – it records only a prejudice lacking intrinsic justification. But even if we concede this, where is the argument to the effect that on the weaker reading, too, GENUINE records nothing but a prejudice? As far as I can see, no such argument is even attempted by McDowell. Second, if it did turn out that even the weaker reading of GENUINE recorded only 'a prejudice with no intrinsic justification', it is unclear that the non-cognitivist needs to embrace it. It might appear that if non-cognitivism does not have something like GENUINE, on either its strong or weak reading, there will simply be no motivation for the non-cognitivist project to begin with. If moral 'features' do not turn out to be 'genuine' according to some criterion like GENUINE (again, either on its stronger or weaker reading), what motivation could one have for the non-cognitivist project of construing ethical sensibilities as functions from sensitivity to 'genuine' naturalistic features of the world to attitudes evinced towards those features? But thinking that there would be a problem here depends on construing the naturalism underlying the non-cognitivist project, in the terminology invoked in 9.2, as 'hegemonic', as based upon some simple 'test of reality'. Probably some actual non-cognitivist theories have been so based. But just as there was scope for a non-hegemonic version of naturalistic cognitivism, there is also scope for a non-hegemonic version of methodologically naturalist non-cognitivism. Recall that Railton expressed his commitment to a non-hegemonic form of naturalism in the following passage:

> It can be informative to find a reduction basis for a range of properties R within a range of properties S, even without any claim to the effect that S is utterly comprehensive. A reduction of R to S could none the less tell us about the place of R in the world, and would be of special interest if there existed a well-developed theory of properties of kind S, or if properties of kind S were less problematic in some way than those of kind R seemed (before the reduction) to be. (1993b: 318)

Likewise, the non-cognitivist can say: it can be informative to construe ethical judgements as a matter of expressing non-cognitive sentiments in response to a range of properties S, even without any claim to the effect that S is utterly comprehensive. A non-cognitivist account of ethical judgements could nonetheless tell us about the place of our ethical activity in the world, and would be of special interest if there existed a well-developed theory of properties of kind S and of the non-cognitive sentiments we express in response to them, or if properties of kind S and the non-cognitive sentiments in question were less problematic than moral properties and moral beliefs seemed to be. Thus, even if the weaker version of GENUINE turned out to be intrinsically implausible, or the result merely of prejudice, the non-cognitivist project could survive the discovery of that fact.[6]

I conclude that McDowell's argument against ethical non-cognitivism is a failure.

10.2 Second Nature

I have now rejected two arguments against versions of ethical naturalism: Wiggins's argument against naturalistic cognitivism (9.7) and McDowell's argument against non-cognitivism (10.1). Suppose, contrary to what I have argued, that Wiggins and McDowell have been successful in their attempts to undermine ethical naturalism. How plausible is the non-naturalistic cognitivism that Wiggins and McDowell propose as an alternative to naturalistic cognitivism and non-cognitivism? Is their non-naturalism any less implausible than the position of Moore's that we rejected in 3.3? I will now investigate this question. In 10.3, I examine whether the non-naturalist can make any capital out of an analogy between moral properties and secondary qualities; in this section, I ask whether McDowell's notions of *Bildung* and 'second nature' can help assuage the worry that his moral realism really only represents a return to the obfuscatory non-naturalism of Moore and his followers.

McDowell distinguishes between the 'space of reasons' and the 'realm of law'. The 'space of reasons' is 'the structure in which we place things when we find meaning in them' (McDowell 1994: 88), the 'realm of law' is effectively the subject matter of natural science, the structure in which we place things when we try to render them intelligible by seeing them as law-governed. In effect, McDowell's non-naturalism denies that moral facts and properties belong to the realm of law: rather, they must be located in the space of reasons. McDowell argues that Aristotle's view of ethics, properly interpreted, provides a model for his own non-naturalism:

> In Aristotle's conception, the thought that the demands of ethics are real is not a projection from, or construction out of, facts that could be in view independently of the viewer's participation in ethical life and thought, so that they would be available to a sideways-on investigation of how ethical life and thought are related to the natural context in which they take place. *The fact that the demands bear on us is just, irreducibly, itself.* (1994: 83, emphasis added)

But if moral facts and properties are not to be found in the realm of law and are viewed as irreducible and belonging to the space of reasons, don't we end up with Moorean *sui generis* non-natural properties and all the metaphysical and epistemological difficulties that follow in train? If moral facts and properties are not to be found in nature, the realm of law, or the subject matter of the empirical sciences, doesn't it follow that they are supernatural and accessible only via mysterious 'intuitional' faculties? And doesn't this take us straight back to Moore? McDowell answers that non-naturalism leads to supernaturalism only given the equation of nature with the realm of law. If we 'expand nature beyond what is countenanced in a naturalism of the realm of law' (1994: 88) we can deny that moral facts and properties form part of the subject matter of the empirical sciences whilst avoiding the charge of supernaturalism. McDowell calls this expanded conception of the natural a 'naturalism of second nature':

> Since ethical character includes dispositions of the practical intellect, part of what happens when character is formed is that the practical intellect acquires a determinate shape. So practical wisdom is second nature to its possessors. (1994: 84)

Moral facts, according to McDowell, are facts about reasons for action (so McDowell is a rationalist by the lights of 9.10). If we can be brought to appreciate something as a reason for action via a proper human upbringing, education, or, in general terms, a process of *Bildung*, then we can see that fact as 'natural' even though it would not figure in the subject matter of a natural or empirical science.[7] Thus, at a stroke we avoid supernaturalism and any associated allegation of disrespect for natural science:

> Second nature could not float free of potentialities that belong to a normal human organism. This gives human reason enough of a foothold in the realm of law to satisfy any proper respect for modern natural science. (1994: 84)

Thus, non-naturalism threatens to degenerate into Moorean intuitionism, or some disrespectable supernaturalism, only if we equate nature as such with the realm of law. If we block that equation via a 'naturalism of second nature', we can avoid any such lapse.

Does this actually do the trick? It seems not. Jerry Fodor expresses the worry nicely:

> Having situated ... the ethical ... outside the realm of law, McDowell needs to face the embarrassing question how, by any natural process, do we ever manage to get at it? (Fodor 1995: 11)

Of course, McDowell attempts to side-step this potentially embarrassing question: if the ethical is accessible to 'second nature', itself the upshot of *Bildung*, education, or proper upbringing, the fact that empirical science has no useful story to tell about how we manage to access the facts in question needn't leave us open to the charge of supernaturalism. So what does McDowell have to say about how *Bildung* manages to do this?

> The picture is that ethics involves requirements of reason that are there whether we know it or not, and our eyes are opened to them by the acquisition of 'practical wisdom'. (1994: 79)

> The rational demands of ethics are not alien to the contingencies of our life as human beings. Even though it is not supposed that we could explain the relevant idea of demandingness in terms of independently intelligible facts about human beings, still ordinary upbringing can shape the actions and thoughts of human beings in a way that brings these demands into view. (1994: 83)

And 'naturalism of second nature' is described as

> [a] conception of our nature that includes a capacity to resonate to the structure of the space of reasons. (1994: 109)

But passages like these are unhelpful. As Fodor points out, all we have here are *metaphors*:

'Bringing into view' is a metaphor; only what is in Nature [on the usual characterization] can literally be viewed. And 'resonating' is also a metaphor; only what is in Nature [on the usual characterization] can be literally attuned to. (1995: 11)

Likewise, Fodor might have pointed out, one can only have one's eyes literally opened to what is in nature (on the standard characterization). It looks as though McDowell is attempting to counterfeit the explanatory value of what natural science tells us about visual and aural perception and then spend it in an area (ethics) where, in the absence of a naturalistic story in the more usual sense, it literally has no cash value. As Fodor might have put it, the trouble with viewing moral demands as items we can access via some capacity that can be imparted to us by *Bildung*, is that 'nobody has the foggiest idea how to do so unless both [the demands and the capacity] are contained in the natural order [as standardly characterized]' (1995: 11).

Thus, for all McDowell has said so far, his form of non-naturalistic cognitivism appears to be no less mysterious than the view of Moore's which is nowadays routinely derided. McDowell makes some other attempts to dispel this impression. We can train human children to be sensitive to moral demands, and there is nothing in this process to which a naturalist (as standardly characterized) need take exception:

Human infants are mere animals, distinctive only in their potential, and nothing occult happens to a human being in ordinary upbringing. (1994: 123)

Although realizing this 'distinctive potential' is conceived in terms of the child being brought to a point where she is genuinely receptive to ethical demands, where neither the capacity to be receptive nor the demands admit of any explanatory story in terms of natural facts as standardly conceived, there is no mystery in the claim that this distinctive potential can in fact be realized:

This transformation [the realization of the 'distinctive potential'] risks looking mysterious. But we can take it in our stride if, in our conception of the *Bildung* that is a central element in the normal maturation of human beings, we give pride of place to language. In being initiated into a language, a human being is introduced into something that already embodies putatively rational linkages between concepts, putatively constitutive of the layout of the space of reasons, before she comes on the scene. This is a picture of initiation into the space of reasons as an already going concern; there is no problem about how something describable in these terms could emancipate a human individual from a merely animal mode of living into being a full-fledged subject, open to the world. A mere animal, moved only by the sorts of things that move mere animals, could not single-handedly emancipate itself into possession of understanding. (1994: 125)

However, pointing out that 'human infants are mere animals, distinctive only in their potential . . .' doesn't help at all. If one found the idea that we can be responsive to moral reasons underexplained when neither the relevant facts about reasons nor the capacities allegedly responsive to them are conceived of as belonging to the realm of law, it helps little to be told that acquiring the relevant capacities is a way of realizing our 'distinctive potential'.[8] To say all of that is simply to *paraphrase* the claim that human beings are capable of making ethical judgements: it is not something that can even begin to help us understand what ethical judgements are or how it might be possible for us to engage in a practice of making them. Likewise, the analogy with language-learning in the passage about the potentially mysterious transformation does little to help. We are trying to understand how it could be that human beings are capable of speaking intelligibly where this is conceived of as a matter of acquiring a capacity to be responsive to facts about meaning, where neither the capacity nor the facts about meaning can be rendered intelligible from the viewpoint of the realm of law. Does it help to be reminded that humans, but not, say, gerbils, can acquire the capacity to converse intelligibly?[9] Of course not.

I conclude, then, that McDowell's deployment of the notions of *Bildung* and 'second nature' does little to help him see off the charge that his non-naturalist ethical cognitivism falls prey to the sorts of worries which have prevented metaethicists from accepting the non-naturalism of *Principia Ethica*.

10.3 Secondary Qualities, Cognitive Access and Working from Within

In this section, I'll investigate whether a defender of McDowell might make progress by exploiting an analogy between moral properties and *secondary qualities*. Recall that in chapter 7 we saw that weak cognitivism, in attempting to run such an analogy, eventually came unstuck. In order to see how a defender of McDowell might try to use the analogy whilst avoiding the problems which beset weak cognitivism, I will begin by thinking about how an objection raised by McDowell against Blackburn's quasi-realism appears parallel to the main worry we saw raised in chapter 7 for judgement-dependent, weak cognitivist accounts of morals. We'll see that quasi-realism and weak cognitivism appear to have an assumption in common, and that it is the rejection of this assumption which characterizes McDowell's own metaethical view. I'll then argue that this manoeuvre, as it stands, does little to deal with the worries left outstanding from the previous section.[10]

McDowell has argued that there is a problem which faces any philosopher who attempts to develop a version of (ambitious) quasi-realism along the lines of the position advocated by Blackburn (chapter 4). Such a philosopher wants to claim *both* that moral claims can be true or false and that they are attitudinal rather than cognitive in nature. Blackburn's proposed solution to this problem turns on the idea that the attitudes expressed by moral judgements are the product of sensibilities that are themselves subject to *rational criticism*, and that in evincing the canons of criticism appropriate for such sentences we thereby *earn the right* to use the notion of truth with respect to moral discourse. This sort of story contrasts, on Blackburn's view, with an intuitionistic conception of ethics, such as that standardly associated with Moore, which simply helps itself to an *unearned* notion of truth. McDowell makes very clear his desire to reject this intuitionistic appeal to an unearned notion of truth:

> [Intuitionism] purports to equip us with special cognitive faculties by whose exercise we become aware of this special field of knowable fact. These special cognitive faculties are vaguely assimilated to the senses, but no detailed account can be given of how they operate such as might make it clear to us – as clear as it is in the case of the senses – how their exercise affords us access to the relevant range of circumstances. The assimilation to the senses gives this intuitionistic position the superficial appearance of offering an epistemology of our access to valuational truth, but there is no substance behind this appearance. (1998: 154)

In developing his projectivist alternative to this disreputable position, Blackburn – according to McDowell – requires that *in evincing the relevant canons of criticism we do not draw on the characteristic concepts of the region of discourse for which we are attempting to earn the right to use the notion of truth*. In McDowell's words:

> A serious projective quasi-realism about (e.g.) the comic would construct a conception of what it is for things to be really funny on the basis of principles for ranking senses of humour which would have to be established from outside the propensity to find things funny. (1998: 160)

According to McDowell, the basic quasi-realist idea is that since our sentiments are prior to the features which they project, we cannot view our sensitivity to the projected features as playing a role in determining the pedigree of the sensibilities from which those sentiments are thought to flow. We thus cannot appeal to moral standards in ranking the various sensibilities from which our sentiments issue, since the whole point of the quasi-realist exercise is to provide a construction of moral standards (moral truth) on a purely sentimental basis.

Now perhaps there is a connection between this sort of quasi-realism and the distinction between extension-determining and extension-reflecting construals of best opinions that figured in chapter 7 in our discussion of judgement-dependent, weak cognitivist accounts of morals. Just as Blackburn's quasi-realist requires that the responses which feature in his putatively deflationary explanations be individuated without drawing on the concepts whose extensions the deflationary explanations are supposed to explain away, the weak cognitivist requires that the cognitively ideal conditions which characterize the extension-determining best opinions be such that their satisfaction is logically independent of facts about the application of the concepts whose extensions the best opinions are thought to determine.

McDowell claims that it is wrong to view our projective sentiments as explaining away, say, ethical or comical features of the world, because the sentiments in question do not have the required conceptual priority over the features which they allegedly spread (see 4.9). So McDowell's claim is, in the case of comedy, for example, that the sentiments involved cannot be adequately characterized otherwise than as the upshots of a propensity to find things funny; or, in the case of colour, for example, that they cannot be adequately characterized otherwise than as the upshots of propensities to experience objects as red. Once we realize this, McDowell goes on to claim, there is no obstacle to employing our acquaintance with such features as playing a part in the construction of our rational ranking of our comical and ethical sensibilities; truth in ethics, as McDowell puts it, can be earned from a viewpoint firmly located within a scheme of ethical concepts.

So, if we concentrate our attention on the idea that we have to earn the right to use the notion of truth with respect to moral discourse, it seems that we can lay out as follows the main views as to how we can earn it.

For the *weak cognitivist* who tries to give a judgement-dependent account of morals, we have the choice of accepting an extension-reflecting account of best opinion, viewing best moral opinion as merely tracking the moral facts (helping ourselves to an unearned notion of truth); or we can attempt to earn truth by giving an extension-determining account subject to the *independence* condition, an account which undercuts the need for a substantial epistemology in terms of tracking or cognitive access.

For *Blackburn's quasi-realist*, we have the choice of adopting intuitionism (the view that moral opinion merely tracks the moral facts) and again helping ourselves to an unearned notion of truth; or we can attempt to earn truth by providing an account of the sorts of rational criticism to which our sensibilities may be subject, where that account is constructed *without* the aid of specifically moral concepts and *without* reference to distinctively moral standards.

For *McDowell's cognitivist*, too, intuitionism merely helps itself to an unearned notion of truth. But we also have the option of attempting to earn the right to use the notion of truth with respect to moral discourse by providing an account of the sorts of rational criticism to which our sensibilities may be subject, *and in constructing which we may draw on as many distinctively ethical concepts as we find necessary: the right to employ the notion of truth in ethics can be earned by 'working from within'.*

So, McDowell sees that the main problems for judgement-dependent and quasi-realist accounts of morals stem from their attempting to earn truth in ethics from a position 'as of outside ethics': in the former case via the imposition of the independence condition, which it turns out that morals cannot satisfy (7.5); in the latter case via the demand that we do not use moral concepts or standards in the ranking of the various sensibilities which issue in the sentiments which form the basis for the construction of moral truth (4.9). McDowell wants to avoid these problems, as well as the problems associated with an unearned appeal to truth in the style of Moorean intuitionism, so he proposes that we attempt to earn the right to the notion of truth in ethics from within an ethical viewpoint.

Can we flesh this out? McDowell is a cognitivist: he thinks that moral judgements express beliefs. I suggest that he is also a strong cognitivist: for McDowell, the formation of a correct moral judgement is a way of cognitively accessing a moral fact. But doesn't this appeal to 'cognitive access' or 'cognition', just taking us back to the bad old days of Moorean intuitionism and all the problems we saw that view facing in chapters 2 and 3? McDowell will want to say that it does not: the intuitionist use of the notion of cognitive access, like the intuitionist appeal to the notion of truth, is *unearned*: but McDowell's use of the notion of cognitive access, like his use of the notion of moral truth, is earned, though from a viewpoint firmly located within a scheme of moral concepts. But what does this mean? One way to get a handle on this is to go back to the judgement-dependent account of morals (chapter 7), and the distinction between extension-reflecting and extension-determining conceptions of the role of best opinion. What must be the case, according to the best-opinion account, in order for us to speak of our best opinions as tracking, detecting or cognitively accessing the facts in any given case? Recall from chapter 7 that, according to the judgement-dependent account, we can only properly speak of cognitive access when there is no substantial, a priori correlation between best opinion and fact which meets the independence and extremal conditions. Now I suggest that McDowell turns this conception of cognitive access on its head: McDowell wants to say that if we have an a priori, substantial correlation between best opinion and fact, we have all we need in order to bring in talk of cognitive access. And, moreover, we do not require that the correlation between best opinion and fact satisfy the independence condition. So, we earn truth in morals by showing that there is a substantial a priori correlation between best moral opinion and best moral fact, and this counts as earning truth from *within* morals because we do not require that the correlation in question also satisfy the independence condition.

But can this actually be done? Can we provide a provisional equation for the moral case which satisfies the a prioricity and substantiality conditions? Recall the biconditional for 'culpable insensitivity' (Wright 1988a) from chapter 7:

MORAL: Act x is culpably insensitive if and only if for any S: if S scrutinizes the motives, consequences, and, for John, foreseeable consequences in the context of the remark; and does this in a fashion which involves no error concerning non-moral fact or logic, and embraces all morally relevant considerations; and if S gives all this the fullest attention, and so is victim to no error or oversight concerning any relevant aspect of his/her deliberation; and if S is a morally suitable subject – accepts the right moral principles, or has the right moral intuitions or sentiments, or whatever; and if S has no doubt about the satisfaction of any of these conditions, then if S forms a moral evaluation of John's remark, that evaluation will be that x is culpably insensitive.

Does MORAL satisfy the constraints on the anti-realist conception of extension-determination? Wright thinks that 'it is a good candidate for refinement into an a priori truth' (1988a: 23), and that the C-conditions 'are not wholly unsubstantially specified' (ibid.). Recall that the main problem with MORAL is that when we proceed to attempt to give a substantial account of what the 'moral suitability' of the subject S is to involve, we will find ourselves violating the independence condition: 'the satisfaction of the C-conditions in moral is not independent of the extension of moral concepts – S's moral suitability, in particular, is itself, presumably, a matter for moral judgement' (ibid.). Alternatively, 'proper pedigree for moral judgements . . . is a matter of meeting conditions the satisfaction of some of which is, irreducibly, a moral question' (1988a: 24). The conclusion drawn is that a judgement-dependent account of morals is not a plausible option: 'the extension of the truth-predicate among ascriptions of moral quality may not be thought of as determined by our best beliefs' (ibid.).

So, according to Wright, a judgement-dependent account is not a plausible position on morals, since we can only achieve substantiality and non-triviality in the specification of the C-conditions at the price of violating the independence condition. But now we can see how space for McDowell's position opens up. Since McDowell, in 'working from within', is explicitly rejecting the independence condition, the fact that we can satisfy the substantiality condition only by violating the independence condition poses no threat to McDowell: in giving our substantial account of what moral suitability comes to, we are permitted to draw on facts which are not independent of the extensions of moral concepts. This means that we are free to say what a morally suitable subject is in the way we would normally do, as someone who is just, fair, courageous or whatever. Of course, this is only the *starting point* in our attempt at self-conscious moral reflection, and there is no guarantee that that reflection will not eventually force us to jettison the whole idea of a specifically moral way of thinking. But likewise, McDowell will say, there is no guarantee that it will force us to jettison it either:

> No particular verdict or judgement would be a sacrosanct starting-point, supposedly immune to critical scrutiny, in our earning the right to claim that some [moral] verdicts or judgements stand a chance of being true. That is not at all to say that we must earn the right from an initial position in which all such verdicts or judgements are suspended at once, as in the projectivist picture of a world that does not contain values. (McDowell 1998: 163)

We may well have to discard the judgements in whose truth the satisfaction of the C-conditions consists. But, if so, this will be because they do not stand up to the self-reflective scrutiny which the moral outlook is obliged to direct at itself, and not because the truth of those judgements violates the independence condition. So, McDowell will argue, pending the unlikely event of the moral outlook's discarding all such judgements, the view that we can cognitively access the moral facts, in a sense of cognitive access different from that which defines the judgement-dependent account, remains a competitive form of non-naturalist moral realism.

Can such an account be made to work? If it could, the payoffs could be substantial. Recall that at the end of chapter 6 we saw that if a dispositional theory of moral value was plausible, we would have a cognitivist account of moral judgement which would provide a partial response to the *metaphysical* aspect of Mackie's argument from queerness and accommodate the *phenomenology* of moral experience.[11] An account such as the one just outlined would – since it too involves the idea that there is a substantial and a priori correlation between best moral opinion and fact – inherit these two features of the dispositional account. We saw at the start of chapter 7 that a weak cognitivist position, based on a dispositional theory of moral value, would, because of its lack of play with the notion of detection or cognitive access, provide an effective response to the *epistemological* aspect of Mackie's argument from queerness. However, the fact that the judgement-dependent account of moral truth could not satisfy the independence condition on extension-determining accounts of best opinion ensured that these attractive payoffs could not be obtained via a judgement-dependent account of moral truth. However, McDowell rejects the conception of cognitive access via which the judgement-dependent account defines itself, and in his account of 'working from within' there simply is no analogue of the independence condition. So McDowell's account, via its replacement conception of cognitive access, avoids the problems the judgement-dependent account faced with respect to the independence condition, provides a response to the epistemological aspect of the argument from queerness, and inherits the judgement-dependent account's response to the metaphysical aspect of the argument from queerness as well as its capacity to accommodate the facts about the phenomenology of moral experience.

Unfortunately, though, this attempt to reconstruct McDowell's position in such a way that the problems of the previous section are avoided is unconvincing, at least as it stands. To begin with, and as we have already seen in 4.9, McDowell misinterprets the quasi-realist's position by ignoring the fact that in the quasi-realist project there is an explanatory aspiration which is best kept separate from a justificatory aspiration. McDowell interprets the quasi-realist as moving from:

(a) Our sentiments are prior to the features which they project;

to:

(b) We cannot appeal to moral standards in ranking the various sensibilities from which our sentiments issue;

and from thence to the view that we must, in attempting to justify the idea that some particular moral judgements are true, begin from a standpoint in which all our current moral judgements are suspended. But, in doing so, McDowell illegitimately transposes a requirement which the quasi-realist imposes on an *explanatory* project to apply to a *justificatory* project. Since one of the aims of quasi-realism is to *explain* what we are doing when we make a moral judgement in terms of a sentiment or attitude expressed, we are not allowed to use ethical concepts in that explanation, on pain of rendering the explanation vacuous: in using ethical concepts to characterize putatively ethical concepts, we would be presupposing an understanding of the very phenomenon – moral judgement – that we were attempting to explain. The explanatory project thus works under a constraint of *non-circularity*. But the quasi-realist imposes no similar constraint on the justificatory project. As far as the justificatory project goes, the quasi-realist, like McDowell's non-naturalist, advocates 'working from within'. I have already argued that this is the case and I shall reiterate what I said in 4.9 by considering how Blackburn advocates dealing with the threat of *ethical relativism*. Blackburn imagines the 'pit of relativism' opening up in the following train of thought:

> [Y]ou should see yourself as one amongst many putative shoppers in the marketplace of values. You pick or have foisted upon you a basket of values, and you then affirm and reaffirm them, even handing yourself the dignities of knowledge and certainty. But you must recognize that others, carrying different baskets, will be doing the same, and in none of this is there more than the contingent conscience or clash of attitude. There is no independent criterion of right or wrong or good or bad, and therefore no certification that you are reliable as an indicator of them. (1996: 89)

Blackburn argues that the way to deal with this relativistic threat is to question the notion of external standpoint which it presupposes. In words that might easily have been written by McDowell, he says:

> The objector asks us to occupy an external standpoint, the standpoint of the exile from all values, and to see our sensibilities from without. But it is only by using our sensibilities that we judge value. So it is as if we are asked to judge colours with a blindfold on, and the inevitable result is that values are lost, and our sense of ourselves as reliable indicators of them is lost along with them. (1996: 89)

Suppose I form a favourable attitude towards Alaric's jumping in, regardless of danger and at some cost, to rescue the drowning Berth. What is the significance of the fact that there may be sensibilities different from my own which form a different, negative attitude towards Alaric's behaviour? Blackburn writes:

> This challenge [to our idea of ourselves as reliable indicators of value] is not posed by the mere actual or possible existence of a different way of taking things. It is of no interest that there might be someone who thinks that Alaric's behaviour was indifferent or even shocking. By itself such a personality poses no threat to my values: it merely itself invites some kind of regret or condemnation. What would be of interest would be a sensibility that cannot be dismissed as inferior, and which issues in this attitude. But in assessing the chances of there being such a thing, we are back working from within. We are no longer playing the fake externalist game of trying to certify values without using values. (1996: 89)

Blackburn thus openly repudiates the very idea which McDowell attributes to him: the idea that we must find a justification for ethics 'from a position as of outside ethics'. What consequences does this neglect of the distinction between the explanatory and justificatory aspects of Blackburn's project have for the reconstruction of McDowell's view attempted above?

The main consequence is that while McDowell may have a plausible story about how we might 'work from within' to a justification of particular ethical claims or to a justification of a choice of particular sensibilities and conditions of judgement as ideal for moral appraisal, that story *entirely neglects* the need for an explanation of what it is we are doing, and why, when we make moral judgements. We can distinguish at least three questions to which the quasi-realist project as a whole attempts to provide answers:

(i)   What are we doing when we make a moral judgement?
(ii) Why do we do what we do when we make a moral judgement?
(iii) Which particular cases of what we do when we make a moral judgement are justifiable?

Quasi-realism attempts to provide answers to all three: (i) when we make a moral judgement we express non-cognitive sentiments towards acts, situations, ethical sensibilities and so on; (ii) we do this because of 'the need for social devices for putting pressure on choice and action' (Blackburn 1993b: 374); and (iii) we may well be able to justify certain of our ethical commitments by 'working from within'. McDowell appears only to attempt to answer (iii) and, as we saw, his answer is essentially the same as Blackburn's. This means that as things stand McDowell has given us no satisfactory answer to the question: what do we do when we make a moral judgement, and why? McDowell cannot answer (i) by saying: a belief with a *sui generis* and irreducibly moral content. As yet, we have no understanding of what that content might be or how we might come to possess knowledge of it.

At this point, McDowell may reply that we only find explanatory questions like (i) and (ii) compelling because we are wedded to the conception of cognitive access which shaped the weak cognitivist's distinction between extension-reflecting and extension-determining accounts of best moral opinion. Once that conception has been dislodged, he might suggest, the worry that we lack answers to (i) and (ii) ought simply to wither away. But this seems premature: we can only rightfully shrug our shoulders at the explanatory questions when we have (a) provided a philosophical argument to the effect that the notion of cognitive access used by the weak cognitivist is incoherent, (b) developed – within a non-reductionist framework – an alternative notion of cognitive access which satisfies our pre-theoretical demands on the notion of cognition, and (c) shown that on that alternative conception, we can indeed have cognitive access to some of the facts in question. 'Working from within' may help with (c). However, McDowell's non-reductionist cognitivism will remain an ultimately unsatisfying metaethical position until he provides satisfactory answers to (a) and (b).[12]

10.4 Humean and Anti-Humean Theories of Motivation

The Humean Theory of Motivation has cropped up at various places in the book so far (e.g., 1.8, 4.2, 9.5, 9.6). As I mentioned in 9.9, a full exposition and evaluation of this theory would probably require a book as long as the present one. So in this section my aims are quite limited. I will attempt to say what the Humean Theory of Motivation is, and then attempt to evaluate one line of argument that has recently been developed in its favour, that suggested by Michael Smith in his 1994a. I will argue that, although Smith's objections to Anti-Humean theories seem plausible, his own positive argument in favour of the Humean theory is at best highly inconclusive.

We can give a rough statement of the Humean Theory of Motivation as follows: motivation is a matter of having beliefs and (independently intelligible) desires, where beliefs and desires are 'independently intelligible' if they are 'distinct existences'. There are various ways of sharpening this up, but for our purposes the key claim at the heart of the Humean theory is the following, as suggested by a formulation of Smith's (1994a: 92):

HUM: R at t constitutes a motivating reason of agent A to G iff there is some H such that R at t consists of an appropriately related desire of A to H and a belief that were she to G she would H, where the beliefs and desires in question are 'distinct existences'.

To say that beliefs and desires are 'distinct existences' is just to say that they can be pulled apart modally: in other words, for any belief B and desire D, it is always possible for an agent to have B in the absence of D and vice versa. A 'motivating reason' is a psychological state capable of playing a role of explaining why an agent acted as he did: a psychological state that is potentially explanatory of behaviour. Thus, HUM amounts to the claim that when an agent has a psychological state that is potentially explanatory of his behaviour, that state must always consist in a combination of a belief with an independently intelligible desire.[13]

Typically, HUM is subscribed to by those who feel a tension between cognitivism and internalism: non-cognitivists (chapters 3, 4, 5) typically accept HUM and internalism and reject cognitivism; cognitivists who accept HUM (chapters 8, 9) typically accept HUM and reject internalism. Non-naturalist cognitivists such as Platts, Wiggins and McDowell typically attempt to hold on to both cognitivism and internalism, and correspondingly reject HUM. Smith considers one line of objection to HUM that has been suggested by McDowell, who writes:

> I suspect that one reason people find . . . [HUM] . . . obvious lies in their inexplicit adherence to a quasi-hydraulic conception of how reason explanations account for action. The will is pictured as the source of forces that issue in the behaviour such explanations explain. This idea seems to me a radical misconception of the sort of explanation a reason explanation is . . . (1998: 213)

A 'quasi-hydraulic' conception would try to see psychological states combining to produce action in a manner analogous to the way in which, in Newtonian mechanics, different forces acting on a body combine to cause that body to move (Hume himself described himself as attempting to apply 'experimental philosophy to moral subjects' (1739: xvi)). Now Smith suggests that we put on one side the question whether there is anything wrong with the 'quasi-hydraulic' conception as McDowell describes it. His main claim is that even if some proponents of HUM have actually subscribed to a quasi-hydraulic conception, there is no *necessity* for a defender of HUM to do so:

> Far from being committed to a quasi-hydraulic conception of reason explanations, the Humean is not even committed to a causal conception of reason explanations. Given that a quasi-hydraulic conception is one form a causal conception might take, it follows that the Humean is simply not committed to a quasi-hydraulic conception of reason-explanations. (1994: 102)

In order to see this, Smith invites us to look again at Davidson's famous argument in favour of the causal conception (Davidson 1961). It could be true of an agent that she G's and has a reason to G even though it is not true that she G's *because* she has a reason to G. So what is added in the case where an agent G's, has a reason to G, and also G's *because* she has a reason to G? According to Davidson, the difference is that in the latter sort of case the agent's reason *causes* her to G. Smith now argues that the Humean and Anti-Humean can both reject and accept Davidson's causal conception of reason explanation, so that there is nothing in the Theory of Motivation per se to force one to embrace a causal theory of reason explanation. The plausibility of HUM is thus independent of the plausibility of the causal theory, so that (since the quasi-hydraulic conception is simply one form of the causal theory), it cannot be the case that the defender of HUM is committed to the quasi-hydraulic conception.

First, then, Smith argues that the Humean and the Anti-Humean may *both* agree that:

[T]here is something more basic and yet still illuminating to say about the 'because' in 'She G's because she has a reason to G'. For, we might say, the 'because' here signals the availability of a *teleological* explanation of the agent's G-ing in terms of her reason for G-ing, an explanation that is not necessarily available when all we know is that the agent G's and has a reason for G-ing. (1994a: 103)

So both may *reject* the causal theory of reason explanation. Second, the Humean and the Anti-Humean may both *accept* the causal theory of reason explanation, since if the causal theory is correct:

[W]e must conceive of some psychological states as possessing the causal power to produce behaviour. But, again, we need not think that desires are the only psychological state that possess such causal power. We might think instead that only certain beliefs, or some other psychological states altogether, possess such causal power. (1994a: 103)

If the debate between the Humean and the Anti-Humean is not about whether or not to accept a causal theory of reason explanation, what is it about? According to Smith, the debate between the Humean and the Anti-Humean is most fundamentally

a dispute concerning what it is about the nature of reasons that makes it possible for reason explanations to be teleological explanations. (1994a: 104)

Accordingly, the main thrust of Smith's pro-Humean argument is going to be that the Humean, and not the Anti-Humean, can make sense of motivation as the pursuit of a goal. The argument proceeds as follows. Smith considers two conceptions of the nature of desires, a *phenomenological conception of desires*, and a *dispositional conception of desires*. The phenomenological conception, which looks as though it might mesh with the Anti-Humean Theory of Motivation, turns out to be independently implausible. The dispositional conception, which Smith argues is plausible, implies HUM as a consequence. I will now briefly review Smith's arguments concerning phenomenological and dispositional conceptions of desire.

A phenomenological conception of desire is a view on which 'desires are, like sensations, simply and essentially states that have a certain phenomenological content' (1994a: 105). According to this conception, desires are like pains, states which are usually held to be simply and essentially states that have a particular phenomenological 'feel'.[14] As Smith points out, this conception of desires faces a number of serious difficulties. First of all, it gets the *epistemology* of desire wrong. It is a truth about a sensation such as pain that if a subject sincerely believes she is in pain, then she is in pain, and if she is in pain, then she believes that she is in pain. In fact, it is this sort of fact that leads philosophers to think of pains as simply and essentially states with a certain phenomenological content. But, at least as far as our folk-psychological practice is concerned, it would be wholly inappropriate to hold that a subject has a desire to G if and only if she sincerely believes she has a desire to G. It is a commonplace of folk psychology that people can be *mistaken* about the desires they possess: because of self-deception and the like people can think they have desires (e.g., to give up smoking, to drink less) which in fact they do not possess. And, likewise, people can have desires (e.g., to ingratiate themselves with those they perceive as social superiors) which they sincerely do not believe they possess. Second, in addition to this worry about epistemology, there is a more fundamental worry. Desires are propositional attitudes; they have *propositional* content. One desires that such and such is the case: I desire that I have this book finished by the weekend, the propositional content of my desire is *that I have this book finished by the weekend*. Now the propositional content of desires is of crucial importance when it comes to citing desires in explanations of human behaviour: it is because the propositional content of my desire is *that I have a beer* (and not, say, *that I have a cigar*) that it can be cited in an explanation of why I opened the fridge door. But the phenomenological account of desire can have nothing to contribute to an explanation of the propositional content of desire: sensations do not *have* any propositional content, so modelling desires on sensations in the manner of the phenomenological conception a fortiori will be of no help in explaining the propositional content, and the epistemology of the propositional content, of desires. Even if we try to accommodate the fact that desires have propositional content by weakening the phenomenological conception to the claim that desires are states that have their phenomenological content essentially as well as propositional content (so that they are not *simply* and essentially states with phenomenological content), we will face the problem that – paradoxically – the phenomenological conception of desires gets the *phenomenology* of desires all wrong. Some desires, sometimes, have a particular qualitative 'feel'. But many don't:

> Consider, for instance, what we should ordinarily think of as a long-term desire: say, a father's desire that his children do well. A father may actually feel the prick of his desire from time to time, in moments of reflection on their vulnerability, say. But such occasions are not the norm. Yet we certainly wouldn't ordinarily think that he loses this desire during those periods when he lacks such feelings. (1994a: 109)

Thus, phenomenological conceptions of desire get the *epistemology* and *phenomenology* of desire wrong, and cannot explain the fact that desires possess *propositional content*.

Why does Smith think a phenomenological conception of desire lies in the background of Anti-Humean Theories of Motivation? Take even an Anti-Humean who claims to reject the phenomenological conception, John McDowell. According to McDowell, a morally virtuous person may be motivated to act morally simply on the basis of her moral beliefs. Helen believes that honesty is morally obligatory, and is motivated to be honest. According to a Humean, this cannot be the whole story: there must be some desire of Helen's to contribute to the explanation of why she is so motivated. So, for the Humean (according to McDowell), if I try to get Lyn to believe that honesty is good and to be appropriately motivated, I must also try to get her to come to have a certain desire. McDowell takes this to be the suggestion that:

'See it like this' [i.e., see that honesty is required of you] is really a covert invitation to feel, quite over and above one's view of the facts, a desire which will combine with one's belief to recommend acting in the appropriate way. (1998: 86)

McDowell takes the implausibility of this to display the untenability of HUM, but in fact it does so only if we see desires as essentially some kind of 'feeling': once the phenomenological conception of desire is given up, this type of point simply loses its force against the Humean.

Thus, Smith argues, the phenomenological conception of desire in the background of Anti-Humean theories is unacceptable. But what is the dispositionalist alternative? Why is it plausible? And how does it lend support to HUM and the Humean?

Smith's attempt to answer these questions takes off from an observation about the difference between beliefs and desires which Mark Platts, developing an idea of Elizabeth Anscombe's, expounds as follows:

Beliefs aim at the true; and their being true is their fitting the world; falsity is a decisive failing in a belief, and false beliefs should be discarded; beliefs should be changed to fit with the world, not *vice versa*. Desires aim at realization, and their realization is the world fitting with them; the fact that the indicative content of a desire is not realized in the world is not yet a failing in the desire, and not yet any reason to discard the desire; the world, crudely, should be changed to fit with our desires, not *vice versa*. (Platts 1979: 256–7)

Beliefs and desires thus have different 'directions of fit'. Smith agrees with Platts that this talk of 'directions of fit' is metaphorical, but suggests that it can be cashed out literally via a dispositional conception of desires, according to which:

Desires are states that have a certain functional role. That is, according to this conception, we should think of desiring to G as having a certain set of dispositions, the disposition to H in conditions C, the disposition to K in circumstances C*, and so on, where in order for conditions C and C* to obtain, the subject must have, *inter alia*, certain other desires, and also certain means-end beliefs, beliefs concerning G-ing by H-ing, G-ing by K-ing, and so on. (1994a: 113)

On this conception, Smith argues, we have ready solutions to the problems about propositional content, epistemology and phenomenology. *First*, the problem about propositional content can be solved by the dispositional conception, since:

A dispositional conception is precisely an account of what a desire is that explains how it can be that desires have propositional content; for the propositional content of a desire may then simply be determined by its functional role. (1994a: 114)

Second, the problem which the phenomenological conception faced regarding the epistemology of desire is avoided, since, on the dispositional conception, 'the epistemology of desire is simply the epistemology of dispositional states' (1994a: 113), and:

It is implausible to suggest quite generally that if the counterfactuals that are [according to the dispositional conception] true of a subject who desires to G are true of her then she believes they are, and it is likewise implausible to suggest quite generally that if a subject believes that such counterfactuals are true of her, then such counterfactuals are true of her. (1994a: 114)

Third, the dispositional conception can account for both the case where there does seem to be such a thing as the essential 'feel' of a desire and the case where there does not, since according to the dispositional conception:

Desires have phenomenological content just to the extent that the having of certain feelings is one of the things that they are dispositions to produce under certain conditions. (1994a: 114)

So both cases can be accommodated, and there are no implausible implications about the phenomenology of desire. Finally, the dispositional conception allows us to cash out the literal truth in the 'direction of fit' metaphor:

The difference between beliefs and desires in terms of direction of fit can be seen to amount to a difference in the functional roles of belief and desire. Very roughly, and simplifying somewhat, it amounts, *inter alia*, to a difference in the counterfactual dependence of a belief that p and a desire that p on a perception with the content that not-p: a belief that p tends to go out of existence in the presence of a perception with the content that not-p, whereas a desire that p tends to endure, disposing the subject in that state to bring it about that p. (1994a: 115)

We can now reach HUM in three easy steps:

(a) Having a motivating reason is, inter alia, having a goal.

This is so since 'we understand what it is for someone to have a motivating reason in part precisely by thinking of them as having some goal' (1994a: 116).

(b) Having a goal is being in a state with which the world must fit.

This is so because 'becoming apprised of the fact that the world is not as the content of your goal specifies suffices not for giving up that goal, it suffices rather for changing the world'. (1994a: 117)
    We have:

(c) Being in a state with which the world must fit is desiring

courtesy of the dispositional conception of desire, and it now follows from (a), (b) and (c) that having a motivating reason is, inter alia, desiring: in other words, that HUM is true.
    I will now argue that it is much less clear than Smith makes out that the dispositional conception can better the phenomenological conception on the points concerning phenomenology, epistemology, and propositional content. To take phenomenology first, Smith says that his dispositional account can accommodate the cases where desires have their phenomenological content essentially and the cases where desires lack phenomenological content altogether, since:

According to [the dispositional conception], desires have phenomenological content just to the extent that the having of certain feelings is one of the things that they are dispositions to produce under certain conditions. (1994a: 114)

Now 'produce' here looks as though it means 'cause', and this would immediately conflict with Smith's claim that the argument for HUM can proceed independently of the debate about the causal theory of reason explanation. Smith may reply that this talk of dispositions producing feelings is really talk of dispositions having feelings as their manifestations, and it is an open, philosophically substantial question whether dispositions can be viewed as causing their manifestations. As an answer to the original worry this is fine, but now there is another worry looming. What about cases where desires do not lack phenomenological content altogether but do not have a specific phenomenological content essentially: that is, what about desires that have phenomenological content *non-essentially* and contingently? Many desires appear to fall into this category. For example, my desire that I have this book finished by the weekend *can* manifest itself in feeling, but it needn't: I've had the desire all week, and sometimes I've 'felt' it but at other times I haven't. How can the dispositional account accommodate this type of fact about the phenomenology of desire? It seems to me that the only way it can do so is by construing the dispositions which constitute the desires as standing in a *causal relationship* to the relevant feelings: on some occasions the disposition causes the feeling, on some occasions it doesn't. If there is no other way of accounting for the phenomenology of desires that have phenomenological content non-essentially, Smith's claim, essential to his argument in favour of HUM, that the debate about HUM is independent of the debate about causal theories of reason explanation, will be undermined, and thus so will his argument for HUM.[15] Thus, it seems to me that Smith's dispositional account is ill adapted to account for the phenomenological content of at least some of our desires.

In addition, Smith's account sits ill with some facts about the epistemology of desire. To be sure, the dispositional conception does not entail that an agent believes she has a desire to G iff she has a desire to G, and to that extent avoids the problem that Smith raised for the phenomenological conception. But what about the fact that our knowledge of our desires, like our knowledge of our intentions (Wright 1987, 1989), is often non-inferential and first-person authoritative? Consider my claim that I desire to finish this book by the weekend. I do not *infer* the fact that I have this desire from some hypothesis about how I will behave under contrary-to-fact conditions: I know it immediately and non-inferentially. Also, my claim to the effect that I have this desire is the *default* position: the claim can be overturned, for instance, by someone pointing out that I am prey to some self-deception or whatever, but the onus is on someone wishing to overturn my claim to make out such a case, not on me. Unless some overriding condition is adduced, my claim stands. Thus, the epistemology of self-ascriptions of desire is in this way *non-inferential* and *first-person authoritative*. It is difficult to see how Smith's dispositional conception of desire can accommodate this fact. If the epistemology of desire is, as Smith claims, the epistemology of dispositional states, it is hard to see how self-ascriptions of desires could have either of these features. It is difficult to see how one could have non-inferential knowledge of the truth of a counterfactual conditional. And if desires are constituted by dispositions to behave in certain ways, it is difficult to see how I could have first-person authority with respect to the content of my desires, given that a third party has in principle as good a chance as I do of knowing about which counterfactual conditionals hold true of me. Thus, although the dispositional conception does not face the epistemological worries of the phenomenological conception, it faces serious and so far unresolved epistemological difficulties of its own.

Finally, Smith claims that the dispositional account of desires can account for their propositional content. But in saying this he omits to mention the serious, and again, unresolved problems faced by dispositional theories of content determination. Even in the simplest sort of case, where we are attempting to account for the meaning of a term such as 'magpie', for instance, there is no satisfactory dispositional account of its content. Can we say that the meaning of 'magpie' is determined by my dispositions to apply it? This seems implausible, since 'magpie' means *magpie*, and I am disposed to apply it to things other than magpies, perhaps currawongs on especially dark nights. Can we say that the meaning of 'magpie' is determined by my disposition to apply it to certain things (the magpies) *under certain conditions* (not including especially dark nights, and so on)? The problem is that none of the attempts that have been made by philosophers of mind and language to specify the relevant conditions in non-semantic and non-intentional terms have worked (see, e.g., the paper by Boghossian reprinted in Miller and Wright (2002)). It may be that philosophers of mind and language will eventually come up with a plausible dispositional theory of content determination, but the important point here is that they are at best some considerable distance from doing so. Smith thus presupposes a particular resolution of a highly controversial philosophical debate which is nowhere near to being resolved. Smith writes that 'the propositional content of a desire may then "simply" be determined by its functional role' (1994a: 114, scare-quotes added). But there is nothing 'simple' about it. Smith is not entitled to the claim that the dispositional conception of desires can account for their propositional content.

It seems to me, then, that Smith's argument for HUM fails, based as it is on a dispositional conception of desires. That said, the debate between Humean and Anti-Humean Theories of Motivation is very much a live one, and much work remains to be done before we can make an informed choice between them.

10.5 Scientism, Curiosity and the 'Metaphysical Understanding'

In this final section, I want to return to McDowell's 'Projectivism and Truth in Ethics'. In 4.9, I looked at two of the objections McDowell raised against Blackburn's quasi-realism, and here I want to look at a third objection McDowell raises. This concerns the following passage:

> [W]e try to place the activity of moralizing, or the reaction of finding things funny . . . In particular we try to fit our commitments in these areas into a metaphysical understanding of the kinds of fact the world contains: a metaphysical view that can be properly hostile to an unanalysed and *sui generis* area of moral or humorous . . . facts. And relative to this interest, answers which merely cite the truth of various such verdicts are quite beside the point. This . . . is because there is no theory connecting these truths to devices whereby we know about them. (Blackburn 1993a: 163)

McDowell now claims that the 'metaphysical understanding' which Blackburn refers to here – which 'blankly excludes values and instances of the comic from the world in advance of any philosophical enquiry into truth' (McDowell 1998: 164) – lacks good philosophical credentials, and is at any rate undefended by Blackburn. McDowell castigates the 'metaphysical understanding' he ascribes to Blackburn as follows:

> Surely if the history of philosophical reflection on the correspondence theory of truth has taught us anything, it is that there is ground for suspicion of the idea that we have some way of telling what can count as a fact, prior to and independent of asking what forms of words might count as expressing truths, so that a conception of facts could exert some leverage in the investigation of truth. (1998: 164)

The 'metaphysical understanding' is thus:

> [a] matter for diagnosis and exorcism, not something that can be allowed without further ado to be a good starting point for a philosophy of ethics or humour. (1998: 165)

What can the quasi-realist say in response? McDowell describes the 'metaphysical understanding' that he takes to underpin quasi-realism as blankly excluding 'values and instances of the comic from the world in advance of any philosophical enquiry into truth', as assigning natural science 'a foundational status in philosophical reflection about truth', and as holding that 'there can be no facts other than those that would figure in a scientific understanding of the world'. Put on one side the question of whether the views here attributed to the quasi-realist are acceptable. It should be clear, especially in the light of my remarks at the end of 10.1, that nothing as strong as this is required to motivate the quasi-realist project: indeed, a view which 'blankly excludes' values and instances of the comic from the world is presumably inconsistent with a view which attempts to earn us the right to see them as belonging to the world. What has happened here? I think that McDowell in fact falls prey to the sort of mistaken interpretation of the quasi-realist project of which he himself convicts Wright (4.9).

The attribution to Blackburn of the 'metaphysical understanding', as McDowell understands it, appears to be justified by the first passage quoted above. But this, in the context of the whole quasi-realist project, is not intended as a bar on including values and instances of the comic in one's inventory of the sorts of property and fact the world can rightfully be viewed as containing; rather, it is intended as a guide to where we might require the *right* so to include properties and facts in this inventory to be earned, rather than assumed. That McDowell misses this shows that he has not himself fully absorbed the distinction – which he accused Wright of overlooking – between earned and unearned uses of the notion of truth. The passage might be rewritten, with its place in the overall quasi-realist project signalled more explicitly, as:

> [W]e try to place the activity of moralizing, or the reaction of finding things funny . . . In particular we try to fit our commitments in these areas into a metaphysical understanding of the kinds of fact the world can be supposed, *ab initio*, to contain: a metaphysical view which can properly be hostile to the assumption, *ab initio*, of an unanalysed and *sui generis* area of moral or humorous . . . facts. And relative to this interest, answers which merely cite the truth of various such verdicts are quite beside the point. This . . . is because there is no theory connecting these truths to devices whereby we know about them.

Properly understood, this needn't be viewed as an expression of a 'scientistic' attribution of foundational status to natural science in philosophical reflection about truth, but can be viewed as stemming, rather, from a perfectly reasonable curiosity about a range of apparent truths and the nature of our dealings with the facts apparently corresponding to them. Science has nothing to say on the matter (we may suppose), the appeal to an unearned notion of truth strikes us as philosophically disrespectable, so we attempt to earn the right to the notion of truth in a manner independent of any *assumption* of an unanalysed and *sui generis* area of moral or humorous facts. A sound motivation for quasi-realism needs only natural curiosity plus a decent and healthy respect for natural science, not a form of 'scientism'.[16] Indeed, this curiosity is arguably expressed by McDowell himself (1998: 165) when he admits that there are 'good questions' about how 'ethics and humour relate to the scientifically useful truth about the world and our dealings with it'. If I am right, all we need to underpin quasi-realism is the thought that these questions are good, not an attribution of 'foundational status' to natural science in 'philosophical reflection about truth'.

McDowell, in considering Blackburn's idea (1984: 146) that the quasi-realist project may be motivated by doubts about particular kinds of subject matter, writes:

> [T]here is a striking lack of concern with the origin of the doubts, and this leaves no room for addressing the question of their merits. It is as if any

bit of philosophy that comes naturally to us must be all right, ahead of
any inquiry into why it comes naturally to us. (1998: 164, n.20)

I have suggested that, in the first instance, the quasi-realist project can
be motivated by natural curiosity about an area of thought, as opposed
to philosophically motivated doubt or anxiety about that area. What if
McDowell replies that we ought to be concerned with the *origin* of the
curiosity, and investigate this before we attempt to satisfy it? I think we
should reject this as a reactionary attitude. If a child asks 'How does
this work?', it would be churlish to reply: 'Why do you want to know?',
'What makes you think that that is a good question?', or 'Come back
and see me when you have investigated the source of your curiosity.'
The right thing to do is to take the curiosity seriously, and attempt to
answer the question.[17] Of course, there can be such a thing as *unhealthy*
curiosity. But in my view, given a piece of natural curiosity, the curiosity should be regarded as healthy in the absence of a positive reason to
think otherwise: in the absence of such a reason, the curiosity stands as
the default position. McDowell's assumption that a piece of curiosity
has no standing unless we have a demonstration that it is healthy gets
the onus the wrong way round. Adopting that view of natural curiosity would leave us prone to a conservative and ultimately self-serving
complacency.[18]

10.6 Further Reading

McDowell's difficult but rewarding essays on ethics are collected in
his 1998. Other philosophers who have developed metaethical views
broadly consonant with McDowell's include Mark Platts (1979), David
Wiggins (1987, 1991), Sabina Lovibond (1983), David McNaughton
(1988), and Jonathan Dancy (1993, 2000). For useful discussion of
McDowell, see David Sosa's 'Pathetic Ethics' in Leiter (ed.) (2001b), and
the chapter on value judgements in Thornton (2004). For Blackburn's
response to the 'Disentangling' argument, see Blackburn (1991 and
1998a, chapter 4). See also Kirchin (2010), Roberts (2011), and Väyrynen
(2013). There is a good discussion of non-naturalistic cognitivism in
Arrington (1989, chapter 4). For some debate on the Humean Theory of
Motivation, see Pettit (1987), and Smith (1988). Sobel and Copp (2001)
provide some useful discussion of the attempt to distinguish between
beliefs and desires in terms of 'direction of fit'. For an alternative non-
naturalist perspective, see Schafer-Landau (2003b and 2006).

Appendix: Sense, Reference, Semantic Value and Truth-Conditions

At various places in the book (2.3, 9.7, 10.1) I have relied on some distinctions and theses introduced in the work of the German philosopher and mathematician Gottlob Frege (1848–1925). In this appendix I briefly run over some of these distinctions and theses. For a full exposition of Frege's philosophy of language, see chapters 1 and 2 of Miller (2007).

Consider the names 'Mark Twain' and 'Samuel Clemens'. Intuitively, we know what 'Mark Twain' means and we know what 'Samuel Clemens' means. But 'Mark Twain' and 'Samuel Clemens' mean the same thing, the same person. Since someone who understands 'Mark Twain' knows its meaning, and someone who understands 'Samuel Clemens' knows its meaning, it is mysterious how someone could know the meaning of 'Mark Twain is Samuel Clemens' but not know that it is true. This is a problem because it plainly is possible to understand the identity statement and then discover that it is true. Frege responds to this problem by distinguishing between the *sense* ('Sinn') and *reference* ('Bedeutung') of a name. The sense of a name is what *determines the reference* of that expression; it is whatever someone has to grasp in order to understand it. The reference is given by the object the name stands for. Thus, Frege will say that although 'Mark Twain' and 'Samuel Clemens' have the *same reference*, they nevertheless have *different senses*. Since one can know the sense of an expression without knowing its reference, this explains how one could understand 'Mark Twain is Samuel Clemens' and yet not know that it was true.

So:

(A) The reference (semantic value) of a proper name is the object that it stands for.
(B) The sense of a proper name determines what object it refers to.
(C) Someone who understands a proper name grasps its sense.

(D) The sense of a proper name is to be distinguished from its reference: it is possible to grasp its sense yet not know its reference.

It is important to bear in mind that although we've introduced Frege's distinction between sense and reference by considering proper names, it can be generalized to other sorts of linguistic expression, including predicates and sentences. In fact, the idea that the reference of a proper name is the object it stands for is a consequence of the following definition (I use 'semantic value' instead of 'reference' to translate the German 'Bedeutung', since it can sound odd to talk of predicates and sentences having a reference):

The semantic value of an expression is that feature of it that determines whether sentences in which it occurs are true or false.

Intuitively, it seems right to say that the feature of 'Mark Twain' that determines whether sentences in which it occurs are true or false is the fact that it stands for this individual rather than that: it is this that determines why 'Mark Twain was an author' is true while 'Mark Twain was Scottish' is false.

Just as we can distinguish between the sense and reference of a proper name, we can distinguish between the sense and semantic value of a predicate. Consider the predicate expression '... is even'. Frege views this as a functional expression, since it has a gap into which a numeral can be slotted. What is the result of slotting a numeral into the gap? It will be a *true* sentence, if the number denoted by the numeral is even; it will be a *false* sentence, otherwise. Thus, we can view the predicate '... is even' as standing for a *function* from numbers to truth-values (the two truth-values are *true* and *false*). There are also functions which take objects other than numbers as their arguments. Consider '... is round'. This has a gap into which a proper name may be slotted, and the value delivered will be true if the object denoted by that proper name is round, false otherwise. Thus '... is round' can be viewed as standing for a function from objects to truth-values. So:

(E) The semantic value of a predicate is a function from objects to truth-values.
(F) The sense of a predicate determines which function is its semantic value.
(G) Someone who understands a predicate grasps its sense.
(H) The sense of a predicate is to be distinguished from its semantic value.

Finally, Frege thinks that sentences can be viewed as possessing both sense and semantic value.

(I)   The semantic value of a sentence is a truth-value.
(J)   The sense of a sentence determines its truth-value.
(K) Someone who understands a sentence grasps its sense.
(L) The sense of a sentence is to be distinguished from its semantic value.

Often, the sense of a sentence is said to be its *truth-condition*, the condition that obtains in the world if and only if the sentence is true. Just as I can grasp the sense of a proper name without knowing which object it refers to, I can grasp the truth-condition of a sentence (*what it would be for the sentence to be true*) without knowing whether it *actually is true*.

Notes

Chapter 1 Introduction

1 I'm not suggesting that questions in metaethics are entirely independent of questions in normative ethics. Many contemporary theorists believe that there are interconnections, although the types of question are distinct. See, e.g., Smith (1994a) and Brink (1989: 4–5).
2 As will emerge later, especially in chapters 4 and 6, this description of the cognitivist/non-cognitivist debate is something of an oversimplification.
3 Again, as we'll see later in the book, particularly when we come to discuss Blackburn's quasi-realism, this type of characterization of moral realism is not very helpful. Like the cognitivism/non-cognitivism distinction introduced above, I use it here merely to get things started.
4 For a good account of how arguments along these lines get going, see Smith (1994a: 1.3).
5 As Schroeder (2009: 257–8) notes, the idea that there is a binary distinction here has recently come under scrutiny: perhaps moral judgements can be viewed as expressing both beliefs and non-cognitive sentiments? Schroeder (2009) provides a state-of-the-art overview of these recent developments, although it's best to read Schroeder (2010: chapter 10) first.

Chapter 2 Moore's Attack on Ethical Naturalism

1 See Baldwin (1993: 102–3). For some opposing thoughts, see Brink (1989: 109–10).
2 Note that the idea that facts about meaning could in this way be independent of facts about the use of linguistic expressions is not unproblematic. See the articles in Miller and Wright (2002).
3 These examples correspond to the applications of the open-question argument made by Moore: see 1903: 15ff and 66ff.
4 Moore's argument strikes me as having some affinities with the argument Socrates gives in Plato's *Euthyphro* to the effect that since the gods love what

is good because it is good, we cannot define good as that which is beloved of the gods. Moore's argument is generally scorned, while Plato's is generally accepted. It is an interesting question why the two arguments should have received such differing assessments.

5 The objection does not have to assume that these controversial philosophical analyses are *true*: it is enough that their unobvious nature does not by itself establish that they are false. In this section I lean heavily on Smith (1994a).

6 For more on this, see Snare (1975) and Smith (1994a: 37–9). For the distinction between knowledge how and knowledge that, see Ryle (1949, chapter 2). The matter is probably more complicated than it appears: see Dummett (1993: Preface).

7 For an introduction to Frege's notions of sense and reference, see the Appendix.

8 Note that 'internalism', as I understand it here, is what is sometimes referred to in the literature as 'judgement-internalism', as opposed to 'existence-internalism'. For the distinction, see Darwall (1983).

Chapter 3 Emotivism and the Rejection of Non-Naturalism

1 For a full discussion of this worry, see Miller (1998a). I argue there that Ayer cannot consistently avoid embracing moral nihilism.

2 For example, Smith writes: 'a non-naturalist *has* to able to use the intuitionist, perceptual account of how we come by knowledge of the claim "This object with natural features N has moral feature M" to somehow ground or explain the a priori truth that any object with exactly the same natural properties as this object, that is N, will have M as well' (1994a: 22, emphasis added). Thus, if the non-naturalist can't use the intuitional, perceptual model to do this, her theory ought to be rejected. The overstatement in Smith's argument is clear: the non-naturalist has to give some explanation of the a priori supervenience of the moral on the natural which is *consistent* with the intuitional, perceptual model. But there is no need for that explanation to flow from the model itself.

3 To what extent does this problem for the non-naturalistic cognitivist arise in virtue of his *non-naturalism* as opposed to his *cognitivism*? Doesn't a similar problem arise for the naturalistic cognitivist?

4 Of course, this is not to suggest that perception plays no role at all. We may need it in order to know what pointless, deliberate cruelty involves, or maybe even to acquire the relevant concepts in the first place. The important point is that once perception has made this sort of contribution, there is nothing *more* for it to do as we proceed to the general moral claims or standards.

5 Perhaps unsurprisingly, some non-naturalists decline this challenge on the grounds that general standards do not play the sort of role in moral deliberation described in the objection: that is, non-naturalists attempt to blunt the force of the challenge by arguing for ethical *particularism*. For a useful collection of articles on the issue of particularism, see Hooker and Little (eds) (2000). For definitive works in the particularist tradition, see Platts

(1979: chapter X); Dancy (1993, 2006); and McDowell's 'Virtue and Reason' (reprinted in his 1998).

6 For some doubts about this type of argument, see Brink (1989: 110). But compare Mackie (1973: chapter 1).

7 For an interesting argument that ethical emotivism must inevitably collapse into ethical subjectivism, see Jackson and Pettit (1998). See also Mautner (2000) and Suikkanen (2009).

8 Note, though, that the projective error which threatens emotivism is actually more radical than the common-or-garden examples I have used to illustrate the threat. When I say (with Wordsworth) that the sea bares its bosom to the moon, my error is one of saying something that is strictly and literally false. But when I say that murder is wrong, on an emotivist construal, the mistake I make is not that of saying something false, but rather of treating something not apt for *either* truth or falsity as if it were actually truth-apt.

9 In the remainder of this section I draw on and develop Miller (1998a).

10 That is, no worries over and above the worries which a verificationist faces relating to third-person ascriptions of mental states in general.

11 Ayer may claim that although he is, for the reasons just outlined, unable to capture all of the distinctive features of our ethical language – given that one such feature is that ethical discourse is distinct from discourse about aesthetic merit or gustatory appeal – he can nevertheless be interpreted as suggesting a *revisionary* account of our ethical practices, suggesting, in other words, that our actual ethical language be replaced by a surrogate. The problem with this suggestion is that, by Ayer's own admission, it would place the emotive theory of ethics in no better a position than the naturalistic versions of cognitivism – subjectivism and utilitarianism – which Ayer rejects. Speaking of these cognitivist theories, Ayer writes: '[W]e are not, of course, denying that it is possible to invent a language in which all ethical symbols are definable in non-ethical terms, or even that it is desirable to invent such a language and adopt it in place of our own; what we are denying is that the suggested reduction of ethical to non-ethical statements is consistent with the conventions of our actual language' ([1936] 1946: 105). Clearly, Ayer thinks that the emotive theory – unlike naturalistic cognitivism – does have the advantage of being consistent with the conventions of our actual language, and this advantage will be lost if Ayer pursues the revisionist line. The adoption of the emotive theory over the adoption of a naturalist cognitivist theory would then seem unmotivated.

12 Nor could Ayer respond that moral sentiments are those with distinctive causes (as opposed to reasons): if it is the fact that a sentiment is caused by certain types of states of affairs that *make it a moral* sentiment, aren't those states of affairs really just *moral* states of affairs? In other words, doesn't this response just take us back to cognitivism, and therefore fail as a defence of emotivism?

13 That the main claim of Ayer's emotive theory does concern an analytic equivalence or a deliverance of conceptual analysis is clear from his remark that 'A strictly philosophical treatise on ethics should therefore make no ethical pronouncements. But it should, by giving an *analysis* of ethical terms, show what is the category to which all such pronouncements belong' ([1936] 1946: 103–4, emphasis added).

14 Note that the reapplication of the open-question argument (17)–(21) does not make the mistake of construing Ayer's position as a subjectivist one. The claim is not that for Ayer 'x is bad' is equivalent to something like 'Jones expresses disapproval of x', which would be subjectivist, but rather that for Ayer the different judgement, 'Jones judges that x is bad', is equivalent to 'Jones expresses disapproval of x'. The latter claim is at least prima facie independent of subjectivism about 'bad'.

15 As before, the *ceteris paribus* clause will rule out Jones's being weak-willed, depressed, or prey to some form of practical irrationality.

16 Kantians would disagree with what I say here, so far as aesthetic judgements are concerned. According to them, the judgement that Jones has made that the *Missa Solemnis* is sublime (say) does sustain a conceptual link to the expectation that Jones will demand that you share his non-cognitive inclinations towards the *Missa Solemnis*. As a *descriptive* account of our practice of aesthetic judgement, this strikes me as very implausible, but I cannot argue the point here. In any event, even if the Kantians are right about aesthetic judgement, the argument could still proceed by pointing out that the beings in question may genuinely wonder whether Jones has expressed some other non-moral and non-aesthetic form of approval.

17 Note that in his 1954 Ayer wrote: 'To say, as I once did, that these moral judgements are merely expressive of certain feelings, feelings of approval or disapproval, is an over-simplification. The fact is rather that what may be described as moral attitudes consist in certain patterns of behaviour, and that the expression of a judgement is an element in the pattern. The moral judgement expresses the attitude in the sense that it contributes to defining it' (238). It is not at all clear to me, though, how this can save Ayer from the moral attitude problem. In order to get at the attitude, one would already have to have some conception of what a moral judgement was; so how could we *explain* moral judgement in terms of the expression of the attitude?

18 It is an interesting question whether there are arguments for the modified internalism of (22) which are as strong as the arguments for the internalism in, e.g., (16) in the version of the open-question argument proposed by Darwall, Gibbard and Railton.

Chapter 4 Blackburn's Quasi-Realism

1 Note that these entitlements are not the same as the entitlement to talk and think as if moral judgements are true even though they are not. See 4.7 and 4.8.

2 Blackburn prefers to distance himself from the label 'non-cognitivism'. Non-cognitivism is the view that moral judgements do not express beliefs, whereas the quasi-realist, although he *starts out* by assuming that moral judgements express desire-like states, *ends up* saying that moral judgements do express beliefs. See, e.g., Blackburn (1996).

3 This is Wiggins's description of what he calls 'explanatory or Humean Naturalism' (Wiggins 1992a, 1993a, 1993b). A 'substantive naturalist', by contrast, is someone who claims that moral facts are identical or reducible

to natural facts. See also Railton's distinction between 'methodological' and 'substantive' naturalism, Railton (1989), and ch. 9 below.

4 This argument may share some of the defects of the COQA, as outlined in chapter 2. For example, someone who holds to the idea that the moral is conceptually necessitated by the natural may hold that Blackburn's assumption that, e.g., Johnson was not confused about any of the naturalistic concepts implicated in N simply begs the question against the claim of conceptual necessitation.

5 The difference between necessitation and supervenience can be captured formally as follows:

Necessitation: $\Box$ ((Na & Ma) $\rightarrow$ $\Box$ $\forall x$ (Nx $\rightarrow$ Mx))
Supervenience: $\Box$ ((Na & Ma) $\rightarrow$ $\forall x$ (Nx $\rightarrow$ Mx))

6 If you accepted necessitation you wouldn't face this challenge, because on your view God could not have created a world such as W1.

7 See also the remarks in Hare (1952: 134).

8 See the passages from Hume, quoted by Brink (1989: 145).

9 This is the account given in Blackburn (1984: chapter 6): as we'll see, Blackburn later modifies this account.

10 I am indebted here to Bob Hale's 2002. For Blackburn's reply to Hale, see Blackburn (2002).

11 We can assume, courtesy of the second part of the strategy, that there are states of accepting and rejecting attitudes such that to accept and reject the same attitude is to involve oneself in inconsistency. This is not a trivial concession, as Hale points out: why should this sort of inconsistency necessarily signal illogicality or irrationality?

12 Might Blackburn evade the difficulty by emending the account so that the assertion of 'If p then q' expresses the commitment to either not accepting p or accepting q (as opposed to the commitment to either accepting not-p or accepting q)? Hale argues that this would cause problems for the account's capacity to secure the validity of *modus tollens*. To see this, consider:

(G) If P then Q.
(H) Not-Q.
So:
(I) Not-P.

What of the commitments held by someone who endorses both of the premises yet fails to endorse the conclusion? In this case these are:

Commitment to either not accepting that P or accepting that Q.
Commitment to accepting not-Q.
Lack of commitment to accepting not-P.

The two branches are:

Branch 2c
Commitment to accepting that Q.

Commitment to accepting not-Q.
Lack of commitment to accepting not-P.
X

Branch 1c
Commitment to not accepting that P.
Commitment to accepting not-Q.
Lack of commitment to accepting not-P.

But there is no inconsistency on this branch. As Hale points out, it would be perfectly rational to have this combination of commitments if the available evidence warrants neither P nor not-P. Again, the account appears to be unable to secure the validity of *modus tollens* even in cases where the ingredient sentences are all factual.

13 Of course, I mean only that an interpretation of an agent is *epistemically* indeterminate, given a scarcity of the relevant sort of background information. This is independent of any claim (such as that of Quine 1960) to the effect that interpretation is *constitutively* indeterminate.

14 I'm not claiming that Blackburn's (1984) account is immune to all difficulties, but just that the central objection to that account might be less of a knock-down argument than it initially seems.

15 See also Blackburn (1993a: 55–8).

16 The alert reader may already be wondering how this ambitious project can be married to the projectivist core of Blackburn's position. Doesn't the ambitious project, if successful, undermine the projectivism? See below.

17 For some scepticism about Blackburn's strategy for dealing with this worry, see Hale (1986).

18 See also Sturgeon (1992, n.12).

19 Blackburn (1993a: 373) christens this objection that of the 'contaminated response'.

20 Though see Kalderon (2005a: 130–5) for the idea that a non-cognitivist needn't accept a constraint like McDowell's.

21 I will return to this issue in chapter 10. See also 4.10.

22 In this regard, note that the term 'quasi-realism' can start to seem like a misnomer. Allan Gibbard (in Gibbard 1996) has suggested 'sophisticated realism' as a more apt title for Blackburn's view, in at least some instances. Blackburn (1998a: 313) records a willingness to embrace the name, though he cautions that 'the overall package . . . matters rather than the label'.

23 Indeed, as the discussion of the Frege-Geach problem earlier in this chapter shows, Blackburn's problem is not that he can't rely on ethical claims in the process of executing the quasi-realist project, but rather that the reliance on ethical claims may extend too far: the main criticism of Blackburn's (1984) account of moral *modus ponens* arguments, recall, was that it turned what ought to be a logical failing into an ethical failing.

24 Law's objection is foreshadowed in Brink (1989: 30). See also Sturgeon (1986b: 140, n.43), Kirchin (1997).

25 I'll leave out 'can be assumed *ab initio* to' when the context makes it clear that this is what the quasi-realist intends.

26 I am not attributing this suggestion to Blackburn himself, but merely

exploring whether it could provide a plausible account of moral attitudes for the quasi-realist.

27 The view of Lewis's which Smith is here criticizing can be found in Lewis (1989).

28 Perhaps, though, the problem is not with the aspiration to have a 'strict' definition (as Blackburn seems to suggest, hinting that a less 'strict' definition may do), but with the aspiration for a 'definition' at all. This should come as no surprise: recall that the reply to McDowell's 'contaminated response' objection was that McDowell was prejudging, a priori, that psychology would provide no adequate characterization of the responses 'projected' on the world in moral judgement. But if discovering the nature of the relevant response is in this way dependent upon the a posteriori deliverances of psychology, the quasi-realist ought not to be in the business of providing, via philosophical *analysis*, an a priori characterization of distinctively ethical sentiment. So the apparent failure of the strategies explored in this section needn't embarrass the quasi-realist. For more on this, see the discussion of McDowell's 'disentangling' argument in chapter 10 of this volume. For more on an a posteriori non-cognitivist position, see Miller (2010c).

Chapter 5 Gibbard's Norm-Expressivism

1 I oversimplify deliberately in the interests of letting the general shape of Gibbard's theory emerge more clearly. For example, Gibbard thinks that we need something like 'impartial anger' in the analysis just proposed, since anger and resentment may have connotations of there being hurt to the person feeling them, a connotation clearly not necessary to moral judgement: I can judge a person's actions to be immoral even if those actions have done nothing to hurt me personally. See Gibbard (1990: 126).

2 This doesn't sound right. If I judge that murder is wrong, I seem to do more than express my acceptance of norms which permit one to feel guilty on having committed murder: rather, I express my acceptance of norms which *prescribe* feeling guilty at having committed murder. Gibbard in fact makes this move himself: he talks of permission at 46 of 1990, but switches to talk of prescription at 47.

3 I owe this way of framing the Frege-Geach problem to Wedgwood (1997).

4 Note that Blackburn's commitment-theoretic approach (4.5 of this volume) is designed to do this too: the 'tree-tying' semantics given for the conditional is the same whether or not the sentences embedded in it contain moral vocabulary.

5 Can this worry be applied to Blackburn's own commitment-theoretic response (4.5) to the Frege-Geach problem?

6 In other words, not prey to objections such as that it convicts those guilty of a logical mistake of only a moral shortcoming, and so on. The objection we are considering here is meant to bite even if Blackburn can see off this other type of worry.

7 Of course, Blackburn cannot without begging the question use a similar argument to respond to the original Frege-Geach problem, since the

assumption used in this context is precisely that his account of indirect contexts constitutes an otherwise successful solution to that problem.

8 See also Blackburn (1998a: 14–21).

9 There is in fact a vigorous debate in the philosophy of language as to whether meaning is genuinely normative or not. See Whiting (2007); Hattiangadi (2007); and Miller (2010a) for some discussion.

10 In fact, Gibbard advocates a straightforwardly cognitivist theory of representation. See his 1990: 35, 108–10. It is a good question whether Gibbard can provide a compelling response to the 'sceptical paradox' about meaning developed in Kripke (1982). See Gibbard (2012) for an extended outline of his views on meaning. I'll leave as an exercise for the reader the matter of how Gibbard (2012) answers questions (1)–(4) here. For an argument that non-factualism about meaning is self-defeating, see Miller (2010b).

11 To be fair to Gibbard, he has much more to say on the issue that we can't consider here: so this section – and indeed this whole chapter – is intended only to get the reader started on Gibbard's rich but difficult oeuvre.

Chapter 6 Mackie's 'Error-Theory', the Argument from Queerness and Moral Fictionalism

1 This characterization of non-cognitivism would of course require some emendation in order for it to cover Blackburn's quasi-realism, perhaps along the lines of: (i) moral sentences cannot be assumed, *ab initio*, to be truth-apt; and (ii) moral judgements cannot be assumed, *ab initio*, to express beliefs. See the previous chapter, and Blackburn (1996). When I describe Blackburn's position as non-cognitivist, I have something like this more sophisticated formulation in mind. For discussion of how (a) and (b) can come apart, see 6.7 of this volume.

2 I include the qualification 'positive, atomic' here for a reason. The error-theorist will of course say that non-atomic moral sentences (those which contain occurrences of logical operators) can be true: 'It is not the case that murder is wrong' would be an example. I'll henceforth omit the qualification and take it as read.

3 I cannot defend the claim that this reconstruction is an accurate representation of Locke's own thought on the matter. But it is certainly one line of thought which Locke might have embraced en route to the error-theory. For discussion of Locke, see Mackie (1976: chapter 1).

4 Note that many philosophers would question whether *properties* – as opposed to *ways of picking out* properties – can intelligibly be characterized as categorical or dispositional. For an example, see section I of Weir (2001). Needless to say, I cannot resolve this issue here, nor consider how 'dispositional' theories of colours and morals would turn out if views such as Weir's were correct. Note, too, that the account of the categorical/dispositional distinction that I am working with here is far from uncontroversial. See, e.g., Lewis (1997) for discussion. For an influential book on dispositions, see Mumford (1998).

5 Note that this is a different use of 'categorical' from that used in the categorical/dispositional distinction in the preceding section.

6 Mackie tends to write of 'objective' and 'subjective' as if they were mono-
lithic concepts. Recent writers have been more sensitive to the complexity
involved in these notions. Wright (1992, 1996); Rosen (1994); Wiggins (1996);
and Railton (1996b) are good examples of this.

7 When I first read Mackie, I took 'objective' and 'categorical' to be inter-
changeable and equivalent, but now I think he intends them to be *distinct*
features. For example, he writes 'Kant in particular holds that the categorical imperative is not only categorical and imperative, but objectively so'
(30), which clearly implies that objectivity is a further feature which may be
attributed to a fact in addition to categoricity.

8 In addition to the argument from queerness, Mackie provides another argument for moral scepticism, the 'argument from relativity'. I concentrate on
the argument from queerness in the text, as this is the argument of Mackie's
that has generated most philosophical discussion. But a full account of
these matters would have to include some discussion of the argument from
relativity (see Railton 1993a).

9 Samuel Clarke (1675–1729) was a well-known English theologian and
rationalist.

10 Note that in the passage quoted, Wright is also arguing against the error-
theory about pure mathematical statements, as developed in Field (1980
and 1989).

11 The distinction made here can be explained in terms of a distinction in the
philosophy of language between *meaning* and *force*. Take a sentence whose
meaning might uncontroversially be given in terms of a truth-condition:
'Divers is Scottish'. Despite the fact that this is typically used with the
force of an assertion – to express the belief that Divers is Scottish – in some
circumstances it can be used with interrogative force (i.e., to express a question). Suppose that, on seeing Divers pulling on an England football top or a
Morris dancing costume, I utter, 'Divers is Scottish' with an inflection in my
voice that signals I am asking whether he is actually Scottish. The fictionalist
point mentioned in the text is that a type of sentence might have a truth-
condition and yet be conventionally used to perform a linguistic act other
than an assertion or expression of belief. For more on the notion of force, see
Miller (2007: 2.7).

12 For a discussion of hermeneutic moral fictionalism, see 6.10 of this volume.

13 Whether or not truth is a genuine norm for belief is not uncontroversial: see
Bykvist and Hattiangadi (2007) for discussion.

14 Joyce approvingly cites Garner (1993) on this matter.

15 Although see 6.10 of this volume: the problem that the hermeneutic fictionalist faces with (what is there called) FG2 will also be faced by the position
that the revolutionary fictionalist urges us to adopt.

16 Joyce even admits that 'asking him [Boyce] in an ordinary context whether
he is asserting that [it is obligatory to hand in the wallet] is likely to meet
with an affirmative answer' (2005: 292). His response to the worry that this
is evidence that Boyce does believe that it is obligatory to hand back the
wallet is that '*that* claim – "Yes, I am asserting that [it is obligatory to hand
in the wallet]" – may be just another part of the fiction' (ibid.), which is obviously question-begging in the context of the worry.

17 For a good book-length treatment of 'companions in guilt' style arguments, see Lillehammer (2007).

18 Note that what I say about redness and to-be-seen-as-red here does not on the face of it generalize to any sort of property. For example, it appears not to apply to traditional primary qualities such as squareness. Although the fact that an object is square gives me a reason for judging that it is square, the fact that an object is square does not have 'to-be-judged-as-square' somehow built into it. The connection between squareness and to-be-judged-as-square is not *internal*, since there is no non-trivial but a priori connection between an object's being square and its being judged to be square by a suitable subject in suitable conditions. See chapter 7 of this volume.

19 I should try to dispel the impression that I am being unfair to Boghossian and Velleman by saddling them with such a crude mistake about the nature of dispositions. But why else would they object to the idea that a red object's manifesting the disposition to look red constitutes a way of its redness revealing itself as opposed to being activated? Alternatively, suppose that their complaint is that if our concepts of colours were concepts of dispositions, then there would be a difference in our experience between these dispositions being 'dormant' and their being 'activated', when in fact there is no such difference. Then the dispositionalist could reply that since the disposition in question is the disposition to look red, we do in fact experience the activation of this (previously dormant) disposition when we switch the lights on.

20 This charming description of rotten meat is taken from an unpublished paper by Mark Johnston.

21 Those reading this book for the first time may wish to skip this section and return to it when they have read chapter 10.

22 Although Kalderon's view doesn't incorporate an error-theory, this chapter seemed the most natural home for our discussion of it.

23 See also Kalderon (2005a: 8–9). Kalderon's comments at 2008b: 34–7 are especially pertinent here. If, as he suggests, non-cognitivism based on his 'argument from intransigence' is inherently unstable, it is all the more important for moral fictionalism to hold on to motivational internalism and Humeanism about motivation.

24 See Eklund (2008: 711): at this point it also becomes difficult to differentiate between moral fictionalism and the kind of 'Ecumenical Expressivism' outlined in Ridge (2006a).

Chapter 7 Judgement-Dependent Accounts of Moral Qualities

1 I'm deliberately glossing over some details here. Wright himself would not wish to see judgement-dependent accounts as dispositional accounts: see the appendix to chapter 3 of his 1992. But this is unimportant for our present purposes.

2 Wright is here assuming that substituting a priori equivalents within an a priori context preserves a prioricity.

3 It may be that Smith is more concerned with the issue of the triviality of

the equation as opposed to its violation of the independence condition. In fact, it may be that the equation violates both conditions. An interesting question is whether the defender of a judgement-dependent account of culpable insensitivity could make any headway by removing the triviality-inducing reference to 'moral suitability' that causes the problems just noted, then replacing it with whatever account appears in his favoured normative ethical theory of what makes for a morally suitable subject. Clearly, the matter calls for further discussion. In addition, it might be wondered whether the imposition of the independence condition is legitimate for an area – such as morality – whose epistemology is broadly coherentist: given a coherentist epistemology one would expect facts about the extensions of moral properties and facts about the moral suitability of agents to be *interdependent* anyway. This suggests that for areas where the epistemology is coherentist, if we are to raise metaphysical questions about the mind-dependence of properties in the way that Wright does, we need some suitably refashioned analogue (or generalized version) of the independence condition rather than the simple formulation deployed by Wright. I hope to pursue this issue in future work.

4 See Heal (1988).

5 Unless we say that a certain shaping of one's affective nature can be required to open one's eyes to an objective requirement that applies to agents independently of those affective natures. Something along these lines appears to be proposed by John McDowell: see chapter 10 below for discussion.

Chapter 8 Naturalism I – Cornell Realism

1 I speak of 'Natural' properties here rather than 'non-moral' properties to avoid making reductionism false by definition: of course, moral properties can't be identical to non-moral properties. Where nothing hangs on this I'll drop the capitalization.

2 The standard view is that multiple realization blocks reduction, and I'll follow the standard view in this chapter. But there are serious doubts about the standard view. See Leiter and Miller (1998: esp. 171–3).

3 I'll say, schematically, that an explanation is 'best' if its unavailability would lead to a genuine explanatory loss. In this sense, it is possible for two distinct explanations to count as 'best'.

4 There are some doubts about the plausibility of one half of the biconditional expressed by (1), namely:

(1*) If P figures ineliminably in the best explanation of experience then P is a real property.

For an account of these difficulties (concerning the relationship between 'inference to the best explanation' and questions about realism), see Leiter (2001a: 80). Note, though, that Leiter overstates the case when he writes that 'explanatory relevance is irrelevant to realism' (79). Certainly, an explanation's being relevant is not sufficient to its being best; but presumably, its being *irrelevant* is sufficient for its *not* being best. So, given that irrelevance could count *against* realism, it is not quite correct to say that questions about explanatory relevance are irrelevant. Note too that some of those sympathetic to Cornell Realism have doubts about this half of the bi-conditional as well. See, e.g., Sayre-McCord (1988: 5). But I propose to ignore these worries here, and will let (1) stand for the purposes of this chapter. I aim to show that Cornell Realism can be undermined even if it is granted both halves of the bi-conditional expressed by (1). Accordingly, the main focus of this chapter will be on (2) and (2a).

5 The talk of 'observation' here isn't really necessary: the real question concerns whether moral facts are necessary for the best explanation of moral beliefs and other non-moral facts. See Sayre-McCord (1988: 2).

6 Note that some philosophers question the assumption – apparently shared by Sturgeon and Harman – that reductionism would be sufficient to earn moral properties explanatory credentials. See Quinn (1986).

7 Sturgeon attributes this argument to Richard Boyd.

8 How would a reductionist of, e.g., Railton's stripe reply to arguments like Sturgeon's?

9 If you think 'cruelty' is a moral term, replace it here by 'infliction of pain'.

10 Note that Sayre-McCord's call to consider explanatory potency rather than explanatory relevance is similar to the point made by Harman. Even the moral epiphenomenalist, on Sayre-McCord's definition, could say that moral properties are explanatorily relevant to facts about moral beliefs: but the moral epiphenomenalist, by definition, views moral properties and facts as explanatorily impotent. Of course, Sayre-McCord goes on to attempt to justify the idea that some moral properties and facts are in fact explanatorily potent, and I'll come to this shortly. (Note that where Harman and Sturgeon speak of 'counterfactual dependence', Sayre-McCord speaks of 'explanatory relevance'; where Harman and Sturgeon speak of 'explanatory relevance', Sayre-McCord speaks of 'explanatory potence'. This is just a terminological difference.)

11 Darwall, Gibbard and Railton suggest that the talk of causal constitution in the quote from Sturgeon just given in the text smacks of reductionism: isn't the claim that chemical facts are *constituted* by physical facts just the claim that chemical facts are *reducible* to physical facts? This appears to sit very uneasily with Sturgeon's desire to *avoid* reductionism. As they put it:

> One might wonder whether in this setting supervenience is genuinely distinct from (messy) reducibility . . . Supervenience between two seemingly disparate classes of properties is in some respects a quite strong and surprising relation; it is the kind of relation that would appear to call out for explanation. If the [Cornell Realist] held that nonmoral properties wholly and exclusively *constitute* moral properties, that would afford some explanation, but it would also make it more difficult to contrast such a view with some species of reductionism. (1992: 172)

But, in the absence of an argument against the standard view that multiple realization blocks reducibility (see Fodor 1974), this is a strange comment. Sturgeon will argue that just as chemical facts are multiply realized by

physical facts, and so not reducible to physical facts, moral facts are multiply realized by non-moral facts, and so are not reducible to non-moral facts.
12 I have changed the example which Jackson and Pettit actually use in this
   quote.
13 But perhaps not impossible. What about worlds in which he is sufficiently
   mentally ill that he cannot be viewed as responsible for his actions?
14 Blackburn makes a similar point to Copp at 119–21 of his 1998a. For another
   objection to Copp's treatment of Cornell Realism, see Leiter (2001: 89). See
   also Railton (1989: 162–3).
15 To be honest, I'm not sure if all of the philosophers typically called 'Cornell
   Realists' do hold to this sort of claim about the semantics of 'good'. What
   follows applies only to those who do. Those who don't still owe us some
   story about how the reference of 'good' gets fixed.
16 Horgan and Timmons note (1992b: 173, n.22) that Hare runs a similar argument against definitional naturalism in his 1952, at 148–9.
17 So in effect, here and below (justice and allegiance), Leiter could only state
   his competing explanation by actually using moral terms to narrow down
   the explanatory claims in the appropriate way. So if using moral terms for
   that purpose is a problem for Sayre-McCord, it is also a problem for Leiter.
18 Likewise, see my earlier comment on the Hitler case.
19 In effect, the program explanation story constitutes a reply to Leiter's
   claim – in his discussion (98–101) of Cohen (1997) – that the best the Cornell
   Realist can do by way of justifying the use of explanation in terms of moral
   facts and properties is that the classificatory scheme afforded by moral concepts makes things 'look different'. Program explanation allows the Cornell
   Realist to make out a case that explanations in terms of moral facts are such
   that their unavailability would result in an explanatory loss.
20 Strictly speaking, we should speak here of lower-level *and other sorts of
   higher-level properties*, but I've suppressed this in the text to keep the presentation manageable.
21 In the debates between Cornell Realism and its opponents, the reality of the
   relevant lower-order facts and properties is not in dispute. So the important
   question is: *given* that there are lower-order properties and process explanations in terms of them, can program explanations earn ontological rights for
   higher-order properties? So 'God' here is just a heuristic device: someone
   assumed to know all of the facts about the distribution of lower-level
   properties.
22 For an account of some styles of naturalistic explanation of moral beliefs,
   see Leiter (2001: 83–90).
23 It is consistent with the argument of this section that there is nothing amiss
   with invoking program explanations in terms of higher-order properties
   once the ontological rights of those properties have been earned in some
   other way: that is another matter entirely. So my remarks in the text are
   not meant to be critical of Jackson and Pettit's use of the notion (in their
   story, ontological rights are earned via the kind of 'network-style analysis'
   outlined in 9.9 of this volume).
24 Another potential problem for the use of the notion of program explanation in this context is the intelligibility of the supervenience relation held
   to obtain between the higher-order moral properties and the lower-order

natural properties. As we saw in 4.2, there are some genuine difficulties about this. See also Horgan and Timmons (1992a).

25 In this I closely follow Leiter (2001: 80–3).

Chapter 9 Naturalism II – Reductionism

1 See Brandt (1979: chapter 1).

2 See Leiter (2001: 80, n.9).

3 See Hobbes (1651: 120).

4 See also Sidgwick (1907: 105–15); Brandt (1979: 10, 113, 329); Gibbard (1990: 18–22).

5 See also the example of Beth, the successful and happy accountant (1986b: 12–13, 26).

6 Of course, a Berkeleyan idealist might deny this latter claim, but in the present context this is not to the point: we are assuming that some form of realism about the external world is true, and investigating the place morality might have in such a world.

7 See also Railton's example of Henry the accountant (1986b: 26–7).

8 We'll see that Railton does not agree with the corresponding claim about specifically *moral* value. Note, too, that 'internalism' as used here is a different notion from 'internalism about moral judgement' as discussed in 9.9 of this volume.

9 Note that Railton is careful not to overstate the strength of the connection: 'There is no logical contradiction involved in embracing wholeheartedly a desire that one knows one would want not to be effective in one's actual life were one fully informed and rational. The sort of conflict that is basic to the criticism of desires is psychological rather than logical' (1986b: 14–15). See also 1986a: 178 and 1989: 168.

10 An intrinsic nutrient is something that directly nourishes the organism (e.g., calcium), a non-intrinsic nutrient is something that is nutritious only insofar as it is a vehicle for an intrinsic nutrient (e.g., cakes and ale). The distinction between intrinsic and non-intrinsic, non-moral goodness is similar. See Railton (1986b: 10–11).

11 Of course, I may have a more pressing *moral* obligation to do something else which means that I have no time to help (suppose I'm rushing to the hospital with an antidote to the poison that has just seeped into the city's water supply).

12 Note that since absolutism about moral value flows from the combination of rationalism with the categoricity of moral reasons, in rejecting rationalism Railton frees himself from commitment to absolutism. In addition, it is important to be clear that Railton is not claiming that moral imperatives are hypothetical. According to Railton, moral imperatives are *non-hypothetical*: one cannot exempt oneself from them by pointing to one's contingent inclinations. But since our concept of a moral fact is not, according to Railton, a concept of a reason for action, we can say that moral imperatives are non-hypothetical even though reason is always hypothetical.

13 Wiggins is here transposing claims about properties into a Fregean framework. For an introduction to the framework, see Frege's essay 'Function and

Concept', in Mellor and Oliver (1997), the Appendix below, and chapters 1 and 2 of Miller (2007).

14 This is all the more puzzling, since Wiggins himself seems keen to ascribe to methodological naturalism (see, e.g., 1992a, 1992b: 637–8). I suggest that we take the point about question-begging that I make in the text as throwing doubt on how serious a methodological naturalist Wiggins actually is.

15 See Railton (1989: 159), where he argues that his style of naturalist cannot be accused of scientism, in any pejorative sense.

16 Sobel (1994).

17 Interestingly, the manoeuvre I suggested in the intrapersonal but cross-temporal case appears (initially at least) to work in the interpersonal case when, for example, Smith's pursuing Q undermines or rules out Jones's pursuing R and vice versa. Perhaps the difference is that in the intrapersonal case Jones+ is ideally placed to ensure that Jones does not develop into someone whose idealized self wants himself to want R, while in the interpersonal case Smith+ *already* wants Smith to want R. The matter clearly calls for a fuller investigation.

18 Railton actually makes a point similar to Fodor's (which is made in an entirely different context concerning semantic dispositionalism) at 24-5 of his 1986b.

19 To say that a belief and a desire are independently intelligible is to say that they are 'distinct existences', in other words that it is always possible to have one in the absence of the other.

20 Smith himself attempts to show that The Moral Problem can be solved by developing a position which consistently holds (1), (2) and (3). See his 1994a, *passim*.

21 This general sort of worry will be familiar to those who know the literature on 'response-dependence' and 'judgement-dependence' (see ch. 7 of this volume). The requirement that the weak internalist provide a substantial characterization of 'practically rational' is roughly equivalent to the requirement that a judgement-dependent account of colour provide a characterization of 'suitable subjects' and 'ideal conditions' which does not reduce to the trivial characterization of, e.g., 'suitable subjects' as 'those who have whatever it takes is necessary to form correct judgements about an object's colour'.

22 Note that when Smith speaks of the good person, he does not mean those who are good in the sense of 'having the motivations that the one true morality tells them that they should have' (Smith 1996: 177), but rather those who have 'the virtue of being disposed to conform their motivations to their moral beliefs in a reliable way, at least absent weakness of will and the like' (ibid.). Smith clarifies this in response to my 1996. See also Stratton-Lake (1998).

23 'I want to do what is right' when read *de dicto* amounts to 'I want it to be the case that $(\exists x)(x$ is right and I do $x)$'. 'I want to do what is right' when read *de re* amounts to '$(\exists x)(x$ is right and I want to do $x)$'.

24 See Williams (1976).

25 One way in which an internalist might try to blunt the force of this would be to adopt a very basic form of non-cognitivism, according to which George's judgement is *identical* to the relevant motivational state

(as opposed to a more sophisticated version of non-cognitivism in which George's judgement expresses a *disposition* to have motivational states). Since the judgement is identical to the motivational state on this view, it would not seem right to say that the motivational state was derived from the judgement. But even if this option worked for the most simple forms of cognitivism, it is hard to see how it could be utilized by a cognitivist or a more sophisticated non-cognitivist. And Smith's argument is intended to be a defence of internalism in general, not just the form of internalism exemplified by this most basic form of non-cognitivism.

26 Again, the most basic form of non-cognitivism might be exempt from this.

27 In addition, it is not clear to me that the non-cognitivist need accept the 'platitude' in the last but one passage quoted.

28 In what follows, I use some material from McFarland and Miller (1998b). I am grateful to my co-author and the editors for permission to do this.

29 See Jackson (1992, 1998); Jackson and Pettit (1995). Jackson and Pettit, unlike Railton, are internalists about moral judgement (in the sense of 9.9). See especially their 1995.

30 On the face of it, there is an asymmetry here with what Smith says about the platitudes in the moral case. Are the 'platitudes' concerning 'substance' really a priori?

31 Kripke (1980); Putnam (1975). It goes without saying that 'gold', as it appears here, refers not to a particular colour, but to a *kind of stuff* or a *substance*.

32 To avoid misunderstanding, I am here talking only about the phenomenology of colours: some of them *seem* or *appear* composite in ways that others do not. I am not concerned here with the empirical results of mixing physically instantiated colours.

33 For example, although I argued that Railton's account of non-moral value could see off the worries about intrapersonal commensurability, the problem of interpersonal commensurability remains to be solved.

Chapter 10 Contemporary Non-Naturalism – McDowell's Moral Realism

1 This is a very slight modification of what appears in McDowell's paper: he actually formulates the denial of SHAPEFULNESS, and I have altered this in the obvious way to obtain a formulation of the thesis itself.

2 For an introduction to these notions, see the Appendix.

3 Strictly speaking, the semantic value of a predicate, for Frege, is not an extension but a function. But since, in the Fregean framework, functions have extensional identity conditions, we can harmlessly talk here of predicates having extensions as semantic values.

4 One way of viewing what the non-cognitivist is doing here would be to see him as attempting a *reforming definition*: not of 'x is good' (that is the naturalistic cognitivist's strategy) but rather of 'Jones judges that x is good'. If the non-cognitivist kept in mind the idea that he is giving a reforming definition, just as Railton avoided the open-question argument applied to claims about moral goodness, the non-cognitivist could avoid the analogues

of the open-question argument directed against the quasi-realist in 4.10. For a development of this thought, see Miller (2010c).

5 Although McDowell does not (to my knowledge) explicitly discuss Wiggins's argument, it seems to me that his strictures against what he calls 'bald naturalism' in his 1994 are of a piece with Wiggins's argument against substantive naturalism.

6 As far as I can see, in his discussions of McDowell's argument in his 1981 and 1998, Blackburn himself does not distinguish between DISENTANGLING* and DISENTANGLING** (and the intensional and extensional versions of SHAPEFULNESS, etc.), and this makes it hard to see which of the two options I've outlined for the non-cognitivist he would prefer. I will not try to decide here which of the two options is ulti- mately best for the non-cognitivist: I have not argued in favour of the first option, that involving DISENTANGLING** and the extensional version of SHAPEFULNESS, but merely that the rule-following considerations leave them untouched. However, if the non-cognitivist takes the second option, and disavows even DISENTANGLING** and the extensional version of SHAPEFULNESS, the notion of an ethical sensibility that he relies on will begin to appear vacuous. We can see this by considering the case of humour. If we disavow the analogues of DISENTANGLING** and the extensional version of SHAPEFULNESS, we will still be able to avoid accepting a non-naturalist version of cognitivism about judgements of humour, since 'this does not entail the lack, on any particular occasion of humour, of an objective feature to which we are reacting. We might want to regard it as true that on any occasion the comic reaction is a reaction to some perceived set of features. It is just that all these sets form a class which independently of our tendency to find them funny, has no shape . . . we may know to which features a person reacts on particular occasions yet still have a disjunctive and partial class which could not enable the outsider to predict the comic effect of new occasions' (1981: 167–8). But it looks as though the explanatory value of the notion of a comic sensibility will then be compromised. As Blackburn himself says: 'Since we are after all only animals in a natural world, whose reactions, however complex, are elicited by the things we come across, surely there must be some explanation pos- sible of why we react as we do. This explanation must proceed by trying to find common elements in the things eliciting the reactions' (1981: 168). This suggests that the first option – involving DISENTANGLING** and the extensional version of SHAPEFULNESS – is preferable. But again, my aim here is not to argue for this, but merely to argue that the rule-following considerations do nothing to foreclose this option for the non-cognitivist. See also Lang (2001).

7 In German, *Bildung* means 'education'.

8 I am grateful here, and in the rest of this paragraph, to the useful discussion in McCulloch (1996: 317–18).

9 Of course, McDowell may reply that the demand for an explanation here is misbegotten, perhaps because it depends on some unreasonable 'scientistic' prejudice. I have already commented on this in 10.1, but I will return to the issue of 'scientism' in 10.5.

10 In this section, the dividing line between *exegesis* of McDowell and *recon-*

struction of McDowell's position is somewhat vague. Those who are sceptical of it as McDowell's exegesis can view it as an attempt to reconstruct a metaethical position roughly consonant with McDowell's. I hope, though, that the material in this section does not seem completely off-beam as exegesis: it should be at least distantly recognizable to readers of McDowell's 'Values and Secondary Qualities', reprinted in his 1998.

11 I say 'partial' here because of the point noted at the end of chapter 7: on its own, the dispositional theory of moral value doesn't appear to make any headway with Mackie's worries about categoricity. This suggests that, so far as the argument from queerness goes, McDowell's play with the notion of second nature is more fundamental than the analogy between values and secondary qualities.

12 It may be that McDowell would cite his 'rule-following' argument against SHAPEFULNESS, GENUINE and so on as undermining the notion of cognitive access underlying the distinction between extension-reflecting and extension-determining accounts of best opinion. But, as I argued in 9.1, McDowell's attack on GENUINE and the like appears to fail to connect with his intended target. For a distinct suggestion as to how a defender of McDowell might attempt to make progress here, see Miller (1998b).

13 Smith's discussion is set up in terms of a distinction between 'motivating reasons' and 'normative reasons', where the latter are conceived of as *propositions* in terms of which an agent's behaviour can be *justified*. Smith goes on to argue that a Humean theory of motivating reasons can be combined with an anti-Humean theory of normative reasons, and that this allows us to defend a metaethical position that is at once cognitivist, internalist and Humean in its view of motivating reasons. Some philosophers have denied that the distinction between motivating and normative reasons can be drawn in the way in which Smith draws it: see, for example, Dancy (1995 and 2000). Since I am going to argue that *even if* we grant Smith his distinction between motivating and normative reasons his argument in favour of Humeanism is inconclusive, I do not enter into these further questions about the distinction between motivating and normative reasons.

14 Not everyone would agree with the usual view of the nature of sensations. See, for example, McDowell's essay 'One Strand in the Private Language Argument' (reprinted in his 1998).

15 Might Smith avoid this point by saying that the desires in question are dispositions to have certain feelings in some circumstances but not in others? This seems implausible. Given any set of circumstances, my desire to finish the book by the weekend could, or could fail to, manifest itself in feeling.

16 Note that it doesn't follow from this that natural science itself is exempt from philosophical scrutiny: whether, and if so how, we are to earn the right to the notion of truth as applicable to scientific judgement is a separate, and perhaps more difficult, question. Also, in what sense does this motivation manifest a decent and healthy respect for natural science? Well, in the sense that we would reject the analogue for something like astrology: a reasonable person would presumably not hold that if the apparent subject matter of an area of thought doesn't figure in the world as described by astrology, then we have to earn the right to view thoughts from that area as potentially true or false.

17 Of course, if we repeatedly found that our curiosity couldn't be satisfied, this may eventually lead to doubt about the area in question. But that is how it should be.
18 See Blackburn (1998a: 102), and also the epigram from Joseph Conrad at the start of the book.

Bibliography

Altman, A. 2004: Breathing new life into a dead argument: G. E. Moore and the open question. *Philosophical Studies* 117.

Arrington, R. 1989: *Rationalism, Realism and Relativism*. Ithaca, NY: Cornell University Press.

Athanassoulis, N. 2000: A response to Harman: virtue ethics and character traits. *Proceedings of the Aristotelian Society* 100.

Ayer, A. [1936] 1946: *Language, Truth and Logic* 2nd edn. London: Gollancz (Second Edition).

Ayer, A. 1954: On the analysis of moral judgements. In his *Philosophical Essays*. London: Macmillan.

Ayer, A. 1984: Are there objective values? In his *Freedom and Morality and Other Essays*. Oxford: Oxford University Press.

Baldwin, T. 1990: *G. E. Moore*. London: Routledge.

Baldwin, T. [1903] 1993: Editor's introduction to Moore *Principia Ethica*, rev. edn. Cambridge: Cambridge University Press.

Benn, P. 1998: *Ethics*. London: University College London Press.

Blackburn, S. 1981: Rule-following and moral realism. In S. Holtzman and C. Leich (eds), *Wittgenstein: To Follow a Rule*. London: Routledge and Kegan Paul.

Blackburn, S. 1984: *Spreading the Word*. Oxford: Oxford University Press.

Blackburn, S. 1988: Attitudes and contents. *Ethics* 98. Reprinted in Blackburn 1993a.

Blackburn, S. 1991: Reply to Sturgeon. *Philosophical Studies* 61.

Blackburn, S. 1992a: Gibbard on normative logic. *Philosophy and Phenomenological Research* 52(4).

Blackburn, S. 1992b: Wise feelings, apt reading. *Ethics* 102.

Blackburn, S. 1993a: *Essays in Quasi-Realism*. Oxford: Oxford University Press.

Blackburn, S. 1993b: Realism, quasi, or queasy? In Haldane and

Wright (eds), *Reality, Representation, and Projection*. Oxford: Oxford University Press.

Blackburn, S. 1993c: Circles, finks, smells, and biconditionals. *Philosophical Perspectives* 7.

Blackburn, S. 1996: Securing the nots. In W. Sinnott-Armstrong and M. Timmons (eds), *Moral Knowledge*. New York: Oxford University Press.

Blackburn, S. 1998a: *Ruling Passions*. Oxford: Clarendon Press.

Blackburn, S. 1998b: Wittgenstein, Wright, Rorty and minimalism. *Mind* 107.

Blackburn, S. 1999: Is objective moral justification possible on a quasi-realist foundation? *Inquiry* 42.

Blackburn, S. 2001: *Being Good*. Oxford: Oxford University Press.

Blackburn, S. 2002: Replies. *Philosophy and Phenomenological Research* 65.

Blackburn, S. 2009: Truth and a priori possibility: Egan's charge against quasi-realism. *Australasian Journal of Philosophy* 87.

Bloomfield, P. 2009: Moral realism and program explanation: reply to Miller. *Australasian Journal of Philosophy* 87.

Boghossian, P. and Velleman, D. 1989: Colour as a secondary quality. *Mind* 98.

Boyd, R. 1988: How to be a moral realist. In G. Sayre-McCord (ed.), *Essays on Moral Realism*. Ithaca, NY: Cornell University Press.

Brandt, R. 1979: *A Theory of the Good and the Right*. New York: Oxford University Press.

Brighouse, M. 1990: Blackburn's projectivism – an objection. *Philosophical Studies* 59.

Brink, D. 1989: *Moral Realism and the Foundations of Ethics*. Cambridge: Cambridge University Press.

Burwood, S. Gilbert, P. and Lennon, K. 1999: *Philosophy of Mind*. London: University College London Press.

Bykvist, K. and Hattiangadi, A. 2007: Does thought imply ought? *Analysis* 67(4).

Campbell, J. 1993: A simple view of colour. In Haldane and Wright (eds), *Reality, Representation, and Projection*. Oxford: Oxford University Press, 1993.

Carruthers, P. 1986: *Introducing Persons*. London: Croom Helm.

Carson, T. 1992: Gibbard's conceptual scheme for moral philosophy. *Philosophy and Phenomenological Research* 52(4).

Casati, R. and Tappollet, C. (eds) 1998: *European Review of Philosophy 3: Response-Dependence*. Stanford, CA: CSLI Publications.

Cohen, J. 1997: The arc of the moral universe. *Philosophy and Public Affairs* 26.

Conrad, J. 1914: *Chance*. London: Folio Society (2001).

Conrad, J. 1915: *Victory*. London: Folio Society (1999).

Copp, D. 1990: Explanation and justification in ethics. *Ethics* 100.

Copp, D. 2000: Milk, honey, and the good life on moral twin earth. *Synthese* 124.

Cowie, C. 2009: *Truth in Ethics: The Minimalist Challenge to Quasi-Realist Expressivism*, MPhilStud dissertation (King's College London).

Dancy, J. 1991: Intuitionism. In Singer (ed.), *A Companion to Ethics*. Oxford: Blackwell.

Dancy, J. 1993: *Moral Reasons*. Oxford: Blackwell.

Dancy, J. 1995: Why there is really no such thing as the theory of motivation. *Proceedings of the Aristotelian Society* 95.

Dancy, J. 2000: *Practical Reality*. Oxford: Oxford University Press.

Dancy, J. 2006: *Ethics Without Principles*. Oxford: Clarendon Press.

Darwall, S. 1983: *Impartial Reason*. Ithaca, NY: Cornell University Press.

Darwall, S., Gibbard, A. and Railton, P. 1992: Toward *fin de siècle* ethics: some trends. *Philosophical Review* 101.

Davidson, D. 1963: Actions, reasons, and causes. *Journal of Philosophy* 60(23). Reprinted in his *Essays on Actions and Events*. Oxford: Oxford University Press 1980.

Divers, J. and Miller, A. 1994: Why expressivists about value should not love minimalism about truth. *Analysis* 54.

Divers, J. and Miller, A. 1995: Platitudes and attitudes: a minimalist conception of belief. *Analysis* 55.

Divers, J. and Miller, A. 1999: Arithmetical Platonism: reliability and judgement-dependence. *Philosophical Studies* 95.

Dreier, J. 2000: Dispositions and fetishes: externalist models of moral motivation. *Philosophy and Phenomenological Research* 61.

Dummett, M. 1993: *The Seas of Language*. Oxford: Clarendon Press.

Dworkin, R. 1996: Objectivity and truth: you'd better believe it. *Philosophy and Public Affairs* 25.

Egan, A. 2007: Quasi-realism and fundamental moral error. *Australasian Journal of Philosophy* 85.

Eklund, M. 2008: The Frege-Geach problem and Kalderon's moral fictionalism. *Philosophical Quarterly* 59.

Eklund, M. 2011: Fictionalism. In E. Zalta (ed.), *Stanford Encyclopedia of Philosophy* (Fall 2011 edition).

Ekman, G. 1954: Dimensions of colour vision. *Journal of Psychology* 38.

Field, A. 2010: *Can Program Explanation Confer Ontological Rights for the Cornell Realist Variety of Moral Realism?* MPhil dissertation (University of Birmingham).

Field, H. 1980: *Science Without Numbers*. Oxford: Blackwell.

Field, H. 1989: *Realism, Mathematics and Modality*. Oxford: Blackwell.

Fisher, A. 2011: *Metaethics: An Introduction*. Durham, UK: Acumen.

Fisher, A. and Kirchin, S. 2006: *Arguing About Metaethics*. London: Routledge.

Fodor, J. 1974: Special sciences. *Synthese* 28.

Fodor, J. 1990: *A Theory of Content and Other Essays*. Cambridge, MA: MIT Press.

Fodor, J. 1995: Encounters with trees. *London Review of Books* 17(8).

Frankena, W. 1938: The naturalistic fallacy. *Mind* 48.

Gampel, E. 1997: Ethics, reference, and natural kinds. *Philosophical Papers* 26.

Garner, R. 1993: Are convenient fictions harmful to your health? *Philosophy East and West* 43.

Geach, P. 1960: Ascriptivism. *Philosophical Review* 69.

Geach, P. 1965: Assertion. *Philosophical Review* 74.

Gibbard, A. 1990: *Wise Choices, Apt Feelings*. Oxford: Clarendon Press.

Gibbard, A. 1992: Reply to Blackburn, Carson, Hill, and Railton. *Philosophy and Phenomenological Research* 52(4).

Gibbard, A. 1993: Reply to Sinnott-Armstrong. *Philosophical Studies* 69.

Gibbard, A. 1996: Projection, quasi-realism, and sophisticated realism: critical notice of Blackburn 1993. *Mind* 105.

Gibbard, A. 2003: *Thinking How to Live*. Cambridge, MA: Harvard University Press.

Gibbard, A. 2012: *Meaning and Normativity*. Oxford: Oxford University Press.

Gundersen, E. 2007: *Making Sense of Response-Dependence*. PhD thesis (University of St Andrews).

Haldane, J. and C. Wright (eds) 1993: *Reality, Representation, and Projection*. Oxford: Oxford University Press.

Hale, B. 1986: The compleat projectivist. *Philosophical Quarterly* 36.

Hale, B. 1993a: Can there be a logic of attitudes? In Haldane and Wright (eds), *Reality, Representation, and Projection*. Oxford: Oxford University Press.

Hale, B. 1993b: Postscript. In Haldane and Wright (eds), *Reality, Representation, and Projection*. Oxford: Oxford University Press, 1993.

Hale, B. 2002: Can arboreal knotwork help Blackburn out of Frege's abyss? *Philosophy and Phenomenological Research* 65.

Harcourt, E. 2005: Quasi-realism and ethical appearances. *Mind* 114.

Hare, R. 1952: *The Language of Morals*. Oxford: Oxford University Press.

Hare, R. 1991: Universal prescriptivism. In Singer (ed.), *A Companion to Ethics*. Oxford: Blackwell.

Harman, G. 1975: Moral relativism defended. *Philosophical Review* 84.

Harman, G. 1977: *The Nature of Morality*. Oxford: Oxford University Press.

Harman, G. 1986: Moral explanations of natural facts – can moral claims be tested against reality? *Southern Journal of Philosophy* 24 Supplement.

Harman, G. 1999: Moral philosophy meets social psychology: virtue ethics and the fundamental attribution error. *Proceedings of the Aristotelian Society* 99.

Harman, G. 2000: The nonexistence of character traits. *Proceedings of the Aristotelian Society* 100.

Hattiangadi, A. 2007: *Oughts and Thoughts: Scepticism and the Normativity of Content*. Oxford: Oxford University Press.

Heal, J. 1988: The disinterested search for truth. *Proceedings of the Aristotelian Society* 88.

Hempel, G. 1965. *Aspects of Scientific Explanation and Other Essays*. New York: Free Press.

Hill, T. 1992: Gibbard on morality and sentiment. *Philosophy and Phenomenological Research* 52(4).

Hobbes, T. [1651] 1981: *Leviathan*. Edited by C. B. McPherson. Harmondsworth: Penguin.

Hood, C. 2010: *Ethics, Intentions and Judgement-Dependence*. MPhil dissertation (University of Birmingham).

Hooker, B. (ed.) 1996: *Truth in Ethics*. Oxford: Blackwell.

Hooker, B. and Little, M. (eds) 2000: *Moral Particularism*. Oxford: Oxford University Press.

Horgan, T. and Timmons, M. 1990: New wave moral realism meets moral twin earth. *Journal of Philosophical Research* 16.

Horgan, T. and Timmons, M. 1992a: Troubles on moral twin earth: moral queerness revived. *Synthese* 92.

Horgan, T. and Timmons, M. 1992b: Troubles for new wave moral semantics: the 'open-question argument' revived. *Philosophical Papers* 21.

Horgan, T. and Timmons, M. 2000: Copping out on moral twin earth. *Synthese* 124.

Horgan, T. and Timmons, M. (eds) 2006: *Metaethics After Moore*. Oxford: Oxford University Press.

Horwich, P. 1993: Gibbard's theory of norms. *Philosophy and Public Affairs* 26.

Hudson, W. 1970: *Modern Moral Philosophy*. London: Macmillan.

Hume, D. [1739] 1968. *A Treatise of Human Nature*. Oxford: Clarendon Press.

Hume, D. [1742] 1903. Of the standard of taste. In *Essays: Moral, Political, and Literary*. London: Grant Richards.

Hussein, N. and Shah, N. 2006: Misunderstanding metaethics. *Oxford Studies in Metaethics* 1.

Hussein, N. and Shah, N. 2013: Metaethics and its discontents: a case study in Korsgaard. Forthcoming in C. Bagnoli (ed.), *Constructivism in Ethics*. Cambridge: Cambridge University Press.

Indow, T. and Ohsumi, K. 1972: Multidimensional mapping of sixty Munsell colors by non-metric procedure. In J. Vos, L. Friele and P. Walraven (eds), *Color Metrics*. Soesterberg, Netherlands: Institute for Perception TNO.

Jackson, F. 1992: Critical notice of Susan Hurley's natural reasons. *Australasian Journal of Philosophy* 70.

Jackson, F. 1998: *From Metaphysics to Ethics*. Oxford: Oxford University Press.

Jackson, F. and Pettit, P. 1990: Program explanation: a general perspective. *Analysis* 50.

Jackson, F. and Pettit, P. 1995: Moral functionalism and moral motivation. *Philosophical Quarterly* 45.

Jackson, F. and Pettit, P. 1998: A problem for expressivism. *Analysis* 58.

Jackson, F., Oppy, G. and Smith, M. 1994: Minimalism and truth-aptness. *Mind* 103.

Jackson, F., Pettit, P. and Smith, M. 2004: *Mind, Morality, and Explanation*. Oxford: Oxford University Press.

Johnston, M. 1989: Dispositional theories of value. *Proceedings of the Aristotelian Society*, Supp. Vol. 63.

Johnston, M. 1993a: Objectivity refigured: pragmatism without verificationism. In Haldane and Wright (eds), *Reality, Representation, and Projection*. Oxford: Oxford University Press.

Johnston, M. 1993b: Remarks on response-dependence. Unpublished MS.

Johnston, M. 1998: Are manifest qualities response-dependent? *The Monist* 81.

Joyce, R. 2001: *The Myth of Morality*. Cambridge: Cambridge University Press.

Joyce, R. 2005: Moral fictionalism. In Kalderon, *Fictionalism in Metaphysics*. Oxford: Oxford University Press.

Kalderon, M. 2005a: *Moral Fictionalism*. Oxford: Clarendon Press.

Kalderon, M. 2005b: *Fictionalism in Metaphysics*. Oxford: Oxford University Press.

Kalderon, M. 2008a: Summary. *Philosophical Books* 49(1).

Kalderon, M. 2008b: The trouble with terminology. *Philosophical Books* 49(1).

Kalderon, M. 2008c: Moral fictionalism, the Frege-Geach problem, and reasonable inference. *Analysis* 68(2).

Kant, I. [1785] 1964: *Groundwork of the Metaphysics of Morals*. Trans. J. J. Paton. New York: Harper and Row.

Kirchin, S. 1997: How Blackburn improves: a reply to Iain Law. *Cogito* 21.

Kirchin, S. 2000: Quasi-realism, sensibility theory, and ethical relativism. *Inquiry* 43.

Kirchin, S. 2010: The shapelessness hypothesis. *Philosophers' Imprint* 10.

Kirchin, S. 2012: *Metaethics*. Basingstoke: Palgrave Macmillan.

Kirchin, S. and Joyce, R. (eds) 2010: *A World Without Values: Essays on John Mackie's Moral Error Theory*. Dordrecht: Springer.

Kivy, P. 1980: A failure of aesthetic emotivism. *Philosophical Studies* 38.

Kivy, P. 1992: 'Oh boy! You too!'. Aesthetic emotivism reexamined. In H. Hahn (ed.), *The Philosophy of A. J. Ayer*. La Salle, IL: Open Court.

Kolbel, M. 1997: Expressivism and the syntactic uniformity of declarative sentences. *Critica* 29(87).

Kolbel, M. 2002: *Truth Without Objectivity*. London: Routledge.

Kripke, S. 1980: *Naming and Necessity*. Cambridge: Cambridge University Press.

Kripke, S. 1982: *Wittgenstein on Rules and Private Language*. Cambridge, MA: Harvard University Press.

Lang, G. 2001: The rule-following considerations and metaethics: some false moves. *European Journal of Philosophy* 9.

Law, I. 1996: Improvement and truth in quasi-realism. *Cogito* 10.

Leiter, B. 2001a: Moral facts and best explanations. *Social Philosophy and Policy* 18.

Leiter, B. (ed.) 2001b: *Objectivity in Law and Morals*. Cambridge: Cambridge University Press.

Leiter, B. and Miller, A. 1998: Closet dualism and mental causation. *Canadian Journal of Philosophy* 28.

Lewis, D. 1970: How to define theoretical terms. *Journal of Philosophy* 63.

Lewis, D. 1972: Psychophysical and theoretical identifications. *Australasian Journal of Philosophy* 50.

Lewis, D. 1989: Dispositional theories of value. *Proceedings of the Aristotelian Society*, Supp. Vol. 63.

Lewis, D. 1997: Finkish dispositions. *Philosophical Quarterly* 47.

Lillehammer, H. 2007: *Companions in Guilt*. Basingstoke: Palgrave Macmillan.

Little, M. 1994a: Moral realism I: naturalism. *Philosophical Books* 25.

Little, M. 1994b: Moral realism II: non-naturalism. *Philosophical Books* 25.

Locke, J. [1689] 1975: *An Essay on Human Understanding*. Edited by P. H. Nidditch. Oxford: Clarendon Press.

Lovibond, S. 1983: *Realism and Imagination in Ethics*. Oxford: Blackwell.

Lowe, E. 1995: *Locke on Human Understanding*. London: Routledge.

McCulloch, G. 1996: Dismounting from the seesaw. *International Journal of Philosophical Studies* 4(1).

McDowell, J. 1994: *Mind and World*. Cambridge, MA: Harvard University Press.

McDowell, J. 1998: *Mind, Value, and Reality*. Cambridge, MA: Harvard University Press.

McFarland, D. and Miller, A. 1998a: Jackson on colour as a primary quality. *Analysis* 58.

McFarland, D. and Miller, A. 1998b: Response dependence without reduction? *Australasian Journal of Philosophy* 76(3).

Mackie, J. 1973: *Ethics: Inventing Right and Wrong*. New York: Penguin.

Mackie, J. 1976: *Problems from Locke*. Oxford: Clarendon Press.

McNaughton, D. 1988: *Moral Vision*. Oxford: Blackwell.

Majors, B. 2007: Moral explanation. *Philosophy Compass* 2(1).

Mautner, T. 2000: Problems for anti-expressivism. *Analysis* 60.

Mellor, D. H. and Oliver, A. (eds). 1997: *Properties*. Oxford: Oxford University Press.

Menzies, P. (ed.) 1991: *Response-Dependent Concepts*. Working Papers in Philosophy. Canberra: RSSS.

Menzies, P (ed.) 1998: *Response-Dependence* (special issue of *The Monist* 81).

Merli, D. 2002: Return to moral twin earth. *Canadian Journal of Philosophy* 32.

Miller, A. 1996: An objection to Smith's argument for internalism. *Analysis* 56.

Miller, A. 1998a: Emotivism and the verification principle. *Proceedings of the Aristotelian Society* 98.

Miller, A. 1998b: Rule-following, response-dependence, and McDowell's debate with anti-realism. *European Review of Philosophy* 3.

Miller, A. 2002: Wright's argument against error-theories. *Analysis* 62.

Miller, A. 2007: *Philosophy of Language*, 2nd edn. London: Routledge.

Miller, A. 2009: Moral realism and program explanation: reply to Nelson. *Australasian Journal of Philosophy* 87.

Miller, A. 2010a: The argument from queerness and the normativity of meaning. In M. Grajner and A. Rami (eds), *Truth, Existence and Realism*. Ontos: Verlag.

Miller, A. 2010b: Rule-following skepticism. In D. Pritchard and S. Bernecker (eds), *The Routledge Companion to Epistemology*. London: Routledge.

Miller, A. 2010c: Noncognitivism. In J. Skorupski (ed.), *The Routledge Companion to Ethics*. London: Routledge.

Miller, A. 2011: Jackson, serious metaphysics and conceptual analysis (critical notice of Ravenscroft 2009), *Analysis* 71.

Miller, A. 2012a: Ethics and minimalism about truth. In H. Lafollette (ed.), *The International Encyclopedia of Ethics*. Oxford: Blackwell.

Miller, A. 2012b: Judgement-dependence, tacit knowledge and linguistic understanding. In P. Stalmaszczyk (ed.), *Philosophical and Formal Approaches to Linguistic Analysis*. Frankfurt: Ontos Verlag.

Miller, A. and Wright, C. (eds) 2002: *Rule-Following and Meaning*. London: Acumen.

Moore, G. E. [1903] 1993: *Principia Ethica*, rev. edn. Cambridge: Cambridge University Press.

Morgan, S. 2006: Naturalism and normativity. *Philosophy and Phenomenological Research* 72.

Mumford, S. 1998: *Dispositions*. Oxford: Oxford University Press.

Nelson, M. 2006: Moral realism and program explanation. *Australasian Journal of Philosophy* 84.

Nolan, D., Restall, G. and West, C. 2005: Moral fictionalism versus the rest. *Australasian Journal of Philosophy* 83.

Pettit, P. 1987: Humeans, anti-Humeans, and motivation. *Mind* 96.
Pettit, P. 1991: Realism and response-dependence. *Mind* 100.
Plato. 1981: Euthyphro. In *Five Dialogues*. Indianapolis, IN: Hackett.
Platts, M. 1979: *Ways of Meaning*. London: Routledge and Kegan Paul.
Putnam, H. 1975: The meaning of 'meaning'. In his *Mind, Language, and Reality*. Cambridge: Cambridge University Press.
Quine, W. V. O. 1960: *Word and Object*. Cambridge, MA: MIT Press.
Quinn, W. 1986: Truth and explanation in ethics. *Ethics* 96.
Railton, P. 1986a: Moral realism. *Philosophical Review* 95.
Railton, P. 1986b: Facts and values. *Philosophical Topics* 14(2).
Railton, P. 1989. Naturalism and prescriptivity. *Social Philosophy and Policy* 7.
Railton, P. 1992: Nonfactualism about normative discourse. *Philosophy and Phenomenological Research* 52(4).
Railton, P. 1993a: What the non-cognitivist helps us to see the naturalist must help us to explain. In Haldane and Wright (eds), *Reality, Representation, and Projection*. Oxford: Oxford University Press.
Railton, P. 1993b: Reply to David Wiggins. In Haldane and Wright (eds), *Reality, Representation, and Projection*. Oxford: Oxford University Press.
Railton, P. 1995: Made in the shade: moral compatibilism and the aims of moral theory. *Canadian Journal of Philosophy*, Supp. Vol. 21.
Railton, P. 1996a: Moral realism: prospects and problems. In W. Sinnott-Armstrong and M. Timmons (eds), *Moral Knowledge*. New York: Oxford University Press.
Railton, P. 1996b: Subject-ive and Objective. In Hooker (ed.), *Truth in Ethics*. Oxford: Blackwell.
Railton, P. 2003: *Facts, Values and Norms*. Cambridge: Cambridge University Press.
Ramsey, F. 1931: Theories. In F. Ramsey (ed.), *The Foundations of Mathematics*. London: Routledge and Kegan Paul.
Ravenscroft, I. (ed.). 2009: *Minds, Ethics, and Conditionals: Themes from the Philosophy of Frank Jackson*. Oxford: Oxford University Press.
Ridge, M. 2006a: Ecumenical expressivism. *Ethics* 116.
Ridge, M. 2006b: Saving the ethical appearances. *Mind* 115.
Roberts, D. 2011: Shapelesness and the thick. *Ethics* 121.
Rosati, C. 1995a: Persons, perspectives, and full information accounts of the good. *Ethics* 105.
Rosati, C. 1995b: Naturalism, normativity, and the open question argument. *Nous* 29(1).
Rosati, C. 1996: Internalism and the good for a person. *Ethics* 106.
Rosen, G. 1994: Objectivity and modern idealism: what is the question? In M. Michael (ed.), *Philosophy in Mind: The Place of Philosophy in the Study of Mind*. Dordrecht: Kluwer.
Rosenberg, A. 1990: Moral realism and social science. *Midwest Studies in Philosophy* 15.

Ryle, G. 1949: *The Concept of Mind*. London: Hutchinson.

Sayre-McCord, G. 1985: Logical positivism and the demise of 'moral science'. In N. Rescher (ed.), *The Heritage of Logical Positivism*. New York: University Press of America.

Sayre-McCord, G. 1986: The many moral realisms. *Southern Journal of Philosophy* 24 Supplement.

Sayre-McCord, G. 1988: Moral theory and explanatory impotence. In G. Sayre-McCord (ed.), *Essays on Moral Realism*. Ithaca, NY: Cornell University Press.

Schillp, P. 1942: *The Philosophy of G. E. Moore*. Evanston and Chicago, IL: Northwestern University Press.

Schroeder, M. 2008: What is the Frege-Geach problem? *Philosophy Compass* 3(4).

Schroeder, M. 2009: Hybrid expressivism: virtues and vices. *Ethics* 119.

Schroeder, M. 2010: *Noncognitivism in Ethics*. London: Routledge.

Schueler, G. 1988: Modus ponens and moral realism. *Ethics* 98.

Shafer-Landau, R. 2003a: *Whatever Happened to Good and Evil?* New York: Oxford University Press.

Shafer-Landau, R. 2003b: *Moral Realism*. Oxford: Oxford University Press.

Shafer-Landau, R. 2006: Ethics as philosophy: a defence of ethical non-naturalism. In Horgan and Timmons (eds), *Metaethics After Moore*. Oxford: Oxford University Press.

Shafer-Landau, R. and Cuneo, T. 2007: *Foundations of Ethics: An Anthology*. Oxford: Blackwell.

Shepard, R. 1962: The analysis of proximities: multidimensional scaling with an unknown distance function. II. *Psychometrika* 27.

Sidgwick, H. [1907] 1991: *Methods of Ethics*, 7th edn. Indianapolis, IN: Hackett.

Sinclair, N. 2011: The explanationist argument for moral realism *Canadian Journal of Philosophy* 41.

Singer, P. (ed.) 1991: *A Companion to Ethics*. Oxford: Blackwell.

Sinnott-Armstrong, W. 1993: Some problems for Gibbard's norm-expressivism. *Philosophical Studies* 69.

Smith, M. 1988: On Humeans, anti-Humeans, and motivation: a reply to Pettit. *Mind* 58.

Smith, M. 1989: Dispositional theories of moral value. *Proceedings of the Aristotelian Society*, Supp. Vol. 63.

Smith, M. 1993a: Objectivity and moral realism: on the significance of the phenomenology of moral experience. In Haldane and Wright (eds), *Reality, Representation, and Projection*. Oxford: Oxford University Press.

Smith, M. 1993b: Colour, transparency, and mind-independence. In Haldane and Wright (eds), *Reality, Representation, and Projection*. Oxford: Oxford University Press.

Smith, M. 1994a: *The Moral Problem*. Oxford: Blackwell.

Smith, M. 1994b: Why expressivists about value should love minimalism about truth. *Analysis* 54.

Smith, M. 1994c: Minimalism, truth-aptitude, and belief. *Analysis* 54.

Smith, M. 1996a: The argument for internalism: reply to Miller. *Analysis* 56.

Smith, M. 1996b: Internalism's wheel. In Hooker (ed.), *Truth in Ethics*. Oxford: Blackwell.

Smith, M. 1998: Response-dependence without reduction. *European Review of Philosophy* 3.

Smith, M. 2001: Some not-much-discussed problems for non-cognitivism in ethics. *Ratio* 14.

Smith, M. 2002: Which passions rule? *Philosophy and Phenomenological Research* 65.

Smith, M. 2004: *Ethics and the A Priori*. Cambridge: Cambridge University Press.

Snare, F. 1975: The open-question as a linguistic test. *Ratio* 17.

Snare, F. 1984: The empirical bases of moral scepticism. *American Philosophical Quarterly* 21.

Soames, S. 2003: *Philosophical Analysis in the Twentieth Century, Volume 1: The Dawn of Analysis*. Princeton, NJ: Princeton University Press.

Sobel, D. 1994: Full information accounts of well-being. *Ethics* 104.

Sobel, D. and Copp, D. 2001: Against direction of fit accounts of belief and desire. *Analysis* 61.

Stevenson, C. 1937: The emotive meaning of ethical terms. Reprinted in A. J. Ayer (ed.), *Logical Positivism*. Glencoe, IL: Free Press.

Stevenson, C. 1944: *Ethics and Language*. New Haven, CT: Yale University Press.

Strandberg, C. 2004: In defence of the open question argument? *Journal of Ethics* 8.

Stratton-Lake, P. 1998: Internalism and the explanation of belief/motivation changes. *Analysis* 56(4).

Stratton-Lake, P. 1999: Why externalism is not a problem for intuitionists. *Proceedings of the Aristotelian Society* 99.

Sturgeon, N. 1986a: Harman on moral explanations of natural facts. *Southern Journal of Philosophy* 24 Supplement.

Sturgeon, N. 1986b: What difference does it make whether moral realism is true? *Southern Journal of Philosophy* 24 Supplement.

Sturgeon, N. 1988: Moral explanations. In G. Sayre-McCord (ed.), *Essays on Moral Realism*. Ithaca, NY: Cornell University Press.

Sturgeon, N. 1991: Contents and causes: a reply to Blackburn. *Philosophical Studies* 61.

Sturgeon, N. 1992: Nonmoral explanations. *Philosophical Perspectives* 6.

Sturgeon, N. 1995: Critical notice of Gibbard 1990. *Nous* 29.

Sturgeon, N. 2006a: Ethical naturalism. In D. Copp (ed.), *The Oxford Handbook of Ethical Theory*. Oxford: Oxford University Press.

Sturgeon, N. 2006b: Moral explanations defended. In J. Dreier (ed.), *Contemporary Debates in Moral Theory*. Oxford: Blackwell.

Suikkanen, J. 2009: The subjectivist consequences of expressivism. *Pacific Philosophical Quarterly* 90.

Suikkanen, J. Forthcoming 2013: Moral error theory and the belief problem. *Oxford Studies in Metaethics* 8.

Surgener, K. 2012: *Korsgaard on the Status of Moral Norms*. PhD thesis, (University of Birmingham).

Thagard, P. 1978: The best explanation: criteria for theory choice. *Journal of Philosophy* 75.

Thornton, T. 2004: *John McDowell*. Chesham: Acumen.

Van Roojen, M. 1996. Expressivism and irrationality. *Philosophical Review* 105.

Väyrynen, P. 2013. Shapelessness in context. Forthcoming in *Nous*.

Velleman, D. 1988: Brandt's definition of 'good'. *Philosophical Review* 97.

Warnock, M. 1960: *Ethics Since 1900*. London: Oxford University Press.

Wedgwood, R. 1997: Noncognitivism, truth, and logic. *Philosophical Studies* 86.

Weir, A. 2001: More troubles for functionalism. *Proceedings of the Aristotelian Society* 101.

Whiting, D. 2007: The normativity of meaning defended. *Analysis* 67.

Wiggins, D. 1987: A sensible subjectivism. In his *Needs, Values, Truth*. Oxford: Blackwell.

Wiggins, D. 1991: Moral cognitivism, moral relativism, and motivating moral beliefs. *Proceedings of the Aristotelian Society* 91.

Wiggins, D. 1992a: Ayer on morality and feeling: from subjectivism to emotivism and back again. In H. Hahn (ed.), *The Philosophy of A. J. Ayer*. La Salle, IL: Open Court.

Wiggins, D. 1992b: Ayer's ethical theory. In A. Phillips-Griffiths (ed.), *A. J. Ayer: Memorial Essays*. Cambridge: Cambridge University Press.

Wiggins, D. 1993a: Cognitivism, naturalism, and normativity. In Haldane and Wright (eds), *Reality, Representation, and Projection*. Oxford: Oxford University Press.

Wiggins, D. 1993b: A neglected position? In Haldane and Wright (eds), *Reality, Representation, and Projection*. Oxford: Oxford University Press.

Wiggins, D. 1996: 'Objective and subjective' in ethics. *Ratio* 8.

Williams, B. 1976: Persons, character, and morality. Reprinted in his *Moral Luck*. Cambridge: Cambridge University Press.

Wright, C. 1984: Kripke's account of the argument against private language. *Journal of Philosophy* 81.

Wright, C. 1985: Review of Blackburn 1984. *Mind* 371.

Wright, C. 1987: On making up one's mind: Wittgenstein on intention.

In *Proceedings of the 11th International Wittgenstein Symposium*. Vienna: Holder-Pichler-Tempsky.

Wright, C. 1988a: Moral values, projection, and secondary qualities. *Proceedings of the Aristotelian Society*, Supp. Vol. 62.

Wright, C. 1988b: Realism, antirealism, irrealism, quasi-realism. *Midwest Studies in Philosophy* 12.

Wright, C. 1989: Wittgenstein's rule-following considerations and the central project of theoretical linguistics. In A. George (ed.), *Reflections on Chomsky*. Oxford: Blackwell.

Wright, C. 1992: *Truth and Objectivity*. Cambridge, MA: Harvard University Press.

Wright, C. 1996: Truth in ethics. In Hooker (ed.), *Truth in Ethics*. Oxford: Blackwell.

Wright, C. 1998: Comrades against quietism. *Mind* 107.

Yang, S. 2009: The appropriateness of moral emotion and Humean sentimentalism. *Journal of Value Inquiry* 43.

Zangwill, N. 1992: Moral modus ponens. *Ratio* 5.

Zangwill, N. 1994: Moral mind-independence. *Australasian Journal of Philosophy* 72.

Zangwill, N. 1997: Against analytic moral functionalism. *Ratio* 13.

Index